CW00709254

TRAVELS WITH MY NAN

By

Mark Thompson

Copyright © Mark Thompson 2019
This book is sold subject to the condition that it shall not, by way of trade or otherwise, be lent, resold, hired out, or otherwise circulated without the publisher's prior consent in any form of binding or cover other than that in which it is published and without a similar condition including this condition being imposed on the subsequent publisher.
The moral right of Mark Thompson has been asserted.
Photographs remain the property of the author.
ISBN: 978-1-9160016-0-2

While all the stories in this book are true, some names and identifying details have been changed to protect the privacy of the people involved.

My Nan

DEDICATION

For my wife.

CONTENTS

CREDITS AND REQUEST

I wish to thank my friend, Trevor Heaton, himself a published author, for his patience and tolerance in proof-reading my book and for being honest and forthright in his opinions. I wish to thank my mum, Norma Bye, for also taking time to proof-read my book. She has a particular passion for reading biographies and travelogues, and her advice has proved invaluable. I wish to thank my friends, Steve Wayne and Will Allen, for their insights and advice, and for being willing stooges in my story. In particular, I want to thank all the people who I met on my trip for making it such a wonderful experience. In a troubled world, it is encouraging to note that at its heart beats a common humanity, where people have an innate desire to be friendly, welcoming and social and to help and guide our fellow man, even if they are complete strangers.

It should be noted that, save in a very limited respect, I have deliberately used first names only in this book, so as to maintain some semblance of anonymity and to protect privacy. Any person who reads my book and is mentioned in it is likely to recognise themselves, but hopefully their friends and family will not; and it will be up to that person to tell them if they so wish. But for any person out there who thinks that they are mentioned in my book, and who wishes to do so, I hope you will contact me. Whether it be to berate me, correct me, update me or simply to get in touch, I would love to hear from you.

Mark Thompson
m_thompson_03@yahoo.co.uk

FOREWORD

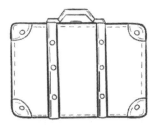

At the beginning of 1999, I was 38 years old, an average guy, of average height, of above average weight, in an OK, but ultimately dead-end job, and was single, having come out of yet another failed relationship the year before. I cannot claim that I was so ambitious as to say that I was in search of excitement in my life. My ambitions simply extended to wanting to break out of a rut, since my life was going nowhere. An initial germ of an idea, though, ultimately evolved into a firm decision to take six months out to go backpacking through parts of Eastern Asia, Australia and New Zealand. This book is about those travels and it turned out that I had the trip of a lifetime. Things happened to me on that trip that wouldn't normally happen to a regular guy like me. The great Alan Bennett succinctly once said in that self-deprecating and witty way that only he can do, "Life is generally something that happens elsewhere." That could normally be said about my life, but for once, during these six months, life happened to me.

On the way, I kept a daily diary. Discounting work diaries, I've never been one for keeping a personal diary, save for one six-month stint when I was a teenager, and the thought of doing so on this trip was initially anathema to me. Not only did it seem too self-serving, but it was the sort of thing only girls and geeky, spotty teenagers – like me – did. However, when a couple of trusted close friends independently advised that I should, the idea gradually grew on me. I had in any event already purchased a diary, because, since I would be travelling on a very tight budget, it was going to be necessary for me to keep a daily log of my expenses. In addition, in a pre-digital age, the diary contained all the usual helpful information that I would need along the way; including, exchange rates, details of consulates in

1

the event of an emergency, addresses and telephone numbers for people that I had planned to meet on the way, and, likewise, addresses and telephone numbers for family and friends back home, to whom I intended to send postcards. Consequently, the notion of using that diary to keep a daily log was a natural extension.

I am so glad that I did keep a diary. At the time whilst travelling, it allowed me to sit back at the end of each day and take stock, to step outside and look objectively at what I'd experienced. On returning home, it turned out that I had kept such a comprehensive diary that I have re-read it over the years, taking me back on that journey and allowing me to enjoy the experiences all over again.

Although at the time I had thought that my trip had been full of adventure, I didn't consider that my experiences were much different to any other traveller in my circumstances and didn't consider that other people would be particularly interested in my stories. However, it has struck me over the years that the more I hear about other people's stories, the more I think that I appear to have had more adventures than most.

There are a number of reasons why I now think that was so. The first is that I was mostly travelling on my own. I had nobody to have to cater for or comply with. It meant that I was a much easier target for local people to be able to come and talk to. I had an outward look on life all around me, whereas if I'd travelled with somebody, I would have been constrained to take account of my fellow traveller and would have looked as much inwards as outwards. The second is because, although it was finite, I had plenty of time – a full six months – before I needed to return to the UK. The third is because I had a job to return to in the UK. This might seem inconsequential, but it gave me the confidence to enjoy my time, and to be able to properly budget and relax in the knowledge that I would have funds to return to in the UK. Freeing me up from the normal constraints of my daily drudge in the UK, it allowed me to fully immerse myself quickly into the rhythms of daily life. The fourth is that I am somebody who is notoriously accident-prone and clumsy. I seem to attract trouble, and, by extension, invite adventure.

My story is not a typical travelogue. I am always interested to hear about other people's travels and I am a keen reader of books by travel writers. Most authors, though, tend to be academics and view their travels in the context of their particular academic interest, be it in archaeology, history, geography or ethnography. I genuinely love the academic slant to their stories and learning about other cultures, but I also enjoy reading about the chance encounters and the local characters they meet on their way. The latter was something that I was lucky to do in abundance on my own travels. Whilst I was keen to learn about their history and culture, I simply loved meeting new people. My story, therefore, is not told from the perspective of an academic. Instead it is told from the perspective of a backpacker and gets down to the nitty gritty of my daily experiences and interactions with persons I met along the way. Friends and family have claimed to enjoy hearing about my tales. Consequently, I thought that others might enjoy hearing about them too.

In writing this book, I have moved from copying pages directly from my diary to turning those stories that I consider to be the most interesting into a longer narrative, although even here I have retained most of what was in my original diary. I have, of course, tidied it up a bit. I have removed some – though not all – of the vernacular, and I have removed most – but again not all – of the 'got up, had breakfast' bits. You, the reader, will note that there are many references to loose bodily functions, to my getting close and personal with members of the fairer sex on my travels and to various references to encounters with ladies of the night. I felt very wary – shy perhaps – about revealing such personal details to you, the reader. Indeed, a trusted old friend of mine took the trouble of proof-reading the first draft of my work and suggested that the regular references to such material could become grating after a while. Having given it much thought, whilst I have tidied these up a bit, I have decided to keep most references in, mainly because my decision to tell my story was meant to cover all aspects of daily life, warts and all. For example, loose bodily functions were a regular occupational hazard in this part of the world and everybody who has backpacked through these areas of Asia will almost certainly have had the same experience at some point. So, in a sense I hope that my account will resonate.

My writing about sexual encounters is not intended to seem like some proud boast. Far from it. This sort of thing simply didn't happen to me, or to guys like me. I didn't go out looking for love and sex, but these things did happen. Again, they were part of my story.

Also, I never went out to Asia, as a middle-aged bachelor, intent on indulging in the sex industry, but it is something that evolved as my trip continued. In the end, in deciding whether to reveal such intimate details in this book, I have applied what I think of as 'the mother test.' If I don't mind my mum reading about them, then I don't mind others doing so too.

However, if all this sounds like I am trying to get my apologies in early, then that is probably correct, because the last thing I would want to do is alienate you, the reader, from the very beginning. It is helpful, and perhaps even important, though, to understand the context in which these things happened.

At the end of the day a diary is a diary is a diary. Again, plagiarising something that Alan Bennett observed, you get the truth with a diary. I hope that I don't alienate you or upset you, but I apologise if I do. I hope that you will sit back and enjoy travelling on a journey with me back in time on what turned out to be the trip of a lifetime.

CHAPTER 1

Evolution of an Idea

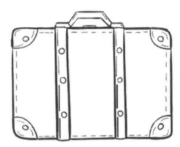

It was a dark and stormy night. I have always wanted to begin a story with these words. They conjure up in my mind images of the windswept West Yorkshire moors up behind Haworth in Wuthering Heights. Although in truth – I believe – those words are the start of a slightly more obscure piece of literature, I am achieving my ambition. However, in doing so I am telling only a half truth. It *was* dark and stormy, that part was true, but I was still a good way off night. It was 4 o'clock in the afternoon and, in theory at least, there was plenty of daylight left in the day. I was in the back of a Malaysian taxi cab on the way from Kuala Lumpur airport to the city itself, a journey of 70 kilometres. And outside the cab a little over to our left I could see a violent electrical storm with streaks of lightning dancing horizontally, first left, then right, across the blackening sky. The lightning was steadily increasing not just in ferocity but also in frequency, so much so that it seemed surreal, like a scene from a film, or maybe I was imagining a Tom and Jerry cartoon where a fireworks factory has exploded, except that this was frighteningly real. I thought to myself that this is perhaps what Armageddon would be like.

But, just as the thunder bolts were increasing in intensity, so too the sky was getting darker and darker, so that it was exactly like night. Outside, the temperatures only moments ago had been a sweat-dripping sultry 40 degrees centigrade. Even though, guided by my Lonely Planet guidebook, it had taken me only a matter of minutes to go from the sub-Arctic cool of the air-conditioned terminal to this taxi, the humidity was so tangible that my shirt was already beginning to cling to my back. Inside the taxi, an ominous rattling sound and even the odd clunk was coming from the cab's own air-conditioning system as it was struggling to try and cope, with only minimal success. For a while, as we were treated to the spectacle, the temperature, if anything, seemed to increase, though that was almost certainly, to my untrained eye, down to a sharp increase in humidity. For a good portion of the journey there was no rain. The taxi driver did not exactly instil confidence. He seemed to sit a little lower in his seat, leaning forward and looking up at the sky, whilst ducking his head, as if somehow that would protect him if a lightning bolt came our way. And he was occasionally mumbling away to himself. Moments of complete silence were interspersed by sharp static crackles on the radio, followed by those short bouts of unintelligible mumbling. Perhaps he was cursing. Perhaps he was praying.

And as we scuttled along, I noticed that the violent weather, which previously was at right angles to us over to our left, now appeared to be a little nearer and sitting diagonally to our left – at 10 o'clock navigationally – such that I got the impression that it was racing towards the city and competing with us to see who would get there first. Then suddenly the rain started, a few large globules of it by way of warning before suddenly it was coming down in torrents, sheeting across at times almost horizontally. The poor taxi had almost every electrical device in it running at maximum strength. Windscreen wipers at maximum speed were frantically trying to wipe the deluge away. All lights were on full beam. And the air-conditioning was still struggling to keep the internal temperature that single, solitary, one degree cooler than outside. Welcome to Asia!

Looking back on it, I should have known that these were ominous portents, as I had never seen such a powerful electrical storm before (and I have never done so since).

I was about to start a six-month adventure, backpacking through seven countries. I cannot claim that I was about to do anything truly intrepid, trusting as I invariably did a succession of Lonely Planet guidebooks, and there was nothing particularly unusual about my experience, since thousands, if not hundreds of thousands, of old-time travellers and new-age backpackers had tramped these very routes before. However, this was going to be *my* story, and each individual patchwork of my adventure would combine into a quilted whole to create a trip that was going to be unique. On this journey I would see angels and demons, pirates and dragons, I would nearly be shipwrecked, I would enjoy small oases of sublime sexual ecstasy, set in deserts of sexual frustration, I would suffer moments of sheer terror, I would have four accidents, on one occasion coming off a motorcycle and on another being the victim of a hit-and-run accident, suffer numerous cuts, bites, dubious diseases and severe sunburn to my back. I would fall in love (more than once), I would swim with turtles and sharks and I would stumble across paradise at a stunning waterfall with no less than seven beautiful young girls. I would be the victim of a theft. And in the last few weeks of my journey, I would experience a supernatural spectral phenomenon in one of the Maoris' most sacred places on earth.

I was a solicitor, commencing work after qualifying in 1991, and by the February of 1999, at the age of 38, I had been with my then current employer for five years. They were a good firm to work for and I forged many close friends there, not least because I was an active member of the social committee. However, I was becoming more and more disillusioned by the way that my career was stagnating. Back in 1994 I had joined the firm to assist in mixed litigation, that is crime, family, and all types of civil litigation. There were several others practicing both family and civil litigation work, but I was the only person throughout the entire firm practicing crime. Naturally, therefore, all the crime that came to the firm came to me. Over the five years that I was there the crime had developed so much that essentially in my last three years I was nigh on a crime only specialist. I sometimes say that I did not choose to do criminal work. Rather, it chose me. That's not to say that I did not enjoy this type of work. I did and still do. The problem was that the management were not keen to expand this department any further. They were happy to be able to provide a service to their regular clients, noting that even their mostly highly-prized (read highly-paying) commercial customers sometimes would come criminally unstuck by, for example, speeding, drink-driving or, as in one case, allowing industrial waste to seep into the river network. Naturally, they also did not object to other non-regular clients coming in off the street and asking for my services, but no more. As with many in a solicitors' practice, my wages depended in part on bonuses, which in turn depended on the income I brought in. However, there was no possibility of improving my lot, since the firm was against expansion of my department. Also, there was no scope for partnership, the firm having made it clear when I asked that my prospects for becoming a partner were presently nil. I had found myself in a career cul-de-sac. Also, about one year earlier I had split with my then long-term girlfriend. Both my career and my personal life seemed to be in limbo.

Then by chance in late 1998 I just happened to be talking to a solicitor from another local firm, one which already had a much larger criminal presence in the area. There might have only been two criminal solicitors or partners in the firm, but they luxuriated in being able to describe themselves as having a criminal department. One day that autumn I was sitting at the back of a Magistrates' Court idly talking to one of the solicitors from that firm, both of us waiting for our cases to be called on, when I jokingly said to him, "Do you have any jobs?" Although I accept on reflection that my subconscious self might well have been doing a job that my conscious self was incapable of doing, I truly meant it as a joke, as at that point, I had not contemplated a life beyond my present employer. The next day, however, he rang me to say that he had been chatting to his partner and they were interested in talking to me.

I met both partners soon afterwards and before too long they readily offered to take me on. Not only could I carry on doing the work that I enjoyed but also an equity partnership would definitely be in the offing within a fairly short space of time. It was too good an opportunity to miss. I ensured that I left my previous firm on good terms. Both my immediate boss at that firm and most of the senior partners understood my motives for moving on and I am pleased to say that I have maintained good relations with them, even to this day.

It occurred to me, however, that it would be a good opportunity to have a holiday between jobs. Not being tied to the usual maximum of two weeks, I asked my new employers if they would mind if I took a sabbatical of between three and four weeks before I started with them. They were more than happy for me to do so. I had several destinations in mind.

Malaysia

Between 1978 and 1983 I spent five years ploughing through what should have been a four-year degree course in Public Administration at Leicester Polytechnic. My best friend in the final year of my course was a Malaysian lad of Chinese origin. His name was Siew Leong Lam. It was Leong who gave me my first SLR camera, taught me – after a fashion – to use chopsticks and inspired me to get out my dusty old school atlas to have a good old gawp at the Orient.

I was 23 when I finished my degree and I decided to take a year off to go backpacking before continuing with my solicitor training. My original plan was to travel to Malaysia to visit Leong. Unfortunately, however, even though I had spent around eight months in a local canning factory and had managed to save pretty well, as I was hoping to be able to travel for six months, there was no way that I would be able to fund the whole trip from savings, no matter how cheaply I was intending to travel and how flea-bitten the accommodation would be that I was prepared (in theory) to use. I needed to be able to work. However, I was unable to obtain any type of work visa for Malaysia.

As a result, having already been hooked on the desire to travel, I decided that I would instead go to Australia where I knew that I could get a work visa and where I also had family dotted around many of the main cities, who I knew could support me. I always vowed, though, that someday I would go to Malaysia. I had kept in touch with Leong for a while after leaving college, but in the intervening years we had lost touch. I thought it would be quite an adventure to try to find him.

Australia

So it was that in 1984, having abandoned the idea of going to Malaysia, I spent six months backpacking through a good deal of the Eastern part of Australia. By late 1998, although there were one or two areas of the country that I was still keen to visit sometime, Australia as a whole was low on my 'to do' list. However, one of my best friends, Steve, from my home town of King's Lynn, had emigrated to Australia in the late 1980s and had been pestering for me to go out to visit him. Then in 1994, when he had come back to England to visit his family, Steve again started haranguing me to go out to see him, and, as a consequence, I made a promise to visit him in 1999. I cannot say that I reluctantly made that promise, because I was genuinely keen to visit him. However, to this day, I have no idea why I specifically said it would be in 1999. It is one of life's uncanny coincidences that the opportunity for me to keep my promise opened up that very year.

I, therefore, originally thought that I would visit Australia and Malaysia only, spending approximately four weeks in total. However, there were other countries in that part of the world that I wanted to visit.

New Zealand

During that very same trip to Australia in 1984 I met a lad called Will and he became one of my best friends thereafter. Will's father was a Kiwi by birth, but moved over to the UK when he was young. Will conversely was born in England but when he was 13 his recently-widowed father moved back to New Zealand, taking Will with him. I met Will in 1984 when we worked together on a beautiful coral-fringed island called Hayman Island, part of the Whitsunday group in tropical Queensland. He moved back to live in England two years later and we had kept in touch ever since. In the mid to late 1990s Will and I had started to do some serious long-distance walking together and when I met up with Will on one of these walks in the autumn of 1998, he told me that he was planning to visit his father some time in 1999. For several years he had been trying to persuade me to travel out to visit him in New Zealand, so the idea of doing so in 1999 also seemed like a good idea. Will claimed to know of some truly great walks in New Zealand.

Indonesia

I first went to Indonesia almost by accident in 1984. Having decided that my backpacking adventure that year should be in Australia rather than Malaysia, in planning how to get to Australia, and with my limited funds, I naturally flew with the cheapest airline, Garuda, Indonesia's national airline. It was only later, when part way through my trip, as I was kicking my heels waiting for a bus at one of Brisbane's main bus stations, and when I was getting so bored that I was even reading the small print on my return flight ticket, that I realised that I was entitled to a stopover in either Jakarta or Bali on the way back. I thought it would be a lovely way to end my trip. It had to be Bali.

Arriving in Denpasar, Bali, some three months later, my trip got off to the worst of starts. Armed with heaps of information from fellow backpackers who had already 'done' Bali, but being on my own for the first time in a non-English-speaking country, I was rather nervous. At the airport, I put my camera down for a moment whilst I fumbled in my daypack for my notes, but when I went to pick up my camera it had gone. No amount of soul-baring to the airport police was going to change anything, but I tried all the same. Although they seemed genuinely sympathetic, the slight twitching of their arced black eyebrows spoke volumes, intimating that they were wondering how this foreigner could be so stupid. But they were only reflecting back to me what I was thinking myself. Indeed, how could I have been so stupid? Little was I to realise how the loss of that camera would shape my destiny.

I headed, as I had been advised by the backpackers' jungle drums, to the North side of the island to a village called Lovina Beach, where I very quickly fell in love with the place and the people. All my senses seemed to come alive. The sounds were of happiness and laughter, clanging gamelan music, the soothing swish of the sea, which was never far away, croaking toads in the paddy fields at night-time, garrulous geckos in the roofs and yet more laughter. The smells were of flowers, bad drains, Hindu incense, wood burning and of rice and chicken cooking. The tastes were of Nasi Goreng, Balinese duck, chicken satay, freshly cut pineapple, coconut taken straight from the tree, and of barbecued fish taken moments before from the sea. The sights were of Hindus and Muslims mixing freely at a wedding, of emerald green chequerboard rice terraces, of flowery batik shirts, intricate wood carvings and of smiling faces. And then there were the touches of people always wanting to shake hands, of pats on the back, and my very own little massage lady, always ready to soothe away the stiffness and aches after a busy (or more often lazy) day.

The loss of my camera had two main effects. Firstly, I am a keen photographer. I accept that over the years I have come to realise that my interest in photography and my desire to try to take the perfect shot has on the odd occasion led to me missing the moment, but that was not the case in Bali. I do not believe that my senses would have been quite so deeply scored if I had had my camera on the go all the time. I was forced, in a way, to let myself go, to observe and experience life whilst being immersed in it thus exciting all my senses, rather than as a two-dimensional image as an outsider, where the visual would have been most dominant. Secondly, stubborn bugger that I am, I was still pretty determined to take my photographs, but that would require me to go back later. That is what I vowed to do.

I returned in 1988, then again in 1990, and finally in 1995. On each occasion that I went back I always made a point of ensuring that, as part of my trip, I took time out to visit the same village at Lovina on the North side of Bali, where my friendships with several local people became deeper and stronger each time. On each of those trips I also explored further afield, which included a good deal more of Bali itself, as well as the neighbouring islands of Java and Lombok. Always, always, always, I was amazed at the unending kind-heartedness of the Indonesian people, who were unerringly so generous of spirit and who genuinely wanted to share whatever they had with me, even if invariably it was very little. I wanted to spend some time in Indonesia, not just visiting my friends in Bali, but also exploring much more of the country.

I was clearly going to need more than four weeks. In fact, I was quickly coming round to the idea that I might need three or four months. However, I was still not finished with the countries that I wanted to visit.

China

China was a country that had always fascinated me, particularly with it being closed off from the outside world for so many years. It had recently become more open to people wanting to travel but it was still well off the tourist map for most travellers. However, being away from the main tourist or traveller drag was one of the main attractions for me. Also, I was very keen to visit Hong Kong, primarily to indulge in my love of horse-racing. In Sha Tin and Happy Valley, Hong Kong boasts two of the most famous and iconic racecourses in the world of horse-racing and I wanted to visit them both. Also, Hong Kong had been in the news recently, as it was handed back by the British to the Chinese in 1998. I thought it would be a great time to visit, immediately after the transfer back.

Laos

Laos is one of those forgotten little corners of the world, where most people have heard of their neighbours – Thailand, China, Vietnam and Cambodia – but few people know what goes on in the land in between. And yet, although most people might not know much about Laos, most people have heard of the Mekong, a river that runs the entire length of the country (plus a few thousand kilometres before reaching Laos and a few hundred kilometres thereafter as it basins out into the South China Sea). I remembered reading about Laos when I was at primary school studying geography. I had always wanted to visit.

Thailand

Thailand too had always had a fascination for me, and it seemed perfectly logical that, if I was going to visit Malaysia and Laos, I should travel overland between the two through Thailand. The only problem was whether I would have enough time to explore it properly.

I now realised that I was going to need six months.

I knew that I would be pushing my luck, but, on the basis that if you do not ask you do not get, I approached my prospective employers, explained my ideas and asked if they would object to me taking a six-month break before joining them. To my surprise they not only agreed, but with immense good grace they said they understood my reasons and wished me good luck. I could not believe my luck. The beauty of it was that I could properly budget for my six months away, knowing that I had a full-time well-paid job to come back to.

A few weeks spent checking itineraries, visa requirements, routes and timetables resulted in me deciding that my route would be as follows: I would fly to Malaysia, where I would spend approximately four weeks; travel overland quickly through Thailand, taking three to seven days; travel North through Laos, spending two weeks; cross the border into China where I would spend one month, winding up in Hong Kong; fly to Indonesia, where I would spend two months; fly to Australia, for two weeks; and finally to New Zealand, where I would spend four to six weeks. I arranged to meet up with Steve in Australia. I arranged to meet up with Will in New Zealand. I would attempt to find Leong in Malaysia.

However, all my arrangements were loose, as I wanted to be flexible with my time, so that I could spend more time in places that I particularly enjoyed, and move on more quickly from those places that I did not. In fact, the only two items on my itinerary that were fixed were my flights to and from the UK and my trip to China. So far as the former was concerned, I booked return flights to Auckland, via Kuala Lumpur. I would 'lose' the outward leg from Kuala Lumpur to Auckland. I would leave London on the 27th February, arriving in Kuala Lumpur the next day and I would leave Auckland on the 25th August. What happened in between was anybody's guess. The visa requirements for all the countries were very straightforward, save for one. For China, I would be required to fully plan my itinerary, to state exactly when and how I would arrive in the country and precisely when and where I would be throughout all my time in China, naming all the cities I would visit and all the hotels I would stay at, and finally to confirm exactly when, and from where, I would leave. This was no easy task, considering I was organising everything myself with the help only of a Lonely Planet guidebook.

Having already paid for my return ticket to Auckland, I was left with a budget of £3,000 to cover the whole of the remainder of my trip. That meant that I was on an average daily budget of £20 and that would need to cover *all* expenses, including accommodation, food and transport, which itself would include at least three flights.

Organising what to take was a task of Gordian Knot proportions. On the one hand, I was going away for six months and I needed to be as self-sufficient as possible. On the other hand, I was going to have to carry it, so I also needed it to be as light as possible. Some of the items that I took that perhaps were more interesting or unusual, or which had some relevance to events later were as follows. I took the recently-published book of 'The Nation's Favourite Poems'. I imagined that I would be visiting some inspiring places and if I was struggling to express myself then maybe the book would help me. I reckoned on trying to read a poem every day.

I took my Reiki certificate with me. I had been a Reiki practitioner for slightly less than three years, having been 'tuned in' during the summer of 1996. For the uninitiated, the way Reiki works is that I receive Reiki energy through my hands, which I can then pass on to others, or transmit to myself, by the laying on of hands. Reiki is a universal energy that is naturally all around us and, by being tuned in, my hands act like a magnifying glass, magnifying the energy through my hands. Reiki is a harmonising, healing energy which works to redress the physical, emotional, spiritual and mental imbalances in our lives. I got into it myself through a friend, Chris, who was struggling with ME, or 'yuppie flu', as it was often described. There were no modern remedies and Chris had already tried a number of other 'alternative' ones, which were also unsuccessful. A friend of mine had recommended Reiki as a cure for ME, and when I mentioned it to Chris he decided to give it a try. I went along with Chris mainly to give him some moral support, but I had been experiencing some extremely stressful situations in my job, and I thought that Reiki would help me to relax and to cope. To be honest, even though I had been 'tuned in' to and practising Reiki for three years by the time of my trip, I was still struggling to fully believe in its power and could not quite bring myself to take that final leap of faith in being able to say that I was a fully-fledged convert. However, I persevered in using it and although I had seen some remarkable results of my own work, the biggest testament of all to its success was the fact that within a year Chris was completely cured. I thought that there were likely to be opportunities to use Reiki on my travels, at least by performing it on myself, and maybe on others, and if I needed to be able to confirm my credentials to a dusky maiden before laying my hands on her winsome body, then the Reiki certificate might do the trick.

Will was a good source of useful objects, items that I would not have considered taking myself but for his advice. They included a washbasin plug, a money belt, and a sleeping sheet, which is like a sleeping bag, but much lighter, and, therefore, good for the tropics; it also might afford me some semblance of protection if I was staying in any less-than-clean establishments and did not want to sleep directly on their sheets. Will also lent me a short-wave radio, which was very lightweight and compact and, by connecting me to the BBC World Service, would help me keep in touch with the outside world. This was particularly important in view of the fact that I would be heading to some areas where the Foreign Office had advised caution – there were pockets of unrest, for example, in several parts of Indonesia – and the

14

radio might help to keep me informed. I was still determined to go to those places, noting that I just needed to be sensible about where exactly I visited and who I pointed the camera towards, and reassuring myself that I was many times more likely to be hit by a bus in the UK than to suffer real problems in Indonesia. I was particularly keen to go to Indonesia in this year of all years because the country was due to have its first proper elections for over 20 years, and maybe the first truly fair ones ever. It was due to be run in early June and I had hoped to be able to manoeuvre myself to be there at that time. Nevertheless, I decided that I should pay close attention to advice I would pick up along the way about the situation in Indonesia and elsewhere by listening in to the BBC World Service.

The weeks leading up to my trip were especially taxing and poignant as two of my closest relatives died. The first was my Great Uncle Durrant on my mum's side. We were very close. When I met up with his widow, Olga, in mid-February shortly after his funeral, she gave me his camera. I already had one SLR camera, a Fujica ST605, which, although I had had to change various parts on it, was essentially the one Leong had given me back in 1982. The Fujica was entirely manual. The all-singing all-dancing camera that my great aunt gave me was a Canon EOS 500, which, although it had a manual function on it, had many automatic features. Although I knew it would take me a while to get used to it, this camera had to come with me. I would, therefore, be equipped with two cameras, 50 rolls of film, and various lenses, including a zoom lens. My great uncle had been a very keen and very good photographer, and by having his faithful trusty camera with me, I felt that spiritually a part of him would be with me on my travels.

The second relative to pass away was my nan, my grandmother on my father's side. Again, we were very close. She was everyone's idea of a typical grandmother, being kind and caring and always seeming to have some just-baked cake or home-made biscuits ready and waiting whenever anybody visited. She had a deep love of family and she was the matriarch around whom her relatively large family revolved, especially after her husband, my grandfather, had died 12 years earlier. She was never outspoken, and never one to proffer her opinions unless asked, but she had very wise and helpful advice for those who sought it. She always seemed to have a warm and friendly smile on her face. I took one of my favourite photographs of her with me on this trip, which was the very first item I took out of my rucksack everywhere that I went and which I then placed strategically somewhere in the room so that we could see each other.

Finally, I took with me a pocket-sized daily diary. Not only did I want to record anything interesting, but I also needed to keep a careful note of my daily expenditure so as to stick as close as possible to my budget.

CHAPTER 2

Malaysia

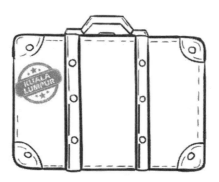

<u>Sunday 28th February – Meeting Anna</u>

Left London yesterday. Sad way to go, saying goodbye to mum, Barry, Sheryl and Robbyne.

On arriving in Kuala Lumpur proper, the stellar electrical storm had passed and the city was bathed in late afternoon sunshine. The heavy rain had left a glossy sheen over the entire city, making it look fresh and new. I had left London yesterday, waving goodbye at the airport to my mum, my stepfather, Barry, my sister-in-law, Sheryl, and my eight-year-old niece, Robbyne. Robbyne had given me a letter, which she insisted I did not read until I was on the aeroplane. In it she very touchingly said she would miss me, wished I would stay safe and asked me to send her a postcard from everywhere I visited. I vowed that I would.

On the flight itself, I was crammed in cattle class between a hijab-wearing young girl wedged into the window seat on my left, who seemingly spoke no English, despite smiling politely and nodding repeatedly whenever I attempted a conversation, and a hoity-toity Singaporean lady on my right, the aisle seat, who clearly did speak good English, but who was in no mood to make conversation. I slept very little.

Lovely letter from Robbyne. Good flight – cramped. Arrived at KL – fantastic electrical storm, then very heavy rain, followed by brilliant sunset...

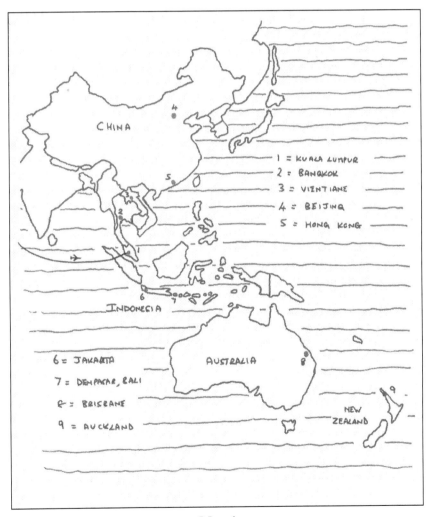

Map 1

I was stopped at customs coming into Malaysia, as I had brought too much wine. My sister-in-law, Sheryl, had told me about a work colleague whose daughter was living in Kuala Lumpur. When she had told the colleague about my plans, he had contacted his daughter to ask if she would mind me staying over. She said that I could. Although I would have been happy to have found my own accommodation, I thought it would be churlish not to take up the offer. In any event, I would probably be paying for the privilege of staying in some flea-infested dumps at various points on my journey, so it seemed crazy to reject the prospect of having some decent accommodation for free. I had brought some wine for her, my enquiries having revealed that she was missing good European wine.

Anna had a condominium in a central part of Kuala Lumpur, which turned out to be very plush. The taxi took me virtually to the front door leading to the communal entrance. Anna was extremely friendly and made me feel very comfortable from the beginning. She told me that I could stay for as long as I needed and that I should not stand on ceremony when wanting to use the bathroom, or to make something to eat or drink in the kitchen. On being shown to my room, the first thing that I did was take out the photograph of my nan, which I had kept safe, wedged between two books, and stand it on the bedside table. "Hello Nan," I silently mouthed and immediately became dewy-eyed. I gave Anna the two bottles of wine that I had managed to salvage. She was pleased at the gesture.

Anna's boyfriend, Gerald, arrived about 20 minutes after I did. He was the complete opposite of Anna, being cold, quiet and unfriendly, almost to the point of being hostile.

Although I had never met Anna before, she was from my home town of King's Lynn and, as a consequence, we had plenty to talk about. I quickly came to the conclusion that Gerald felt threatened by the fact that Anna and I had a common background. In truth, he had nothing to fear, but I was too tired to let it worry me too much.

After I had taken a shower and freshened up, Anna had prepared a delicious Thai meal and in the course of our conversation I learnt that Anna was part of a brand-new project in Kuala Lumpur, that being the creation of a Malaysian Philharmonic Orchestra. The organisers had tempted in talented musicians from all over the world to be part of the new venture. Anna was taken on as a librarian. In my ignorance, I never knew such a position existed. My re-education was swift. Anna made sure that I understood that the librarian is almost as important as the conductor, as he or she is responsible for organising the sheet music for each individual member. Gerald was a percussionist in the orchestra. The project was initially intended to run for two years, with the possibility of extensions if it was successful. It was clear that so much effort – and money – had been ploughed into the project that failure was almost unthinkable. I had managed pretty well to stay awake into the evening but my eyes were starting to glaze over. I did just catch the exciting news that the home of the orchestra was in the newly-built Petronas Towers before Morpheus led me into the ether.

Monday 1st March

First full day – Anna brought me a cup of tea in bed. This morning I feel full of shit. I couldn't sleep but I couldn't wake up either. I eventually got up.

I went to the roof – took photographs of KL's skyline.

I went walking – saw mosque – Merdeka Square – very pretty with cricket pitch in the middle. Very colonial. Then walked along river to railway station – very attractive, white – minaretted building – pushed a chap in a wheelchair to platform 4. Walked back via swimming pool and plaza. Girls very pretty.

Went for Cajun meal in evening – met Sally, very nice. Gerald not there. Anna apologised for him. Good food. Anna's a really lovely girl.

Tuesday 2nd March – Rehearsal

Felt like shit yesterday morning – feel much better today.

Leisurely morning – met Anna at 12 noon at Petronas Towers – at first glance not as grand or as high as I had imagined. However, it grew on me, with its impressive stainless steel structure with gardens and fountains and patterned mosaic-style stone work on the ground. I went up to the bridge in the middle. Had fantastic views over the golden triangle and the rest of the city. Then went to watch the Malaysian Philharmonic Orchestra rehearse – I believe Tchaikovsky's Swan Lake. Anna left me while she worked.

Had lunch at a Chinese diner – good.

I went to gardens later, went to Birdland and a butterfly park. Birdland was best.

Evening with Anna and friends – Anna's lovely – Gerald's a real jerk. Total dickhead – she can do a lot better than him (I hope Anna doesn't read this). Great Chinese.

Booked ticket for Ipoh tomorrow.

Wednesday 3rd March – "An interesting diversion."

I left KL today. The rucksack was very heavy but manageable.

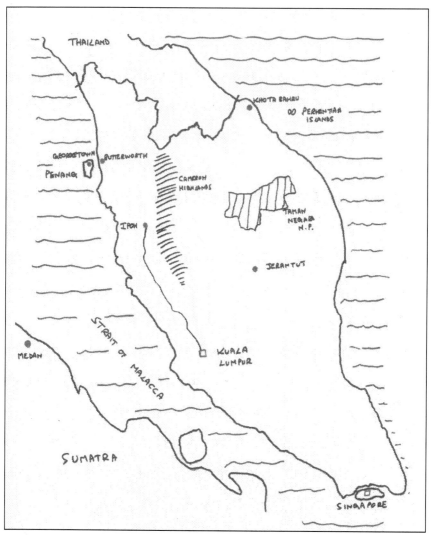

Map 2

Went to Ipoh – met a group of Japanese men from Osaka – old man gave me prawn crackers. At Ipoh had meal – the Japanese beckoned me to join them. They are on their way to Penang.

Found hotel Winwah (pronounced Winner) – grubby but not too bad.

Later met a very nice man.

At the beginning of the day, Anna had dropped me off early at the bus station for buses heading North out of Kuala Lumpur and the journey was pretty uneventful, save for meeting up with a very friendly group of eight Japanese men on my bus. They spoke very little English, which meant that I did not manage to find out their main purpose of travel, but they seemed in good spirits so I guessed they were tourists. When we arrived at Ipoh a little after midday, I learnt that the Japanese would remain on the bus, which was continuing further North. However, the bus driver decided to take a lunch break at Ipoh and his bus would wait at the bus station for a little over 30 minutes, so the Japanese took the opportunity to quickly grab something to eat. I accepted their kind offer to join them. How could I resist? They chose half a dozen dishes of Chinese food from a roadside diner, which were laid out in the centre of the table and before I knew it a pair of chopsticks, still bound together in a sterilised paper sleeve, was thrust in my hand. There was no standing on ceremony with personal plates, since everybody was mucking in and eating communally directly from the platters of food, skilfully and rapidly stretching over and taking chopstick-laden portions at a time. I dived in too, giving the appearance of shedding my English inhibitions, whilst underneath trying hard not to let them show. The food was delicious. When it was all over they resisted all my attempts to make a financial contribution.

My purpose in coming to Ipoh was to try and find my old friend from my Polytechnic days, Leong. I had two addresses for him in Penang, which would be my next stop, and one here in Ipoh. Before I went looking, I needed to find some accommodation. With the help of Lonely Planet, I had in mind a shortlist of three hotels and as I made my way from the bus station to my preferred first choice, I was struck by how unfit I was.

With the glaring sun beating down from a cloudless sky, it was quite a struggle carrying my heavy backpack in the stifling heat of the early afternoon. When the first hotel turned out to be less than inspiring, and I stumbled off to the second, the struggle intensified.

I was reminded of something my Kiwi pal, Will, who was more experienced in backpacking, had said just before I left. He told me that as I travelled around I would get fit very quickly, but it would be difficult at the beginning. He reminded me that there is an inverse correlation between the weight of my backpack and my level of fitness. At the very beginning, my pack would be the heaviest it would ever be on my entire trip, with, for example, my full complement of books and all my bottles of shampoo, contact lens solutions and other toiletries being untouched. At that point, I would also be at my least fit. However, in the coming weeks as my load would lighten, my fitness levels would increase. With my discovery that the second hotel was worse than the first, and noting that the third hotel was a little way off, as I trudged wearily back to take a room at the first hotel all I could think of was, "Bloody know-all!"

Having placed my nan's photograph strategically in the room where I could see it and having organised myself, there was still plenty of time left in the afternoon so I decided I would immediately start looking for Leong's address. I hopped into a taxi, showed the address to the driver, and only ten minutes later I was standing outside it. When I knocked on the door, there were a great many dogs barking from somewhere nearby, but nobody was in. At least the dogs ensured that there was no chance that the owner would not have heard me. I went back into town, changed and had a Chinese meal that disappointingly was not a patch on the lunch I had enjoyed with my Japanese friends. I then went back in the evening to the address I had found earlier. This time I found a gentleman in. By banging at the gate to attract his attention, I had re-awoken the hounds from hell, which, to my horror, not only disturbed him but, from the various windows being opened, the numerous twitching of the curtains and the switching on of lights, disturbed all the neighbours in the area too. Unfortunately, the man I found was not Leong. The dogs turned out to be his and he had five in all, including a Rottweiler. When I explained my mission to him, he very kindly invited me in and made me green tea. He was a softly-spoken, slim, older Chinese man, possibly in his 60s, for whom the word 'inscrutable' had probably been invented and he appeared to live alone (apart from his dogs). His accent was strong but his English was very good. He informed me that he had lived in the house for five years and before that it was owned by a person who ran a pub and who apparently had been a very noisy neighbour, which he relayed to me whilst leaning forward and frowning. I couldn't help but wonder what the neighbours must have thought when this man moved in with his dogs! The man told me that the area had changed a great deal and the address of my friend might have done so too. Despite my protestations of, "You've made me tea, you've welcomed me into your home," and, "you've been very kind already," he insisted on later driving me back to my hotel.

When I thanked him, he said in his slowly-delivered, deliberate, thick Chinese accent, "You're welcome, it has been an interesting diversion."

I tried to telephone Leong on a number I had for him in Ipoh but I had no luck.

Thursday 4th March – Manchester United 2 – Inter Milan 0

Food today was great – had Chinese sweet dumplings with meat for breakfast, fried noodles for lunch and an Indian meal in the evening. I had my first loose stool today. But I don't feel too bad. The prices for my meals today were 50 pence, 50 pence and £2.00 respectively.

The bus from KL to Ipoh was 9.50 ringgit (£1.55), for Ipoh to Penang it will be a further 9 ringgit.

Today was hot, I believe in the thirties but I don't know for sure.

I went to the Ipoh Parade Mall and I spotted a sports shop that had a television on in the window showing Manchester United playing Inter Milan in the European Cup. Before I knew it, there were five others alongside me watching it from the outside. We were quite a crowd oohing and aahging as shots went amiss. United beat Inter Milan two nil.

I then went to the Perak Tang Temple – which was a cave with Buddhas and paintings and alters lit with candles inside the cave. I went up the steps to the top of the hill which was a rocky limestone outcrop. I met a Singaporean girl and her cousin there and we talked for a while. I saw monkeys near the tourist shop at the bottom. My feet were smelly for the first time. I have gone through two pairs of pants.

Friday 5th March – Stilt Houses

I left Ipoh today and I arrived in Georgetown, Penang.

Much more lively place than Ipoh which I have only now discovered is a dead, defunct tin mine town.

My hotel – Cathay – is much nicer than at Ipoh but a bit more expensive too at 69 ringgit (£11.50) – I need to watch the pennies.

I tried to find Leong. I went to 53 McAlister Road – it's either a deserted run-down house (unlikely) or what looks like a Pakistani school or mosque. Then I went to 88q Green Lane – it's in a residential area. However, the house is now a business. There was nobody there who knew Leong but the girls did try very hard to help me by ringing directory enquiries. We had no luck.

I saw the harbour and the esplanade area in the evening. The harbour was particularly interesting. An entire community, comprising probably fifty or so individual dwellings, live in rickety wooden shacks built on stilts directly above the water.

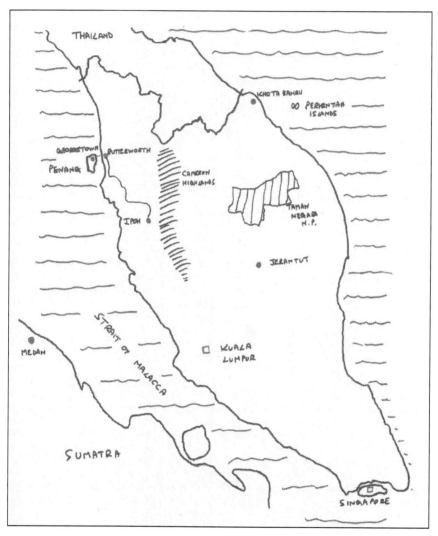

Map 3

Saturday 6th March

Slightly more inspiring day. Yesterday I had a touch of the 'what am I doing here?' blues. Today I felt better despite a bad night's sleep.

Found a shop called Lam Leong – which was a clothes shop. It was a nice try but he was not there and nobody knew him. A lady there referred me to a biscuit shop called Leong Nam. I went there but again nobody had heard of him. I then went back to 53 McAlister Road again. I asked around.

Saw man who I had seen working in my hotel last night on opposite side of 53 McAlister Road. Had chat with him and explained what I was trying to do, whereupon he offered to try to help me – asked at three or four places about Leong – one was possibly a good lead. A neighbour said that 53 used to be a camera shop (possibility, because Leong was good with cameras). Apparently, he left about five years ago. I was directed to a nearby shop where I was told that a man now works who was previously an employee at the camera shop. He was not there and I was told to go back on Monday. I may well try.

Had stomach trouble again and only just made it back to my hotel. Went to the esplanade, saw Fort Cornwallis and I wandered around the waterfront in the evening.

Sunday 7th March – Med-Angels

Great day – best yet. Went to Komtar – booked bus for Khota Bahru for tomorrow evening. Then went to top of Komtar tower – great views across the straits and everywhere. Then got bus to Batu Ferringhi...

My first week had not been bad. I had met some interesting people and seen some interesting sights but today was the day that my adventures truly started.

I had long since been planning to travel to one of the tropical islands off the East coast of Malaysia early in my trip. I thought it would do me good to wind down and relax, to take a holiday within a holiday. The Perhentian Islands had a good write-up. So, midmorning I went to the Komtar – the bus station – and I booked my ticket for the following day to travel to Khota Bahru, the town on the mainland on the East coast for the boats out to the Perhentian Islands. I was looking forward to it. Perhentian Kecil (small Perhentian) sounded particularly idyllic, "[The Perhentians are] arguably the most beautiful islands in Malaysia... Long Beach on Perhentian Kecil is a beautiful long white sandy beach... as far as things to 'see and do' go, it's simply a case of lazing around and watching the coconuts fall" (Lonely Planet). I was going to have some of that.

Having booked my ticket I climbed my way to the top of the Komtar Tower where I was afforded extensive views towards the palm-fringed coast in the West, the ramshackle shanty town of old Georgetown directly below and South-East across the sandy straits that separate Penang from mainland Malaysia. In the distance, I could see the 8 ½ mile long Penang Bridge. Outside, the sun was beginning to sizzle.

I was keen on getting a little taste of beach life and, having read about some nice beaches on the Northern Penang coast, on descending from the tower, I hopped on a local bus headed for Batu Ferringhi. The bus was almost full, with me being the only Westerner on the bus. I was sat towards the back.

On the way, I became aware of a group of young girls, who were sat a couple of seats in front of me, who were animated and excited. I noticed (or was that just imagined) that one of them glanced my way whilst talking furtively behind her hand to her friend and then seeming to giggle. I smiled and she half smiled back, and then turned away, seemingly more out of disdain than embarrassment. Hey ho! Then about ten more minutes into my journey another girl in the same group also looked my way, smiled and simply said, "Hello." I smiled back. What else could I do?

Travelling in a North-Westerly direction away from the city, out of the windows over to the right I caught the occasional glimpse of a tiny sliver of startling blue sea behind the curious mix of new office blocks and old shanty town; gradually the sliver became thicker and more iridescent as the road headed diagonally towards the coast until it reached a point where the bus turned a dog-leg West, as the road started to run parallel to the sea, which was then about 50 yards away. Leaving behind the bustle of Georgetown, the bus rattled on for another 35 minutes. I had no idea where I should get off, but when the bus stopped and about half of the bus got off I followed suit as I assumed I would be somewhere about right. I was last off the bus, and paused to consult my guidebook. As the small crowd dispersed the same group of young girls was standing around. One of them approached me whilst I had my head in my guidebook and asked me in very good English, "Where are you going?"

I replied, "I was trying to find the beaches at Batu Ferringhi, but apart from that nowhere in particular."

She said, "Would you like to join us? There is a waterfall just behind the beach; would you like to come?" Well, it would have been impolite to refuse. What else could a gentleman do?

We initially walked on along the main road, with the sea still to our right, before we very soon branched inland off the main road onto a dusty track that did not look too promising. There were seven girls in total, to my eyes all of them beautiful, some stunningly so. I really thought I had died and gone to heaven. Five of them spoke very good English, and as we walked on I was the centre of attention as I was treated to a barrage of questions from those five. What was my name? Where was I from? Was I married (it did not take them too long to ask that question)? Why was I not married? Did I have a girlfriend? What job did I do? There really was no messing about, no standing on ceremony. Suddenly, we had arrived at the waterfalls, and I had been completely unaware as to how we had got there.

There was Ropida, the oldest one in the group and not unattractive in her own right, who seemed to cosset and fuss over her friends like a mother hen. She spoke very good English. There was young and pretty Erlina, in white top and green shorts, who spoke no English. Her cheeky laughter was very infectious and brokered any language barriers. There was the dreamily gorgeous Titin, in blue top and blue shorts. There were Liza and Ratna, who seemed welded together. I believe they were good friends back in their home town of Medan and, being quite young, they seemed to cling to each other for support. There was Julita, also pretty, who also spoke little English. And last but not least was the skinny, enigmatic, and oh-so-sexy – with her little black-framed spectacles, choke-chain round her neck and wet fringe falling across her brow – Ayu.

To be honest the falls were none too spectacular, comprising a series of mini rapids, but they were clearly popular with other locals. Even so, with the simmering heat starting to boil over, the cooling waterfalls were delightfully refreshing. The setting was perfect.

On arrival, it was really very sweet and trusting how behind their towels they very discreetly, but equally uninhibitedly, changed into their swimwear right in front of me. They were very endearing.

I was then treated to a magical couple of hours. We swam about. We laughed. We took photographs. Each of the girls insisted on taking it in turns to slide down the rapids with me. There were quite a few other people – all locals, no tourists – who were swimming there too. And many of the boys threw envious glances at me. I guess it was a bit greedy of me to have the company of these seven girls all to myself. But I speak only with hindsight, because I have to concede that I was blissfully oblivious to this at the time. They also shared their food and drink with me, and at one point when I – with typical English reserve – politely declined their invitation to eat, one of them, refusing to accept my answer started feeding me with her hands. With this act, in my very first week I had fulfilled a fantasy that I had harboured in relation to this trip, but which I had never imagined in my wildest dreams would come true. Probably my favourite book about Indonesia is 'Ring of Fire', by Lawrence Blair, which was also turned into a television series aired on the BBC in the 1980s. It is about two brothers, Lawrence and Lorne Blair, and their journey of exploration through the Indonesian archipelago for ten years during the 1970s and early 1980s. They described Indonesia as "Perhaps the last truly undiscovered area on earth." I found their exciting tails both fascinating and inspirational. One of their stories describes the occasion when the Blair brothers had arrived on the island of Buton, a small Indonesian island off the East coast of Sulawesi and one of my intended destinations later. They wrote about the reputation of the Biranese girls on the island:

"[They] warned us about the girls' reputation as practitioners of a dangerous form of magic which could trap a man on the island forever. We soon realised that the girls' magic was of a very straightforward kind. Almost without exception they were breathtakingly beautiful; their every movement a languid dance, their smiles open and confident... [On being invited to meet the Sultan at his palace that evening for dinner] we were sitting cross-legged on either side of the Sultan with a vast array of tiny dishes on finely worked brass trays stretching before us... I wish I could describe the Sultan's appearance but my eyes were elsewhere, for on my other side sat Sadria, one of his radiant daughters. In an island where most of the girls looked like princesses, the princesses looked like goddesses – and Sadria was no exception. She dipped her fingers delicately into a dish and, to my astonishment, popped a morsel of food into my mouth instead of her own. Sadria leant back on her heels, smiling at me expectantly. I shot a nervous glance at our host. He, too, was smiling, but with sardonic ambiguity, and my eyes shifted to his ceremonial dagger. 'Well,' he said, 'if you don't feed the poor girl soon, she will starve.' Not at all sure I was doing the right thing, I fumbled towards the nearest dish for a finger-load of food, and turned to Sadria. The sight of those slightly parted lips was almost my undoing but, with the hollow feeling of a gambler who has laid out far too much on a horse, I plunged the titbit into her mouth before my resolve could falter... 'This,' said the Sultan, 'is how we customarily feed our guests. It shows that we trust each other enough to have no fear of being poisoned.' Trust me enough! My God, I wasn't at all sure I could trust myself."

That was exactly how I felt, a prince amongst princesses, a guest at the banqueting table and, suitably enough, the trust that flowed through this entire adventure was very moving. That they should trust *me*, a complete stranger, so as to be able to change in front of me, to allow themselves to splash into my arms as they tumbled down the waterfall after me and to feed me with their own hands was a powerful uplifting feeling. I was very touched by it all, even more so as I began to find out about their tale.

All seven girls were from Medan on the island of Sumatra, Indonesia. I had always had a very high opinion of the friendliness of the Indonesian peoples and it was the ultimate self-certifying proof of my opinion that the first persons to truly befriend me in Malaysia were Indonesians. They had come over to Penang to work in the clothes sweatshops of Georgetown on a three-year contract. There they worked six days a week, from 8.30 in the morning to 5.30 in the evening each day, with only half an hour for lunch, not inordinately long hours, but in conditions that I understood were very hot, humid and cramped. And they did that for just 45 Rm (equating to roughly £7.50) each week. It was not lost on me that my daily budget on this trip was £20, and I had previously thought that *I* was living frugally. Sure, their accommodation – tiny, communal and none-too-clean – and their food – basic – was provided, so the sum of 45 Rm represented profit in the pocket but I was amazed to discover that the girls were able to save and send money home to their families back in Medan, which was their sole reason for being here in Penang. It was little wonder, therefore, that, with this being a Sunday and their one day off each week, the girls had been in such an excited mood, so excited in fact that they allowed me to be swept along on their tidal wave of elation.

I learnt that they had used some of their hard-earned money to purchase special foods to eat on this picnic. Not that it was barely possible, but I felt even more humble to think that they were perfectly happy – nay insistent – on sharing their food with me.

After a while – the time flew by, but I reckon it was about two hours later – everything suddenly changed. The girls stopped talking and the mood became subdued. When they started to dry their hair I realised that it was because it was probably time to go. The contrast seemed to emphasise the downtrodden sort of lives they lead in their sweatshops. They were clearly not looking forward to going back. And who could blame them? They would be working long hours, for little money, in cramped Dickensian conditions, in the stifling heat of the day, no doubt having to do close needlework so as to ensure their garments were of a sufficiently high standard, but having to work nimbly and quickly so as to ensure they made a profit for their employers. Perhaps they were on piecework. And all this away from their families. Little wonder that every now and again they would steal away for a couple of hours to breathe fresh air into their lungs and to breathe life back into their very existence.

We walked back to the bus stop. I hung around for a bit until their bus arrived but we didn't say a great deal. I felt like I should be making some sort of grand gesture as a way of thanking them for making my day so special. But I couldn't think of anything. I simply said thank you.

After they had gone, I hung around on the beach at Batu Ferringhi. It was a nice beach but nothing particularly special. Maybe my perceptions were themselves subdued as they reflected the feeling of anti-climax sweeping over me after the earlier excitement. I walked to the University Science building, and saw a number of monkeys clambering about the trees. In the evening, I managed to catch a little bit of a football match between Manchester United and Chelsea in one of the bars. But to be honest my mind was elsewhere. As my head hit the pillow that night I couldn't stop thinking about those little angels from Medan.

Monday 8th March

Not a huge amount done today as counting time down to tonight's trip to Khota Bahru.

I went to the camera place as recommended on Saturday to ask about Leong. Nobody had heard of him there. I then went to the post office to the telephone section.

I went through all the telephone directories for Leong Lam's address. I found six possibles but not one had the full Siew Leong Lam name. I tried ringing all the numbers just in case but I had no luck. I used a phone card but there was either no number or no answer or the person answered in Malay or Chinese and could not speak English. It was a very hot day but also very windy. The film, The King and I, starring Jodie Foster is being shot in Penang right now. I saw extras for that film. I did not see Jodie Foster.

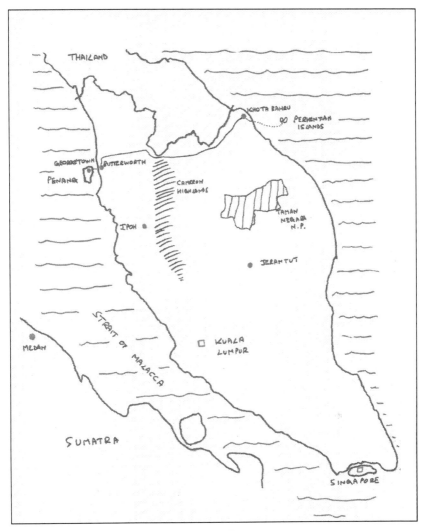

Map 4

<u>Tuesday 9th March – Perhentian Islands</u>

    I left Penang on the night bus last night at 9.00 pm and arrived in Khota Bahru at 5.00 am, having almost certainly not slept a wink. It was an extremely full bus and an extremely bumpy ride and I am not sure that my plan to save money on accommodation by travelling overnight was really worth it. I will need to catch up with my sleep. It might be better to take the night train to Bangkok, rather than the bus.

I met Pierre from Sweden. He has a French father. He's a truck driver and he is in Malaysia for six weeks travelling around. He does a trip every year. He is going to the Perhentian Islands too. Also on the bus were four Danes — one female who I got talking to later and got on well with (I don't recall seeing her since I landed on the island). At Khota Bahru I had a coffee at 5.00 am whilst waiting for the taxis to start at 6.00 am. The bus was 19.40 ringgit — taxi 6 ringgit. Then waited for the ferry to take us out to the islands. I went to Perhentian Kecil — Pierre went to Perhentian Besar. I stayed on Long Beach — the chalet is basic — 15 ringgit. It is a beautiful white, sandy beach — palm tree fringed — coral reef providing a natural barrier and therefore calm water — blue water — not very busy, but almost all backpackers. Got plenty of sun.

Wednesday 10th March

Got a little burnt yesterday — I'll be very careful today. I really seem to have struck into the backpacker's trail. I am in a chalet which is very basic and has an old mosquito net and a thin mattress. I discovered what I thought were rats running around on my ceiling which eventually turned out to be squirrels. Funny how a little bushy tail turns a nightmare scenario into an idyllic one. As I'm writing this a traveller is practising on his guitar. I have to share the toilet and bathroom which are 30 yards away and to get to which I have to pass other chalets, where invariably the occupants are sitting around outside reading — lovely! If I am carrying a towel they know I'm going for a shower, if it's a toilet roll it's something else. Everybody is sitting on the balconies of their chalets pretending to read books but secretly watching and declaring, "I know what he's doing." Did my first dobi-ing today. Dad refers to washing as dobi-ing. I am not sure where he gets it from but I have seen several signs here in Malaysia with the word 'dobi'. Water's drawn from a well. It is a little disconcerting that the well is five yards from the toilets!! There were several firsts — I used the padlock for the first time as none on the door — I used matches to light a mosquito coil and I used the torch at night. I met several travellers, including a lovely girl with somebody who I thought was her mum. How to prise her away? Also, a rather fat but quite attractive German in the sea — but I'm not exactly slim myself so at least we've got something in common. Lonely Planet talks about the Cempaka Chalets, where I am staying, being run by the "ever friendly" Musky.

I have yet to meet hm!!

PS I also had to use my first aid kit for the first time today, as I cut my hand on rocks when I was climbing up for a view.

Thursday 11th March – Turtles and Sharks

Great day, though got very burnt at the end. Saw squirrels, an osprey and a 4-foot-long monitor lizard.

I had booked to go on a snorkelling trip today, together with Jim and Brigs, a fun young couple from Southampton, who I had met and made friends with yesterday.

Both Brigs, who was naturally very pretty, not to say curvy, with her mousey-blonde hair and her super red bikini, and Jim, with his salt-and-pepper dyed hair and fake tiger teeth necklace, were happy to show off their lightly-toned, shiny bronzed torsos. They were backpacking through South-East Asia.

There were in all eight of us on the boat and the plan was that we would be taken to four different snorkelling sites, two in the morning and two in the afternoon, with lunch in the middle. The first site was a coral reef only a few hundred yards out to sea from Perhentian Kecil. Despite being so relatively close to our island, the reef was teeming with life and the fish seemed to be of every hue, from the brilliant orange and white banded clownfish, to fluorescent blue-green chromis and vibrant yellow butterflyfish.

On my first venture into the sea, as I went overboard, my goggles were knocked out of my hand, which then slowly sank down to the seabed some 12 feet below. I was contemplating how I was going to retrieve them since I was wearing my contact lenses, which meant that I would not be able to open my eyes and see where I was going if I swam down to get them. Jim immediately noticed my predicament and, after I had explained about my lenses, without hesitation he swam down to get them. As he did so, however, he cut his back quite badly on some coral. It was not particularly deep, but it did look very sore. I offered to Reiki him, explaining that I was a Reiki practitioner, and how the laying on of hands often works particularly well on bruises, burns and cuts. Had Brigs not been sat beside him, in my shyness, I might not so readily have offered to lay my hands on his naked torso. Had Brigs not been sat beside him, he might not so readily have agreed! But he did. Sitting on the boat as it made its way to the second site of the morning, I Reikied his back for a good 20 minutes. True to the way that Reiki seems to work, Jim told me that for the first couple of minutes the pain intensified, but then it started to cool quite rapidly and by the end he could not feel a thing.

With each swim both the sea-life and the experience as a whole became progressively better. The second site was in a shallow stretch of water between the two Perhentian islands. It did not seem to be particularly promising but we were advised that this would be a good chance to see turtles. True to their word, within a minute of entering the water I was swimming beside a magnificent large turtle. It was probably not large enough to be a leatherback, and was more likely to have been a greenback. He – or she – seemed not to be at all perturbed by my presence. In fact, if anything it was the opposite and he seemed almost to be just as curious about me, as I was of him. Or her. As I went up for air, he surfaced with me and then he quickly dived down again.

Back on the boat, we headed to the only village on Perhentian Kecil and moored up for a spot of lunch. By now Jim's cuts were feeling sore again. Without prompting, Jim asked me to Reiki him again. I did so for the best part of 30 minutes. This time the pain and heat disappeared much more quickly and, thankfully, never returned.

In the afternoon, we swam at two more reefs, and at one of them I suddenly spotted a shark, some five or six feet in length, which came within three or four yards of me directly below where I was snorkelling. It was a reef shark, which I was assured was harmless.

It was gliding effortlessly just above the reef itself, looking for prey. Before long it was joined by a number of other reef sharks and in all I counted six separate individuals. Absorbed as I was by the multi-coloured spectacle below me, my initial alarm very quickly ebbed away.

My otherwise brilliant day had a sting in its tail. I had swum and snorkelled all day without any top on, oblivious to the fact that I had exposed my naked back to the tropical sun at its strongest, over a period of three or four hours. I only realised when it was much too late that the water washing over me had magnified the sun's power, and the coolness of the water on my back betrayed the reality of what it was truly doing to me. My back was lobster-red raw as a result. So painful was it that I could not even enjoy the reciprocal laying on of hands on *my* back by the gorgeous, still curvy Brigs, lashing after-sun by the bottle over my back.

Friday 12ᵗʰ March – Monitor Lizards

After burning my back so badly yesterday, I made sure that I stayed in the shade all day today. I also decided that I would stay here two more days than I had originally planned to give my back a chance to heal. It would be no great hardship to hang around this idyllic place.

For the second time now I have been asked if I am a travel writer. I said, "No," but perhaps I ought to pretend that I am. It would be fun. I was told that I look intelligent! I suspect the reason why people think that I work for Lonely Planet is because I am avoiding the sun to give my back a chance to heal, and thus spending the vast majority of my day sitting in the shade on the veranda of a restaurant where I am regularly topped up with either freshly-squeezed orange juice or coconut milk. And I am sitting catching up with writing some postcards to my niece and others as well as writing this diary. I guess people are assuming that I am writing up my notes for publication later!

I moved chalets after the first night – I now spend 25 ringgit per night, 10 ringgit more, which means that I am spending approximately £4.20 as opposed to £2.50. It's a much better chalet and in a much better location. As cheap as it still is for me, it represents over half a week's wage for my Indonesian friends in Penang.

I saw several lizards today – the islanders call them iguana but they looked more like monitor lizards. There was one near my chalet last night – he was right beside my door tonight – three-foot long. But I saw several bigger ones on the other side of the dunes. I later tried to stalk one to try to take a good photograph – and I was failing, having spent a good 50 minutes or more – but then I heard the sound of crackling leaves to my left and a huge monitor lizard approached from my left unaware that I was there. I stood still. He came to within eight feet of me and stopped and looked at me, his tongue darting out. I should have some brilliant photographs. I saw my first really big spider today – four inches wide – which was in my bathroom. My burns are getting better. I did nothing today. I have done 17 postcards so far. When I got back to my chalet in the late afternoon my friendly local monitor lizard was waiting for me.

Saturday 13th March – Stuck on top of rock

I saw my local monitor lizard in the morning – it looks like he had managed to find something to eat. I take comfort from the fact that he is probably keeping me safe from something undesirable entering my chalet.

My shoulders came up in ugly blisters today. Still it is a good sign that my body is repairing itself. I was getting restless so I got a taxi boat to Perhentian Besar. I was dropped off at the Northern tip of the island – 7 ringgit. I then walked along a path which seemed to follow just inland from the sea, heading South. I lost the path at one point and I clambered up on a rock only to find a sheer 12 foot drop diving straight down to the sea on the other side and going back suddenly became very difficult. I was stuck.

I was trying to find a way down when a small boat came lumbering past. Rather than suffer the ignominy and embarrassment of asking for help I pretended that I was admiring the view and I squatted there. The boat and his passengers seemed to take an age to move off. I was about to try again when along came two snorkelers. I felt a real twat. I eventually had to jump into the water. Thankfully, it wasn't too deep. I had protected my camera and other belongings by placing them in my rucksack which I held above my head but my shoes, shorts and underpants got a right soaking. I felt a right fool. I found my way out and carried on walking. I had a drink and bite to eat on Perhentian Besar. Then I got a taxi boat back to the village on the Southern part of Perhentian Kecil and I walked all the way back. It took nearly two hours to walk back from the village to Long Beach. I saw more lizards and at dusk an extremely large bat – probably a fruit bat. As I was planning to leave early in the morning, I said goodbye today to Brigs and Jim, who had decided to hang around for a day or two longer.

Sunday 14th March – met German woman in Malaysia who teaches English to Indonesians

I left Perhentian Kecil on the first boat this morning at 8 o'clock. I had to get a small boat to take me from the beach to the main boat 100 yards offshore (2 ringgit). Then it took two hours for the boat to get to Kuala Besut. From there I arranged a share taxi with a Brit and a German woman who I learnt is teaching English to children in Kalimantan (the Indonesian side of Borneo). She was quite austere and brusque – seemed a typical German type – but quite a character. Then when the Brit left us we shared the taxi one step further to the train station at Wakaf Baru. I sorted out a ticket for the train for tonight – third class, 17 ringgit. I went back to Khota Bahru. I left the German woman and I wandered around to kill time, being the best part of six hours. I did a lot of sitting and reading. Then I got a taxi to the train station which left at 6.45 pm and is due to arrive at Jerantut at 2 minutes past midnight. We'll see. Finished off my third book – today was Charity (Len Deighton). My first was Faith in the same series and then a Margaret Yorke book – pretty poor in my opinion. Stayed at Jerantut – 25 ringgit.

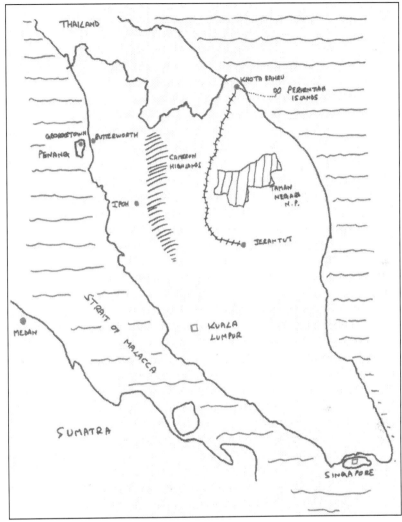

Map 5

<u>*Monday 15th March – Riverboat Trip*</u>

My reason for coming to Jerantut was because I was intending to spend a few days exploring the Taman Negara National Park, being Malaysia's biggest and most important nature reserve. The description of it as one of the oldest and most pristine primary rainforests still existing in the world was one of its biggest draws, the description being apt since it has never been affected by any of the ice ages of the previous 130 million years, and it has also been generally free of the geological upheavals prevalent in other parts of East and South-East Asia. Access was strictly controlled and limited in terms of both numbers of people allowed in and the areas readily accessible. In fact, the only way to get to the park's headquarters was by way of a 60 km upriver boat trip.

I left Jerantut today – eventually – got up late. Given talk at 12.55 pm to explain what we could expect in the nature reserve. Taxi shuttle to Kuala Tembling – 6 ringgit – got permit – 5 ringgit – camera licence – 1 ringgit – and 2 x ferry tickets – 38 ringgit.

The boat trip was great – long, narrow boats, flat to the water. The river was very wide and the sediment made it very muddy looking. Saw some Orang Asli people – also loads of kingfishers, many of them diving, a hornbill, swallows, a monitor lizard on the bank, water buffalo and domestic cattle. It was a great journey. The boat conked out at one point as it was attempting to go over rapids. We were drifting back down stream and the two crew members were obviously a little concerned. But they got it going again, and we made it. I decided to stay on the village side – we arrived at about 5.15 pm – barely time to adjust to what's going on. My room's ok – had to get it down to 43 ringgit – took out Nan's photograph. The main part of the village is separated by the river from the resort itself, so to get to the resort side we need to take a boat each time – half a ringgit.

My sunburn is now peeling very badly.

Tuesday 16th March – Terrapin

I saw a hornbill outside my chalet today. I had a busy day walking. It was supposed to be a gentle loop, approximately 3 – 4 hours – but it took me from 11.00 am to 5.45 pm. I did stop at several places but it was still a lot more arduous than I had anticipated. The extreme humidity meant that my t-shirt was dripping with sweat within minutes of entering the forest. I didn't see a huge amount of wildlife – a two-foot terrapin was the highlight – it was enjoyable though. Saw several birds that I couldn't properly identify. I walked on the canopy walkway – at times it was very high up and a little unnerving. I think it was the sounds of the forest that more than anything else were amazing. I walked to one of the hides and it was derelict. At one point, I was following the river which was very pleasant, when I saw a boat go down and I thought I saw Jim and Brigs – the male person in the boat had got grey/white flecks in his hair and was topless – and the female was very fair with a red bikini – their trademarks. They said that they were coming to Taman Negara but they would have had to follow on very quickly to get here by now. At night there always seems to be lightning flashing in the distance somewhere.

Wednesday 17th March

Today was a do-nothing day, although not intentionally. I had been regularly crossing paths with a singularly unattractive, rather obese, French girl. I don't know her name. Somehow, she knocked me out of my stride. I had intended to make an early start but I bumped into the French girl in the morning and she seemed to be coming on to me, dropping hints about trekking together. It was 10.30 am by the time I had broken free and I was ready to go off trekking, only to discover that the river bus had left at 10.00 am and the next one wasn't due to leave until 3.00 pm. I enquired about chartering my own but it would have cost me 70 ringgit. I had met an Aussie couple from Perth – the woman being French and the man, I believe, Singaporean – on the day that I arrived. They were in the taxi that a group of us shared to get from Jerantut to the ferry. I bumped into them today and they told me that later they were going on a boat trip so I asked to join them and they agreed. So I relaxed until at 2.00 pm I went up river with them.

We shot seven major rapids. I saw no real bird or animal life on the way. It was, however, a pleasant trip. Back in the village, I got talking to a local girl called Narani who works in a shop near me. We attempted to talk for an hour or so. There was a very interesting night market today. I intend to do my trek tomorrow.

Thursday 18th March – Jungle Trek

This time I went trekking today as planned. I thought that I had managed to give the French girl the slip but when I got down to the river and got on the 10 o'clock river bus the French girl was already there. I discovered her name is Nicole. A Japanese lad was on the bus too. They were both going to the same hide. We got to Bumbun Kumbang at around 11.30 am. I hung around until 1.00 pm. I didn't see a huge amount whilst there – not that I really expected to. I saw a monkey, two hornbills and a squirrel. The Japanese lad was planning to stay for five nights. He'd got some pretty fancy photographic equipment. I then made my way back by walking. To my horror, the French girl came too. There were just the two of us. I later saw a wild boar, more monkeys, a monitor lizard, some hornbills, spiders, butterflies and a variety of other birds and insects. I saw a dead five-inch-long millipede. It was a great walk but very taxing. We must have gone about eight or nine miles, which doesn't sound too bad but it's up and down, some of it very difficult underfoot and we had several streams to cross including one where we couldn't avoid getting up to shin deep. I also had to contend with several boggy areas and leeches. I saw some try and climb my boots but a combination of kicking them off and the insect spray that I liberally covered them with earlier seemed to repel them. The heat was extreme and the humidity was over 90%.

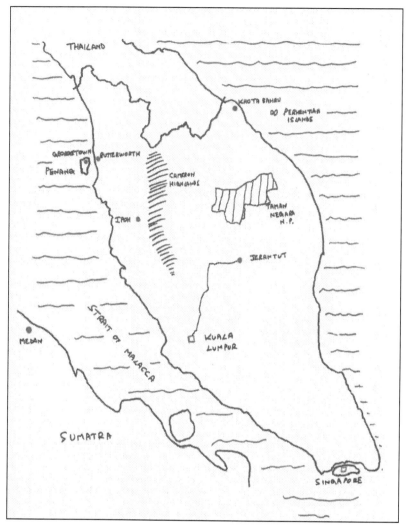

Map 6

I was soaked with sweat within five minutes of walking, not that it seemed to deter the obese, still singularly unattractive French girl.

Friday 19th March

During the week, my groin had been aching and was very painful on Wednesday night and again last night. I gave my groin an intensive Reiki and today it was virtually perfect.

I left Taman Negara today.

The French girl was there to see me go. I feel mean describing her the way that I have but there was something ever so irritating about her. I got the ferry boat back which left at 9.00 am. The French and Singaporean Aussies left today too and at the other end we shared a taxi to Jerantut and then on to Kuala Lumpur. Walked to Anna's. Got there at 3.45 pm. Went into shops – having left rucksack – and I bought some new soft shoes plus insoles plus shoe spray. This should do the trick. I went back and met Anna. Had promised to see a concert with the Malaysian Philharmonic Orchestra. Can't get a ticket for the concert tonight but there is a good chance for tomorrow. Apparently, it should be a good concert tomorrow. Coming back to KL I first saw the twin towers from about 17 miles away. They were very clear. I saw rubber farms on the journey back. At Anna's I did my washing.

Went out on my own in the evening. Wandered around. Was approached by countless prostitutes (and male pimps). Got a bit tedious after a while. Most girls were unattractive. Had good (though expensive) Chinese in the evening, including duck (not Peking).

Saturday 20th March – Classical Concert

Great day. Having had a pleasant breakfast with Anna of tea and toast, she booked me in for a massage. I went and booked my train and bus tickets to go to Bangkok tomorrow. Then bought a Chinese phrase book.

I then went back and had the massage – traditional Chinese massage, so I was told – with a Chinese lady by the name of Jenny, which lasted one and a half hours. At times very painful but I felt great afterwards. It was really very relaxing and my body felt very supple and relaxed afterwards.

I had a meal of duck and rice for about 75 pence. A lot cheaper than yesterday but it was just as nice.

I then freshened up and I went to the concert in the evening. Not being a classical music aficionado, I have to admit that it was a really brilliant evening and I found some of the music quite moving. Firstly, there were several samples of Bizet. Then there was a violin concerto with a French soloist performing a piece from Saint Saens. He was brilliant – I couldn't stop applauding. He did five or six bows and even an encore, which was clearly not planned for. His music was very passionate. The little Chinese lady who *was sat next to me was crying. In the second half, there was the second symphony by Sibelius. Again, very good. Both Anna and her friend Sally were equally enthralled by it – Anna calling it one of the best she had seen.*

We then went on to a bar to watch the England v France Five Nations rugby match. I had a few beers and it was all very good. Anna was really very sweet. Even Gerald was a bit better than before. Though that is almost certainly because he knows that I will be leaving tomorrow. A great night. The music had been French and Finnish and the guest conductor and violinist had both been French too.

21ˢᵗ March – Lad Knocked Unconscious

I spent all day on the move. I got a taxi to the bus station (3.20 ringgit – 60p), then got bus to Butterworth (17 ringgit) then I got the long-distance night train to Bangkok (60 ringgit). On the train, there was a bit of drama that could have led to a fatality. As we were approaching the border with Thailand there were some young kids playing around close to the track. Some of the kids threw mud and bricks at the train, presumably for a laugh. All the windows were down and a lad who was sitting directly behind me was struck by something. There was dried mud and stones everywhere on the floor in the carriageway. I looked behind me and I saw the lad had slumped. I didn't twig at first what was happening. He looked like he was leaning over but then it became clear that he had been knocked unconscious. I was just about to get up to go to his aid when a person sitting nearer to him caught him and very quickly the conductors on the train raced to him too. He came round fairly quickly although he was a bit delirious at first. The poor lad, who could only have been about 14, seemed OK.

I made it into Thailand.

CHAPTER 3

Thailand

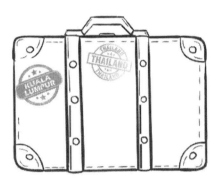

<u>Monday 22nd March – New Suit</u>

The night train into Bangkok was late arriving – one and three-quarter hours. I took quite a few photographs on the way. Had a reasonable sleep on the train. By the end I was really filthy with dust that had blown in through the open windows. My nails were full of it. I got a taxi to my intended hotel – 60 baht (£1.00) – the room was quite reasonable with a bath, 250 baht (£4.20). After a shower, I went wandering. I met one lad who told me that today was a Buddhist holiday and that many temples were closed. He gave me directions to one that was open and he also recommended that I should go to a clothes factory named Diana, where there were some really good deals. I went to the temple – Wat In – whilst there, another man got talking to me, and he too recommended that I should visit the same clothes factory as the earlier guy had suggested. Thinking that it was too much of a coincidence that they had both said it, and, thinking there might be something in what they said, I went there and ended up buying a new suit (plus a shirt and tie thrown in). It will be made to measure and posted to the UK in about three weeks. Paid by card. It cost 13,500 baht (£225.00) which is cheap for what I am

43

getting. (Did I really write that?!) Then I went to a second temple. I got talking to a man there too. He advised me that I should visit Patpong, Bangkok's most notorious red-light district, as it would be an experience for me but he recommended that I should go elsewhere for sex!

I hadn't realised it but I stumbled on a cremation ceremony earlier today. I saw the back end of it. I had Thai food in the evening – what else – which was very spicy but very delicious. In the evening, I was approached by several men offering to find me a girl. During the evening, it was difficult not to look at a girl and wonder if she's a prostitute. The girls are so beautiful that I am half tempted to indulge but I am afraid.

Tuesday 23rd March – Nakhom Pathom

I got up, which was very difficult as I felt very lethargic. I tried to go to the bus terminal but I lost an hour when a tuk-tuk driver took me on an unscheduled and unrequested detour via another clothes shop. This was similar to the shop I went into yesterday. The rhetoric sounded remarkably similar, "Our suits are all made to measure... we will get you a client number and you will be sent a catalogue later... this is your last chance because they are only available for one week." This was everything that I had heard at Diana. This made me wonder whether yesterday I had been duped. However, if so, it was very clever because it seemed as though I had met up with the two men yesterday apparently randomly and entirely separately. They were seemingly ordinary members of the public and were clearly not tuk-tuk drivers!! Thinking it through and trying to apply logic, I convinced myself that precisely because they were so credible, they were entitled to be believed and perhaps I had not been duped after all. But a question mark would remain until I returned home.

I eventually made it back to the bus station and travelled out to Nakhon Pathom, the largest, and one of the oldest, Buddhist temples in the world. It was very impressive. I met and talked to a Buddhist monk in his orange robe who was 39 and spoke good English having been to the UK and elsewhere. He invited me to sit with him and he gave me some Chinese tea, and we sat chatting for over half an hour. I later got the bus back. I had intended to see the floating market but I was too late.

I thought of going to Patpong in the evening but I chickened out. I saw police and firemen at the scene of what must have been a serious fire. Temperatures today touched 40 degrees in Bangkok. I had a delicious soup on the roadside – very good – 35p.

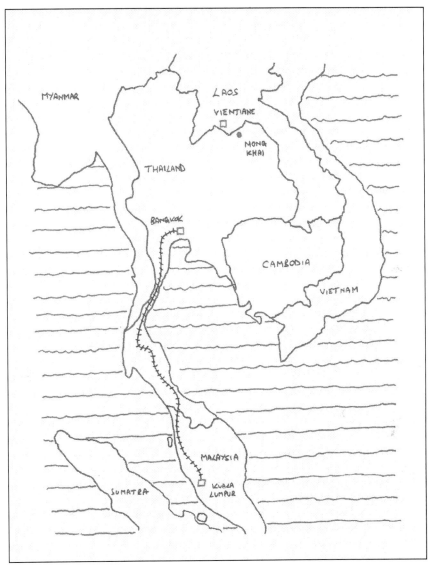

Map 7

Wednesday 24th March – Thai Massage

Woke up to a major thunderstorm – one clap was really, really loud. Poured with rain. At just before 12 noon I booked a train ticket for the night train to Nong Khai *leaving later today. The train was due to leave at 8.30 in the evening. However, I could not pick up the ticket until 4 o'clock in the afternoon, thus leaving me four hours to kill before picking up the ticket and four hours to kill thereafter.*

Before ....

I went to the floating market at Wat San – not there, as I was too late. It had ended at around 9.00 am. Cost 420 baht (£2.00) by taxi going, 3½ baht (5p) by using the bus coming back. Then went on riverboat – the views of Bangkok from the river were good. Went back to the booking office and collected my ticket.

After ....

Although I would have liked to have spent more time in Bangkok and Thailand, my timings were tight if I wanted to get up to Laos and China. Having arrived into Bangkok on the night train from Malaysia two days ago, I was about to take another night train, this time to go to Nong Khai, a town very close to the Thai border with Laos.

With a little over three hours to kill, I decided that I would take the plunge and indulge myself with a Thai massage. I had passed an unprepossessing place close to a busy highway two days before, which had advertised as offering a traditional Thai massage and which was about a 20-minute walk from my hotel. By this stage, being nearly four weeks into my trip, the wisdom of Solomon, i.e. my friend Will, was coming true in that I was acclimatising and getting fitter with each passing day. I would never be a Mr. Universe or a David Beckham but I was becoming tanned and toned and I cannot deny that my male hormonal juices were starting to flow. I had previously met and engaged in conversation with several very beautiful girls in Malaysia. Here in Thailand the girls seemed to be one notch up and were even more stunning. Consequently, I had found the discussions with the tuk-tuk drivers somewhat titillating in that it was hard not to think of the blissful pleasures that might be waiting for me at the other end. "You want suck or f***?" they would say, or, "You want one girl or two girls... you want to have a bath with a girl... you want girl with baby oil?" However, the horrors of what might await me at the other end and, even if the fantasies were to come true, the potentially dormant and dangerous diseases that might lurk and fester within my body only to erupt in a pestilential way some weeks or months later was, thankfully, more than enough to persuade me to keep away from the fleshpots of Bangkok.

It was with this background that I found myself at the door to the Thai massage parlour. It had looked reasonably authentic when I had passed by it two days earlier but there was no way of telling whether it would be truly authentic or would be a knocking shop unless or until I went in. Walking to the door, I momentarily hesitated before plucking up the courage and entering.

Inside there was darkness and I thought it was closed, but very quickly some strip lights flickered on to illuminate a corridor and a man and woman, both in their thirties, and of the Orient, came towards me. I said to them exaggeratedly slowly, one word at a time, "I... want... Thai... massage... no... sex."

"Yes... yes," the man said, equally slowly. "You... choose... girl."

Before I had fully taken on board what was happening, I had been ushered down the corridor where over to my right bright lights came on inside a room behind a window, which I quickly learnt was one-way mirrored glass. Inside the room were sitting 50 or so Thai girls, all fully clothed and of differing ages, though mostly were young and very pretty. They were each carrying a number. Immediately thinking that it did not feel right, I repeated to the man, "No sex."

"Yes, yes," he again replied and he pointed to several of the girls and said, "She good massage, she also good massage."

So, like a child in a sweet shop who was spoilt for choice, I took my time to look over the sugar candy before selecting one. Some of the girls were truly stunning, but I decided to go for one of the slightly older and slightly less attractive girls, on the pretext that she was likely to be a better masseuse. Although she was not the best-looking girl, she was still very pretty which I thought would be my insurance policy just in case.

"I will have number 95," I said, making me feel like I was ordering special chow mein. The price would be 180 baht (£3.00) for two hours. *Great*, I thought.

The lady who had accompanied the man when I first entered took me further down the corridor and through a door into another corridor at the rear, where there were cubicles on the right. She stopped outside one of the cubicles, bowed forward with her hands clasped together in front of her prayer-like and she then went out the back. Very soon thereafter number 95 came through holding a basket. She too bowed and also put her hands together prayer-like. In the basket, I could see towels and what looked initially like a linen cloth, but which turned out to be a very large and loose-fitting pair of shorts. Number 95 spoke no English, but she gestured for me to remove my boots and socks, and then for me to enter the cubicle. Inside the cubicle she showed me the loose-fitting shorts and after performing a mini version of charades I understood that I was meant to remove all my clothing and put on the shorts. She left the cubicle pulling across a curtain to protect my modesty and, like an obedient puppy that has just been house-trained, I did what I was told.

A couple of minutes later she returned with a stool and a bowl full of soapy water. She pointed to the stool. I sat. She knelt down on the floor, picked up my left foot and put it in the bowl of warm soapy water. With her hands, she carefully washed my foot. Her touch was soothing and sensual and I slowly started to relax. After about five minutes of gentle massage she reached for one of the towels, placed it on her lap, took my foot out of the water and dried it. She then patted my right foot, and understanding the drill I lifted it and placed it in the water. No words had been spoken as she performed the same ritual to my right foot. Having patted it dry, she pointed to a thin mattress that was laid out towards the back of the cubicle, gesturing for me to lie down on my back. I laid. What then followed was what I believed to be a truly authentic Thai massage. She used all of her fingers to dexterously apply pressure to all points of my body, she pulled all my limbs, stretched all my muscles, twisted my back round clockwise, before then twisting it anticlockwise, she cricked my neck more than once and again in both directions and she walked all over my back. She stretched me so much that I imagined this must have been what it was like in the Middle Ages to have been on the rack.

She had started initially with my legs, before moving to my arms, upper body, back and my head. Whilst she was working on my legs at times her hands applied pressure to various points high up into my groin such that despite the excruciating pain I could not avoid getting an erection. I considered this was maybe why the shorts were designed to be so loose.

Once she had walked over my back and completed her realignment of my skeleton I thought that was it. However, before I knew it, there was one more manoeuvre to do and she gestured for me to again lie down on my back. She then knelt down between my legs and pulled me close towards her, so that my legs were straddling her such that my backside was on her legs and my groin was perched perilously up in the air. Putting her hands up inside my shorts, she proceeded to apply finger pressure deep inside my groin area again. Instantly my flagging erection re-inflated, bulging through my loose shorts. She pointed to the shape that it was making and compared it to the thickness of her wrists, seemingly in awe of its size. Prostrate as I was, and being petrifyingly vulnerable, I was in no position to strut, but she triumphed in playing to my vanity and peacock-like my member proudly did the strutting for me. She then continued to search for pressure points so far up into my groin that it almost felt as though she was physically inside me.

Once she had finished working me in the 'presenting' position, she slowly rolled her knees from under me and then came and laid down beside me on my left side. I was still lying on my back. She paused and again I believed it was over, but her small soft-skinned hand moved slowly and snake-like inside my shorts, took hold of my member and started to masturbate me. Truly it would not have taken much longer to finish me off, but as I turned towards her I could also see just beyond her the dials of my watch, which was lying on the side. A cold frisson ran tingling down my spine as I registered what I saw. It was now 7.45 pm with my train due to leave at 8.30 pm. To my amazement, I had been there for over three hours. I sat up in a panic, looked at my watch to make absolutely certain and realised that, with about a 20-minute walk back to my hotel, time spent finishing my packing and then a 20-minute taxi ride going through the busy city centre to get to the train station, which was about four kilometres away from my hotel, not to mention the time it would take me to find the correct platform and locate my train, I was almost certainly going to miss it. When I quickly sat up, I startled number 95 so much that she must have thought that she had caught a hang-nail on me or something. Striving to reassure her, I picked up my watch and pointed to the time and then also quickly took out my train ticket, which had been poking out of my jeans pocket nearby, and I showed this to her too. She immediately understood what was happening and she could not stifle a giggle at my predicament. She jumped up and went out of the room to let me quickly get dressed. Looking back, I can only imagine what passers-by must have thought when they saw this panic-stricken mad Englishman running out of the massage parlour still tucking his shirt in.

On the way out, I gave the appearance of doing the honourable thing by paying number 95 a tip, being 120 baht more than was agreed, but frankly I was in too much of a hurry to wait for any change. She seemed very pleased, but maybe she was still struggling to stifle a giggle. Squeezing all the segments of my frantic journey into 44 minutes, I managed to catch the train, but only just.

As I sat on my seat and the train slowly edged out of the city and into the night, I felt as though my body which had reached boiling point back at the massage parlour, and which had remained at a rolling boil in the course of the 44 minutes that it had taken me to get to the station, was only now able to begin to simmer down. I was entranced and transfixed by the physicality of what I had just experienced and despite all my frustrations, I glowed at the self-indulgent sensuality of it all. She certainly knew which buttons to press. Literally.

As the flames of the conflagration inside me gradually died away and as I slowly came out of my trance and rejoined the real world, I realised that the Westerner sat opposite me was talking to me. It turned out that he was a middle-aged Aussie expat, named Adrian, who was married to a Thai girl and who was living and working in Thailand as a horse riding instructor. He turned out to be a 'been there, seen that, done it' type of guy, exactly what I did not need at this precise moment in time! When I unguardedly told him about my visit to the massage parlour with the room full of 50 girls, he rolled his eyes, licked his lips and took great delight in lecherously informing me, "Jeez, mate, you've just been in the chicken shed." Pausing only momentarily, he continued, "There are some real beauts in Nong Khai and Laos," grinning as he did so and exposing yellowing tobacco-stained teeth.

Thankfully Adrian got off the train two stops down the line and I limped off into the Thai night in peace.

Thursday 25th March

Today was always going to be a rum day after the frustrations of yesterday, and it was. By the time that my train arrived it was 8.45 am.

Went to a hotel in Nong Khai recommended by Adrian, known as 'Meeting Place'. All shut up. I went and had a coffee and then went back to the hotel and this time it was open.

The owner is an Aussie, and a Geordie lad from Newcastle, UK, was managing it for him. Room 200 baht – shared bath and toilet. Tried to sleep for half an hour or so. Had breakfast. Then wandered. At lunch I had soup, very good – 30 baht.

Walked down to riverside market – very good. Then hired tuk-tuk to see sights – agreed a price of 40 baht with one driver. He took me to one temple of a Hindu or Buddhist design. Then he took me to a beautiful sculpture park and gardens – Sala Kaew Ku – with giant concrete sculptures depicting Buddhas, Hindu gods and a seven-headed snake, very good. Then to another temple in Nong Khai town centre. Then he took me down to the riverside community. Then he took me back to town. In the end, he asked me for 200 baht. I refused and I gave him only 50 baht (being the 40 baht we had agreed plus a small tip). He was not very happy. Back at the hotel a bloke there told me that the tuk-tuk driver was correct and 40 baht would have been the price for going to only one of the temples. Felt very guilty and wandered around in evening to see if I could find the driver. No luck.

Later went to a shop advertising massage. Yesterday I wanted a massage but got sex (sort of). Today I would not have minded sex but all I got was a massage. It was very good – two hours and girl very pretty. Several times she teased me and at one point she kissed me and said, "I love you," and ran her hands over my chest. But that was as far as it went. Later found a karaoke bar. Later back at the hotel, I heard a strange sound coming from outside my room and when I looked outside I discovered the Geordie pissing over the balcony.

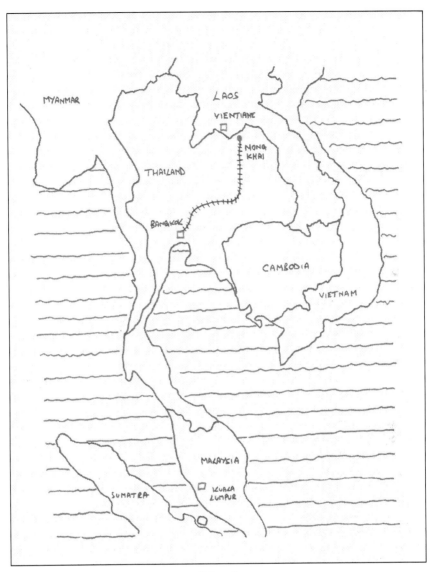

Map 8

CHAPTER 4

Laos

Left Thailand today and arrived in Laos. Although I thoroughly enjoyed my four days or so in Thailand, I think the old-Aussie-ex-pat/ugly-pissed-Geordie-with-young-pretty-Thai-girl scene depressed me a bit. Is it because they seem pathetic or is it perhaps because I am jealous? I guess it could be a bit of both.

Stool loose but not too bad.

Crossed into Laos fairly quickly via the Friendly Bridge over the Mekong – cost 120,000 kip (£15.00) for the visa. Met and crossed over with two Austrians – one a typical junkie and the other had two deformed hands. Found place to stay at Vannasinh guest house 70,000 kip – (£9.00). Room quite good. After placing Nan's photograph on the chair beside my bed, it struck me how seeing it somehow makes a plain room seem more homely. Went wandering. Laos seems a very friendly place. People are not pushy but are friendly and smile a lot. Met and talked to a number of girls in the marketplace – changed money. Better rate of exchange on the black market – 135 kip per baht in the bank, but 200 kip on the black market, and 5,000 kip for 1 US dollar in the bank as compared to 6,000 in the street. Also, you pay no commission. Talked to some girls at a market stall and they shared some of their food with me, encouraging me to feed off the same plate as them. Through open door of a house saw woman working on a loom. Stopped, talked and took photographs. She charges 100,000 kip (£12.00) for a garment which appeared to be very good. The children are very friendly and it seemed just like Bali fifteen or so years ago. Went to the Samlo pub in the evening and got talking to a girl called Sa. She was dressed a little bit tarty which is not to my taste but she seemed very pretty. We talked for a while and she pecked me on my cheek, before disappearing off into the pub. I left a short while later.

Saturday 27th March – Lao Massage

A good day. There haven't been many days thus far where I have enjoyed the localness of somewhere but today was one of those days. I think I am falling in love with Laos. Got up late. Tired. Don't know why. Wandered round all the Wats in the main part of the town. Talked to one young monk in orange robes. Then stopped to help some kids knock some fruit out of trees. One of the girls showed me what to do and I copied her. Not sure what the fruit were – they looked like limes but the skin was not so leathery. Saw the Victory Monument which is known in Laos as Patuxai, which looks like a smaller version of the Arc de Triomphe.

I forgot to mention that a bird shit on my head earlier (which is relevant because...)

When trying to find their inner selves, some people try meditation, others turn to Hinduism or Buddhism or other religions, some access other forms of spirituality and some, like my very dear Uncle Patrick, try them all. For me, few practices in life other than travelling over time come close to providing the feeling you get when your surroundings come alive, and your pace of life slows down so that you appreciate everything around you, every little nuance. You have time to notice the position of the sun in the sky, to feel the breeze in your face and to observe droplets of rain. Every little smile fills your heart, you can hear the laughter of children playing, you can enjoy the smells of flowers and breathe them deep into your lungs and not only do you absorb all life around you, but you feel part of it. That's how I felt on this day. Laos was the complete antithesis of Thailand, and for the first time in my trip I truly felt that I was travelling, properly travelling.

My guidebook had been full of glowing praise for a temple by the name of Wat Sok Pa Luang, which was located a few kilometres outside of Vientiane and situated in a forest. The temple was known for its rustic sauna, administered by eight precept nuns, as Lonely Planet described them. Amazing, I thought, not just nuns, but precept nuns. To this day – and in my shameful ignorance – I am still not sure what precept nuns do that other nuns do not. My dictionary tells me that the word 'precept' means a rule of conduct or moral instruction, but is that not what most nuns do, or at least subscribe to do, anyway? In any event I was sufficiently impressed that I decided to go there in the afternoon.

It transpired that the temple would have been easy to find, but it was made easier by my decision to take a tuk-tuk. Having been dropped off at the edge of a forest, as I walked along the track into the woods, I sensed the air of calm that exuded from the temple complex almost immediately. Shafts of sunlight beamed down through the forest canopy to illuminate the track before me, unidentified birds, hidden high up in the trees, were singing, I could hear the gentle distant hum of happy humans conversing and I could occasionally smell wafts of burning wood infused with incense. As I approached there were a little over a dozen people milling around an open wooden veranda under a thatched roof and one of them, an older lady with a wet sarong wrapped tightly around her, came towards me and bowed. I presumed that she must be one of the precept nuns, though she was dressed nothing like any of the nuns that I had ever seen before. She spoke only a little English, so she was never going to satisfy my curiosity about what a precept nun is (or does!). A gesture and a warm smile from the crinkled face of the sweet diminutive lady, reminding me of my dear departed nan, made me quickly understand that I needed to change out of my clothes behind a curtained area a little way off from the veranda and wear the sarong that was being passed to me. She also gave me a towel.

The action, or, more appropriately, inaction, took place back on the veranda. The group of people that I could see appeared to include one or two backpackers like me but also a gratifyingly large number of locals, reassuring me of its authenticity. The air of calm continued to be palpable. Some were quietly chatting, some were sitting back eyes closed, some were waiting their turn to use the sauna and some were sipping tea having already used the sauna. The sauna room itself was located in the middle of the veranda and was very small, in a dark wooden shed slightly larger than a telephone box and I could see steam drifting out of small holes in the walls. People had had to wait their turn to go in, because the room was so small and only big enough for two to fit in. I did not have to wait long before a rather attractive Lao woman in her 30s came out and it was my turn to go in. I could not help wondering if a similarly attractive friend of hers was waiting inside but when I got in, though it was almost pitch black except for tiny shafts of light coming in through the same small holes in the walls, I could just about make out the shape of a bear-like creature not unlike a huge Samoan rugby player. The room was only just big enough to hold the two of us and our knees knocked as I clumsily sat down. The air inside was steamy and pungent with herbs, making the atmosphere wholly conducive to relaxing, such that it was impossible to prevent my mind from drifting off almost trance-like.

Afterwards, the soporific ambience was maintained by the nuns' provision of copious amounts of herbal tea. I sat back on the wooden bench with eyes closed, arms outstretched on the wooden rail behind me, allowing the late afternoon sun shining and dappling through the surrounding trees to dance across my face.

I also took up the opportunity of having a Lao massage, which was occasionally brutally painful. The massage was performed by a small but extremely strong monk who was very good but was very tough. He clearly took no prisoners, with the neck cricking being the worst. I was given more herbal tea to calm me down afterwards.

I had already said a few polite hellos and had idly chatted to a number of people when I began speaking to a girl called Valda, who was there with a person who I presumed to be her boyfriend. She told me that they were from England and they were on holiday for one year travelling from India through to Vietnam. I then learnt that both Valda and her brother, Adrian, back in England, have links to the *Eastern Daily Press* newspaper, one of my local newspapers in Norfolk. Valda told me that she used to work there, and that her brother still does. When I asked her if she knew one of my friends, Trevor, who also worked for the same newspaper, she replied that both she and her brother knew him well and were very good friends with him. She explained that she used to live and work in King's Lynn, being a town in Norfolk where Trevor worked, and Thetford, a town where I lived at the time. It was truly amazing to meet somebody in such a remote place who had so many connections with me and knew one of my best friends.

The coincidence of meeting someone so far away from home, but with a connection to that home, is something I call my pianola theory. The 'pianola theory' is not so much a theory as a way of thinking. I first thought of the idea about 15 years or so previously when on a visit to London, which is a hundred miles from my home town, I first bumped into an old friend from school, who I hadn't seen for 15 years jogging down the Bayswater Road, followed 30 minutes later by seeing another friend walking further along the same road, who I hadn't seen for three or four years, followed shortly thereafter by walking past the great Sir David Attenborough. I couldn't claim that Sir David was a personal friend, but it was an amazing coincidence nevertheless. All of us have probably shared the same experience of seeing somebody we know so well in a strange place so far away from their familiar setting. However, as we make our way through life, we must over the years meet hundreds, if not thousands of different people, be they family, friends, work colleagues, acquaintances or friends of friends. None of us are staying still in one place and it struck me, therefore, that with all those thousands of people moving about all over the place, the statistical probability of meeting somebody we know at some point in a strange place is not that remote and that for every one occasion when we might actually meet somebody in these circumstances, there are probably hundreds of occasions when we have a near miss. I imagine what it would be like, if at all possible, to go back over our lives and trace our every movement and compare it with the movements of somebody else, a loved one perhaps, and see how close we might have come in the past. Maybe we were in the same street, or maybe we were in two different shops next door to each other, or maybe we even bumped into each other. I coined the phrase 'pianola theory' to describe this idea, the pianola, of course, being a self-playing piano, with its turning mechanism operating the piano via pre-programmed music recorded on perforated paper or metallic rolls. I imagine the width of the sheets of perforated music as being space, the continuous turning of the rolls as being time and, though this is stretching the analogy somewhat, our movements through time and space being plotted on the rolls like a graph. Experiencing pianola first hand through meeting Trevor's former work colleague Valda in a steaming, sweaty sauna, in the middle of a forest on the outskirts of Vientiane in un-touristy Laos was a humbling, poignant experience.

Having explored other shared connections with Valda, I sat back again with eyes closed and reflected on how the world sometimes seems so small. The ambient tranquillity of the temple sauna, being situated in an enchanted forest, with its magic enhanced by my meeting up with someone with direct links back to home, created such a gravitational pull that it was almost impossible to drag myself away.

As I walked back into town, I remembered that I had omitted to find out what a precept nun is. Frankly I was not too bothered anymore and I was content to remain in blissful ignorance.

In the evening, I decided to go back to the Samlo pub. At the time that I made the decision to return I wasn't really sure why, because the previous evening had been relatively uneventful and, having been there once, I had no real desire to go back. However, it seems quite obvious to me now looking back that I was half hoping to see the girl called Sa, who I had spoken to the previous day. I guess also that I was still riding on the crest of the high wave that I had been on since the afternoon, and didn't want the day to end.

Before I did so, I had a meal in one of the French restaurants in Vientiane, which had been recommended to me. Laos, of course, is a former French colony. The meal made a change from Asian fare and was tasty without being overly inspiring.

I then made my way to the pub. Sa was there and seemed to be the life and soul of the party. When she spotted me at the bar, her wide smile was disarming, and within a minute of arriving she started talking to me again. I very quickly learnt that her name is Dao, not Sa. Dao was 25 years old, was a little taller than most Lao girls, with strong, rather than soft oriental features. She was slim, and had long shapely legs, which she was not slow to show off. She seemed always to be on the go. The pub tonight was reasonably busy but she seemed to know, and talk to everyone. Her English was good and, even to my untrained eye, she seemed very keen on me. However, the evening took a nasty turn. Some expats came in and started talking to her. Disconcertingly, they all seemed to know her too. Everything was calm to begin with, but then suddenly one of them started shouting and swearing at her. I could not hear what was being said and, therefore, could not tell what the argument was about, but Dao stood her ground, and in arguing back to him she was giving as good as she was getting. It continued with her goading him and him letting rip. He seemed seriously angry. A Swedish bloke, who was sat at the bar next to me, advised me not to get involved even though she was my girlfriend. Up to that point I had only been talking to Dao and, even then, only for about 20 minutes, so I was shocked, though quietly pleased, that the Swede should make this connection. Frankly, I had not intended to get involved in the argument anyway. The conflagration fizzled out almost as quickly as it had started and the man left the pub.

Despite all the outward appearance of bravado, the argument clearly had shaken Dao. She was subdued and seemed to have lost some of the spark that I had seen in her earlier. Dao suggested that we go on to a nightclub and I agreed. We later moved on to a second club. Whilst there we started kissing and, as we did so, Dao brushed against me very provocatively. Reading my mind, Dao suggested that we get a room for the night. Before I could remind her that I already had a room, she explained that she was concerned that the staff at the Vannasinh hotel where I was staying might not be happy if she stayed there. She soon found us a room in a different hotel. We were both tired, and slightly groggy with alcohol, but after a quick shower we made love and we stayed the night. Sleep that night, when it finally came, was deep and satisfying.

Sunday 28th March – Lazy Day

Today was another good day. They come thick and fast here. I love Laos.

I woke up beside Dao this morning and although I enjoyed being in her company she was starting to become clingy. She came back to my hotel and I couldn't really shake her off. At the guesthouse, she remained downstairs and I went up to my room to sort myself out. I took over an hour – I confess by design – and by the time that I had come down she had left. I felt a bit guilty about us parting in this way.

Later ate Laap, which is a fiery local dish of meat with salad and herbs and was very good. I then walked along the banks of the Mekong River. The water in the river was very low and there were numerous sandbanks in the river. I was about to go down from the riverbank onto one of these sandbars when I saw a girl in the distance that looked just like Dao walking up from the river's edge. As I walked towards her I realised that it was indeed her. Vientiane is not exactly the biggest city in the world, but it is still a city and it was an amazing coincidence that I should meet up with her so soon again – a mini pianola. We spoke. She was with a friend who was older but also very pretty. They both walked back to the river edge with me. I enjoyed being with them and was actually enjoying Dao's company again after having had a short break from her. She appears to know everybody she meets, they all say hello to her and she appears to be well liked.

There were many rudimentary stalls, sited along the banks of the Mekong, frequented almost exclusively by locals and as we wandered along we ate and shared a mango, pistachio nuts, crab apples, barbecued chicken, sticky rice (which she fed me by hand) and coconut juice. It was all very enjoyable.

Dao's friend had a stomach ache and I Reikied her and she said she felt better. Today was a slightly cooler day which I quite liked. The Mekong here is very wide. I will see Dao later tonight. I cannot get over the fact of how friendly the Lao people are.

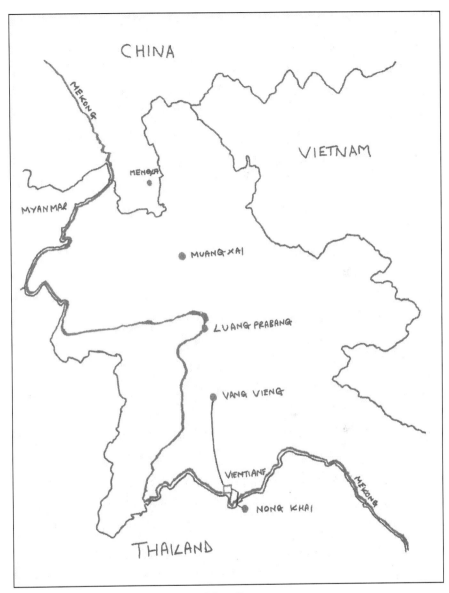

Map 9

Monday 29ᵗʰ March – Met Genevieve

Saw Dao this morning and she is actually growing on me. She is very funny and so full of life. Although I had met up with her last night we did not stay over in any hotel and it was quite endearing to see her waiting for me outside my guesthouse this morning. I was due to leave Vientiane today to head North to Vang Vieng. Dao came with me and we went and got some money; we shared a local pate baguette, I sent some postcards and I sorted out the bus ticket. We then had about an hour and a quarter to wait. We looked at each other and we both knew what we wanted. Dao found us a hotel room. It was really very funny because the normally fearless and unashamed Dao suddenly became very shy when she went to book the hotel room. Afterwards she suggested that we leave separately as she was a bit shy about us both going out together. She suggested that she would follow me. I left her to go and get my bus but I didn't see her later. Perhaps she didn't come. Perhaps she thought it would be easier this way.

On the bus, there was a gobby Yorkshireman who wouldn't stop talking to an American couple. The bus arrived at Vang Vieng and, as I got off, a girl on the bus, who had evidently seen me reading my Lonely Planet, latched on to me and asked if my book had any recommendations for accommodation. She came with me and we looked at a couple of places together. The second place was much better even though it was the same price as the first one, being 20,000 kip per room (£2.50). The girl suggested sharing. I was inwardly startled but outwardly tried not to show it, making out as if her suggestion was the most natural thing in the world. I agreed observing that the room only had one double bed. She is quite good looking but I don't want to try anything. It just would be nice to have somebody friendly and trusting. Toured Vang Vieng which is a great place. I love it already and everyone is friendly and smiling. The prices in Vientiane had included 55 pence for half a chicken, 88 pence for Laap, 28 pence for a baguette, 33 pence for a tuk-tuk across the town, 7 pence for tea and the room I shared with Dao for a little over an hour was £5.00.

Tuesday 30ᵗʰ March – Swim in Stream

The sleeping arrangements last night were civil and wholly innocent, despite the fact we shared the double bed. My roommate is called Genevieve, aged 23 and from Sydney. She is not unattractive.

Dao had yesterday given me things to give to my mum and I was starting already to reminisce about her and to think about the things we had talked about. She told me that her own mother died three years ago. She has eight brothers and sisters. She says that she is not like them and has often questioned her parentage, but I had reassured her that it sometimes happens. She sometimes smokes and she often swears but otherwise she reminds me of my very close cousin, Stephanie. Dao, like Steph, wears short shorts – which might be OK in the West but not here where women dress more conservatively – likes clothing and fashion, is money-orientated and likes shopping – all things that are not my cup of tea. She is married but separated. She has a son who is with his father in Norway. She telephoned him last night and she was really happy afterwards. Like Steph she is caring and has a lovely nature and if it sounds like I am quite taken with her I believe that I am.

Today was another great day. Got up later than planned. Breakfast was two eggs, baguette, coffee and orange juice – 66 pence. I hired a bicycle. Genevieve stayed in or around the hotel. Saw and spoke to an American lad by the name of Dayna, who was one of the Americans who had been pestered by the Yorkshireman on the bus yesterday. After we had got chatting we decided to cycle off together. The start of the journey involved clambering over a 100-metre-wide rickety bamboo bridge over the River Song at the edge of town before making our way along dusty tracks. On the journey, we saw a cave which was quite impressive. The temperature was very hot and we found a lovely running stream. We both went swimming and it was very refreshing. Then we found a local village which was amazing. Me and Dayna were the only two Westerners there. Pigs were running around near the children and both sets of mammals were filthy dirty. It was just great. On the way back, we split up and went our separate ways. I saw a woman and her daughter collecting grasshoppers for supper. There was a great sunset in the evening. I am missing Dao. I might ring her. The Song River was very beautiful. A beautiful river with a beautiful name. Had tea. I saw Genevieve and she is not too well. She thinks she had a very bad joint two days ago and she may need to go to the hospital in Bangkok. I had noodle soup in the evening and lemon juice. Genevieve had a banana shake. Not sure that it helped her. My arse is very sore from the biking. In the evening, I gave Genevieve a full body Reiki massage. It was very endearing that she so readily trusted me. She seemed to improve a great deal but later was poorly again. I discovered that the village that Dayna and I had visited earlier was a Hmong tribal village.

Wednesday 31ˢᵗ March – Accident in Shorts

Quiet day – made quieter by the fact that I was very loose today three times.

When I was with Dayna yesterday I apologised to him on behalf of the English race for the Yorkshireman who had collared him on the bus the day before. In fact, I discovered that his encounter was even worse than I had thought. His girlfriend and he had been backpacking together through Asia but were having some problems and at one point they had split up. He very quickly met another girl in Bangkok, but his girlfriend found out and wasn't best pleased. She had evidently thought that their separation was more temporary than he had thought. Thereafter, they had patched things up shortly before moving on together into Laos and onto Vang Vieng. Although they were together, their truce was, however, a fragile one. He told me that she is also a very strong feminist and is always moaning about the plight of Asian women. I then learnt that the Yorkshireman was the typically bigoted male chauvinist variety and he had told Dayna that he lives in the Philippines with two or three girlfriends or wives who cater for his every need. They wash his feet and clothe and feed him. After Dayna's dalliance in Bangkok this Yorkshireman was the last person that he needed to bump into. It was very funny in a black-humour way. The plot thickened today as I also found out that the Yorkshireman had brought a Lao girl with him but she wouldn't leave the room they were staying in.

Today I had a little walk. I saw children beside a school climbing a tree. Then somebody clanged a metal drum and the kids all cheered, clambered down and ran out to go home – so it seems as though the climbing of the trees was part of the school curricula. I later saw a very cool stream and I dipped my toes in it. I took a tablet in the evening to ease my looseness and I felt better.

I was missing Dao, so I later managed to locate the telephone number for the Samlo pub in Vientiane. I used the telephone at our guesthouse and I called the pub at 8.30 pm, but Dao was not there. I then telephoned at 10.30 pm and this time she was there but she sounded very drunk. We had a conversation and it ended up with me inviting her to come over to Vang Vieng. She said that she would come up tomorrow. Now that I have called her I am not sure that I have done the right thing.

Thursday 1ˢᵗ April

A waiting day. It would have been my nan's birthday today. She would have been 95. I lingered a little longer over my photograph of her before venturing out. Genevieve is feeling better today and may decide to stay on rather than go back to Bangkok. I was a bit loose again in the morning but I too felt better later. I realised that if and when Dao arrived I would need to change hotels. I had told Genevieve that I would be leaving, but I had not mentioned to her that I had asked Dao to join me because I was a little bit embarrassed to tell her. I thought it best if I tried to be discreet. I only ventured out at around 3 o'clock in the afternoon after I had packed and when I felt I was safe to be able to go more than 100 yards from my room without having an accident – took a walk along the river. Every day I see it, every day it gets more beautiful. I got back to my hotel later than planned – much later than when the bus from Vientiane was due to arrive – and I couldn't see Dao and I thought that I had missed her. In one sense I was relieved but moments later I saw her coming down the road and when I did I felt good. She was again wearing shorts but I didn't care. She seemed genuinely pleased to see me. She agreed to my suggestion to change hotels even though she knew the people at the hotel where I had been staying and thought they would be okay for her to stay there. As we walked through the village, me with my laden rucksack, and Dao with her smaller backpack, Genevieve was sitting at a restaurant, looking out of the window and saw us. She looked surprised.

Sheepishly, I waved to her. So much for discretion. Dao and I went to a different hotel deeper in the village beside the river. This seemed just as good as my previous hotel, but it was still only 20,000 kip, same as before, though it seemed better. Dao and I talked, ate and made love. It was a hot day. Earlier when I had walked down to the river and seen how pretty it was I thought that I would have liked to have organised an inner tube ride down the river. However, I have no time left to do it as I am planning to leave early tomorrow.

Friday 2nd April – Bus Trip

I finally left Vang Vieng today, and Dao was coming with me. Had a shock at first. The accommodation that I thought was very good for 20,000 kip (about £2.50) turned out to be $20.00 – five times more. By the time that I had paid for soft drinks and breakfast it was $29.00 or just short of £20.00, my budget for the entire day. I paid by card. The 233 kilometre bus journey to Luang Prabang was remarkable, but arduous, as the rickety bus zig-zagged up and down mountains on pothole-laden roads. Both the girl in front of me and the girl beside me were sick. I saw some amazing mountainous scenery. I also saw gorgeous villages on top of hills. I shared the bus with live chickens, sacks of rice, a lady breastfeeding her baby, army chaps with machine guns and I saw oxen and buffalo in the road holding up traffic. The scenery was fabulous. The journey was seven hours with a lot of ups and downs. When we arrived in Luang Prabang Dao and I took quite a while to find somewhere to stay. We did so eventually. Didn't see a huge amount of Luang Prabang in the evening. Dao won the prize for the best quotation on my trip so far, "My husband Jan – I opened pussy first time for him." Great! She can't say, "th" as in "thanks" – instead she says "sanks," which I find endearing. Dao seems to know and is friendly with just about everyone, even here in Luang Prabang. She is certainly quite a character (and I like characters). She's a real gem. In the course of a very delicious but amazingly cheap meal in the evening, Dao observed me using a toothpick Western-style, that is by openly digging in. She advised me that it was regarded as very impolite to do it this way and demonstrated to me how to do it discretely behind my hand. (It's a method I continue to use to this day).

Saturday 3rd April – Lao Meal

Another great day. Didn't start off too well as my stool is still a bit loose. However, we had a good breakfast. Yesterday on occasions I was regretting bringing Dao. Today I am very glad.

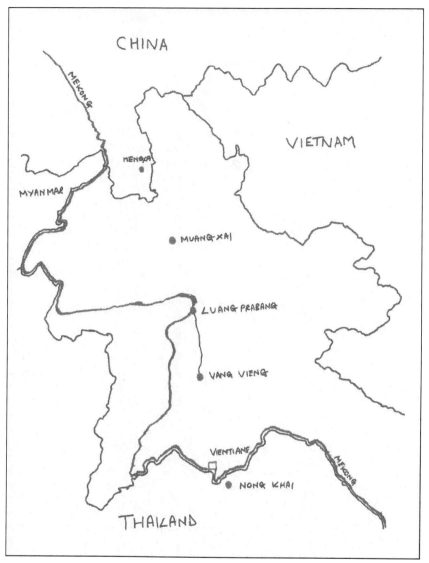

Map 10

Looking back on it, my 'regrets' were simply minor irritations. One minute, there I was, on my own, minding my own business doing my own thing at my own pace. Next minute, Dao had blown into my life and was dragging me along in her enthusiasm, ensuring that we were the centre of attention. Yesterday, Dao had been so lively and so full on, chatting to everyone on the bus, laughing raucously out loud and bouncing around the roadside stalls like a kid in a sweetshop when the bus stopped to allow the regular obligatory comfort stops, that it chafed against my English reserve. However, it was precisely because Dao was so lively and so full on that my misgivings very quickly evaporated. Dao ensured that we did not sit still for too long, which, once my initial misgivings had evaporated, I did not mind in the slightest, keen as I was to explore and discover. More importantly, Dao was opening up doors, and creating opportunities, that I would never have come across on my own. She was not only my friend, and girlfriend, but she had become my very own personal tour guide, and today's events would show just how invaluable she had become.

We decided to hire a tuk-tuk to take us to the Kuang Si Falls, located approximately 20 miles out of town. Dao was intending to wear her shorts today but I persuaded her to dress more modestly and to wear a sarong instead, which really suited her. She wore a light pink sleeveless top, a yellow and pink patterned batik-style sarong, and she pinned her hair up. If anything, her more modest appearance made her even more alluring.

On the way, we discovered that the 'water splashing season' had started early and we became some of the first victims. The 'Water Festival' takes place in Southeast Asia and forms part of their New Year celebrations. Although it has religious foundations, it is called the Water Festival by Westerners because people splash water at one another as part of a cleansing ritual and to welcome in the New Year. Traditionally people would gently sprinkle droplets of water on one another as a sign of respect, and the act of pouring water was also a show of blessing and good wishes, but in more recent times many people, especially children, had become not quite so subtle, resulting in them dousing strangers and passers-by in vehicles in boisterous celebration, their motivation no doubt enhanced by the fact that the New Year falls during one of the hottest months in South-East Asia. My understanding was that it was meant to take place between the 14th and 16th April, but we were *lucky* in that we received our 'blessing' early this year.

Thankfully we were more damp than drenched, and in any event the temperatures today were scorching and the water splashing provided some relief.

The journey out to the falls was interesting in itself, as the whole gamut of indigenous rural life was laid out before us, from the many untethered and seemingly dispossessed buffalo plodding lazily along the road, to the several Hmong tribal villages that we passed through, which Dao promised we would visit on the way back, and to the numerous paddy fields in varying stages of preparedness, some bone dry, some thickly green and lush and some flooded, that we observed in the countryside between the villages.

The Kuang Si Falls themselves were very beautiful and clearly very popular with both Lao and Westerners alike. The water cascades over three tiers, from a wide shallow basin atop a cliff, down through lush verdant green vegetation to a larger deeper pool halfway up the hill, before tumbling into a series of shallow turquoise green pools at the base. Being surrounded by trees and other flora, the air was refreshing and cool, but enough sunlight was able to penetrate in through the canopy to ensure that this beautiful oasis sparkled with colour. The site was clean and well-maintained.

The route to the Falls had been mainly along a dirt track, so that we were covered in dust by the time we had arrived. A swim at the end was very welcome. I bathed in the lower pools first before clambering up to the pool halfway up the hillside. The route up was neither arduous nor long, but it was enough to deter most of the visitors. There were only half a dozen of us up there, mostly Lao. Dao did not join me, and instead had her own private dip in a large pool away from the rest. Her reasoning was based on the fact she had not brought any swimwear, so she bathed in her bra and knickers, and accordingly she preferred to swim away from prying eyes. Indeed, she had this pool to herself. To see the normally brazen, bold-as-brass Dao behave in such a shy and demure way was very touching and paradoxically made her seem even more sexy.

The Falls were so beautiful and pleasant that we hung around for a while and at a nearby stall we devoured a spicy salad dish, shared a mango and chomped through sunflower seeds. Dao found it very amusing when in my ignorance I chewed on the seeds shell and all. She showed me what to do and, having placed several seeds in her mouth, with a dexterous twist of her tongue, one by one Dao was able to separate each seed from the chaff, expertly spit-puffing the shell into a dish.

As agreed, Dao asked our tuk-tuk driver to stop at one of the Hmong villages on the way back and after Dao spoke briefly to some of the elders, and their ultra-smiling faces had confirmed we were more than welcome, she was able to take me deep inside the village. This was something I would almost certainly never have been brave enough to have done myself, feeling that I would be voyeuristically intruding into their space. However, in Dao's presence, my inhibitions abated and our communication with the villagers seemed very natural, meaning that I was able to get right in there and meet, greet, and engage with the indigenous people. To them, no doubt, they were simply going about their daily lives, but for me I was enchanted at being able to observe the rhythms of daily village life whilst effectively at close quarters being a part of it. One woman was studiously weaving, an open-shirted young man with a moist sheen on his hairless chest was cutting wood, another woman was pounding beans of some description, young girls were carrying sheaves of sticks back from the forest, and older women, their faces etched with character, were sitting around chewing betel nuts until their mouths turned blood red. One younger girl was idly chatting to her friend, her blouse open at the front with one baby hungrily tucking into her left breast and an erect nipple enticingly peeking out on the right. Their soft features made them naturally very beautiful people and the older women were attractively dressed in sarongs and blouses of blues and greens.

As we were leaving, Dao took me by the arm, kissed me tenderly on the cheek and thanked me for encouraging her to wear her sarong. She admitted that she would not have felt so comfortable coming to this village wearing her shorts.

On the way back into town, the driver picked up one of his friends and they invited Dao and I to join them for a meal in the evening at a place a little way out of town. On arrival, the place seemed very uninspiring, since it looked like just any other wooden shack beside a mud courtyard, both of which were common in this area, with its dusty dried-mud floor, bamboo walls and the ubiquitous flea-bitten dog roaming around. Certainly, there was nothing by way of advertising or even décor to suggest that we could get a meal here. However, the faintest waft of something meaty being barbecued hinted that all would not be lost. In fact, I was about to be treated to the most delicious and memorable meal I would have on my entire six-month trip. Sitting on wooden benches at a table which was high up on the bank overlooking the confluence of the Mekong and one of its tributaries, the River Nam Khan, with the setting sun igniting the sky and turning it crimson – a common occurrence, it seemed to me, in Laos – plates of food were suddenly produced. The focus of the meal was barbecued duck which turned out to be crispy and juicy, without being fatty. Large plates laden with Chinese lettuce leaves, fresh mint, spring onions, chopped fresh coriander and sliced cucumber were produced alongside a bowl of chilli sauce and a large bowl of sticky rice. Being a variation of Peking duck, it involved taking a lettuce leaf, placing some of the duck in the centre of it, followed by a small amount of each of the herbs and salad, rolling the salad leaf up and then dipping it into the chilli sauce before devouring it. The combination was exquisite and moreish, with the fusion of cool fresh herbs and salad, hot and tangy chilli sauce and perfectly succulent barbecued duck. There was no cutlery, and everything was done by hand, taking the food from communal plates. Copying the others, I would scoop up a small portion of the sticky rice with my hand, and then roll it into a ball before popping it into my mouth with the duck. It was very ethnic, very rural and very tasty. Before long both Lao whisky and Lao beer had also been produced.

Dao was utterly charming, as she had been throughout the day, never once complaining when translating for me. Again, I would never have found this place without being with Dao.

Later, as we made our way back to the hotel at the end of the evening, sitting in the tuk-tuk as it bounced through the dark streets of the now-quiet town, with Dao sleeping with her head resting on my shoulder, my face softly glowing, part from the whiskey, part from the sun, and my mind glowing from the experiences of the day, I mused that I had actually been proud of Dao today. She was definitely a people person, engaging naturally with anyone and everyone we met, be it the young things at the falls or the elders in the village, and it was clear from the laughter and smiles on their faces that everybody seemed to love responding to, and engaging with, her. She seemed simply to light up their lives. It had been a long and blissfully happy day and I would sleep well again tonight.

Sunday 4th April – Wat Xieng Thong

Spent the day wandering around Luang Prabang with Dao. I had been thinking about leaving today – my Lao visa was running out and I still had to make my way North to the border, plus my Chinese visa was fixed in time and was about to start – but I wanted to maximise my time with Dao and so decided to stay one more day and go tomorrow. Waking up with Dao is so cosy and so good. We had a lazy breakfast. We met a woman from Udon Thoni (Northern Thailand) who Dao made friends with and she was visiting with her husband or boyfriend who is either French or Swiss and who was chain smoking cannabis joints. It was a very hot day approaching the mid-30s at least. We walked a little way – then flaked out – then walked a little more. We had a very nice soup for lunch and Dao and her new friend put all sorts of condiments into their soup – chillies, chilli sauce, soy sauce, peppers, fish sauce, vinegar and something else indescribable. I dived in and did the same except for the fish sauce – it was very nice but fiery. We then walked on to Wat Xieng Thong. It was the most impressive Buddhist temple that I've seen so far in Laos. It is over 400 years old so there is some real history to the place. We then went to Phou Si which is an important hillside with a temple on its slopes. We went to the top of the hill. I learnt that this was the first time that Dao had been. She thought that it was very beautiful and I entirely agreed with her, although I wished that we had gone there earlier when it was brighter and clearer and would have made for better photographs. Dao bought a fresh coconut drink – straight from the nut – which she shared with me – very nice. We went out in the evening after Dao had telephoned her son. Tonight's meal was not so good. We started bickering a little later on because Dao had been talking about getting a flight back to Vientiane. "I will get sore *arse!" she complained. At first, I hadn't realised that she had been expecting me to pay for her, but when the penny dropped I reminded her that I was on a tight budget. Although I learnt that it would only be around $50.00, not only had I not budgeted for it but I had also not changed enough money to be able to pay for it. Dao understood and we later made up.*

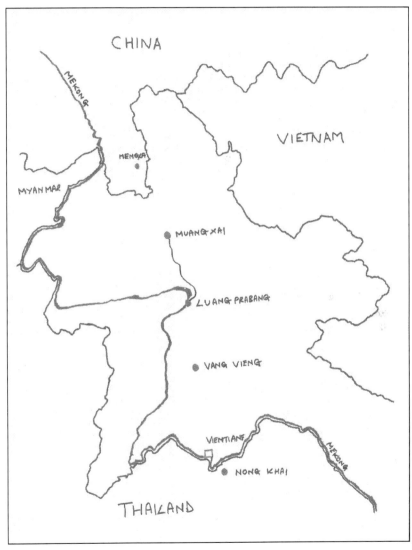

Map 11

Three of the Medangels at Penang

Me with six of the Medangels at Penang

Perhentian Kecil

Buddhist Temple at Nong Khai, Thailand

Hindu Sculpture Park at Nong Khai

Vang Vieng, Laos

Hmong village near Vang Vieng

Kuang Si falls near Luang Prabang

Monday 5th April – Saying Goodbye to Dao

This was a sad day and was one which I felt as though I had made worse. After last night's little argument, Dao and I made up and everything was OK. I had agreed to give her 100,000 kip which would have easily paid for her trip back to Vang Vieng and Vientiane with a little bit on top. She asked me for a further 20,000 kip. I said no. She went quiet and would not speak to me. My bus would soon be leaving and I had no time to properly make it up. She was lying back on the bed in our room with her arms folded. I kissed her on the forehead and I said goodbye. She said nothing to me as I paused at the door and looked back at her. Now I feel mean. As I write this I know I am feeling a little emotional because Dao got under my skin in a much bigger way than I would ever have originally imagined. I guessed that I was not the first person that she had met in this way and I probably would not be the last, but, except at the very end, she was never demanding which is one of the reasons why I now feel so guilty. I guess I will write to her and I will make it up to her and I may even try to see her again. I do get attached to people very quickly and I knew beforehand that I would be feeling this way when we eventually went our separate ways, so I know that this is me talking with my heart on my sleeve but I can't help feeling guilty.

This was obviously a day that I had not been looking forward to. Moving on has its pitfalls as well as its pleasures. I had also clearly felt particularly guilty at the way that we eventually parted. I had only known Dao for nine days, and even then we had been apart for three of them, but I had grown attached to her very quickly. Looking back, I now realise that some of my initial reluctance for Dao to join me in Vang Vieng was because I knew deep down that the longer I would be with her, the harder would be the parting of the ways at the end. However, I also now understood that, whether by design or by pure instinct, not talking to me and not even acknowledging me as I went out of our room in Luang Prabang, was Dao's way of coping. She had, after all, behaved in a similar way back in Vientiane, when she had promised to come to the bus station to see me off, but didn't. No matter how often I go over the machinations in my mind or however much self-psychoanalysing I do, my memories of Laos will run strong and deep, thanks to Dao.

Today's bus ride was very bumpy and very uncomfortable in the back of a bus that looked more like a pick-up truck. I was well and truly wedged in and the sack in front of me that was digging into my knees seemed to be full of bricks. The people in the bus were mostly Lao and they included a monk, but there were two Spaniards on my left and there was a very interesting older French gentleman. He was aged 77, was well travelled and

fought in World War II in the desert campaign. During it he lost one eye and had a deep wound to his cheek, which was still very apparent, and he had shrapnel in his leg. I had not needed any convincing but he felt compelled to tap his glass eye with his fingernail to make sure that I believed him. I understood that he was travelling and had seemingly been just about everywhere – he was a great character. Keeping a straight face but with an obvious twinkle in his eye, he could not resist some Anglophobic political jousting in commenting on the UK's reluctance to be part of the common currency in Europe, "You say you want to be part of Europe, but then you don't, you should make your minds up."
The bus went through some amazing rustic scenery today. In one village, we saw some dead deer being hacked up on a wooden bench. We stopped – for the Lao to buy some meat – for me to take some photographs. The people are very friendly and attractive and more and more women seem to wear traditional costumes. We eventually arrived in Muang Xai (also known as Udomxai), where I found a hotel for 25,000 kip.

Tuesday 6th April – Arrived in China

Left Udomxai – still upset about Dao – wrote letter last night and I posted to her the balance of my kip, being 70,000. I had budgeted well and it turned out that I could have paid her more after all. I may go back and see her later – perhaps even on this trip. Today was another arse-breaking journey – first to the border at Boten. Apart from the typically uncomfortable journey, with my knees wedged into yet another brick-filled sack, it was a great trip. There was fabulous mountain scenery, fields full of watermelons, buffalo, turkeys, ducks, chickens, dogs, pot-bellied pigs, colourful ethnic costumes and very interesting villages. Yesterday I saw a woman dragging a pig by its leg. I had a meal last night but I haven't got a clue what meat it was. This was a worry because I was told that they were selling rat meat in the market and I saw what looked like dried rat and dried dog meat today. I was the only foreigner on the bus to the border and beyond.

It was dead easy getting across into China. My visa was checked on the Lao side and there were one or two questions but it was all OK. There was a half mile walk to the Chinese side where I had to fill in a form and then walk through. It took only three minutes.

Immediately on getting across the border I was keen to go to the toilet and I made the mistake of going to the loo. It was absolutely dreadful and stank to high heaven. The fact that women were segregated from men was the only cap-doffing to common decency, as the toilets were all completely open to the elements and open to each other. They were also of the squat variety. Pissing seems to be in a ditch over to the left whilst shitting seems to be in deep troughs gouged out of concrete. The excrement is piled high within every trough. I thought, "Welcome to China!"

China was instantly definitely different. There was a lot more hustle and bustle, with people constantly moving around. I got a bus intending to go to Jing Yong and I had asked somebody to let me know when we got there but they failed to do so and I ended up at Mengla. On the way, some armed police boarded the bus and were checking ID and passports. They looked very stern and the passengers seemed on edge but everything turned out okay. The town seemed drab and the hotel was grubby but it was 30 Yuan (just over £2.00). I had Chinese meatballs in the evening which weren't very good.

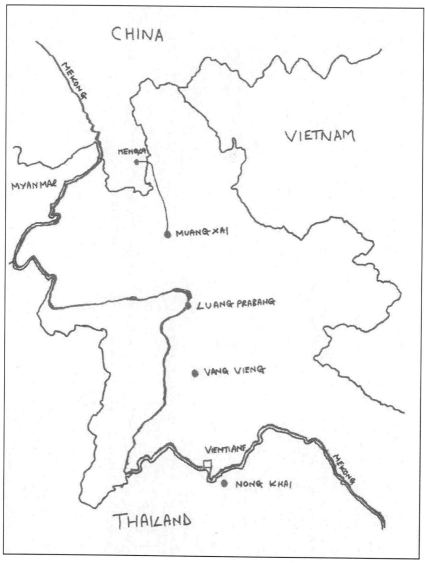

Map 12

CHAPTER 5

China

Wednesday 7th April – Melon Sharing

Saw and heard a fight last night. Riot police with helmets arrived quite quickly and I thought it would get ugly but it seemed to die down as quickly as it had started.

On my arrival yesterday, I found dry, dusty, concreted Mengla to be uninspiring and I wasted no time in booking a seat on a bus to Kunming leaving today. The price was 150 yuan – about £11.00 – for what I was told would be a journey of about 24 hours, but was warned that it could take as long as 30 hours. We got off to a bad start immediately as the bus was meant to leave at 8.30 in the morning but left instead at 9.30. China was evidently not immune to Asian rubber time. The bus also had to be bump started by rolling it down a hill. This was not an ideal beginning.

Once we had emerged out of the grey concrete of Mengla the views beyond were fabulous with an ever-changing landscape of shard-like mountains, fertile green valleys, mile upon mile of rice fields, homesteads with pigs and buffalo roaming around, and farms selling abundant produce on the side of the road. We passed several stalls selling watermelon, which were evidently in season, piled up invitingly like huge bowling balls. I was the only Westerner on the bus, which made me feel like a true pioneer.

The views outside partially allowed me to take my mind off the inside of the bus. My seat was actually a forward-facing bunk, a comfy fit for the diminutive Chinaman, but rather a squeeze for me. The fabric – if that's what it was – on the seats was so worn that parts of it were black and shining. Duvets and blankets were provided but they were filthy dirty. There were no women on the bus, and all the men seemed to smoke; and constantly too, such that my clothes quickly reeked of cigarette smoke. As bad as the smoking was, the aspect of their behaviour that I found even more disgusting, however, was that they spit, all of them, and that included the bus driver. There was no attempt at discretion when they did so as every single Chinaman at repeated intervals would reach deep down as far as their solar plexus and loudly hawk up all contained therein. It seemed impossible that there could be anything left in there but ten minutes later each one would be hawking it all up again. Some were spitting on the floor of the bus, which was totally unnecessary, and which became a disgusting mess. If it wasn't one person, then it was another, so that the constant hawking up from somebody somewhere on the bus sounded like a chorus of bullfrogs in a paddy field.

I was told that we had traversed through the city of Jinghong and that we had passed by the Mekong as it made its way through its China phase. However, when I checked my books later, that turned out to almost certainly not be correct. Looking out of the window I observed numerous working elephants with their mahouts, saw several fast-flowing streams, and noted that there was virtually no farm machinery in use, save for the very occasional and extremely ancient tractor. From the literature that I had read I understood that this had been Mao's way of ensuring that everybody had a job.

The weather outside was baking hot – we were after all still in the tropics. I was sat on the left side of the bus as it headed in a generally Northerly direction and for most of the morning I had been sheltered from the sun, but as we headed into the afternoon the shifting sun started to blaze down on my side of the carriage. Thankfully, the breeze coming in through the open window beside me provided some relief.

At one point as I was idly reading I felt some spots of what I thought was rain coming in through the window. However, when I casually looked outside I could see an almost cloudless azure sky. Thinking that I must have imagined it, I went back to my book. A few moments later the same thing happened again. In the knowledge that I had not been mistaken, I made a closer inspection of the sky and the landscape on both sides of the bus, but I could still not see any sign of precipitation nor could I locate any other source. I wondered if it had been some type of irrigation sprinkler system (even if such a thing ever existed in China) but I could see nothing. I turned back to read my book and very shortly thereafter the same thing happened again. Suddenly a shot of adrenalin ran through me and horror struck me when I realised that, with this bus being a left-hand drive, and with the bus driver therefore being sat on my side of the bus, the 'raindrops' coincided with the raucous hawking up by the driver who was then spitting out of the window. At that realisation, having instantly shut the window, I froze. Having acquired a touch of the OCDs, needless to say, I handled nothing and did nothing until we stopped for one of the thankfully regular comfort breaks, at which point I speedily strode to the nearest tap to wash my face, hands and arms over and over again. There was one – but *only* one – positive aspect of the way they were so vocal when they spat. It was my alarm call. I was able to sit there reading my book, with one hand on the window, positioned ready to quickly close it when I heard the first rumblings coming from the driver. Then, when I heard the hawking, the hairs on the back of my neck would stand up, I would quickly shut the window, see the gob fly by, before opening up the window again and then carrying on reading.

None of the Chinamen on the bus spoke any English, and my attempts to speak Chinese were clearly a waste of time. However, they seemed friendly enough with their brief respectful smiles. At one stop the chunky moon-faced young lad who was sat in the bunk behind me bought a watermelon and sat down with his pal one bunk further back to devour it. Although I do not mind them, for me a watermelon is an extremely disappointing fruit. They have a gorgeously mottled lime and emerald green skin with a delicious-looking raspberry red centre. However, the taste is almost nondescript and watery, hence why I presume they are called *water*melons. Also, I find that the pips get in my teeth. Whilst I appreciate that pips aid digestion, that was not exactly a problem on this trip.

About ten minutes after we had stopped, I felt a tap on my shoulder, and when I turned around moon-face smiled and offered me a piece of his watermelon. With good grace, I thanked him and accepted. Chomping on my not insignificant segment of the fruit, I realised that this was not going to be a quick job. I would occasionally turn to my neighbour, nod, and smile, to signify that I was enjoying the watermelon, which initially was not entirely untrue. My neighbour, using our rudimentary and only form of communication, nodded and smiled back, biting into his watermelon and loudly slurping and burping as he did so. Chinese manners were going to take some getting used to. The piece of watermelon was too large for me and I began to eat more and more slowly as I struggled to get to the end. When I had finally managed to finish, I turned back to my neighbour to show him the crescent-shaped rind and thanked him again, which was my undoing because he instantly gave me a second piece and no amount of polite refusals was going to deter him. Laboriously making my way through this second piece, my nods and smiles to my neighbour had become cheesy grins through gritted teeth. At the end, my slightly sicky burp to signify my completion of this latest labour of Hercules seemed to please my new friend but, to my horror, a third wedge of watermelon was immediately thrust into my hands. My refusals were a little less polite and a little more forceful, but his equally forceful – almost aggressive – insistence that I take it was impossible to trump. My repeated patting of my full ominously-churning bloated belly made no difference, so through the same gritted teeth I accepted his offer and thanked him again. However, to have eaten the next piece when I still had a very lengthy and bumpy bus journey ahead would have courted disaster, so I made a show of patting my stomach again to signify that I was full and I found a plastic bag in my rucksack into which I made a show of placing the watermelon, attempting to indicate to my friend by pointing to my watch that I would eat it later (or, unbeknown to him, as was more likely, to throw it away). He seemed to understand. However, just as I thought we had finished he then passed me a fourth piece seemingly indicating that I could save this one too for later. *My god,* I thought, *is there no end to this?* This time, I succeeded in insisting that I give it back to him. From the shrug of his shoulders, it seemed that we had reached a position where honour on both sides was satisfied. It was only later that I learned that in Chinese society it is impolite to eat all the food that is offered to you, otherwise the host or donor will think that you are still hungry and want for more, and will see it as a slight on the original gift by not offering you enough in the first place. Despite the rumblings down below, I was moved by the generosity and the attempt by moon-face and his friends to engage with me.

As the day was turning into evening, the bus came to a halt seemingly in the middle of nowhere and the chatter on the bus ceased abruptly. I was initially perplexed, but the reason became clear only a second later when armed police boarded the bus. This time, unlike yesterday, they checked my passport alongside everybody else's documents. The police left as everything seemed to be in order, but we drove on in silence for a while, with even the absence of the frogs' chorus, before eventually the chatter on the bus returned.

Later, the same lad who shared his melon with me also bought and shared a meal with me at one of our stops. He and his friend also insisted on sharing alcohol with me which looked and tasted something like ouzo. I was completely bowled over by how decent they were to me and, even though we could not speak to each other we had great fun trying to communicate.

Thursday 8th April – Epic Journey

Very long bus journey – four stops yesterday for repairs including one for one hour.

This morning our bus had a prang with a lorry and both vehicles remained where they were for one hour blocking the road both ways. Up to 50 Chinese arrived on the scene. There was a lot of loud talking but little else. In the end both vehicles managed to slowly disentangle from each other and drive off without any problems, other than with them both being a bit dented of course. Why they couldn't do that 55 minutes earlier if only to unblock the road I don't know? The journey became very arduous and ended up being nearly 35 hours – very tiring. I felt very grubby. With all the smoking and the spitting, it's making me take a distinct dislike to China already.

On the positive side, it was great that my fellow passengers were so friendly. Once the lads sat near me had broken the ice others tried to engage with me too. At the frequent stops, I became the entertainment – everyone tried to talk to me and my phrase book was passed around everywhere.

The scenery was very rugged and breathtaking at times. I arrived too late in Kunming to see much today. I did not want to spend too much time looking around for a hotel and so I quickly headed straight for one that I had picked out of my Lonely Planet guidebook. In fact, it was a good choice. The price indicated in the guidebook was Y166 (£12.00) which would have stretched my budget but the price turned out to be Y128 (£9.00) and the room was good and even had a bath.

I am thinking of going back to Laos.

Friday 9th April – Bamboo Temple

Yesterday saw two fights, one with two women fighting and the other with two men fighting. I didn't see any Westerners at all yesterday. Have decided I will draw up on an A5 piece of card a list of the most useful words or phrases, together with my attempt to depict the Chinese Mandarin script and my 'pinyin' pronunciation. I am hoping it will help me.

Today was a good day – I feel I am in the swing of it here in China. The weather is much cooler but I understand that the temperatures are still somewhere between 25 and 28 degrees which is quite pleasant. It shows how much heat I have put up with thus far on this trip and how I have become acclimatised to it. After saying hello to Nan and welcoming her to Kunming I went out. The traffic, where motorised vehicles seem to mix with bicycles and pedestrians, is amazing as it seems so random and heads off in all different directions. Somehow, though, it still seems to work.

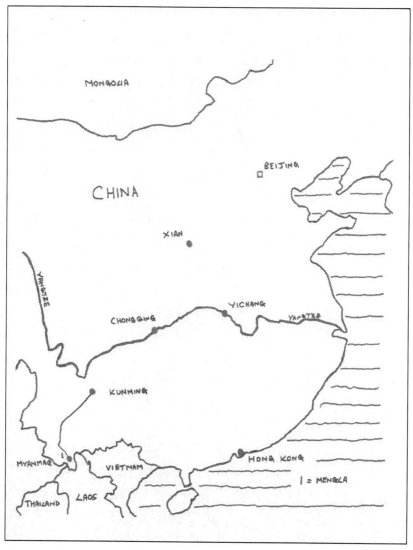

Map 13

After a little wander around Kunming, I managed to find the correct bus to take me out to a place called the Bamboo Temple which Lonely Planet promised would be an amazing experience. It did not disappoint.

Dating from the Tang Dynasty (AD 618 to 906), the temple burned down and was rebuilt in the 15th Century. Consisting of several small temples or rooms, it was restored in the late 19th Century by a Sichuanese sculptor, Li Guangxiu, who created 500 models, known as luohan or noble ones, to sit in or around the rooms. Referring to these life-size clay figures as a sculptural tour de force, my Lonely Planet guidebook did more justice in describing them than I could ever hope to do: –

"Down one huge wall come the incredible surfing Buddhas, some 70-odd, riding the waves on a variety of mounts – blue dogs, giant crabs, shrimps, turtles, unicorns. One gentleman has metre-long eyebrows, and another has an arm that shoots clear across the hall to the ceiling. The statues have been constructed with the precision of a split-second photograph – a monk about to chomp into a large peach (the face contorted almost into a scream), a figure caught turning around to emphasise a discussion point, another about to clap two cymbals together and yet another cursing a pet monster. The old, the sick, the emaciated – nothing is spared; the expressions of joy, anger, grief or boredom are extremely vivid. So lifelike are the sculptures that they were considered in bad taste by Li Guanxiu's contemporaries (some of whom no doubt appeared in caricature) and upon the project's completion he disappeared into thin air."

My book advised that getting into the rooms, which were controlled by nuns, would be difficult. However, this was not the case, and, wandering around, I was mesmerised by what I saw and remained within the temple complex for nearly four hours. The temples and the Buddhas were truly stunning and no amount of clever writing, even by the talented contributors to Lonely Planet, could properly do them justice, since you have to see them to truly appreciate them.

It was only part way through my visit that I discovered that I was not meant to be taking photographs. Earlier, one of the nuns, became quite upset at me but at the time I could not understand why. Later, I walked into another room, oblivious to the attention I had engendered, blatantly armed with two cameras, including one on which I had readied my flash gun. It was only after I had taken some photographs and was on my way out of the room that I noticed a 'camera forbidden' sign. The nun had been looking at me very scornfully before I had seen the sign, but only then did I understand the reason why. Although I had to be very careful thereafter, because the old ladies took it very seriously, I have to confess that their attitude, if anything, made me more determined to try to take photographs. It became almost like a cat-and-mouse game, with me dodging round pillars and waiting for other visitors to distract the nuns. I did in fact later succeed in obtaining several more pictures. The faces on the sculptured Buddhas were so lifelike that it felt very eerie when I was alone in a room in total silence, particularly since I had been skulking around trying to take photographs when nobody was looking and was nervously anxious at the prospect of being caught.

I saw a couple of tourists, but the vast majority of the visitors were Chinese, and I observed that many of them bowed and knelt three times, sometimes at the entrances to the temples and sometimes inside. In one room, there was the sound of a bass drum softly but repeatedly resonating. In another there was a sound of a gong. For all their sobriety, I found the nuns very interesting and their devotion to their task was heartwarming, making me (almost) feel guilty at my attempts to evade them earlier. Having hopefully obtained enough decent photographs – hopefully, of course, because I would not see the developed film for another five months or so – it was very pleasant to sit under the cherry trees full of blossom in the afternoon sun sipping Chinese tea, absorbing the ambience and reflecting on a job well done.

Afterwards I went back to town and I went to the bird and flower market. I had not been looking forward to it, but I felt that I should see it and, although it was not quite as bad as I had imagined, it was still pretty gruesome. It was unbelievable how many live birds they could stuff into a single cage. I also saw a very curious object at several of the market stalls which looked like it was something for people to eat and which from a distance looked like a massive red jelly. However, when I got close to it, the jelly seemed to be moving and it appeared to contain hundreds, if not thousands, of very tiny red worms. I also saw numerous stalls selling fried chicken feet, which seem as popular to the Chinese as burger or hotdog stalls might be to us. Wherever I went I noticed that people kept staring at me. It was very unsettling.

In the evening, I found a place that was serving 'across the bridge noodles' which were recommended by the guidebook as a local speciality. They were very tasty and great fun to eat. I had local Kunming beer which was Y12 (90 pence) for half a litre. I also purchased fruit from one of the stalls which was like a type of raspberry. I saw a huge Chinese cemetery.

Saturday 10th April – Western Hills

Bit loose again today. Made plans to move on to Chongqing, which I have decided I will do on Monday. I had breakfast – good coffee. Then went to Western Hills, intending to visit three temples. Got off the bus at the bottom and walked up. Very pleasant walk – heard two woodpeckers, and a mynah bird. Saw a large kestrel and I believe a squirrel. I went to Huating Temple – very attractive and saw an art exhibition – very interesting. Then went up to the next temple, which was Tiauha – again quite good. Then walked up to Dragon Gate – which was reasonably attractive – but I couldn't find my way to the third and final temple, Sanqing, nor the tomb of Nie Er (a "talented young musician" who had apparently composed the national anthem of the Peoples Republic of China). When I arrived back down, on looking back I saw all three temples away on top of the hills including the third one, which didn't seem all that far from the second one, so I don't know where I went wrong. I was a bit frustrated since I don't like to miss anything. From the top, there had been a great view across to Kunming Lake and the valley beyond. At one point today, I was loose and as I was going up through the woods I had to go native but I had anticipated this by taking paper and having water with which to wash my hands.

There was a strip of land across the head of the lake, which I guessed to be some kind of dam in the event of flooding. When I came down from the hills I walked across this central strip, from where there were great views looking back to the Western Hills. The Western Hills are also known as the 'Sleeping Beauty Hills', because the undulating contours are said to resemble those of a woman lying down. I looked back at them, squinting to try to discern the woman lying there, and although I think that I just about made her out, if those were her hips she would definitely not have been my type! I then returned to the town and to my hotel. In the evening, I had a bath.

I later had a meal at the Chun Cheng Hotel where the food was served buffet style. This included steampot chicken. The buffet was very good but the chicken was not that special. I later heard today on the World Service that Bobby Jo had won the Grand National. I continued working on my card of useful words.

Sunday 11th April

Rum sort of day and one that has left me unfulfilled, frustrated and restless. Tried to find stuff to make my own lunch – I wanted Yunnan ham or goat cheese and couldn't find either. I found bread but it was too sweet for my liking. I then prepared a picnic comprising ham sausage (7p), a tomato (2½p), a pear (7p) and a half box of Pringles (25p). I went to the Yuantong Temple – which was okay but not as inspiring as others I had seen. I then went to Cuihu Park. I understood that Sunday sees the park at its liveliest when it is host to an English corner and there are hordes of families at play. I went there hoping to meet people and have some fun but I couldn't find it. I did manage to find one man who talked to me in English, which was OK at first, but he seemed to cling to me and I couldn't shake him off. I did so eventually. Then tried to find a good spot to sit, read and to try to take photographs unobtrusively. I couldn't find anywhere. I went to the foreign languages book store, hoping to get some new books – no chance. Finally, I tried to order some food in the evening and I tried to speak Chinese – I did my best but the staff were very unenthusiastic and impatient at my attempts. In the end I pointed to rice, to vegetables and to a beef dish and left it to them to select. I just sat down, feeling very frustrated. The meal was quite good in the end.

Everywhere in Kunming there seem to be new buildings going up which is all well and good but means that many of the places in the Lonely Planet Guidebook no longer exist. Apart from my hotel's own restaurant I haven't found a single place mentioned in the book. I later learnt why and that is because Kunming is hosting Expo 99 next month and the city authorities are clearly panicking to get everything done. I assumed that was why everybody seemed to start work early in the morning and finished late and carried on working on Saturdays and Sundays. NB the man I spoke to earlier in the park in English warned me against talking openly about politics to anyone because the PSP, the Chinese intelligence services, have many spies. The man proudly told me that he is anti the PRC. Being a fan of le Carre, I couldn't help wondering if he was being sincere or if he was saying those things to try to flush me out.

After my frustrations earlier in the day, I completed my A5 card with its Chinese script, its 'pinyin' pronunciation and the English translation.

Monday 12th April – Watching Mahjong Sipping Tea.

I wandered around Kunming without feeling I'd achieved much but I guess that I did. I changed enough money to hopefully last me through to Xian. I found the Lao Embassy as I was still contemplating going back there but it was shut for lunch when I arrived. I had intended to go back later but I didn't. I then went to the bus station to check for buses to Chongqing. There are no buses. I then went to the train station and after a huge amount of perseverance I booked a train – a hard sleeper – leaving tomorrow at 4.50 pm. It costs Y185 (£13) and should take about 24 hours – we'll see. Posted card to Robbyne – then wrote and sent card to friends Richard and Kevin. I had a very good noodle soup for breakfast. Again, I had dived in to try to speak to locals but couldn't make myself understood. At least I am trying. The Chinese don't seem to have much patience and I am trying my best. But I am not giving up. I am still diving into local haunts. Whilst it was very hot today – possibly low 30s – and I wore shorts, I had earlier noticed that people were staring at me and my decision to wear shorts today was a mistake as they seemed to stare at me even more. I found it very disconcerting and I stared *back as best as I could.*

Now that I know why there is so much building work I am noticing the building work even more. People seem to be scurrying around like ants. I now understand that the city will also be hosting the Expo International Horticultural Show. I went to the West Pagoda where I spent a pleasant couple of hours sipping tea and watching people playing mah-jong. I would like to learn both that and Chinese Chequers so that I can join in.

Tuesday 13th April – Daguan Park

I forgot to mention that two gay men approached me and tried to seduce me yesterday – needless to say, they weren't successful. Last night I got talking to a lad who said he was a Buddhist teacher from Lhasa, Tibet. He spoke in praise of the Dalai Lama which is a dangerous thing to do in China. I was a bit sceptical, but only because he seemed to talk so openly. At one point, he left but he later came back and when he did so we played snooker at the open-air table nearby. It was I who had suggested to him to play snooker as I thought it would be a good way of trying to encourage him to talk and have an open conversation without it looking too obvious or serious. I saw women line dancing at Daguan Park today.

I am now sitting on a train going from Kunming to Chongqing. I am in a hard sleeper and the carriages on the train are packed. I haven't seen a Westerner all day. Each carriage has ten compartments, all without doors and, therefore, open to a corridor, which runs along one side of the carriage. Everyone is sitting wherever they can and seem to be lounging anywhere and everywhere. Each of the ten compartments has six bunks, three on each side. I booked myself into a middle bunk, just as Lonely Planet had recommended. Blankets, sheets and pillows are provided and girls pushing trolleys with food and tea (and other drinks) regularly travel up and down the carriages.

These trains are like small travelling towns. All humanity can be found on them. Unlike the bus, where it was all male, there's a fair cross-section of people on this train, including girls, old men and children. There's one man in the section in front who got into his long johns almost as soon as we started. There are several girls in my section – I think I'll wait till they go to bed first just to see what the drill is. Although there is not quite as much spitting (or smoking) as on the bus, unfortunately there is still some. It always happens when you least expect it and serves as a reminder. I saw some very beautiful countryside in the first two or three hours. Looking back on my earlier visit to Daguan Park, I again noted that the people were still staring at me. I had decided to stare back and it seems to work in getting them to turn away.

My Lonely Planet Guidebook had talked about the phenomenon of the Chinese people staring. They called it the 'Staring Squad': -

"This is the scene: you walk into a railway station waiting room and everybody (about 300 people) stares at you. Quite literally everybody. From the three-year-old with his fingers in his mouth in the far corner to the octogenarian in the blue cloth cap to the ticket attendant stepping to one side as you enter. Do you wake up in a cold sweat? You'd be lucky. This is the grim reality of the staring squad and you are stuck on a pin. Almost 20 years of exposure to foreign travellers has done little to dull the fascination that welcomes the big noses. The "circus is in town" factor still greets all and sundry. Actually, most people take the staring in their stride and it is certainly a lot better in large cities like Beijing and Shanghai than it used to be. Small towns still go somewhat slack-jawed when the barbarians turn up, and small villages really go to town (metaphorically) at the sight of a foreigner — but look at it this way, if you are self-conscious by nature, this is an excellent aversion therapy."

So it was with me. I was clearly travelling through areas where very few Westerners visit, and accordingly I was constantly subjected to intense scrutiny, which was unsettling and very disconcerting at times.

Wednesday 14th April – Train Journey

Yesterday was hot, as had been the previous two days when I believe temperatures were in the thirties. However, today feels much cooler. I believe that I did get some sleep last night on the train. The decision as to when to retire was made for us as lights went out (completely) at 9.40 pm. Clambering up to my middle bunk in complete darkness was almost impossible to do. I decided to use the toilet – I had tried not to but I know that it is unhealthy to try to stop yourself from urinating. This turned out to be a big mistake as they were extremely dirty and smelly. I seemed to be the only Westerner on the train and nobody else seemed to speak English. The people around me are friendly and some were sharing their biscuits with me. It was a cloudy day but the views were terrific. We went through a whole series of tunnels, three of which were quite long, for a period of two or three hours. Saw some great mountain scenery and followed a river for quite a long way. Every now and again the tannoy plays music which is mostly European classical music, which seems bizarre. Occasionally I sit by the window – which is usually open – and I keep feeling spots of rain even though it does not seem to be raining (a shudder goes down my spine). Even one of the sweet young girls in my compartment keeps hawking up but at least she has the decency to spit hers out daintily into bits of paper and tissue which are now collecting together on a tray in front of me. Delightful!

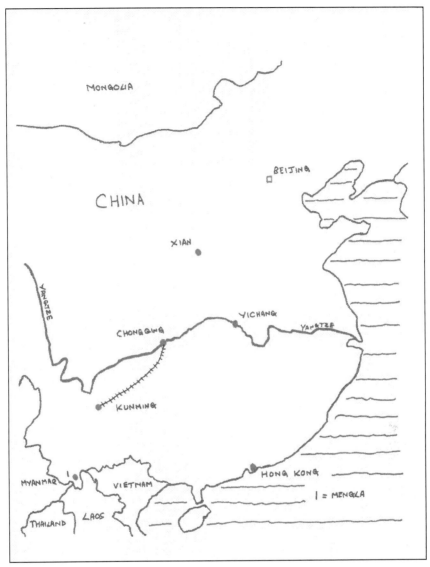

Map 14

It became more and more cloudy and miserable as we closed in on Chongqing which seems very industrial with coal heaps, factories and billowing yellow smoke, which reminds me of Len Deighton's description of winter in his book, Winter Berlin. We crossed the Yangtze. The hotel in Chongqing is not as good as expected – but it will do. I booked a boat to go down the Yangtze leaving tomorrow evening. In the evening, I ate at the Yizhishi Restaurant, which was mentioned in Lonely Planet. I had tea smoked duck.

Unfortunately, it reminded me of smoked haddock, which after a bout of food poisoning a few years ago is not a good memory for me.

Thursday 15th April

Good night's sleep. The train journey yesterday had been 25 hours in all. The hotel was Y130. For my meal last night in addition to tea smoked duck, I ate pork dumplings, broad beans, and white rice, which together with a bottle of beer cost me £1.68. I dreamt of Amita (my ex-girlfriend). I got in a little tizz with my boat ticket. Although I had booked a ticket through an agency, I needed to go to the boat to collect it and on the way down I met a friendly man who spoke good English who seemed quite convincing and sincere. He seemed not to be a tout. In the course of our conversation I mentioned the name of the boat I was booked on and he told me that I had been given a bad boat. He advised me that I should have looked at the boats first to compare them, which made sense. He gave me his telephone number before leaving me to make up my mind. Taking his advice, I went to the boat and cancelled my ticket – for which I had to forfeit 20% (Y44). I then returned to my hotel and telephoned the man and arranged to meet him. He accompanied me back to the boats and attempted to show me the bad boats just to demonstrate to me what I had managed to avoid. However, we couldn't get on. He then helped me to book a place on a 'good' boat. Frankly, I'd hate to have seen the bad one. The only difference appears to be that here you get to shit in a pit on your own rather than to an audience. I went back into the city. I had noodle soup which came still in its clay casserole pot and carried on cooking after I'd got it. Very nice. It was a very humid day today. It was also very overcast – I was told that this is often the case because Chongqing is surrounded by mountains and the pollution in the town within the resulting bowl finds it difficult to escape. I was told that it was 22 degrees centigrade today. I saw people mass meditating. I also saw people playing mahjong. I also saw people playing Chinese instruments and dancing. Also, I saw and heard a man and a woman having a very bad argument last night. I hate to confess it in this diary because I like to think I have a good sense of direction but last night I got lost and a kind man took me back to my hotel. I saw live fish and eels being cut up in the market, I also saw ducks and chickens ready for killing and small roasted whole birds, which looked the size of blackbirds. The Chinese are karaoke mad. Now I am on the boat and we are heading down the Yangtze. I later discovered that there is one other Westerner on the boat, who is a Frenchman. All the rest are Chinese. My eight-bed cabin seems to hold twelve. I earlier bought three books.

Taking this trip was one of the main reasons why I wanted to come to China. I had, of course, heard about the world-famous Three Gorges stretch on the 6,300-kilometre-long Yangtze River, the third longest in the world. I had also become aware that the Chinese government had authorised the construction of the Three Gorges dam. Due to be completed in 2008, it would be the world's largest water storage reservoir. Intended to improve the river's navigability and to protect against flooding, it would also provide electricity and, once completed, it was envisaged that it would increase the whole of China's generating capacity by 20%. Whilst difficult to argue against the economics of it all, its environmental and social impact was likely to be huge. An estimated two million people living in the inundated area would have to be relocated. The building of the dam would cost approximately US$20 billion and with at least two other dams having collapsed in China in recent years there were inevitably concerns about its safety. Also, it would create a 550-kilometre-long lake stretching from Yichang in the East to Chongqing in the West. The Three Gorges would simply disappear, and with it one of China's most important and iconic tourist attractions. I wanted to see the Three Gorges before it was too late.

However, very early into the trip the gorges were the last thing on my mind.

The toilets in China are truly dreadful, and the seemingly indifferent attitude to them by the Chinese is almost as pitiful. With over a billion people in this country defecating on a daily basis, it's got to go somewhere and I guess, therefore, it is not surprising they are so blasé about it. However, I shuddered at the thought of what the toilets on my original choice of ship must have been like, if the ones on my ship were better than those. The gentleman who had given me the benefit of his wisdom the previous day was at least correct in identifying that the toilets on my current ship were single cells allowing some semblance of privacy. At least you were on your own (if you discounted the etymology). The toilets were of the squat variety and the business was deposited into what looked like a shallow trough in the floor. Not that I inspected it *too* closely, but I could not see any outflow so that it looked as though there was nowhere for the excrement to run off or be flushed. Excrement and soiled toilet paper was simply piled on top of excrement and more soiled toilet paper. I could only imagine that at some point someone would have to come along and simply shovel it off into a wheelbarrow. Within one hour of leaving the dock at Chongqing yesterday, every single cubicle was piled up with excrement. It was as if the natives had waited until they were on the boat. I know that it was every single cubicle because, believe me, I checked. Needless to say, the smell was excruciating, and the extremely strong, not to say potentially dangerous, cocktail of methane and ammonia, made my eyes water. Although squatting is not my normal *modus operandi,* I had become quite used to it in the Orient, but it was out of the question here. Even if I could have coped with the smell and had overcome all the other psychological barriers, squatting safely would have been a nigh on physical impossibility in view of the height of the piles of excrement. I had not *been* at all today before I boarded the ship, and in fact my previous evacuation was early yesterday morning, but there was no way on earth I was going to use these facilities.

Friday 16th April – Bear in the Woods

I swear there were 11 people sleeping in our tiny 8-bunk cabin last night, the lights never went out, the television stayed on until very late and the men carried on talking and continuously smoking until the wee hours. I ended up with a sore throat.

When I woke, I felt heavy and lethargic, and, having not *been* for 48 hours, I knew that I really ought to *'use the facilities'*. Not being an attractive prospect, and wondering how I was going to avoid crushing a part of somebody's anatomy with my lumbering size tens, whilst clambering over the sea of humanity in my cabin, I was slow to get up from my bunk. More as a wild fantasy than truly in hope I imagined that the man with the wheelbarrow might have come along during the night. However, on entering the first cubicle, there it was, same as last night, only slightly higher if that were at all possible. The other cubicles were the same. The sphincter-shrinking sight cured me of my need to go quicker than any amount of Imodium.

I went up on deck to get some fresh air and I met up with my sole Westerner comrade on this ship. He was French, a single man in his early 30s, who was on holiday here in China and wanted, like me, to sail through the Three Gorges whilst it was still possible. He told me that he was living and working in the IT industry in Budapest. We spoke mainly in English, but occasionally in French. Being a city I had long wanted to visit, but never had, he expanded on my basic knowledge of Budapest exponentially by telling me it was once two separate cities on either side of the Danube, Buda on the West bank and Pest on the East. I think it was that way round. I broached the delicate topic of the ship's toilets to my new pal, and discovered to my relief that he was just as horrified as I, unwittingly reassuring me in the process that I was not looking at it through entirely atypical ultra-sensitive English eyes. If the French think the toilets are bad, then they must be bad, or so I thought.

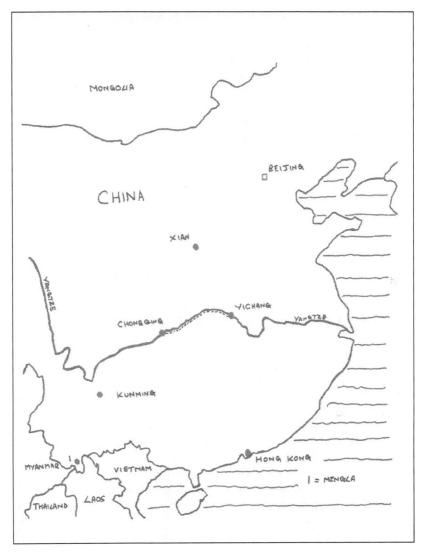

Map 15

As we gazed out over the stern of the boat, after initially noticing that the banks were becoming steeper and more rugged, and the width of the channel was narrowing, and thus coming to the conclusion that we were probably now entering the first of the gorges, my eyes were drawn to the water in the river itself, because there seemed to be a never-ending stream of human rubbish floating down the river: glass bottles, plastic bottles, discarded paper, polystyrene plates, plastic noodle cartons, linen clothes, the skin of half-eaten oranges, polythene wrapping, plastic bottle tops, plastic knives and forks, plastic, plastic and more plastic. For me, this otherwise idyllic scene was ruined by the rubbish floating in the river. The stream of human debris stretched out upriver beyond the back of the boat as far as the eye could see. I walked over to the side of the boat and looked forward. It was exactly the same. My Franco-Hungarian pal saw what I was looking at and simply shook his head. Words were unnecessary. Nobody, save for me and my French pal, seemed to notice, or even care. How could the Chinese be so oblivious of their surroundings? All I could think of was that if there was this much rubbish this far inland, being still more than 2,000km from Shanghai and the open sea, how much more would there be by the time all its tributaries downriver joined up with it and it reached the coast; and if there was this much rubbish on the Yangtze, there was bound to be the same happening down the 5,400km-long Yellow River, the 2,200km-long Pearl River and the 4,300km-long Heilongjiang River, to name but a few; and if we could see this much crap on top of the river what else was going on underneath the surface; and if there was this much detritus pouring out into the ocean day in, day out, how long would it be before the Pacific Ocean itself was usurped into becoming China's very own giant cesspit? I was feeling thoroughly depressed.

The mood was lifted a little while later when the boat pulled alongside a jetty beside a town called Fengdu. By the action of fingers pointing at dials on watches we understood that the boat would remain here for about four hours. My Lonely Planet guidebook told me that there were a couple of interesting temples on a hill running alongside the Yangtze, so I decided to have a look and at least use the chance to stretch my legs. Franco-Hungary said he would follow on a bit later. On the basis that there might also be an opportunity for me to evacuate my bowels, I took some toilet paper with me. The path up to the temples was quite busy but it took only 20 minutes to get to the top, where there was a fine view looking back across the Yangtze. There was also a small tea shop. "A-ha," I said to myself, thinking there might be a toilet here. "Oh no," I sighed, at the realisation when I peered into it that this was as bad as the ones on the boat. I left it.

I decided to try out my Chinese language and order some tea. I sat down at a small table. "Chay," I said to a tiny Chinese waitress, who had tried to avoid eye contact with me as she attempted to surreptitiously slide past my table. She stopped and looked at me, puzzled. Remembering that I had read that the tone by which you speak the Chinese language is as important as the pronunciation, I repeated, "Chay," in a flat tone but it still evoked no response. I tried again using a rising tone, "Chay." Still nothing. "Chay," I said, falling. "Chay," high notes, "chay," low notes, "chay," rising and falling, "chay," falling then rising. There was still no discernible movement in the young girl's visage. Having exhausted in my mind all possible combinations, I pointed in frustration to the word in Chinese script on my handmade card.

"Oh, chay," she said, the penny finally dropping. She said it in such a manner as if to say, "Why the hell didn't you say so in the first place?" to which I wanted to scream, "I did, I bloody did," because to my ears it was the exact same flat tone that I had used the first time. In any event, why she seemed so surprised that I would want tea in a tea shop was beyond me.

The sun was hazy but warm and welcome, and as I sat there sipping my tea and enjoying my pyrrhic victory under a leafless tree, its skeletal shadow waving across my face in the light breeze, I observed that this area was now practically deserted. I had recognised most of the Chinese who had made it up to this level as being people from off my boat. A quick check on my watch told me I had plenty of time. I mused that with typical Chinese efficiency, they had marched like ants up to this level, quickly had their photographs taken in front of the temple, slurped down their tea and en masse hurried back down the steps from whence they had come. As my mind wandered, I suddenly realised that I didn't know Franco-Hungary's name. *I really ought to ask*, I thought. As I looked back down the hill, and saw that there was hardly anybody there either, I noticed that the path I had come up zigzagged along the slope, and between a couple of the zigs and the zags there was a wide ledge where there were ornamental bushes, and plenty of them, beautiful thick bushy bushes. My time had come. Conspiratorially, I checked in my rucksack: bottle of water, check; toilet paper, check; another look at my watch to make absolutely sure I had enough time, check. I looked round for a short sturdy stick and soon found a small branch. All I needed now was to pick the right moment. I made my way down the steps until I found the prime location. I loitered around on the steps, pretending to take in the view, but secretly observing the people around me. I calculated that it had taken me about a minute and a half to walk down from the top, and, as I could see the top from where I was, I knew I had that amount of amount of time before being disturbed from above. At that point, nobody was above me. However, there was a loved-up young couple just a little ahead of me going down the path, arm in arm and lost in their own world, who were descending agonisingly slowly, totally oblivious to the plight of others. "Come on, come on," I yelled in my mind. Eventually, like an impatient sun-worshipper waiting for the sun to come out from between clouds, they disappeared and the path ahead suddenly became clear, and when I looked behind me the path in that direction was also still clear. With my mission having been plotted with military precision, like a bear in the woods, I dived into the bushes, dug my hole, de-frocked my trousers et al, squatted on my haunches, launched my torpedo, wiped, washed, buckled, back-filled and sidled back out onto the path in less than

90 seconds.

Being many pounds lighter, like a young Nijinsky – the analogy works for both dancer and racehorse – I positively flew down the hill back to my boat.

Back on board the boat I returned to my cabin. The people in there treated me like a long-lost friend and offered me some of their pomelo, a very large yellow fruit, much like a grapefruit, but more pithy and less sharp. To my surprise, one lad started speaking English. It was very rudimentary and with a strong accent, but it was very welcome. His English name was Gordon. Stopped at two more places along the river. At one stop the locals attempted to charge me Y55 (£4) to enter a park. Declined to enter that tourist trap. Had a very good lunch, a Chinese buffet.

Saturday 17th April – Horse Beaten

Today should have been a very good day – not great, but still very good – but it was spoilt by a very ugly incident in one of the towns. Having slept a bit better last night, I woke up and was getting washed and changed and as we entered the first gorge, known as Qutang Gorge, I realised that yesterday's scenery was not part of the gorge itself, but a precursor to it. The scenery was very spectacular. Then we arrived at Fengjie, where the boat moored up and those of us who wished to take a tour then left to join up with some smaller boats to go up a tributary leading off from the Yangtze. I learnt that this was called the Three Little Gorges. The scenery was, if anything, even more spectacular. It had been a cloudy morning but later the sun started to come out. I was also warming to a Chinese girl on our boat – I'm not saying that she was coming on to me but she seemed very friendly all the same – who was a tour guide for the Chinese. Both my new friend, Franco-Hungary, and my even newer friend, Gordon, came with me on this trip. The boat rode the rapids as it went further up river and it was difficult at times to cling on. At one point, I nearly did a permanent injury to myself when I discovered that the seats on the boat were not screwed in and I landed on my arse. As the Lonely Planet Guidebook had advised, there were several tourist traps further along the river, and our boat moored up beside one such small village which just by chance had some tourist trinkets. The only thing that I purchased was some nuts. Back on the boat, I shared the nuts with the people on my boat. Several of them wanted me in their photographs. The boat took us back to the town where we waited to rejoin the main ship.

Seemingly our boat was the first to arrive back in Fengjie, where we waited for the other groups to join us before heading back to our main boat. We appeared to be in the centre of town close by a busy street. I was chatting away to Franco-Hungary when our attention was drawn to what sounded like a loud crack followed by a horse whinnying. As we both looked, about 30 metres away an older Chinese man dressed in a dark flat cap and dirty crumpled charcoal-black jacket and trousers was pulling with his left hand on a rein that was taut and on the other end of the rein was a skinny horse that had apparently planted its feet and was refusing to budge. The man had a bamboo cane in his right hand and as we carried on looking he stepped back to the horse, lifted the cane up into the air and with all his might pulled it down with a crack on the horse's shoulder area. The horse visibly winced. The man pulled again on the rein but still the horse would not budge. When the man stepped back, this time he gave the horse two further almighty whacks in quick succession. As each blow landed, the horse yelped at the pain, but still would not budge. I felt a sickening sensation deep inside me.

Gordon, who was with us seemed frozen and the attractive Chinese tour guide put her hand to her mouth. The man struck once more with even more force than before and again the horse did not move. The situation had by now attracted the attention of most people in the street, even all the local Chinese who had previously been scurrying around doing their daily business, but this, if anything, made the situation worse. The man, perhaps embarrassed at being the centre of attention, completely lost his temper and rained blow after blow on the horse, indiscriminately hitting the horse anywhere and everywhere, including on the neck, shoulder, legs and nose. The horse was clearly flinching and attempting to duck away as each blow was about to land. The man must have flogged the wretched creature 40 times. At one point, I was so sickened and adrenalin-fuelled by what I was witnessing that I started to walk over to him. I could not hold back any longer. I had visions of snatching the cane away from the bully and whacking *him* with it. However, Gordon grabbed hold of me and clung on tight and said I should not get involved. Franco-Hungary went to take a photograph, but Gordon let go of me and went to stop him, explaining it would just make the situation worse. The physical abuse only stopped when the cane effectively broke, since the man had used so much force that the previously solid end of the cane had disintegrated into what looked like pieces of string. By this point, the group from the second boat had arrived and we were all ushered away. I could not get the sickening images out of my mind all the rest of the day.

Having rejoined our boat, it then made its way down river and through the two remaining gorges, known as Wu and Xiling. They were very beautiful. However, it was difficult to take my eyes off the river itself which was dreadful and the most polluted river I have ever seen. I was also constantly haunted by the memory of the horse getting beaten.

Arrived in Yichang at the end of our journey. I said goodbye to Gordon. The pretty tour guide helped me and Franco-Hungary obtain a hotel. I was starting to grow quite fond of her but in an instant she said goodbye and was off. The hotel was better than the ones I had become used to up to now on this trip but Franco-Hungary agreed to share a twin room and after a couple of days on the boat I was looking forward to a good scrub.

I continued to feel sick thinking about the horse being beaten earlier, and in fact the horse incident nearly resulted in me taking out my anger on a worker at the port where we disembarked. He was being very abrupt and pushing past people. I was about to confront him and had already fired off a couple of invectives when Gordon again intervened and pulled me away. Good old Gordon. In the evening, I talked to a couple of girls. They really were quite pretty. In all, the boat journey took 51 hours.

Sunday 18th April – sitting on the banks of the Yangtze

Very good day today. Woke up full of cold but had a good sleep after a good shower and getting out of my dirty togs. Performed a Reiki on myself and I had a lie in. I later bought a train ticket leaving this evening for Xian: Y166 for hard sleeper. Went into Yichang town centre with Franco-Hungary – we tried to find a photocopying machine as he wanted to copy a few pages from the Beijing section in my Lonely Planet, as that was where he was heading to next. On the way, we met and got talking to a Chinese man who was very helpful and spoke good English. He helped to find us a photocopier. Franco-Hungary then had to go. I said my goodbyes to him and then the Chinese man asked if I was hungry, to which I said I was. He showed me a good place to eat, where I had 12 small dumplings followed by a dish of rice, vegetables and meat. As I was sitting there, I was thinking about Franco-Hungary and realised that I had still never found out his name. The Chinese man bought a bottle of beer which he shared with me. He then took me to the post office where I bought postcards and stamps. The Chinese man then had to go, so with a generous shake of the hands and a polite bow he went his own way. I wandered down to the river, and, wistfully reminisced about the 'ships in the night' you bump into on the way when you are travelling, some for short periods, some for longer, and then as suddenly as they had originally appeared, they quickly sail away. This is one of the unfortunate side effects of this type of travelling. Both Franco-Hungary and the Chinese man from Yichang had for a brief period been an important part of my life in their own way and just as quickly as they had entered my life they then moved on. I bought some pistachios at a stall together with a bottle of Coca Cola and I went and sat on the wall on the banks of the river. It was sunny and warm and there were kids flying kites. People seemed to be enjoying themselves and relaxing and the scene was not unlike a typical Sunday back home. As I sat there two girls came and sat near me and started talking to me – they were very friendly and quite attractive. I developed a particular attraction for one of them who was wearing glasses. Her name was Ling Zuh. She was aged 30 and was a physicist. Her sister, Ma Yal was 29. The girls were sisters and were both married – Ling Zuh to a policeman – and both had one child each, the official state maximum. Ling Zuh tried to persuade me to stay until Tuesday and it seemed as though she was genuine in wanting me to stay behind. She even suggested that we could go to Xian together – but "as friends," she tried to emphasise, which sounded to my ears like the lady was protesting too much. They also asked me to come to dinner with them this evening. I was very tempted to stay and miss my train and not go to Xian but I had been receiving very mixed messages and I might have been tempted to try it on with pretty Ling Zuh (not a good idea if her husband is a policeman, and a Chinese policeman at that). I was disappointed to leave them and to decline the meal but it was probably for the best. Nearly missed train as a result, just got on and nearly had a punch-up with our carriage conductor. He was very brusque and in fact seemed positively hostile towards me. Feeling thoroughly pissed off, I deliberately barged by him, heavy rucksack and all. He seemed to get the message and then co-operated, albeit reluctantly and showed me to my bunk. An hour or so into the journey he seemed very keen to be friendly, as if he had realised how brusque he had been earlier and was trying to make amends. In its own way, it was very endearing and made me feel a whole lot better, and almost made me regret deliberately barging into him earlier. As I say, almost.

Monday 19th April – Beijing Duck

Nearly had a fight last night – my third altercation in just over 24 hours.

I occupied a bunk on the hard sleeper section of my train, similar to the one I used previously between Kunming and Chongqing. I was again the only Westerner. My journey was expected to take 19 hours. As before, my carriage consisted of ten compartments, in each compartment were six bunks, three on either side, and again none of the compartments had any doors or curtains, and were open to the corridor. Although each compartment provided only minimal privacy, by now I was getting quite used to communal living in crowded China. I had been assigned the middle bunk on the left as you look in. The other middle one on the right and the two lower bunks on either side were all occupied. The top two appeared to be free. I needed somewhere to put my large rucksack, so I placed it on the bunk above me.

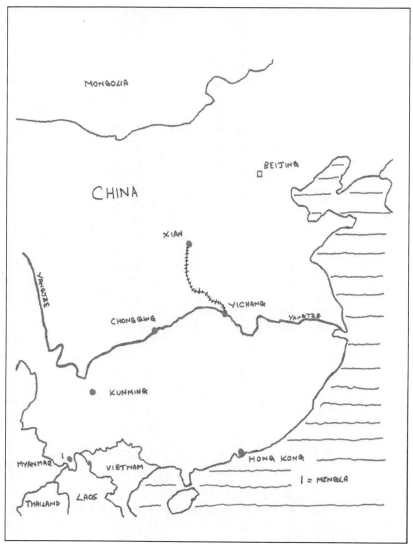

Map 16

In terms of timings and train etiquette, unlike on my previous train ride in China, I now had a rough idea what to expect and had already brushed my teeth, removed my contact lenses and changed down to a t-shirt and shorts over my underpants, when the lights went out at 11 o'clock sharp. The carriage was pumping out hot air from somewhere and underneath my blanket and sheet I was getting very warm, so I stripped down to just my underpants, with the blanket protecting my modesty. I had evidently been tired and fell into a deep sleep very quickly. I was woken a short while later – I guessed it was around midnight – by the sound of loud whispering Chinese voices in the corridor. I was still semi-comatose but I registered the fact that the train was no longer juddering along and when I half-opened my eyelids I realised that we had stopped at a station, which, through the heavy condensation on the window, I could just make out was dimly lit by flickering fluorescent lights. The carriage lights were still off. The whispering oriental voices came nearer and suddenly bright torchlight was being shone towards the top two bunks of our compartment. Looking down at the shadowy figures, my initial thought was that the persons were probably interlopers from the hard seat section of the train, who were looking for somewhere better to sleep, despite the fact they did not have a specific place allotted to them. I closed my eyes. A moment later the bloke on the middle bunk adjacent to me nudged my arm and pointed to the bunk above me where my rucksack was lying. I leaned up and looked. My rucksack seemed to be where I had left it and all seemed in order. Being half-asleep, I still had not registered what was happening. I shrugged my shoulders at the man to gesture that I was not sure how I could help him and laid back down. Next thing I knew, some unusual noises from above disturbed me and when I looked up there was a Chinese man on the top bunk diagonally across from me yanking at my rucksack. My first instinctive thought was that he was trying to steal it. I threw off the blanket and abruptly knelt up to push my bag back. He shouted aggressively at me. I shouted back and in a flash, I jumped up from my bunk, stood across the two middle bunks and shoved him with both hands hard in the chest to get him to back off. He neither shouted nor tried again to remove my bag, but simply sat back on the bunk submissively. Suddenly the lights in the corridor came on, a female conductor appeared and the people from the other compartments in our carriage, men, women and children, some barefoot, some in hair nets, many in vests and long johns, and one holding a teddy, crowded in to see what all the commotion was. There I was in full light, standing legs astride across the two middle bunks, naked apart from my underpants, looking like the Colossus of Rhodes. The buggers had something to stare at now!

As I hurriedly put back on my t-shirt and shorts, the conductor speaking only Chinese was trying to explain something to me and when she wasn't quite getting through to me, she produced a train ticket from her pocket and pointed at it and then at the men above. It was only then that the light bulb in my tiny brain illuminated to make me realise that the train was evidently picking up more passengers on the way and the man and his mate had tickets with these two bunks allocated to them, and, therefore, they had every right to try to remove my bag from their bunk. Feeling very embarrassed, I said sorry over and over again, and from the countenance on my face and my obsequious bowing the Chinese man seemed to understand, as he nervously smiled back at me. At that point, disappointed that it had ended so cheaply and without bloodshed, the crowd seemed to lose interest and they tottered back to their own compartments. I took down my rucksack and the female conductor showed me a space in the corridor where I could leave it. I was very glad when the lights went out again a short while later, allowing the darkness to conceal my embarrassment.

Today, once I had managed to extricate myself from my bunk, quickly splashed some water on my face in the rancid bathroom, accepted a plastic cup of hot steaming water that masqueraded as green tea from the train conductor, nodded and mouthed a further apology to the man on the top bunk who, peering out from under his covers, seemed half afraid to come out of his bolthole and plonked myself on a pop-up seat beside the window, I contemplated my time in China thus far. It had been bloody hard work and I considered that I had not so much enjoyed it, as endured it. There was the spitting, the smoking, the staring, the aggression and the fighting, the numerous birds stuffed in tiny cages, the difficulties with the language, there were the disgusting toilets, there was the smog hanging over polluted Chongqing and the litter in the Yangtze and to cap it all there was the incident of the cruelty with the horse. I like to think of myself as a pretty tolerant chap but I recognised that my levels of tolerance were wearing thin. I had been in this wretched country for two weeks and I still had a further two weeks to go. How was I going to cope, I thought to myself, if the events had brought me to the point where, but for the intervention of others, I could have easily got myself into far deeper trouble with all the potential ramifications surrounding it?

However, I also recognised that, perversely, I seemed to engender a more positive reaction from them when I stood up to them. The guard who I had had the barging match with when I first got on the train yesterday could not have been more friendly later, and that poor shivering wreck of a chap on the bunk above me had become much more compliant after I had shoved him hard in the chest. I realised that I had become in a sense battle-hardened by the experiences of the last two weeks, which, on the one hand, was not such a bad thing, but I also realised that it would be a very dangerous game to allow aggression to be the key to seeing me through the next two weeks. I kept my head down for the rest of the journey.

Train arrived on time – 19 hours. When I arrived in Xian a man at the station persuaded me to accompany him to a hotel – I looked at it but it was very grubby, so I moved on – he then continually pestered me to give him a tip. He was hard to shake off. I went to the Golden Bridge travel agency where the staff were very helpful and spoke reasonable English – booked tour tomorrow which includes seeing the terracotta army. They found me accommodation at the Victory Hotel (Y120) – this hotel was much better than the previous one but for the same price. The hotel has a restaurant that does good tea. In the evening, I went wandering.

Xian was the ancient capital of China, and the focal point at the Eastern end of the Silk Road, the destination, and departure point, for a thousand years for traders between China and the Mediterranean, and all points in between. Extending over 4,000 miles, the Silk Road was not one single road, but an interlocking series of trade routes, the name deriving from the lucrative trade in Europe for Chinese silk. However, whilst silk was probably the main trade item, many other goods were traded, including porcelain from the East to Europe and dates, saffron and glass bottles from the West to China, together with other less tangible commodities such as religions, ideologies, philosophies, technologies, not to mention diseases, including the Black Death. The Xian I discovered in 1999 was clearly a modern metropolis, but enough remnants of the old city remained to fire up the imagination and remind me of its cosmopolitan past.

I firstly came across the Jianfu Temple, which housed the Little Goose Pagoda. The Buddhist temple was originally the home of one of the Emperors in the Tang Dynasty and was converted into a temple in AD 684. I then passed under the South Gate and entered the inner city. Towards the city centre, located incongruously inside a wide roundabout bustling with traffic, I discovered the Bell Tower, an ornate square-shaped building that dated from the Ming Dynasty in the late 14th Century, its three layers making it look like an elaborate layer cake. A short distance away was the similarly designed Drum Tower. The two towers were a type of aide-memoire used to assist old city locals to tell the time. The bell was sounded at sunset and the drum was sounded at sunrise. I couldn't help wondering why, instead of listening out for these sounds, the old folk could not simply look out of their windows! The Drum Tower also signified the entrance to the Muslim Quarter, an area I hoped to explore later. Moving on, I arrived at the West Gate, which I passed under and found a bench a little further along where I could sit and look back at the Gate and the City Wall. The present wall has a circumference of 14km, is 12m high and has a width of between 12m and 14m. Colin Thubron in his book, 'Behind the Wall: A Journey Through China', describes the version of the wall dating from the 7th Century as having a circumference of 22 miles (or 35km), which made me wonder if there might have been both an inner and an outer wall. Certainly, the wall you can see today is very impressive in its own right and is almost intact, so the idea that there was originally an even larger wall was hard to comprehend. Seeing these ghostly reminders of Xian's ancient past, my mind mused on the Xian of myth and legend as most aptly described by Peter Hopkirk in his book, 'Foreign Devils on the Silk Road':

"[China's] capital Ch-ang-an (now Xian), the Rome of Asia and point of departure for travellers using the Silk Road is one of the most splendid and cosmopolitan cities on earth. In the year 742 its population was close on two million ... Ch-ang-an had grown into a metropolis measuring six miles by five surrounded by a defensive wall. The gates were closed every night at sunset. Foreigners were welcome and some 5,000 of them lived there. Nestorians, Manichaeans, Zoroastrians, Hindus and Jews were fully committed to build and worship in their own churches, temples and synagogues. An endless procession of travellers passed through the city's gates, including Turks, Iranians, Arabs, Sogdians, Mongolians, Armenians, Indians, Koreans, Malays and Japanese. Every known occupation was represented: merchants, missionaries, pilgrims, envoys, dancers, musicians, scribes, gem dealers, wine sellers, courtiers and courtesans."

An image of bearded, black-haired merchants sporting loose-fitting pantaloons, thick woollen gowns and turbans, and carrying scimitars in long camel-led caravans crossed my mind. With Xian being the main terminus at the Eastern end of the legendary Silk Road, and one of the places visited by Marco Polo some seven centuries before, logically, these people would have passed through the very West Gate that I was presently looking at. It was a sobering thought.

In the evening, I ate Beijing duck. It was good but I've had better in the UK. After my meal, I was writing this diary and all the staff crowded around to look. Maybe they think I'm a restaurant critic.

Tuesday 20th April – Terracotta Army

Very good day. I went on a day trip. The minibus picked up at my hotel – there were only two other people on this trip – both English – Paula and Helen (not bad looking). We went to the Banpo village, which was much more interesting than I had first thought. The Neolithic settlement was discovered in 1953, and artefacts date back to around 4500 BC. Then we went to a factory shop which I thought would be the usual tourist trap – and probably was – but I found the traditional furniture, painted tiles and folding

Chinese Screens very interesting. I would be half tempted to come back and fit out a house. We then had lunch which was included in the price and was actually very good. We then moved on to the Hauqing hot springs which were okay. Finally, saving the best to last, we then saw the Terracotta Army itself. Having read up about it in advance I had already been forewarned that what you see isn't quite as good as you might have hoped or imagined. They have supposedly found 6,000 warriors so far so you might have expected to see all 6,000 warriors. In fact, only a fraction of them are available to see because many of them are either being repaired, or beyond repair, or are in other museums. However, armed with that knowledge – and perhaps because my expectations had not been great – I found the visit absolutely brilliant. Stunning.

Up with Tutankhamen as one of the archaeological finds of the 20th Century, the army dates back 2,000 years. Excavation of the area is still going on and could take decades still to finish. So far, three chambers and 6,000 warriors have been discovered and sorted. No two warriors look alike, their facial features or expressions differing in some way. At the site, you can see three pits: one of them was very large, with half of it displaying columns of soldiers and the other half still waiting to be dug; the smaller one had a few solders but had been almost completely excavated and was largely empty; the third one still had people digging in as we looked. It was fascinating to observe live archaeology taking place before our eyes.

We were supposedly prohibited from taking photographs, but I managed to take about eight. I had to dodge both the police and security guards and the photographs were taken using guesswork. I will be very lucky, but also very grateful, if I get just one good one. I saw and photographed the gentleman who first discovered artefacts lying beneath his land. He was an old peasant farmer but he is now a celebrity in his own right. Recently, he met Bill Clinton. Lucky him! The tour guide was quite sweet and quite pretty, but she seemed to lose heart (and probably lost commission) after none of us had bought anything at the factory we visited earlier. On the way back, we got stuck in a traffic jam and we were totally gridlocked. The driver became very frantic. I would have liked to have got to know Paula and Helen a little better but my attempts to engage in conversation fell on deaf ears and they were disinterested. As I was walking along a street near to my hotel I decided to dive into a barber's to have a haircut. It was good fun and I enjoyed some banter with the staff. I had earlier given some laundry to the hotel which they gave back to me in the evening. I had my meal in the hotel which was very good. I discovered that our hotel has a massage parlour, which I thought was authentic until I was told that I have to pay Y350 (£25) and was told that the girls were beautiful and young. Dodgy (but I'm tempted!!). I went wandering later in the evening into two bars and I talked to several local people.

Wednesday, 21ˢᵗ April – Two Lessons Learnt

After talking to the English girls yesterday, and having consulted my Lonely Planet guidebook, I pondered the not insignificant topic of whether I had eaten truly authentic Peking duck the other night. Lonely Planet in particular talks about it costing Y180 (about £13) whereas I had paid Y25. I might be confusing Peking duck with aromatic crispy duck, which I had previously thought were the same. I hope to solve this conundrum later.

This has been (and, as I write this, still is) an 'experience' day, a lived-in day, one which I would not forget in a hurry. I had had a restless night – two reasons: 1. I am still getting over a cold, and 2. having become quite friendly with the tour guide on the boat down the Yangtze and having been practically propositioned by Ling Zhu in Yichang, my gander – shall we say – was well and truly up; that, together with the knowledge that my hotel, seemingly like many, if not most, hotels in China had its own sideline in providing personal pleasure, meant that the prospect of having a massage experience like the one I (nearly) had in Bangkok was getting my juices flowing. Laid in just a little. Intended to do walking tour around the walls of Xian, but decided to go to the railway station first to try to book a ticket for tomorrow to head off to Beijing and to change some money before doing so. Went to Singapore Fast Food for breakfast and wasn't that impressed.

When I read my diary now I wonder how I allowed myself to get as involved as I did, but, of course, it is easy to look back in hindsight. It is completely different to actually being there and living the experience. I might have been single and I might have been approaching the ripe old age of 39, but I can honestly say that I never had any intention of indulging in the sex trade on my trip. In that respect, I guess I would have regarded myself as a typically reticent Englishman. However, throughout my time in South-East Asia and China, I had been propositioned, sometimes subtly, sometimes downright blatantly, by girls in the trade, on an almost daily basis. It seemed as though it was woven into the culture and society. In Chinese hotels in particular, it was more like an industry, with most of them offering a massage service. Many of the hotels I stayed in were occupied in the main by young to middle-aged businessmen, and very few women. When I first checked in yesterday, the wiry middle-aged man at the front desk, his open shirt revealing a grimy collar, asked for my passport, bade me to sign the register, asked for money in advance, gave me my room key, told me which floor to head for and informed me in slow broken English, "We heff messarge." He said it without batting an eyelid, like it was as routine as telling me my room number or what time was breakfast. Throughout yesterday and earlier today, I had noticed that there were several girls, many who were downright gorgeous, hanging around the restaurant area in the hotel. On a couple of occasions yesterday one of them in particular had made eye contact with me and had flashed what in other circumstances would have been a shy smile at me. They were experts at their trade, because they were very disarming, and very persuasive, behind their betraying smiles, and although I knew they were more interested in my money than me personally, I was tempted to play along and part with some of my filthy lucre. For a while, I resisted.

On the way to the station, I exited through one of the old city gates and wandered down some of the bustling side streets just before reaching the station. I discovered a street full of what looked on the face of it like barber shops. It seemed as if every sixth or seventh shop was a hairdresser's. Many of them had young girls sitting outside apparently trying to draw customers in. True enough, I did see one or two gentlemen having haircuts, but I also saw displayed in several of the shop windows the word 'massage' in Anglicised script. Although there was no way of telling immediately whether they were providing authentic massages, or were a knocking shop, the very fact that the word 'massage' was being advertised in English, presumably for the tourists, hinted to me that they were the latter.

At one of them a couple of pretty young girls, looking like young professionals in crisp clean white blouses and knee-length tight navy skirts, beckoned me to go in. I hesitated but I went in. I was intending not to succumb to temptation, but I was curious and I was also happy to attempt to engage in conversation and to allow myself to be titillated by the bargaining process. I managed to get the price down to a two-hour massage for Y100 (£7), but I chickened out and left saying I would think about coming back later. Further down the road, invigorated by my first encounter, there was no hesitation this time when a young girl beckoned me into her shop and I strode in full of confidence. Once inside, the first girl was joined by two others, and I was given a small cup of hot green tea before one of them engaged me in a stuttering conversation in English. My imagination was running wild by this time and I tried to negotiate a massage with two of them together, but they were not very keen. The price here for one girl for two hours would have been Y120. I left a short while later. The truth was that at that point I was still far too nervous to truly allow myself to indulge, but I enjoyed the fact that I was playing with fire, and I was starting to feel very horny.

In an attempt to cool down my ardour by returning to the mundane, I walked on to the railway station, where I found out that there were no spare tickets available for tomorrow. I was advised, however, to try out one of the travel agencies back in the city, as they might have some spare.

Turning on my heels, and heading back in the direction of town, I had to pass by the street of hairdressers which ran perpendicular to where I was heading. I was tempted to have another wander. A short distance into the street, I passed by yet another barber's shop where standing in the doorway was a very pretty, tall, slim girl, wearing a miniskirt that revealed shapely long legs, who beckoned me in. At this third shop, I couldn't resist. She proposed charging Y60 (the princely sum of £4.29) for a massage. Like a rabbit caught in headlights, the ridiculously cheap price did not ring alarm bells in my mind at the time, so I agreed and was ushered past a curtain into a dingy back room. She insisted that I pay the money up front, which I did. At that she undid a couple of buttons on her white blouse and pulled aside her bra to reveal small, shapely breasts. She took my left hand and placed it on her right nipple. She then pushed her left nipple towards my mouth gesturing for me to suck. I was like a child being given sweets, and I obediently did what I was told. As pretty as she was, she was routinely going through the motions. Thankfully, she was not chewing gum. That *would* have been the final straw.

After about two minutes, she drew back and by way of a combination of sign language and the language section in my guidebook, she offered to charge me a further Y100, for which she would firstly massage me, I would then massage her, and finally she would masturbate me. This sounded more like it, so I agreed and paid the further Y100. I laid back on the table which was lined with blankets. I was still fully clothed. Although she proceeded to massage my shoulders and torso, it was performed over my clothing and with no real effort being made. She was clearly still going through the motions. She too remained fully clothed, save that the two buttons on her blouse were still suggestively undone. After only five minutes, she went to my jeans, and with speed and precision, she undid the button, pulled down my zip, pulled my underpants to one side, took out my member and started yanking on it. I was semi-flaccid, as I was finding the whole experience thus far devoid of excitement. It was perhaps only the fact that she was so pretty that provided any sort of stimulus. I was also still very horny, however, and I knew that it would not take long to finish me off, so I tried to stop her from doing so, wanting to prolong the experience. Oblivious to my pleadings, she carried on, however, and true enough 30 seconds later, despite being only semi-erect, I came. She applied massage to my shoulders for a further two minutes, then gave me some tissues, turned on her heels and promptly left the room, passing thorough the curtain back into the front shop. There was never even the slightest attempt at conversation.

After cleaning myself up, I went back out front to find that, although she was still not chewing gum, insult was finally added to the injury – she was now filing her nails. I tried to remonstrate with her, pointing out that she had not properly massaged me, and she had not allowed me to massage her. She shrugged her shoulders, intimating that she did not understand what the fuss was all about. A second girl, a friend of the first, then came into the shop and, ignoring my presence, they both started chatting. By now, I was getting quite exasperated, but realising that I could not exactly sue for breach of contract or complain to Trading Standards, and, knowing that I was not going to get anywhere, I left.

Bizarrely, I was able to take my mind off the experience by playing pool. Further up the street I stopped to watch some lads playing on tables in the street and before too long I was invited to join in. The cloth on the tables was threadbare and the pool cues were as thick as broom-handles but, although the lads who I played against spoke no English, they, like me, seemed to find it great fun.

Walking back into town, I passed back under the East Gate, one of the main gates into the ancient city, and tried to access the city walls. However, the steps up to the walls were closed off. I carried on walking back into town and made my way to the Golden Bridge Travel Agency to check out train tickets for tomorrow. They only had hard seat tickets left, but I needed to move on and I booked a ticket paying Y180, including commission. I grabbed a noodle dish and wandered back to my hotel.

I had had a dispiriting, dissatisfying, frustrating day, but I knew I only had myself to blame. As I paused at the front desk of the hotel to collect my key, the girl who had flashed a smile at me yesterday walked past carrying a tray of drinks. She looked at me and smiled, before carrying on to a room at the side. She was wearing the ubiquitous uniform of tight, knee-length, navy blue skirt and white blouse, which made her look not at all like a waitress – more like an upmarket secretary. She went into the room. The receptionist, still wearing the same grimy shirt, must have noticed my ever-so-slight smile in response to the girl's flirting, because he said to me, "You like girl?" his lascivious grin revealing a couple of mock-gold teeth. My mumbling denial fell on deaf ears, and he must have caught my initial momentary hesitation, because he quickly disappeared into a room behind the counter and emerged a moment later with a colleague, a rather rotund middle-aged chap with a round face and the beginnings of a moustache, who was wearing a crumpled brown jacket over his equally crumpled open-neck shirt. The jacket probably signified that he was the boss. The manager spoke better English than his colleague, so that was probably the main reason why he had been summoned. I had to stifle a laugh because, looking at the tall, wiry receptionist and his short, rotund boss, a picture came into my mind of Laurel and Hardy.

"You would like girl?" Hardy asked, but in that instant and before I could answer, the girl emerged from the room with a now-empty tray. He called over to her speaking in Chinese and she sashayed towards the front desk. As she approached, he said something else to her, which was unintelligible to me, but from the beaming smile that erupted on her face and the way that she grinned when she turned to look at me, he had clearly breached my confidence. She seemed genuinely pleased that I had apparently expressed some interest in her. I believed, of course, that I had indicated nothing of the sort, but the receptionist and his boss could obviously read me like a book. Frankly, I was captivated by her beauty and after only a moment's pause that had seemed like time had been suspended, the girl half-winked at me and turned to walk away. I was landed, hook, line and sinker. Hardy cleared his throat to break the spell and said, "You want one hour or two?"

I replied, "How much for one hour?"

"Y500," he said. My daily budget was the equivalent of Y280, so it was more than I could really afford, but I had budgeted pretty well so far and I had built up the equivalent of nine days' surplus. After a little bit of haggling I got him down to Y400, but I insisted that the girl would be with me for one hour. My dirty little mind was already imagining that my first 'go' was likely to be rather quick, and I wanted the luxury of leaving enough time to 'go' again. He agreed, assuring me over and over again that I would get my full hour. He said that she would come up to my room in about 30 minutes.

I went up to my room, took a shower and made myself ready. I wore shorts and a t-shirt. I put Nan's photograph away in my rucksack.

A short while later there was a knock at my door. I went to it and standing outside were the girl and a male aged around 30, who I had not recalled seeing before. It turned out he was there to confirm the terms of the agreement. "You pay 400?" to which I said, "Yes, for one hour."

"Yes," he replied, "you pay now?" I said I would rather pay later. He agreed and left.

I gestured for the girl to come into the room. She walked past me. I closed the door and went and sat on the side of my bed. Close up, the girl was even more beautiful than at first sight. She was quite a lot taller, at around 5' 10", than most of her Chinese counterparts and her features were more chiselled. She had high cheekbones, wide dark eyes, shoulder-length straight dark hair, her nose was more Western and less button-nosed than other Chinese women and she had a long and slender neck. Her close-fitting blouse and her tight skirt promised that I would not be disappointed by the delights that lay hidden underneath. She carried with her a small shoulder bag. She spoke no English.

As I was sitting on the side of the bed my member was fully erect in anticipation and was creating a bulge in my shorts, a fact that did not go unnoticed, as she giggled and beamed from ear to ear. She seemed genuinely pleased at the compliment I was paying her.

She took me by the hand and led me into the bathroom. She gestured for me to wash myself very thoroughly down below. Although I had already showered, I had no problem giving her the reassurance that she sought. She stood at the door to the bathroom as I did so. She then gestured for me to leave the bathroom whilst she then washed *her*self. I went back into the room and sat again on the side of the bed. From the sounds that I could hear she seemed to wash herself several times. A short while later she emerged from the bathroom and stood at the end of the bed. She was still fully clothed. She took me by my hand and pulled me towards her and she placed my hands on her blouse gesturing for me to undo the buttons on it. A feeling of déjà vu flashed into my mind and just as quickly flashed out again. I got on with the job.

In my state of nervous anticipation my hands trembled slightly as one by one I undid the buttons on her blouse to reveal a lacy white bra underneath. I pulled her arms through the blouse and I lay it on the chair in my room. She then turned her back to me and pointed to the top of her skirt gesturing for me to unbutton the top and slide down the zip. I did so and peeled off her skirt, putting it too on the chair. She wore matching lacy white panties, cut high to accentuate her athletic toned legs and reveal the roundness of her buttocks.

Not needing any more guidance, I moved around to face her and I stroked her long neck from her ears down to her shoulders, and as I did so, I slipped the straps of her bra off her shoulders. She half-turned and with what I cannot deny was expert precision, I unclipped the clasp on the back of her bra in one movement (why do we boys puff out our chests in pride at such an achievement!). I placed her bra on the chair. Her breasts were pear-shaped, full and firm and her small, tight nipples were erect. Her cream-toned torso, offset by her dark hair and dark eyes, was long and her stomach was flat and smooth. She was gorgeous.

She took me by my hand and led me to the bed and gestured for me to lie there. She peeled back my shorts to remove them, and as she pulled them over my member it sprung back like a coiled spring. She took hold of her shoulder bag and she took out a small bottle of baby oil. Standing beside the bed she slowly peeled off her panties to reveal close-cropped downy pubic hair. She moved her long legs languidly onto the bed and knelt up in front of me. She took hold of my hand, turned it palm side up and poured a little of the baby oil into the cup of my hand. She then took my hand and placed it under her vagina, gesturing for me to massage the oil into her. I massaged the oil gently around her labia and then briefly slipped a couple of oily fingers inside her. To my surprise she was already quite wet, and she shuddered slightly as I did so. I caressed her clitoris gently squeezing it between my thumb and forefinger. She gave a little moan. I moved my hand up between her legs to play with her perineum.

After about five minutes I was full to bursting and knowing that I still had plenty of time, I pulled away and went to the side table where I had earlier strategically placed a couple of condoms. She nodded with approval, as I tore off the wrapper and gave the condom to her. Lying on the bed, I laid back whilst she expertly peeled back the condom over my phallus. I gently moved her onto her back and I knelt up between her legs and entered her, ecstasy filling my whole body. I did not hold back and the climactic shock that arced through my body moments later was exquisite.

Afterwards, we propped up the pillows and sat back on the bed, still both fully naked. We tried to converse with the help of the phrasebook. I learnt that she was of Uighur descent, but although her ancestral origins lay in the far Western fringes of China in Central Asia, she was born in Harbin, the capital of Heilongjiang province located in the far North-Eastern corner of China bordering on Inner Mongolia and Russia. She was 23.

I glanced at the clock. I still had a full 30 minutes left and I was raring to go again. I put the book down and gestured for her to lie on the bed. She frowned and shook her head. I pointed to the dials on the clock to indicate that we still had another 30 minutes. She held up one finger to suggest that I was allowed one 'go.' I picked up the phrasebook again and I managed to find the words to remind her that I had paid for one hour. She too used the phrasebook to tell me that, yes, I had paid for one hour and she would stay for one hour but she would not have any more sex, emphasising the point by shaking her head. Without saying or doing anything else, she stood up, promptly got dressed and sat back on the bed. Unhappy at the notion that I was apparently about to be ripped off yet again, coupled with me being absolutely certain that Hardy had fully understood my terms earlier, I obtained some satisfaction from the fact I had at least not paid up front this time. *Well,* I thought, *if she is only going to give me half the time, I will only pay her half the money.* I went to my money belt and at the sight of me about to sort out the money she stood up, presumably pleased to be about to be on her way. When I tried to give her only Y200, she looked perplexed, refused to take the money and sat back on the bed, crossing her arms and then crossing her legs. I asked her to leave and held out the money again. She did not react, other than to start swinging her crossed leg. At that point in time, I had decided that there was no way that I was going to pay her another

Y200 to sit there and do nothing, so when I spotted her shoulder bag still hanging over the chair I knew what I had to do. I picked up the bag, opened one of the side pockets and put the Y200 in. I then went to the door, opened it and slung the bag into the corridor. I then went back to the girl, took her by the arm, pulled her off the bed and I dragged her out of the room into the corridor. I shot back into the room and quickly slammed the door shut and put the bolt across. As I stood there leaning with my back to the door, a jolt of sheer terror, like an electric shock, shot through my body and I suddenly thought, "What the fuck have I done?" The adrenalin had clearly got the better of me and maybe I had let out some of the pent-up frustration of my first two weeks in China, but in an instant my heart was pounding in my chest. A moment later there was a knock at the door and I could hear a female voice trying to say something to me in Chinese. I said nothing. There was another knock, this time a little louder. It all then went silent. A minute or two later, there was another knock at the door and this time there were two voices. Firstly, a male voice tried to say something to me. When I didn't answer he spoke to the other person, a female who I presumed to be my companion from earlier. He then knocked on the door again, this time a lot more forcefully. I still did not answer. I could hear footsteps walking away. Far from being relieved I was petrified as to what would happen next.

The only noise I could hear was that of the hammering in my chest. It was dawning on me that since this girl worked at this hotel, she probably had friends or bodyguards to look after her and I imagined Laurel running up the stairs taking them two at a time, armed with a meat cleaver. It occurred to me that maybe they could even be Triads and I imagined hordes of angry Chinese men hammering on my door to break it down intent on revenge. The silence outside was more terrifying than the knocking had been. Panic-stricken, I looked around the room and decided that I needed to barricade myself in. I firstly went to the wardrobe and slid that across and in front of the door. I then put as much of my belongings inside the wardrobe as possible to give it some weight. I picked up the side table and wedged it against the wardrobe. Finally, I pulled the bed across the room and wedged it end up against the side table. Frankly, looking back, my defences would have probably only held back a pack of genuinely baying blood-thirsty Asiatics for no more than two minutes, but psychologically they made me feel safer at the time. All that was left in the room now were me and the chair. However, that was more than enough, because I was in no mood to sleep and I stayed awake right through an anxious but ultimately, and thankfully, uneventful rest of the night. Even before the first sight of dawn I packed my stuff in my rucksack, hastily rearranged the furniture in my room, and sneaked downstairs. It was 4.30 a.m. when I got down to the lobby, and because I didn't want to wait around for change, I paid a fraction over the room price to a bemused and sleepy-eyed Laurel, who was still wearing the same grimy shirt. On exiting out of the front doors, I did not look back.

Lesson 1, do not get involved with ladies of the night as you will just get your fingers burnt. Lesson 2, if you ignore lesson 1, do not pay up front.

Thursday 22ⁿᵈ April – Little Goose Pagoda

Survived last night intact. My barricade stood firm. No repercussions. But it's really put the wind up me. Packed. I went to the travel agents. I had hoped to catch the 6.00am train not least because I thought that the sooner I got away from Xian the better – but unfortunately it was already full up and I had to book to go on the 23.30 train. I decided to use the day to do the walk that I was going to do yesterday and wander around the walls surrounding the city. Saw the bell tower, which was okay but was quite expensive, saw the South Gate, and I wandered through the Little Goose Pagoda which had very attractive grounds. Inside those grounds I saw what looked like a wedding photo session but I discovered that it was not a real wedding and was for some kind of advertising or promotion. It was a very hot day and probably in excess of 29 degrees. The city walls were extensive. After lunch, I wandered around the Muslim quarter, which was very attractive and gave me a taste of what old Xian must have looked like.

I ambled into the Great Mosque, reputed to be one of the largest in China, which had a Chinese architectural style, rather than an Arabic or Turkish one, and was reminded of the observations of Colin Thubron in his book, 'Behind the Wall: A Journey Through China.' He noted the absence of indicators to suggest this was the Muslim area, which would have distinguished it from the rest of the city: -

"They came as merchants and mercenary soldiers, and the houses of their Muslim descendants, who call themselves Hui, still cluster in white-washed lanes; yet the people looked identical to Han Chinese, and when I ventured into the chief mosque I was surrounded by pagodas, dragon-screens and tilted eaves; only when I looked closer did I notice that on some memorials Chinese characters gave way to the dotted swing of Arabic, and the prayer-hall enclosed no plump idol but an empty space, inviting a god only in the mind."

For sure, there was not much evidence to be found within this area to remind oneself of its ancient roots and I fully recognise that my blissful ignorance was my salvation, since I would never have picked up on the absence of fine detail that an eminent scholar like Mr. Thubron would have noticed. However, for me there were enough fragments of clues, including the tightness of the lanes, the number of artisans working from their homes directly onto the street, together with the very fact that there still exists today an area known as the Muslim Quarter together with its mosque, to fire up the imagination and make one think that the one-time Souk in this district might have been a home from home for those intrepid souls who ventured here from the Middle East all those centuries ago. In fact, the same could be said about Xian as a whole, in that behind the concreted modern metropolis there lie clues to its antiquity, found in its bell towers and walls and pagodas. You might need to squint a little bit, you might need to search a lot and you certainly need to use a great deal of imagination, but for me the ghosts of ancient Xian were there to be found.

Back at the travel agency I made further enquiries regarding Laos but it seems like it may be too expensive for me to be able to travel back there. On listening to BBC World Service, I also discovered that there have recently been more problems in Indonesia, including Jakarta and Sulawesi. Caught train. Very clean and no smoking. Seemingly a new cleaner breed of train.

Friday 23rd April – Arrived at Beijing

This was the best train journey yet, despite the fact that I had a hard seat (which was not too hard). It was a relatively new train and as well as no smoking there was no spitting. It was a welcome relief. This was a faster journey which took 16 hours. Again, I did not see any foreigners on the train. Very poor service when I arrived in Beijing. Considering I was in a capital city and had just arrived at one of the major stations, I found myself stuck. Everybody seemed to be rushing around and nobody seemed to be prepared to stop and talk to me when I tried to ask for help. However, I persevered and that was the theme for the rest of the day. Throughout the day it seemed like I managed to get where I wanted to go to but it was all a bit of a struggle, like I was wading through treacle. The people were very unhelpful. A tout irritatingly tried to press me to get a taxi for Y40 but I resisted. I eventually found the bus (for Y2) that I thought would take me to the area that I wanted to go to. Then I struggled to find the travel agents (as recommended by Golden Bridge in Xian). I had to make a telephone call to them to find out where they are. I eventually found them, but I was knackered from lugging my rucksacks around. Whilst I was there I found out details of onward trains to Hong

Kong. I checked a number of hotels but they seemed quite expensive. They eventually found one for me which just about fitted my budget. They gave me directions. I walked to the hotel but on the way my left calf muscle gave way and it was extremely painful. As at that stage I hadn't eaten much in 24 hours and I wondered if I was depriving my body of salt or water or something else which might have caused the problem. The hotel was not very easy to find. It costs Y217 which is 75% of my daily budget. Maybe I will try to find a cheaper one tomorrow. I checked in. I washed and then wandered down to an area where there were market stalls where I had a spring roll at one place, a meat kebab at another and then some noodles. I saw a Chinese version of pick and mix with locusts, scorpions, and all sorts of grubs and beetles waiting to be eaten.

Saturday 24th April – Forbidden City

A very good day. I had the hotel's breakfast – dreadful. I then went to the Forbidden City via Mao's portrait overlooking the Tiananmen Gate and then into the city itself. It is not quite what I imagined. I had pictured cobbled streets, houses close together, narrow lanes and men in dark uniforms cycling through. In fact, it was the Emperors' Palace which for centuries had been totally off limits. Entrance was Y50.00 and it cost Y30.00 for the audio cassette (well worth it because I could go around at my leisure). The narrator was Roger Moore (the Roger Moore of James Bond fame), which was fun in itself and it was strangely reassuring to hear such a familiar voice. There were large and small courtyards, several palaces, statues of lions, ornate rooves, cranes and tortoises and gold and bronze urns. I spent about four and a half hours lazily roaming around there and I had a great time. Although the Terracotta Army was more spectacular I think I enjoyed this more because I could wander around at my own pace. Afterwards I went to Jingshan Park just North of the Forbidden City and to the top pavilion where I was able to get a good panoramic view looking back at the Forbidden City and its red roofs, and of Beijing city beyond. On the way back down from the pavilion, I passed by a locust tree which commemorates the location during the 17th Century where the last Ming Emperor hanged himself after slaying his family before the Manchus took his palace. I learned a week or so back that this year marks the fiftieth anniversary of the founding of the People's Republic of China, so the fact that I have seen a lot of building work going on in this and other cities makes more sense. I noticed in particular that they are reconstructing the moat around the Forbidden City. One of the lesser ambitions that I had had for the trip was to have Peking Duck in Peking and I achieved it this evening. It was delicious. It was served in two courses, with the first being the more familiar boneless juicy sweet honey and sauce glazed duck meat, with its succulent crispy skin, accompanied by shallots, hoisin sauce and pancakes – and plenty of it – followed by duck soup. I was propositioned twice more by girls on the street but I readily, though I like to think politely, declined. In the evening, I went walking over to an area in the North-East of Beijing where there were lots of foreigners. I saw one European woman have her handbag stolen. Otherwise it was *a quiet evening. I estimate that I walked about six miles there and back. I moved room in my hotel and the price is now Y177.00 (£12.50).*

Map 17

Sunday 25th April – Temple of Heaven

I got stuck in my room this morning. The knob on my door turned but wouldn't open. There were no telephones in my room and I had to knock repeatedly and loudly for help which took quite a while to come. I found out that yesterday Manchester United won their semi-final and are through to the European Cup Final. Had another very good day – had good coffee in the morning. Then I went to Tiananmen Gate and on into Tiananmen Square. Much of it was being re-laid and was a building site. I saw the Great Hall of the People, which is proclaimed to be the National Parliament, although effectively it is a rubber stamp legislator. Then I saw the People's Monument, Qianmen Gate and the Mao Zedong Mausoleum. All the monuments were only visible from a distance as they were all being renovated for this year's fiftieth anniversary. I read that Mao's body gets a good makeover several times each year and despite the fact that I found the idea of viewing the body as bordering on the macabre, I was still curiously drawn to see one of the most iconic figures of the 20th Century particularly in this year that closes out that century. The queues into the mausoleum were very long, though, and I decided that I would try to see him later. Whilst wandering around the square I met and got talking to a couple of Chinese girls who spoke very good English. One of them was obviously trying to sell paintings. Even though she very quickly learned that I would not be buying, both she and the other girl were happy to carry on talking to me. The second girl turned out to be an artist herself and I realised that the first girl had probably been trying to sell her colleague's paintings. The artist never pushed me to buy any of her paintings – in fact there was never any mention of it. Her name is Li. She described to me where her shop was located, just North of the Qianmen Gate and I said that I would try to see her later.

I wandered South beyond Tiananmen Square. I had a delicious noodle soup for lunch. I then went to Tiantan Park which was very beautiful and contained many interesting examples of Ming architecture. They included the Fasting Palace, where the emperor would exercise abstinence from meat, drink, music, women and state affairs for a period of three days. I also saw the Hall of Prayer for good harvests, which was used by the emperor to conduct rites and ceremonies. I also saw the Round Altar which is composed of white marble constructed in three tiers. Indeed, the entire geometry revolves around the imperial number 9. The top tier has nine rings of stone with each ring composed of multiples of nine stones so that the ninth ring has 81 stones. The number of stairs and balustrades are also multiples of nine. I also saw the Echo Wall and the Imperial Vault of Heaven. The park is collectively known as the Temple of Heaven. The buildings within generally are round and the bases are square deriving from the ancient Chinese belief that heaven is round and the earth is square. The ground upon which this park was constructed was considered to be highly sacred. It was very interesting and the architecture was very iconic. There were several tour groups wandering around, all of them Chinese visitors and each group carried its own coloured flag or hat to designate which *group they belonged to. Thankfully the park was big enough to absorb these numbers of people and they were not too difficult to avoid. I bought a couple of postcards and arranged to send one to Robbyne. I then headed back North in the general direction of Tiananmen Square and my hotel beyond it and as I did so I walked back past Li's shop. I popped in to see her and her paintings. They were actually very good and I was very tempted to buy one or more, in part precisely because she had never once suggested that I should buy any of her paintings, but was happy for me simply to look, which made me want to buy a painting even more. However, partly because of my tight budget and partly because I would have to carry it throughout the rest of my trip I decided not to. We had a really good conversation and we talked about acrobatics and opera because apparently there is a show in Beijing which combines the two. I asked Li if she wanted to go. Although she said that she would she did not seem overly enthusiastic. I genuinely wanted to go only as friends but afterwards I thought that she might have thought I was coming on to her. She didn't say a definite 'no' and we agreed that we might possibly go on Tuesday. I said that I would ring her.*

Monday 26th April – Great Wall

Yesterday I noticed how heavy-handed the police appear to be. There are plenty of them, they very rarely smile and they are the second most rude and unhelpful sort of people (after train employees) that I have met in China. One poor man, who appeared to be down and out, was told to empty his bag and show it to a policeman on a motorcycle. It was in front of Tiananmen Gate which was a Sunday and which was accordingly very crowded. Later in the Temple of Heaven where smoking was prohibited a man lit a cigarette. I assume he did it without thinking. Almost immediately a policeman was there telling him to stub it out armed with a fines book. The man had to pay an on-the-spot Y10.00 fine. I have seen this fines book come out before. It seems that everybody is afraid of the police because every person who is approached or confronted by the police appears to do everything they tell them to without any discussion or objection. I had big plans for today and I had set my alarm for 5.30 am.

One of my main reasons for coming to this country – no doubt it is on many travellers' 'to do' lists – was to visit the Great Wall of China. The Great Wall is, of course, one of the most venerated and iconic man-made structures on the planet. Estimates as to its length vary from 2,500-6,000km, one of the reasons for the uncertainty being because the whole wall had never been fully surveyed – at least that was the case in 1999. Another reason is because, although much of the Wall follows a general line rising from the Yellow Sea in the East to a border with the great Gobi Desert and Mongolia to the North and West, it is not one long continuous wall. It is rather a series of walls, not all of them connected.

I hoped to be able to view it at two locations and my first attempt was going to be today. Lonely Planet provided various suggestions of access points close to Beijing for viewing the Wall. Several places looked to be very heavily touristic but I had been particularly drawn to one section described as 'Walking the Wild Wall.' The book explained; "this 'Wild Wall' is remote, lonely, unspoilt, overgrown and crumbling; there are no tickets, no signposts, no hassles from trinket-sellers, no coach parks or garbage to spoil the view." It sounded ideal.

Getting there was an adventure in itself, partly because there was no direct transport to the start of the walk, which was about 60km North, and involved several changes of transport, and partly also because by necessity I was mixing it with the locals. Not so many Chinese had resorted to staring at me in central Beijing – presumably because they were used to seeing Westerners. However, only a mile out of the centre I had become an oddity for them and the staring brigade were in full flow. Having got up at 5.30 in the morning it took nearly four hours before I was deposited beside the wall. Rather worryingly, on the final leg of my journey there were only two other persons on the near-empty minibus which dropped me off and it seemed that only a few minibuses used this route from the last main town 12 miles down the road. Consequently, I was a little concerned as to whether I would be able to find connections to enable me to return to the city at the end of the day. I would worry about that later.

It was a cool, grey, overcast day, but it was dry and the clouds were high. Consequently, although it would not make for great photography, visibility was still good and, in any event, the greyness provided a suitably moody and sombre backdrop to the scene. True enough, as the battered minibus, with its exhaust billowing great clouds of white smoke, slowly disappeared into the distance heading North along the narrow road away from me up and over what looked like a mountain pass, I found myself alone besides two large distinct sections of crumbling Wall, one heading East and the other heading West. I could not see a great deal of the Wall from where I was positioned, as I was standing in a small valley effectively underneath where the Wall would have traversed this spot – probably long before there was even a road – many centuries before. All I could see of the Wall from this angle were small sections on either side of me heading up short slopes. It certainly was remote. There was one small building 100 metres back down the road, but apart from that we had passed only tiny settlements and very few buildings since leaving the outskirts of the last town, 11 miles back. There was nobody around, and the only sound came from the occasional distant caw of a crow. To be stood beside one of the world's most iconic and well-known monuments but yet to be completely alone was awe-inspiring, though unnerving at the same time.

Having checked the rudimentary, but very useful, map in Lonely Planet, I decided that I would head West in the morning and then East in the afternoon. As advised in the book, with the section closest to the road being in a poor state, I walked back about 100 yards down the road in a Southerly direction to look for a footpath heading right and up onto a better-preserved section. As I did so, I glanced at the building I had passed earlier, which was now on my left, and noticed a dim but distinctive light on inside. I also noticed that in front of a door there was a weathered whiteboard with writing on it in lines, written in Chinese script, looking suspiciously like a menu. Despite it apparently being incongruously positioned in the middle of nowhere, on looking at my book it confirmed that sure enough there was a restaurant at this location. I assumed that it must have enough passing trade to make it worthwhile. I walked over and knocked on the door before walking into a small room furnished with a couple of tables and three or four chairs. A diminutive slightly hunched middle-aged lady wearing a thick grey woollen waistcoat, over a sweatshirt, saggy jogging bottoms and slippers, appeared out from behind a bead curtain, speaking to me in Chinese as she came through. Immediately realising that I was a Westerner, and concluding that I was bound not to have understood, she stopped mid-sentence, turned on her heels and disappeared briefly back through the bead curtain. She emerged a moment later holding a small, grubby, plastic-coated menu with photographs of the fare on offer. From the stains on the plastic cover, I deduced that there were not just photographs of the food on the menu, but samples of it too. I pointed at the meat dumplings and requested two of them. I had earlier purchased and brought with me a veritable picnic of biscuits, crisps, fruit and water, but the chance to be able to eat something hot before setting off was too good to miss, especially since I had not had any breakfast. Two hot steaming dumplings appeared quickly. Being more dough than meat, it was difficult to deduce the type of meat and impossible to ascertain its provenance. I tucked in, nevertheless. In fact, they were tasty and reminded me of my mum's suet puddings, just the thing for a cold day. I decided I would come back here for lunch before heading East in the afternoon.

Leaving the restaurant, I located the path immediately across the road, which soon turned North-West and almost instantly the brickwork of the Wall was recognisable, and I was heading for a watch tower. Arriving under the tower, I soon found a way up onto the ramparts and the Wall itself. The tower was very well-preserved, with archways, windows and completely intact walls on all sides. The only thing missing was its original wooden roof. Leaving the tower behind, I then walked along the top of the Wall and headed West towards the next watch tower. It involved a tricky climb up a steep slope. Some of the original steps were remarkably intact, but in other places the brick had crumbled away turning it to scree, and it was overgrown with weeds and bushes, some of which had very sharp thorns (which I located the hard way). On arrival at the next watch tower, there was not a great deal left of the tower, but I had gained a good deal of height deceptively quickly and the panoramic views 360 degrees around were spectacular.

Looking West, I was now able to see the Wall snaking ahead for a good two or three miles, initially maintaining its height twisting North, then dropping down to a valley heading South-West, before rising again up and over a couple of ridges in the distance. Ahead of me to the North were a series of craggy mountains, blanketed a racing green by either trees or other foliage – it was difficult to tell. Looking East, beside the road where I had been deposited by the bus, I could see a small reservoir, which I had not noticed before and from there the Wall emerged from the road zigzagging up a steady steep slope past a series of watch towers, before looping away to the North. It disappeared from view for a while before re-emerging and heading steeply up to more crags in the far distance. Away to the South was a relatively flat and wide river valley. The views all around clearly illustrated the strategic importance for positioning the wall between the mountains to the North and the valley to the South. I lingered at this place to try and take it all in. I constantly had to remind myself that this was *the* Great Wall. The ashen sky leant a brooding and spectral atmosphere to the surroundings. I was alone high on this Wall, with the only sounds coming from the continuing occasional caws from crows and the breeze that had picked up, rumbling and whooshing gently past my ears. The melancholy was only enhanced by my reading that the construction of the Wall required hundreds of thousands of workers, many of them prisoners or forced labour, and legend has it that one of the building materials used was the bodies of deceased workers. A shiver ran down my spine. Everywhere was still, that is until a couple of buzzards drifting in from the mountains to the North spiralled towards me.

I moved on, continuing mainly on top of the Wall, but occasionally having to drop off it to circumnavigate sections where the Wall had simply disappeared. Much of this area was overgrown with conifers. I passed two more watch towers before the Wall disappeared steeply down into a valley. I descended and passed through a passageway underneath the Wall. My book told me that this pass was one of three considered to be crucial in preventing large Mongol armies on horseback from so easily approaching old Peking. I took a path, which led off from the Wall, heading first South and then East, before eventually taking me back to the main road and lunch. I had covered 2 ½ miles in 2 hours. Knowing how undemonstrative the Chinese are, I did not expect much of a greeting back at the restaurant, but the very faintest of momentary smiles in acknowledgement on the lady's face when she saw me walk back into her restaurant was practically tantamount to her treating me like a long-lost friend. I pointed to one of the stains on the menu and asked for some of that. Whilst I waited I had a quick read of my book and discovered that this restaurant had a name, 'Shuang Long Zhu Jiu Jia' in Chinese, otherwise known as 'Pair of Dragons Playing with a Pearl Alcohol House.' A steaming hot plate of beef with fried noodles sent me off with enough sustenance for the afternoon.

I walked back up the road to where I had been dropped off by the minibus earlier and turned right – East – across the head of the reservoir before very soon striking up the steep slope I had seen from my vantage point earlier in the morning. This stretch, known as Gaping Jaw, was a long, steady, continuous climb, past a series of ramparts and towers. The fourth tower of seven was particularly well-preserved, with its parapets still standing, its brickwork intact and with its upper storey battlements and loopholes in excellent condition. The wind had dropped when I was on the road, but as I climbed higher the breeze again picked up and it was an eerie experience being alone under the still-leaden, slate-coloured sky. At least I thought I was alone. My heart skipped a beat and I froze when I thought I heard voices. My imaginary whimsies vanished instantly when suddenly, without warning, a group of three young, Western, English-speaking backpackers rose rapidly up from below me on the Wall, bade me a courteous, though peremptory, "Hello," as they passed me and strode on up the rising Wall beyond. I observed rather smugly that they seemed lost in their own little world oblivious of their surroundings and probably more intent on achieving the climb and ticking this trip off their list than in fully appreciating the history and ambience of the place. It also occurred to me that from the fact that their greeting had been so singularly perfunctory they were probably my race, that is, English. I felt glad to be on my own again, except, of course, that the feeling of being completely alone had now vanished.

I carried on and by the time I reached the top the group were thankfully well ahead of me. The section that I had reached was a vantage point on a corner, where, as I had observed in the morning, this part of the Wall turned North. I had a fine panoramic view of a hairpin section of Wall ahead of me, as well as the Wall further West where I had walked in the morning. I now had two choices, either to take the easy route and drop down off the Wall onto a path heading South-East, or to tackle an ominous-looking stretch of Wall on a descent known as Sawtooth Slope. The slope looked very long and steep, pitched at a 45-degree angle and getting to it would firstly involve a 500-yard climb in a generally upwards direction. However, I noticed that two members of the group had already reached the slope and were scrambling down. It couldn't be that bad. Or so I thought. Forty-five minutes later I had reached the top of the slope and looked down. It was frighteningly steep and I was tempted to turn back, but I decided that I would try a small section first to see how I would get on. This was my undoing. Not only was it very steep, but the Wall here was crumbling very badly and it was extremely difficult to get a foothold. I had only gone down about 30 feet, when I realised that it would be harder to go back up than to continue down. To get back, I would have had to have found a firm enough foothold with sufficient grip to be able to climb upwards. However, the Wall was very unstable and whenever I tried to place my feet I could get no leverage and all I succeeded in doing was to send a shower of dislodged stones tumbling down below me. I paused to take stock. I realised that I had no alternative but to tackle the remainder of the down slope. Descending thereafter involved a very slow, painstaking, slippery slide down on my backside. It was with blessed relief that I finally reached the bottom of the slope and left the Wall beside the remains of some ancient army barracks.

As I took a path back to the main road, the sun briefly smiled down on me as it rather cheekily emerged for a moment from behind the otherwise gloomy stone-coloured funereal sky. Fortune continued to favour me, because immediately as soon as I reached the main road a minibus passed by and stopped to pick me up. I had no idea where the English group had gone, since I found myself to be the only Westerner on this bus. For all that this walk had essentially been set up by those amazing people at Lonely Planet, I felt like a pioneer and, as the bus drew off down into the valley, I felt compelled to look back rather wistfully at the Wall slowly disappearing into the distance, as if I was departing an old friend. I had had a thoroughly uplifting spiritual day, when for most of it I had had it all to myself. I hoped to see it again one day before I leave.

I walked back to the hotel from the station which was three or four miles, so, bearing in mind that I had spent a long day trudging up and down the Great Wall, I was looking forward to a hot shower. Unfortunately, when I got back to the hotel I discovered that there was no hot water. I had a long argument with the manager at the desk but I persevered and he at least agreed to give me a discount on my room – down to Y150.00 – for the remaining time that I am here. In the evening, I rang Li to see if she wanted to go to the show. She told me that an emergency has cropped up and she has to shoot back to Xian tomorrow. Blown out!

Tuesday 27th April – Punch Up

Good day – they are coming thick and fast. I wanted to travel to Hong Kong on Thursday but I had no luck today trying to book trains. Instead, after much perseverance on my part, I managed to get the agency to book me a ticket for Guangzhou instead, which is very near to Hong Kong. I thought I would find a way to get to Hong Kong thereafter. I booked a ticket to leave on Thursday, but it was on the proviso that I paid the agency in full tomorrow. I was intending to take another trip tomorrow to see a different section of the Great Wall, so I would have to pay them tomorrow afternoon.

The food that I am eating just gets better and better: yesterday evening I had delicious meat-filled dumplings followed by beef with noodles; today I had hot and sour soup and then fried aubergine and chilli chicken. I have seen a few Westerners in Beijing but not a great number and they almost all appear to be in tourist groups. Except for my Franco-Hungarian pal on the boat down the Yangtze I have seen no other foreigner on any public transport. The great thing with this type of travelling is that I have been able to see a good deal of countryside and I noticed that the farming here is very labour-intensive and it struck me yesterday that I have seen virtually no engine-fired piece of farm machinery. All the machinery that is used is manually operated, and I have seen both oxen and horses pulling ploughs. It seems very mediaeval and that's a word that came to my mind as I wandered through the markets the other day.

I used the underground today (Y2.00) which is quite efficient and right next to where I was sitting was a major punch up. The seats in this carriage were not single seats but were one long bench seat. A man, who I estimated to be in his fifties, got onto the train at one stop and tried to squeeze onto the seat and he beckoned for a lad sat at the end to move up a bit to enable him to do so. The young lad, however, refused. Words were exchanged which quickly became heated and then just as quickly ended up in a full fist fight involving the young lad and an older man, who I presumed to be his father, and the other older man. The single older man appeared to get the upper hand at one point but his face was very bloody. They were in the middle of the carriage as the train was going along and the only reaction that I perceived from my fellow passengers was to draw back to give them more space to fight. When the train got to the next station all three piled out onto the platform where the fight continued as the train drew off. For me it was a frightening and disturbing experience but the other passengers seemed to carry on perfectly normally, just as if this type of experience was common place. This episode was a real live example of a custom I had read about in China known as 'Face'. This could be loosely defined as relating to self-respect and is essentially about avoiding being made to look stupid or being forced to back down in front of others, which we would call saving face. I had read that in China this is critically important. I had, of course, seen another example of it with the man who had beaten his horse. A shiver went down my spine when I considered that the incident when I had confronted the porter at the ferry terminal in Yichang could have ended up much more violently. The same could have applied to my barging match with the guard on my train and with the man who had been about to remove my rucksack from the top bunk of the train that I was on.

In the afternoon, I went by bus to the Summer Palace. Although it was slightly on the cool side, it was a lovely sunny afternoon and I thoroughly enjoyed wandering leisurely around the grounds of the Summer Palace and viewing the architecture therein. Some of the structures have amazing names including the Hall of Buddhist Tenets, the Sea of Wisdom Temple, the Hall of Virtuous Brilliance, the Hall of Listening to Orioles, the Cloud Dispensing Hall, the Boundary Stone of Popular Fragrance and the Bridge of Floating Hearts.

Wednesday 28th April – Meeting Cynthia

Absolutely barnstormingly brilliant day and tomorrow promises to be even better. Got up reasonably early. Had delicious noodles for breakfast at a roadside stall. Now I have worked out how to apply the condiments the dish is both delicious and deliciously cheap. Then went to Qianmen to get the bus to Badaling where I had booked a tour to see the Great Wall again, although the descriptions of this section were that it was much renovated and more touristic. The round trip by minibus was Y36.00.

There were about 15 people waiting for the minibus. I was the only Westerner. Some of the others looked my way when I arrived, presumably because they were surprised to see a Westerner like me on their tour. However, they soon lost interest in me. Or should I say, *most* of them soon lost interest in me. There were a couple of young girls in their 20s waiting in the group and one of them, a very pretty girl sporting a ponytail, politely said, "Hello," to me in English. I said, "Hello," back. She smiled warmly in response and then returned to speaking in Chinese to her friend. The minibus arrived on time. An initial crawl through the city was followed by a 45-mile hour-long drive to the Wall thereafter. On arrival at Badaling the driver spoke to us all in Chinese, whereupon the girl with the ponytail kindly translated what he was saying and explained that the driver had informed us that we would be left to explore the Wall by ourselves but that we needed to be back at the bus by a certain time. The girl suggested that I go with her and her friend. I readily agreed. Her Chinese name was Xia, and her chosen English name was Cynthia. Cynthia was petite, and very pretty with a melt-your-heart smile. Her English was very good. I asked her why so many young Chinese adopt Western names. The primary reason, she explained, was to adapt to the World Wide Web and to make the Chinese more easily identifiable to others on the internet. It was also because Westerners find it difficult to use, pronounce or even understand Chinese names. She introduced her friend as Anita. Anita spoke virtually no English.

Today was a very bright sunny day, and reasonably warm. Cynthia suggested that we walk in a North-Westerly direction along the Wall. It was clear that a lot of work had been carried out to renovate this section of the Wall, and it was remarkable to see it in an almost pristine condition. It did not carry with it the same cache that my Wild Wall walk had done a few days earlier, but it was certainly impressive in its own way. This is the Wall that the Chinese authorities like to promote to the outside world, and many famous dignitaries, including American Presidents and British Prime Ministers, had walked this section of the Wall. However, it was a victim of its own success, because here were the coach tours, the trinket sellers, the merchandise, tickets, signposts, and garbage thankfully missing two days earlier. In addition, just as the Wall itself rose and fell like a rollercoaster for miles in both directions, so too seemingly did the crowds upon it. The car park had been full of coaches when I arrived, not to mention jugglers and acrobats to lure the unwary tourist, and sure enough up here on the Wall were the hordes with their cameras snapping away at each other from every angle, with many different organised tour groups differentiated either by them wearing a different coloured hat – red and yellow were popular – or by carrying a different coloured pennant. When the tour group leader was ready to move on, up went the pennant and that person's group would dutifully follow like herded sheep. It was gratifying and reassuring to see that most of the people here were not foreign tourists, but local Chinese, seemingly much interested in their own history and culture. Many of the groups were of schoolchildren. Almost all of the photographs taken were of the 'proof that I was there' variety, with most of the younger element also feeling compelled to display a V for peace sign in virtually every photograph that was taken of them. Thankfully, though, for many, once they had taken the photographs to prove that they *had* been there, that was mission accomplished and they had no need to move on. Consequently, the crowds were already dwindling down within minutes of walking away from the starting point. Continuing North-West, some of the Wall was extremely steep and difficult to negotiate, despite its good condition. I was armed only with a light day rucksack, so it was difficult to imagine how a soldier in heavy armour at full speed would have been able to negotiate the Wall. However, the steepness had the effect of further filtering down the numbers even more. By the time we had walked a mile and reached a fair height at the furthest point that we realistically could manage in the time allowed, there were only a handful of people around us.

Cynthia was the ever-helpful, perfect personal tour guide, explaining and advising as we went along and endearingly and touchingly occasionally taking me by the arm when she wanted to emphasise something. She seemed to be getting as much pleasure (not to say, pride) out of visiting the Great Wall, as I. With the help of Cynthia's translation, Anita was very kind and helpful too, and seemed to be well-informed. Despite the conduit of the conversation being entirely via Cynthia, Anita at no point seemed to feel left out.

Having taken time out at the top of our walk to pause and reflect on our surroundings, and to soak up some of the sun, Cynthia pointed to her watch and advised us that we needed to return. I would have liked to have spent more time there and, as we headed back, believing that the tour was solely to view the Great Wall at Badaling, it occurred to me that we would get back to central Beijing much earlier than I had anticipated. However, as we wandered back, Cynthia started talking about the Ming Tombs and I soon discovered that there were three legs to this trip, the Wall being the first. My initial delight at the prospect of being able to spend more time with Cynthia and her friend quickly turned to horror at the realisation that we would not be back in Beijing until well after six this evening, which, on the basis that the travel agency operated only during normal office hours, would mean that I would not be able to pay for the train ticket that I had booked yesterday, and which, in turn, meant that I would not be able to leave for Hong Kong tomorrow. I was also concerned that, as I'd already booked the ticket, I might still have to pay for it, even if I could not use it, and I might end up effectively paying twice. Cynthia came to the rescue. Having returned to the minibus, and as we headed to our second destination, I explained my dilemma to her. She suggested that she call the agency when we got to our next stop. When we arrived, we found a public telephone, she made the call and after a little bit of negotiation, the travel agency agreed to change the ticket for the following day, the Friday, for an additional fee of Y100. Not only could I now relax but Cynthia had taken the opportunity to invite me to spend some time with her tomorrow, which I was naturally keen to do. Leaving a day later than scheduled and paying Y100 (£7) for the privilege were prices worth paying.

The second stop was a pedestrian yawn-inducing tour of a waxwork museum. The third leg of the tour involved a visit to the Ming Tombs, which was marginally more stimulating. Though visually uninteresting (accurately described by Lonely Planet as looking like a bombsite), its impact lies in its history. Thirteen of the sixteen emperors of the Ming Dynasty (AD 1368 to 1644) are laid out in this area. As with previous sites in China, the taking of photographs here was strictly prohibited, but I did not take the same risks here as I had done with other sites, as I did not have much opportunity and, frankly, much less inclination. Their value after all lay in their history, not their aesthetics. I had read that, aware that the tombs are not a visual spectacle, the Beijing Municipal Authority was planning to dress up the area with a museum (which was fair enough), but additionally there would be a golf course, an amusement park, an aerospace museum, an archery and rifle range, shops, cafés, a hotel, a swimming pool, an aquarium, a camping ground, a fountain, a fishing pier and a velodrome. The sense of emperors turning in their graves was almost palpable.

As the afternoon had worn on, Cynthia had evolved from occasionally touching me by the arm to practically holding my hand. As we clambered back aboard the minibus after the visit to the Ming Tombs, Cynthia suggested that we sit at the back of the bus. There we sat arm in arm and holding hands, and as the late afternoon merged into dusk Cynthia fell asleep with her head on my shoulder. Cynthia woke up as we approached Tiananmen Square and our final stop. Still with her head on my shoulder, she affectionately squeezed my hand a little tighter and looked up at me and said, "Mark, I…" she paused, "I like you."

Copying Cynthia, I replied, "Xia I…" pausing for effect, "I like you too." She smiled. I asked her if she would like to join me for dinner this evening, but she said she had to get back home to her aunt. I also mentioned about the Chinese acrobatic show that I'd heard was playing in the city and asked her if she would like to go. She said that she would think about it, but she didn't seem overly keen. She then gave me a note with her Beijing telephone number on it and she asked me to ring her tonight. After we had descended from the bus still holding hands, she smiled, gave my hand an extra squeeze and then turned and left. In an instant, she was lost in the crowd. It had been an enjoyable eventful whirlwind of a day and my meal of egg and tomato soup and sweet and sour pork that evening tasted even more delicious as a result.

Back at the hotel, I telephoned Cynthia. She was very sweet and very attentive. She learnt about my travel plans, my work, my education, my interests and, of course, she wanted to know about my love life. I told her the edited highlights, needless to say leaving out the less salubrious aspects of my adventures. I learnt that she is 22, lives in Wuhan, a huge industrial city on the banks of the Yangtze, is a student, studying history and living here in Beijing with her aunt, and wants to be a teacher. Conversation was easy and time flowed by very quickly and we talked for 45 minutes in all. She suggested visiting Beijing Zoo tomorrow. Although I love animals, I am not a great lover of zoos, finding them on the whole to be depressing places. Nevertheless, I agreed.

Thursday 29th April – Beijing Zoo

A rum day and one that might have a sting in its tail. Got up in good time and met Cynthia as arranged at 9.30 at Qianmen.

Today was the chalk to yesterday's cheese. It all started very well, despite the fact that Cynthia had unexpectedly turned up accompanied by her cousin's five-year-old son. I could not understand why. He turned out to be a lovely and loving boy, and once he had got over his initial shyness, he warmed to me, even to the extent of him insisting that I hold his hand. Later, he even kissed me on the cheek on a couple of occasions to thank me.

Although he was easy to take around and made a visit to the zoo more enjoyable, he was also a burden, because his very presence did not give me and Cynthia the chance to talk properly. Maybe that was the whole idea. At first, I thought that it had perhaps been Cynthia's idea to bring him along to create some distance. However, that notion was soon dispelled as we picked up where we left off yesterday. As we walked away from Qianmen, she insisted on holding my hand and leaning on me. She had also clearly made an effort to dress up to meet me, and she wore her shoulder-length hair down today (let it not be said that I too had made an effort and was wearing the one and only decent shirt that I had brought with me). Her dark hair and dark eyes offset her creamy skin and her soft delicately-chiselled features. She looked gorgeous. I was touched by the effort she had gone to. She also said that she would love to go with me later to see the acrobatic show and she had even suggested that I should go back to her house and meet her aunt after tonight's show.

However, as the day wore on, it became clear that yesterday's bubble had burst and her attitude towards me gradually changed. We went to Beijing Zoo, which was not quite as depressing as I'd imagined it to be, since some effort had been made to provide the animals a reasonable amount of space within which to roam and to create some semblance of the animals' original habitats. However, the animals still looked sad and lethargic. Both on our walk to the zoo, and as we wandered around within it, the 'staring brigade' returned with a vengeance. Not only did it seem as though virtually everybody that we passed by looked at us, but they seemed to do so with an almost hostile intensity. To me it was pretty obvious why. By this stage, Cynthia's nephew had warmed to me and when he was walking between us, he was holding hands with both Cynthia and I. We must have looked like the complete family, the three of us hand in hand, except, of course, in complete contrast to me, both Cynthia and her nephew had full Chinese features, undiluted by any Western genes. In a country where the people did not even need a reason to stare, when they were presented with a situation as incongruous as ours appeared to be, the staring rose to a whole new level. This did not go unnoticed by Cynthia and I sensed that she felt very uncomfortable at being the subject of such intense scrutiny. Cynthia stopped leaning on me and was less reluctant to hold my hand. I did later wonder whether at some point, when Cynthia might have been momentarily separated from me, somebody might have said something disparaging to her. Certainly, after leaving the zoo, there was no more talk of going to see the acrobatics. Instead Cynthia suggested that we get a taxi back to my hotel. She obviously wanted to avoid walking down the street with me and being the object of so much attention.

At the hotel, Cynthia and her nephew came up to my room. Her nephew sat there happily scribbling away on a piece of paper whilst Cynthia and I talked. Some serious hard talking then followed. Worryingly, Cynthia even mentioned the word 'marriage' at one point. She explained that she had very quickly developed very strong feelings for me. However, she confessed, she had a male friend, who was very interested in her and who she had known for about two years. Her feelings for him were nothing like her feelings for me. But... Her sentence trailed off. In my mind, I completed the sentence for her. Her other 'friend' represented stability. I, on the other hand, represented an entirely different future for her, a potentially exciting one that could take her in a completely different direction (both metaphorically and geographically) to the one she had probably been envisaging only two days ago. However, she would have to cope with the uncertainties of a mixed-race relationship, especially one that would have to come to terms with the public's seemingly unwelcoming attitude towards it, and we hardly really knew each other having only met a little over 24 hours before. Finally, of course, I would be leaving tomorrow.

We were silent for a moment, deep in our own thoughts. I responded by reminding her that it was difficult for me too, moving on having only just met. I told her that for my part I had quickly developed feelings for her (which was true) and I was honoured and deeply humbled that somebody as beautiful and kind-hearted as she had not only spent some time with me but had taken me into her heart. I told her that I would always treasure the memories of my time with her. I cautioned her against us getting too carried away, what with our different backgrounds, different lives and different ages. She asked me to keep in touch with her and wait for her, and suggested that we should see how things might develop. I agreed that I would try, and I meant it, but deep down inside me was the realisation that there would almost certainly be far too many obstacles in the way. Cynthia left shortly afterwards, with a lingering shake of the hands.

Later, as I sat in my room, contemplating the events of the last 36 hours, a vision of a clever and wily aunt came into my mind. It occurred to me that maybe it was her aunt who had suggested to Cynthia that she should take her nephew with her, knowing that he would present some kind of buffer. I imagined a breathless Cynthia returning home yesterday evening and excitedly telling her aunt all about her meeting with me, and in my mind I could see the aunt sagely nodding her head, and cautioning Cynthia against getting too carried away. Perhaps it was the aunt who had suggested to Cynthia that she might want to take her nephew with her as a way of bringing Cynthia back down to earth, knowing full well, but without saying it, exactly how Cynthia's fellow Chinese might react and thus wanting to expose Cynthia to the realities of the situation. If she could cope with the reaction, then there might be a chance for us. Perhaps, however, her motives were less subtle, and maybe her aunt had suggested the arrangement as a way of preventing this filthy foreigner from laying his dirty hands on Cynthia. In actual fact, her aunt would have had no worries from me on that score, because although I was deeply attracted to Cynthia, she was too sweet for me ever to have contemplated anything more than just enjoying being in her company.

Looking back at my diary, I described the potential for there to be a sting in the tail. Although I could have chosen a better metaphor, it should be remembered that I wrote in my diary every day as I went along, and at the time, taking into account several U-turns I had made so far on this trip, and the mixed emotions running through me at that moment, I wasn't sure if this truly was the end of the story.

The day was warm but it was cooler in the evening.

Friday 30th April – Left Beijing

I finally left Beijing today, a day later than planned. I was told that the statistics for my journey from Beijing to Guangzhou were that I would travel for 23 hours and 58 minutes (was it really so important to shave two off minutes!) and would cover a distance of 2294 kilometres. The cost of the journey, which included the agent's fee and the additional fee for changing trains, totalled Y608.00 which was quite expensive, almost twice my daily budget. I am still thinking about yesterday and Cynthia. She's a really lovely girl but clearly a little immature to be even mentioning the word 'marriage'. She is very bright and ambitious. She's head of her Students' Union. She was obviously initially taken with me but it was also equally obvious that her doubts increased throughout the course of yesterday, when she was clearly quite put out by the constant staring by people looking at us and thinking that we (her, me and her nephew) were family.

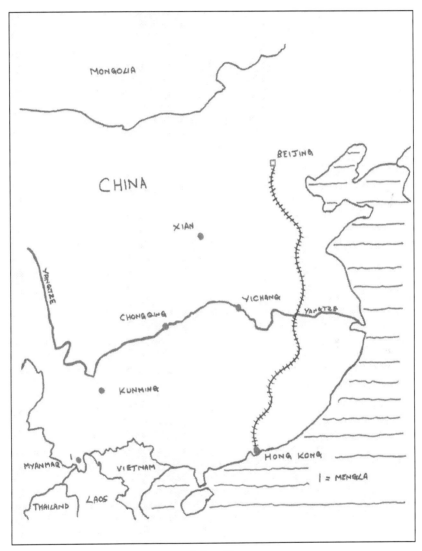

Map 18

It seemed clear to me that she would have felt more comfortable if I had been Chinese. As I say, she's a lovely girl and I cannot deny that she is the sort of girl I could well imagine settling down with (which is what she's clearly contemplating). However, in the circumstances and with my current agenda there is little or no hope of us ever properly getting to know each other sufficiently well to progress any further. You never know, though, so I will correspond with her and I will look to try to help her to come and visit me in the UK.

Once again, I am the only Westerner on the train. At one point, we crossed over the Yellow River which was very broad with very wide low plains either side of it. It is easy to understand how often it must flood. Somebody on the train was sneezing a lot and I gave him one of my hay fever tablets. He immediately accepted my offer and was very grateful, which he said over and over again, and repeated again later when it seemed to have worked.

Saturday 1ˢᵗ May – Carmen

Yet another great day. I am really lucky. The train was an hour late getting to Guangzhou. Last night on the train I was talking in English to a lovely girl called Ding (with the way that she squeezed into her tight fashion jeans she's most definitely not unattractive). She is 27, single, comes from Baotou in Inner Mongolia and she's manager of her own clothes business. She told me that she's pretty good at reading English but she has difficulties in talking and listening. However, from my own conversation with her she underestimates her talents. She was very chatty and friendly. I had a good night's sleep.

Today at the Guangzhou main train station I was getting in a muddle trying to find out how to find trains for onward travel to Hong Kong and I wasn't getting anywhere. Everybody that I talked to kept shaking their heads. This was until a young lad offered to help. He advised me that Hong Kong trains leave from a different station. He offered to take me there and I readily accepted his kind offer. We took a bus across the city to the other station which was about 6 miles away. We were outside that station and getting sorted out when two policemen approached the lad. They were clearly checking to see why he was there and he was eventually carted away. I could not tell whether they were arresting him or whether they were simply removing him from this area. I tried to remonstrate with them but they ignored me and when they moved off I tried to follow. However, they aggressively warned me to stay away. I felt very guilty as the lad had only been trying to help me.

I was trying to sort myself out and having already worked out that I would have a long wait for the direct train to Hong Kong, I decided to at least make my way to the city of Shenzhen instead which was closer to the border with Hong Kong. At that point, with them presumably thinking that I was lost, three girls approached me and, speaking in English, offered to help me. It turned out that they were also heading to Shenzhen and they invited me to go with them. I agreed. I had already purchased my ticket, which had allocated seating, before they got talking to me but they arranged a swap of seats. The girls' Western names were Carmen, Mandy and June. They were really good fun. On arrival at Shenzhen they invited me to hang around and spend some time with them. They took me to a restaurant to have lunch and we shared several small dishes, including a type of meat kebab, dumplings, sweetcorn and vegetables, green vegetable soup, two types of spicy noodles, and a cucumber and tomato salad. After the meal, try as I might they wouldn't let me contribute. At one point, we were joined by a male friend of June's. When I told them that I really should be going the male friend offered to give me a lift back to the station on his motorcycle. Although I had only known them for a short while, I had spent some fun time with them and I was sad to go. Carmen and Mandy gave me a signed bookmark. Very sweet. We exchanged addresses and each girl presented their cheek for me to kiss. Sweet.

At the station, I had to pass through immigration. Despite the fact that Hong Kong was taken back by the Chinese two years previously it is still treated like a foreign country and the transfer involved me showing my passport and completing a departure card on leaving mainland China and an entry card into Hong Kong. I then took the train to Hong Kong itself. On arrival, I looked at several hotels and I found one that was referred to in my Lonely Planet Guidebook. Its normal price is HK$150.00 per day (£12.50) but they said that for today I could have it for HK$100.00 as it was still in use. In the evening, I had a great curry. There was a small but significant Indian community close to where I was staying. Tomorrow I intend to go to Sha Tin Racecourse and on Wednesday I intend to go to Happy Valley Racecourse. Hong Kong is apparently about to be hit by a typhoon.

Sunday 2nd May – Sha Tin Abandoned

Frustrating day. Everything had looked like it had sorted itself out nicely with me going racing today at Sha Tin, then having two free days, then racing again at Happy Valley on Wednesday and then leaving Hong Kong on Thursday. Unfortunately, Typhoon Leo put paid to today's race meeting. I arrived at the racecourse in good time which cost HK$10.00 to get there. I was in the course when it was announced only 25 minutes before the first race that the meeting would be abandoned. The typhoon was described as an 8 on the Beaufort Scale. There were no refunds to the course and I was given a voucher to use again. The next meeting at Sha Tin is not due until next Saturday, meaning that if I want to see Sha Tin I will have to leave two or three days later than planned. One of the main reasons for me coming to Hong Kong was to see the racing at both of their racecourses. Consequently, although the delay would be frustrating, on the basis that I might never get another chance to come back to Hong Kong, I decided that I had no option but to sit it out. Back in town I had a good meal of pork and noodles. I went back to the hotel. Yesterday when I had arrived at the hotel the room was not available and I could not get in until after 9.30 pm. I was then told this morning that they were going to change rooms for me so I had to pack my rucksack and I left it in a holding store. When I arrived back at the hotel they told me that the room would not be *available again until after 5.00 pm. I had had enough. I told the man that I wanted to leave but he got very irate. I ignored him and I went to walk past him to go and get my rucksack but he physically stopped me from entering the room to get it. He nearly tore my shirt in the struggle. Although he was smaller than me, he was physically quite strong and we were an even match. He told me that if I paid him HK$50.00, he could make up the balance of the money by letting it out again. In the end, I agreed rather than continue to have all the hassle.*

The room in my new hotel was little bigger than a shoe-box, but I was glad to be away from the other place. I had a very good meal in the evening of barbecued goose and pork with rice. I saw a sign for a topless bar and I plucked up the courage to go in and have a look. Not a good move. Once inside, I discovered the minimum price for a drink was HK$49.00 (nearly £4.00). The bar was almost empty but there were four girls in there, only one of which was even remotely good looking. There was only one topless female and she was a sad fifty-something saggy-breasted hook-nosed woman behind the bar. I was approached by one of the girls who came and sat on the stool beside me at the bar and she invited me to buy a drink for her. She was clearly working me and it was all getting very uncomfortable. I politely declined, drank my drink very quickly and left shortly thereafter. It was a good job that I did because I discovered that it would have cost me HK$400.00 (£33) to buy her a drink and an extra HK$1000.00 (£83) for her to talk to me too.

Monday 3rd May – Victoria Peak

Hong Kong is a hybrid place and is hard to weigh up, because at times it seems so very different from China but at other times it seems very much like it. Vehicles drive on the left, the people are courteous, there is no spitting, there are double-decker buses and there are separate visas between Hong Kong and China. I tried to ring Cynthia last night, but without success. I did speak to a couple of her relatives one of whom I believe was her mum in Wuhan and the other who I believe was her aunt in Beijing. I understood that she is presently travelling between the two. I enquired about my onwards flight today – the cheapest to Jakarta being HK$1520.00 and the cheapest to Bangkok being HK$1320.00. It was a brighter day today. Typhoon Leo had fizzled out and headed off in a different direction. Seemingly it was potentially a massive one and it had originally been heading straight for Hong Kong. Although it dried out it was still a record breaker as it involved the earliest typhoon warning in the calendar year since records began. I went wandering today. The harbour was very colourful and I took a number of photographs. I then took the ferry from Kowloon, where I was staying, to Hong Kong Island. I then travelled on the hillside escalator link which is an 800-yard moving walkway heading up to the heights of Hong Kong Island. Thereafter I took the tram for my onward journey to High Peak (formerly known as Victoria Peak when under British rule). From there the sight of Hong Kong Harbour and the surrounding islands was very *spectacular. On my journey up to the top, I had met an Indian lad by the name of Noy. He invited me to meet up with him later together with his sister, who is currently going to Cambridge University. Unfortunately, I was an hour late when I headed back down and I missed him. Temperatures today were around the 29°c mark. I learnt that there had been further problems in Indonesia. In Bali, there was rioting over the weekend. I also learnt that Sir Alf Ramsey, Oliver Reed and Jill Dando all died this week. I read that Jill Dando had been shot.*

Tuesday 4ᵗʰ May – Aberdeen Harbour

I planned to go walking today on Hong Kong Island so I got up reasonably early and left the hotel just after 8. I didn't actually start walking until around 10.35 because it took so long to get organised.

My first stop was the supermarket, where I stocked up on water, rice crackers and mangoes, which I had spotted in the store yesterday and which looked ripe and very delicious. Priced at only HK$2 each (14p), I went mad and bought four. I also bought a map. I had read up about a number of walking trails, including the Hong Kong Trail, which runs through Hong Kong Island for 31 miles in total. I was going to do part of it today. I made my way back along the now-familiar route of the ferry to the island, the escalator up the hillside and the tram to High Peak, from where the walk would begin. Measuring only approximately seven miles by five miles, and being the commercial and business centre of the territory of Hong Kong, thereby having more than its fair share of the 6.3 million population of the whole territory, it would be hard to imagine that there would be any room for nature to thrive in the urban jungle of Hong Kong Island. However, much of the Central and Southern parts of the island were surprisingly rural with some parts protected from development by being National Parks. High Peak sits at the Western end of the island and once I had traversed around its Western and South-Western slopes and started heading in a generally Easterly direction, I immediately found myself deep in tropical jungle. The path itself was very well made and provided excellent walking, much of it underneath a canopy of overhanging trees. It was very sunny today and, as a consequence, very hot, so the shade provided by the trees was very welcome. Considering how small and crowded Hong Kong Island is, it was amazing that, save at the very end I saw no other people during my walk, but I did encounter a great deal of fauna, including butterflies, insects and birds, with one particularly striking unidentified bird having extraordinary electric blue plumage. I also saw several different types of lizard, including common skinks, and a changeable lizard, and I came across two snakes. I met the first only 45 minutes into my walk.

There I was, sauntering along, minding my own business, enjoying the walking on a lovely flat, winding section. At this point the path had become quite narrow with grasses, flowers, bamboo, reeds and other flora encroaching onto the path. When I turned a corner, I froze as there only eight or ten feet in front of me on the footpath was a five-foot-long snake. It was standing erect with its head about two feet in the air and looking straight at me. A shot of adrenalin raced through me and a frisson ran down my spine. For about two seconds we both remained perfectly motionless, with the snake seemingly as transfixed by me as I was by it. Then it unflexed itself, dropped down onto the path and slithered away into the undergrowth. I would describe the snake as very thin, coloured lime green and it had two black marks around the area of its lower jaw – I made a note to check it out later. A couple of hours thereafter I saw another four-foot-long snake slip off the path and into the undergrowth. Honeysuckle blossom was in season and the beguiling fragrance provided an intoxicating heady scent throughout much of the trek. Humidity was high in this tropical climate and I soon became very thirsty. I had taken 1 ½ litres of water with me but it turned out to be far too little as I had drunk it all by halfway. I then took a chance by taking water directly from a stream. Although not recommended because of the risk of taking up parasites, I thought it better than to allow myself to dehydrate. Thankfully, there were no repercussions. The walk generally followed the line of the coast and as a result was undulating. By the middle of the afternoon, an elevated section of the path opened up at a headland, hugging the edge of a steep hill, and as I followed it round in an anti-clockwise direction Aberdeen Harbour suddenly revealed itself before me. This natural inlet on the South coast of the island had evolved over the years to become a very busy harbour, chock full of boats of all shapes and sizes, including luxury yachts, ferries, floating restaurants and many traditional sampans with their arced rooves and the occasional distinctive ruffled sails. Perched high above the harbour, I had a superb panoramic view and I decided that this would be the perfect spot to finish off my picnic.

Calculated that I had completed approximately 16 miles of the Hong Kong Trail itself, but taking into account my walk back across the centre of Hong Kong Island to the ferry terminal, I must have walked 24 miles in all. I was exhausted but very happy.

In the evening, I had Singapore noodles which were delicious. I rang Cynthia again and spoke to her sister. She advised that Cynthia is at college. I tried to give her my telephone number to pass onto Cynthia but the telephone ran out before I could repeat it.

Wednesday 5th May – Happy Valley Racing

Woke up to a day pouring with rain. Had a horrible thought that the racing might again be cancelled. I received a call direct to my room from Cynthia this morning. It was a very short conversation and she just had time to give me her number before her money ran out. The number she gave me is her university number. I said that I would try and ring her later.

I wandered around killing time by hopping between cafes to have coffee or to take a snack. I had a good noodle dish for lunch. I saw the jade market, the ladies market, the flower market and the bird market. They were mildly interesting. I then went to the Happy Valley racecourse in the evening. The rain had stopped by late afternoon and in fact the going at the turf-only course was described as "good." There were seven races and I spent HK$280.00 in bets in all. I had no winners but it was great racing and a great atmosphere. The whole meeting was floodlit. The course is on Hong Kong Island, the grass is lush and emerald green and the backdrop to the course is a series of high rise buildings surrounding the course. It gave me the feeling of being in an amphitheatre. I recognised some of the jockeys, one of the horses, and a trainer as being from Britain or Europe – I am pretty sure I saw the horse race at Chester Racecourse last August (a mini pianola). It cost me nothing to get in as I was able to use the voucher left over from Sunday, but I then paid an extra HK$10.00 to upgrade to the Members' Area. No winners.

Thursday 6th May – Booked Flights

A quiet day and rather a wasted day too. It was raining and miserable. I went for a swim in the morning which was the first time that I have been able to use a proper swimming pool since coming on this trip. I did 100 lengths and felt pretty good thereafter. I then had noodles for lunch. I then went across to Victoria Harbour to find a travel agent to sort out my onward flights. I was still debating whether to go straight to Indonesia or whether to attempt to go back to Laos but I concluded in the end that it would be best for me to go straight to Indonesia. I had noted that I am about a week or so behind schedule and going to Laos would have put me back even more. I am also now in deficit with my money (minus £11.00 as of yesterday with the cost of the flight to add to it) and Laos would sting me even further. I also thought that it was probably not a good idea to return back to old haunts and instead I should just look forward and allow the adventure to continue. However, keen as I was to see Dao, I did give fate one last chance to send me to Bangkok, and onto Laos, since I had declared to myself that I would rather go there if I could not fly out to Jakarta on either Sunday or Monday – in the end there were tickets to Jakarta on Sunday, so that put the final kibosh on that. I had to pay HK$1660.00 (£138.00) and I leave on Sunday at 5.00 pm. I was required to return later to collect the ticket so I just wandered around in the rain trying to find shelter wherever I could. I saw the Western Market and I wandered along the intriguingly named Ladder Street but they were not particularly interesting. I wandered into an art gallery where the paintings and photographs were reasonably interesting. Having finally collected my ticket I went back to Kowloon and in the evening, I decided to go back to the Indian restaurant. I discovered that the restaurant is located in the Southern Indian Men's Club. I was the only Westerner there and all the other people visiting were of Indian descent. All bar me ate their food with their hands. I had a mutton curry, rice and a paratha and soup.

Friday 7th May – Deserted Beaches

Good day. I was a little slow in getting up for my planned walk to the Sai Kung Peninsular today. I bought some water and food to take with me and then went to have breakfast. I took the tramline to Hoi Chung, then a bus to Sai Kung and then another bus to Pak Tam Chung. With all the various connections, I didn't start walking until 1.25 pm. I had originally intended to walk the 15 miles to Pak Tam Avenue. At the picnic site that represented the start of the walk, I had to negotiate my way round a bull that was grazing across the path, before heading off around the peninsular. I saw the High Island Reservoir which is very picturesque. I saw several birds, including buzzards and a black bird that looks like a large black version of a kingfisher. I covered the first 5 or 6 miles fairly quickly but after that the going was tough as I was constantly climbing up and around various spurs that marked the coastline. In the end, I had to give up on my planned route and detour back along the reservoir to my origin at Pak Tam Chung. At one point, I took a wrong path and ended up half a mile away from where I really needed to be. I guess with all the detours I must have eventually walked the 15 miles that I'd originally planned. There were great views along the way of several clean white-sanded beaches. All looked totally deserted and had I set off earlier and had I brought a proper picnic I could have enjoyed them even more. I nearly lost my camera as I left it on the bus coming back but as I was walking off somebody on the bus called for the driver to stop and then called me over. I was very lucky. In the evening, I had barbecued goose and pork with rice which was delicious.

Saturday 8th May – Racing at Sha Tin

Great day and what I came to Hong Kong for. I got up in good time. Telephoned and spoke to Cynthia last night. My money ran out quickly so I didn't get to talk to her for very long. I realised yesterday that I had made a mistake about the Chinese visa. I had assumed that the one month visa would apply to my time in both China and in Hong

Kong. However, I discovered – too late – that it only applies to the China leg. Therefore, I could have stayed in China for longer than I had thought. I told Cynthia about this. Cynthia told me that she would like me to try to help her arrange a course swap with either Australia or the UK. I said that I would try. I didn't get time to find out but I presumed that she is looking to forego this – her last – academic year. I bought a newspaper and I went and had breakfast.

Sha Tin racecourse is Hong Kong's newest racecourse. It is not as visually impressive as Happy Valley, but what it lacks in aesthetics it more than makes up for in its prestigious races and has a large number of internationally-famous Group 1 races. These include the most celebrated single race, the Queen Elizabeth II Cup, usually run in April, and a racing festival comprising no less than four Group 1 races – being the Hong Kong Cup, Mile, Sprint and Vase – run on the same day, usually in December. The course regularly attracts the best horses from Great Britain, France, Ireland, the Middle East, Japan, New Zealand and Australia. Unlike Happy Valley, which only has a turf course, Sha Tin has both a turf and an all-weather track. Today's racing was not of the highest quality but it was good nevertheless, with one or two horses which I recognised, having seen them race in England before. The weather was wet and miserable, but it did nothing to dampen my spirits. I love horse racing and it is my favourite sporting pastime. I like the sheer physicality of these magnificent animals, with them padding around the parade ring beforehand flexing their well-toned muscles and with their black, bay, chestnut, grey or shiny mahogany-coloured coats glinting in the sunlight (or reflected in the rain!). I love the fact that a horse can weigh half a ton but yet can run at speeds in excess of 40mph, even with a nine-stone combination of human, saddle and tack on its back. I am always in awe when the earth shakes as a dozen or more animals thunder past on the track. I love the spectacle of the colours carried by the jockeys, the plotting and intrigue pervading the jungle that is the betting ring and the high emotions of winning or losing. I love the fact that the sport is frequented and enjoyed by both rich and poor, by a fairer proportion than most sports of men and women, and can be enjoyed at every level from the rich Arab sheikh and the professional punter down to the £1-each-way stick-a-pin-in once-a-year gambler. I was in my element being back at racecourses like Happy Valley on Wednesday and Sha Tin today.

There were ten races in all scheduled for today. I had budgeted to spend an average of HK$40 (£3.30) per race and I kept rigidly to this. By the end of the ninth race on today's card, the racing had been excellent with several close finishes and a couple of come-from-behind performances. However, whilst I personally had had a couple of near misses, I had had no winners.

This meant that, taking into account all my losers in all seven races on the card at Happy Valley, I had gone through 16 races in Hong Kong thus far with not a single winner. So it came to my 17th and very last race in Hong Kong when I had HK$50 left to spend and I strongly fancied a horse priced a fraction under 13/1. I put it all on to win. For a while during the race it did not look promising, as in a field of 12 horses it was still lying only third last as it entered the long sweeping bend into the home straight. However, it gradually began to make up ground by going slightly wide around the bend and thus avoiding any trouble. By the time it entered the home straight with a little only three furlongs to go, it was lying fourth about three lengths back. A couple of horses that had taken the inside track, and had accordingly saved ground, suddenly darted for home and gained a further two lengths in a couple of strides as a result but the jockey on my horse crouched deeper in the saddle and the horse itself sensed that this was the moment and started to really stretch out. By the two furlongs from home marker it had reduced the distance back down to three lengths and as it went past the one furlong from home marker it had overtaken one of the two lead horses in front and was lying in second place. It kept digging, and grinding away and half a furlong out it forged ahead, holding on to eventually win by half a length. It was a pulsating and exhilarating way to win a race. By the end, although I had only one winner over the two days and 17 races, I had effectively broken even, staking a total of HK$680 and winning HK$695.

I was propositioned twice last night by girls on the street, one of whom was very good looking with a very good figure. In fact, I had seen her on my train back into the city yesterday. I noticed her earlier because she was so pretty so it was quite a coincidence that I should then get propositioned by her later. Despite her good looks, I wasn't tempted. Celebrated tonight by going back to my favourite curry house at the Southern Indian Men's Club.

Sunday 9th May – Left Hong Kong

I certainly seem to have been lucky with the weather for the walking. Generally, throughout the week there has been rotten weather but after my inauspicious start with Typhoon Leo I had been very lucky as the two days which were good were the Tuesday and Friday, which were the days when I walked. After the thrills of China, I wasn't overly enamoured by Hong Kong as it was too modern and too busy. It seems that, like London, people are too busy with their lives to talk to passers-by and they are not particularly friendly (except when they want your money). Last night I went up to the peak again to see Hong Kong at night. White clouds lit up by the bright city lights of Hong Kong were drifting up and over the peak and the wind was howling. Although it was not the most comfortable of evenings to be up on the high peak, it made for some spectacular scenery.

I discovered the first snake that I had seen on Tuesday was almost certainly a bamboo snake, which is venomous, but only really dangerous to those who are vulnerable, such as children or those with a heart condition.

I wandered around again killing time before my flight out tonight. I again had barbecued pork and goose with rice for dinner. I tried to ring Cynthia from the city in the morning and again at the airport but she was not in either time. It was pouring with rain once more today. By a combination of tram, train and airport express I arrived at the airport. At the desk, the girl queried my lack of an onward ticket beyond Indonesia but upon providing proof of the funds that I had and on showing her my itinerary I was let on board. I posted a card to Robbyne from the airport.

There were many very beautiful girls on my plane – both crew and passengers (the vitamin pills are kicking in again)! I met a chap on the plane who was sat near me and after chatting to him and explaining my plans he offered to let me stay at his house tonight in Jakarta. It was obvious that I was not going to arrive early enough to find any onward connections tonight so I agreed. As it would be free accommodation I tried to pay the taxi fare but my new friend only let me pay half. His name is Benny, he is of Chinese descent, and currently lives in Indonesia but works in Hong Kong.

Selling deer meat on the roadside, Laos

Luohan at the Bamboo Temple, Kunming

Relaxing in Daguan Park, Kunming

Exiting Qutang Gorge, part of the Three Gorges on the Yangtze

Terracotta Army, Xian, China

One string violin, Beijing, China

Imperial vault of Heaven, Beijing

Wild and unkempt section of the Great Wall of China

Aberdeen Harbour, Hong Kong

CHAPTER 6

Indonesia

<u>*Monday 10th May – Train to Surabaya*</u>

Nearly didn't get allowed into Indonesia yesterday because of my lack of an onward ticket. Immigration officers told me to go to a private interview room. I was a bit concerned but eventually they agreed to give me a visa and told me not to do it again. Benny is not very enamoured with Indonesia – "Good people, but poor country," he says. Certainly, he is a perfect example of how friendly they are. He would like me to try to help him to get to Australia. I will try.

I had always had a fascination with Indonesia, and a very high opinion of its people, since my first visit in 1984 to the island whose name is synonymous with tropical paradise, Bali. Indonesia is an archipelago, with over 13,000 islands, around 6,000 of which are inhabited. This means that, if he or she managed to visit one island every day, it would take the Indonesian president over 16 years just to see the inhabited ones. The country is vast, with the distance East to West roughly equidistant to that of mainland USA and stretching over three time zones. However, because it is a nation of islands it occupies only a fifth of America's land mass. Names such as Borneo, Bali, Java, Jakarta, Sumatra, Celebes, Lombok, Flores, Makassar, Krakatoa, Komodo, Banda and New Guinea evoke images in the mind that are mysterious, exotic and powerful.

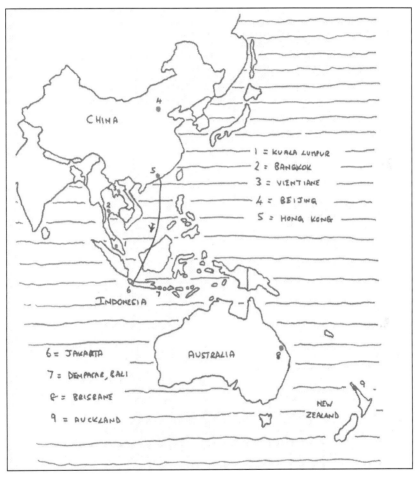

Map 19

The country sits on one of the most volatile volcanic regions on earth, part of what is euphemistically known as the Ring of Fire, which surrounds the Pacific Ocean. Indonesia leads the world in many volcano statistics. It has the largest number of historically active volcanoes, numbered at 127, it has suffered the highest number of eruptions producing fatalities, and two of the most devastating volcanic eruptions in modern history took place in Indonesia. The most famous of them all was Krakatoa, which in 1883 carved itself deeply into the collective memory of mankind, when it is estimated that the severe tsunamis resulting therefrom killed 40,000 people around the world. However, this eruption is still dwarfed by the largest eruption known within the last 10,000 years, that of Gunung (or Mount) Tambora on Sumbawa Island on the 10th April 1815. The volcano erupted more than 12 cubic miles of magma, the caldera collapse at the end of the eruption destroyed seven cubic miles of the mountain itself and formed a new caldera four miles wide and almost a mile deep. Floating islands of pumice three miles long were observed in April 1815, and even four years later these iceberg-like islands still hindered navigation. It had such far-reaching effects on the climate that in 1816 Europe was to experience a year without summer. Indirectly or directly it is also estimated to have killed more than 100,000 people.

In addition to the erupting volcanoes, somewhere within the country an earthquake measuring more than 4.2 on the Richter scale occurs on average three times every day. Furthermore, potentially devastating earthquakes measuring more than 6.0 on the same scale occur on average 16 times every year.

In the midst of all this the people are laidback, hospitable, very friendly, and generous with a laissez-faire attitude to life. Some expert commentators have suggested – this amateur commentator is inclined to agree – that this is not *despite* living in such a potentially inhospitable part of the world, but perhaps in part *because* of it. They recognise the fragility of life in their surroundings and know that devastation might just be around the corner, but they also recognise that the very same forces that at times cause so much destruction are also the ones that created the environment in the first place, with many of the islands literally rising up from the seabed. Also, the very same forces are nurturing ones too because Indonesia is extremely fertile and much of the fertility is borne in the material thrown out and provided by the volcanic eruptions. It is no wonder then that Indonesians have such a *que sera* attitude to life. In their book, 'Ring of Fire', Lawrence and Lorne Blair had observed,

"...it is hardly surprising that the Indonesians have been so profoundly affected by their kinetic environment, for theirs is the most tectonic nation on earth, boasting some 34 per cent of all the world's active volcanoes ... of a total population of some 160 million Indonesians, about 151 million of them dwell on or near volcanoes, thriving on the rich nutrients which make their islands so fertile."

Living on the very edge of nature in all its powerful glory has clearly affected the people's religious psyche. Indonesia is the largest Muslim country in the world by population, but there are also large pockets of Christians living on various islands, and Bali is an oddity being predominantly Hindu, an oddity because it is wedged between its Muslim-dominated neighbouring islands of Java to the West and Lombok to the East and separated from them both by only very narrow straits. Whilst each of these religions would be familiar to their counterparts in the rest of the world, they are at the same time very different, in that within Indonesia each of these relatively modern religions has become curiously infused with the more traditional religions based on an animist philosophy, a belief in the power of the earth, the sun, the moon, the sea and Mother Nature generally. This must in part be explained by the Indonesians living on a knife-edge existence between destruction and survival, between the animate and inanimate, between the body and soul, between life and death itself.

The name 'Ring of Fire' was used by Lawrence and Lorne Blair for their television series and the accompanying book. I had found their stories of travelling throughout Indonesia in the 1970s and 1980s truly inspiring, especially with the series being aired on the BBC for the first time in the mid-1980s, shortly after my first visit to Bali. If their descriptions of their travails were anywhere close to being true – and I should make it clear I have never doubted it – their travels were of the genuinely intrepid kind: sharing their wooden boards-for-beds in the hull of a pinisi (a traditional wooden Indonesian cargo ship) with all manner of insects; travelling deep within Irian Jaya, the Indonesian part of New Guinea, to go native and naked with indigenous peoples who were known to be cannibals (Michael Rockefeller, son of Nelson Rockefeller, allegedly being one of their most recent victims); and trekking deep into the jungles of Borneo in search of head-hunters. I was never going to pretend that my journey would come close to theirs, but I wanted to follow in some of their footsteps and my route would be plotted accordingly.

I would arrive in Jakarta, and, although I would miss out Krakatoa, which was visited by the Blair brothers, I would travel quickly East to the city of Surabaya and visit some of the volcanoes of East Java. I would then head further East and hop across the straits separating Java from Bali to visit my friends there. I would then travel to Sulawesi (formerly Celebes), where I would visit three areas mentioned by the Blair brothers. In Makassar, now known as Ujung Pandang, I would try to locate and meet members of the Bugis tribe, a people who were famously known for being sailors and the builders of the pinisi boats, but who were also infamously known for their treachery and piracy, and from whom the term 'bogeyman' derives. I would head North into the hinterland to visit Tanatoraja, an area of Central Sulawesi where the people were famed for their elaborate funeral and marriage rituals, and for their upside-down arc-shaped houses with an exaggerated bow in the middle, and its ends pointing up to the sky, which is where they believe their ancestors came from. I would then head to the South-East corner of spider-shaped Sulawesi to visit the island of Buton lying just off the coast, where, as I mentioned earlier in my recollection of my travels through Malaysia, the Blair brothers encountered the enchanting and beautiful princesses, daughters of the island's Sultan.

Thereafter I hoped to be able to head South to visit the Island of Flores and to see dragons on its neighbouring island of Komodo. With my visa being limited to two months, I doubted whether I would have time to visit Borneo, or to head to the far East of the archipelago to visit Banda or Irian Jaya. However, I hoped that at some point I might get the opportunity to travel on a pinisi ship. I would then need to head off to Australia somewhere around the first week in July. Although I had plenty of ideas, I had nothing booked and would do it on the way.

Didn't get much sleep last night, partly because I was on the mattress on the floor, but mainly because Benny was restless and had a light on – either full or on dip – all the time. I wanted to get to the train station early and Benny insisted on accompanying me there. We arrived at 6.45 am, and discovered that there was no train until 2.00 pm. Benny said he would make enquiries. He came back to say that there was a seat available for 200,000 rupiah (£18) on the black market for a train leaving at 9.30 am, but we needed to make a quick decision. I agreed but after Benny had left to go and get the ticket, a feeling of regret immediately came over me at the idea that I had been pressured into making a quick decision, not least because the other train would have cost only a quarter of the price at 48,000 Rp maximum and I was not in any great hurry. However, I reminded myself that I had originally been contemplating going by plane which would have cost me about 600,000, so I was still saving money in the grand scheme of things. Once the rational side of my brain had appeased the emotional side I felt better. Benny bought some breakfast, gave me a cufflink and tiepin set, and two key rings – he's a very generous man, and it was sad to say goodbye.

The train arrived at Surabaya spot on at 6.30 pm. I got a becak (a three-wheeled bicycle rickshaw) to hotel Remaja – 10,000 Rp – hotel 85,000 Rp (£5.00). I am 99% sure that this is the same hotel that I stayed in before where I recall sharing a good deal of banter at that time with a friendly female member of staff.

Tuesday 11th May – Wandering

Indonesia's already got a totally different feel about it – everyone very friendly. Girls all say hello. Had an absolutely brilliant day and yet I didn't really do a great deal. I had breakfast at the hotel, then went wandering.

The only Indonesian guidebook that I had brought with me was a generic one for South-East Asia, and I wanted to try and obtain as much information as possible on the ground so to speak, about onward travel within Indonesia and thereafter to Australia.

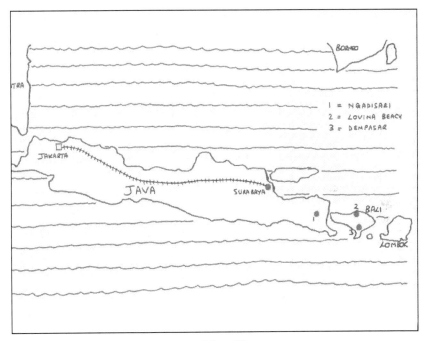

Map 20

Went to the Tourist Information Centre where there was only one man and he told me that unfortunately he had left his brochures at his home. Discovered, though, that they would have only covered East Java. Then bought shampoo. Then went to travel agents to make some preliminary enquiries about planes to Australia. Discovered planes still go from Kupang – on the island of Timor – to Darwin on Saturdays and Wednesdays, therefore I could leave either on the 3rd or 7th July for Australia. Also discovered the best route to go to Gunung Bromo. At the Garuda office discovered planes go direct from Bali *to Brisbane for about £350.00. Surabaya is a major seaport and I wanted to explore options for travelling by boat. At the Pelni shipping office I obtained a copy of the timetable but it was difficult to decipher. I just carried on wandering and stopped and talked to one set of people after another. Although I know from previous experience that the people are very friendly in Indonesia it's still always a pleasant surprise each time to be reminded just how friendly. I found the market which was vibrant and colourful. Everyone wanted me to photograph them. Met several girls in the morning – it is possible that they're on the game, but I had a good chat with them nevertheless. Then I saw and spoke to several groups of girls around the market.*

One lad talked of his hopes for Indonesia's election. I was propositioned by numerous ladies of the night in the evening. Most were almost irresistible – very gorgeous – but the prices (coupled with the still-raw memories of my previous experiences) meant that I was equipped to resist. Great day.

Wednesday 12th May – Downpour

Busy day but without a great deal to note. Got up, had breakfast and then went to the Garuda office – found out the only points of exit into Australia are from Bali, Jakarta and Kupang. Told that I would need an onward ticket before I could enter Australia – I don't believe that's true but it is worrying if it is. Also found a Garuda timetable (for 1998?!). Went back, had a shower, packed and then left. I enjoyed my short stay in Surabaya – however, saw much poverty with people living in the streets, under roofs and beside the river – there are many beggars, but the spirit here is generally very good. Talked to one man who had seen me walking yesterday, and who came over to speak to me today. Everybody is very friendly. Took taxi (30,000 Rp) to the bus station – then bus (5,500 Rp) to Probolinggo. Took another bus to Ngadisari – had been boiling hot but on the way came into really heavy downpour. It was mega heavy – lasted quite a while – large volumes of water were streaming down the roads. My rucksack which had been on the roof was rescued – but it had already become drenched. Then I had to get out into another van and I too got soaked in the process. Got to Yoschi's in Ngadisari. Very nice place – nice staff – very helpful. Managed to obtain a 10% discount on the room – 63,000 Rp total for two nights (which was 22,000 Rp less than for one night in Surabaya). Had a hot shower. It was dry when I arrived but the thunderstorm quickly followed. There was a very loud thunder clap and heavy lightning immediately above us.

Thursday 13th May – Gunung Bromo

Superb day. Set alarm for 3.00 am and as usual on such occasions I did not sleep too well. So I was wide awake when the alarm went off. After breakfast, I left at about 3.40 and went to the crater lip at Cewaro Lawang. From there walked to Bromo itself.

I had travelled through East Java and Surabaya on a couple of previous trips and had always bypassed Gunung Bromo (or Mt. Bromo). My only reason was that there were so many backpackers and travellers who had talked about their trip to Bromo, that irrationally, and rather pathetically on my part, I had reasoned that I preferred to be independent and did not want to follow the crowd. In addition to being pathetic, it was also hypocritical of me, in view of the fact that I was quite happy and ready to be guided – like a prize bull being tugged along by the hook in its nose – by the writings of my various Lonely Planet guidebooks. I decided that I really ought to see what the fuss was all about, and I am so glad that I did.

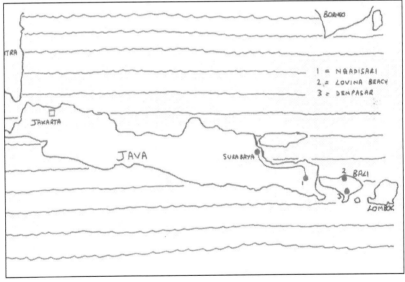

Map 21

It began with a dreary, bleary-eyed rise at 3 o'clock in the morning. The idea was to be at the summit of Mt. Bromo at sunrise. Although I had no guide, I did take the advice of the landlord at my losmen – the Indonesian equivalent of a guest house – the previous day, so as to know where to go.

"Follow the voices," he said, somewhat cryptically. It is a curious phenomenon of the tropics that even where there is a cloudless sky and the Milky Way in all its glory is illuminating the heavens, it is pitch black on the ground. I am so used to being in the UK where, even on the darkest night once your eyes have adjusted, there is usually some residual light so as to be able to see your way. I concede that some of that is light pollution, of which there is very little in Indonesia. Also, in the tropics, unlike in the UK, there is no long, lingering period of gradually increasing light in the period before dawn. The sun seems to go straight up in the morning, and straight down again at sunset, resulting in the shortest possible period of dawn or dusk. There is no messing around. Consequently, making my way to Mt. Bromo, initially along a dusty track outside my losmen, up the gentle slope of a ridge of an outer caldera from a much earlier extremely violent eruption, descending a bit more steeply down the other side of that caldera and along the bed of the dusty, pebbly crater inside the caldera, was a bumbling, shuffling, trial-and-error affair. I was on my own. Having been born clumsy – falling into a vat of road tar, black-bruising half of my face and body having walked backwards into a lamppost and falling into a raging bonfire being some of my more infamous escapades as a child – it meant that I needed only the slightest excuse to fall arse over tit. Thankfully, the surfaces of the road, ridge and crater were relatively flat (and relatively soft).

As I reached the top of the ridge and was about to go down into the crater, I could detect the sound of two whispering, subdued voices a little way off ahead of me. Indeed, as I headed in the general direction of the voices, I was soon able to hear a third and a fourth voice, and then more. They all seemed to be going in roughly the same direction, so, based on the pretext that to be out at such a silly hour of the morning suggested that they too were heading to Bromo, I thought I must be going in the right direction. So, I mused, my landlord was not being cryptic, but was instead talking literally when he had advised me to follow the voices.

Additionally, I noticed up ahead of me a single spot of white light, which looked like a dancing firefly, except that, as I drew nearer, it became a short beam of light, which turned out to be torchlight, in the hands of a person swinging his arms as he walked. Very soon other spots and beams of light could be seen. It appeared as though they were coming from different directions, but from the way the lights were swinging and moving, and occasionally coinciding with the sound of a person's voice, they were also heading in roughly the same direction as us. Hearing the soft murmuring voices was to an extent reassuring, but in the sort of sloe-black night that Dylan Thomas made famous, seeing nothing save for the odd shaft of torchlight was at the same time curiously unnerving.

Arriving just before Bromo itself, its dark conical shape was just about visible. There were now many whispering voices, behind, beside and rising up ahead of me, but all I could just about make out were the shadowy silhouettes of human beings. A set of man-made steps had been hewn into the side of Bromo and I climbed up. The nearer I got to the summit of Bromo the more voices could be heard. Once on top of the volcano the rim appeared to be reasonably wide and using as much of the limited bat-like senses available to me, I managed to find what seemed to be a suitable vantage point without assaulting any of the purveyors of those voices. And then I just stood and waited.

It did not take long for a glimmer of light to appear in the East and very quickly for it to glide into dawn. Seeing the silhouettes sharpening against the growing light, to my surprise I discovered that there must have been more than a hundred people up here on the ridge.

The sun rose majestically, initially turning the sky into an aura of misty haziness, before quickly burning off the moisture in the air, bursting over the horizon and erupting into life. There was a cheer amongst the crowd. It was an awe-inspiring sight and I could fully understand why so many people before me had made such a fuss about it. As the sun rose and caught the faces of all the people around me, I realised that there were as many people behind me and to the side of me as there were in front of me. Although I estimated that there were 15 or 20 tourists or travellers up here, they were gratifyingly outnumbered by Indonesians, gratifying because it was good to observe that seeing sunrise at Bromo was as important and impressive to them as it was to us tourists.

Very soon after the sun had risen most of the people on top of the rim went back down the steps, presumably heading off for breakfast, leaving about a couple of dozen of us lingering behind. I was in no hurry to leave as I was keen to absorb as much of the experience as possible and in the new brightness of the day I could now see everything around me. I was standing on the Northern edge of the crater rim of Gunung Bromo. About 1 ½ miles away in a North-Easterly direction I could see the ridge that I had clambered up and over earlier at the edge of the caldera. Assuming that I was in the middle of the caldera the notion that it measured something in the region of three miles across was a sobering thought, considering the power the erupting volcano must have unleashed to have created it. The outer fringes of the caldera were green and lush, but the area inside the caldera between the outer rim and Bromo was flat, dusty and sandy. Just next door to Bromo, in a North-Westerly direction, I could see another small volcano, with an almost perfect conical shape. This was Gunung Batok, which at 2,440m. is slightly higher than the 2,392m. of Bromo. Both it and Bromo had emerged from the sandy surface inside the huge caldera, like a couple of pustular acne spots, some years earlier, and, by all accounts, were still growing.

Just a little to the North, strategically situated on the sand plain between the foot of Mt. Bromo and the foot of Mt. Batok, I could see a temple. I would later read that this temple, known as Pura Luhur Poten, is the focal point of an annual Hindu ceremony, known as Kasada, where the Tenggerese people of East Java would congregate, before climbing up Mt. Bromo in order to make offerings of fruit, rice, vegetables, flowers and sacrifices of livestock to the mountain gods by throwing them into the crater inside Bromo. The origin of the ritual arises out of a legend where a Tenggerese princess and her husband were childless. After praying to the mountain gods for assistance, their prayers were answered and the gods granted them 24 children but stipulated that the 25th child must be thrown into the volcano as a human sacrifice. The gods' request was implemented. The tradition of throwing sacrifices into the crater to pacify the gods of the volcano continues today, but mercifully no longer involves human sacrifice.

Looking South, inside the broad crater of Bromo itself, small clouds of occasionally dirty white, or sometimes slightly yellow, sulphurous smoke puffed up from the bubbling interior, rising gently up the slopes before pouring over the crater rim and down into the valley outside. Now and again, the breeze would bring a cloud of smoke up to that part of the rim where we were standing, resulting in a very strong, though not entirely malodorous, smell of sulphur and, as it rolled off down the slope, it deposited on me a thin covering of pumice ash, like snowflakes.

As I looked around the rim of the crater, I thought that I could just make out a path around the edge, but some of the edge looked jagged and perilously narrow, so I was not sure if I would be able to make it all the way round. I would explore later.

About ten miles further South, beyond the crater rim, I could see Gunung Semeru, at 3,676m the highest mountain in Java, which is potentially very dangerous. It is a living, breathing fire-dragon of a volcano with its own pulse, since every 20 minutes or so it emits a large plume of malevolent-looking smoke. I later read that Semeru has effectively been in constant eruption since 1967 and what I was seeing was an eruption every 20 minutes.

There wasn't a single cloud in the sky and the vertically-rising sun was heating everything quickly. I was still in no mood to leave and decided that I would, if possible, walk around the entire rim of Bromo. Walking in a clockwise direction, I was soon on my own, or so I thought, because about ten minutes into my walk I came across a group of seven boisterous Indonesian lads, seemingly of student age. They had brought plenty of water, biscuits and other titbits up here with them and it looked like they were having a party. They seemed as taken aback to see me as I was of them, but once they overcame their momentary surprise they seemed genuinely pleased to see me and they offered to share their food and drink with me. I offered them some of the nuts and dried fruit that I had brought with me. They spoke only a little English, and my Indonesian was at that stage still rudimentary, but it didn't seem to matter, as we shared our common humanity, a few photographs and some of my nuts. I did not want to be a party-pooper and after a few minutes I thought it was about time to leave, but before I could do so they packed up their things and headed back round, in an anti-clockwise direction, to where I had come from. Seeing the group disappear off into the distance, waving back at me as they did so, a slight breeze brushed past my face and I had a brooding sense of suddenly being alone with the elements. I continued around the rim.

Some parts of the path were indeed very narrow, and occasionally precarious with steep drop-offs to one side, but it was also well defined. I saw only one other person on my walk round the rim, this being a young Western girl heading in an anti-clockwise direction, who seemed to be in her own zone, as she barely acknowledged my 'hello' with an almost imperceptible nod of her head as we passed by each other. Anyone would have thought we had passed each other by in the middle of Oxford Street, London.

Having circumnavigated Bromo, on arriving back where I had started I saw a group of about nine or ten people, and I soon got talking to one of them, a very friendly middle-aged Indonesian lady by the name of Catherine. I discovered that she was from Ambon, a part of Indonesia over a thousand miles away in the Moluccas Islands, and she was visiting Bromo with her family. She spoke very good English and was both very friendly and very funny. Having interrogated me with the first and more usual gamut of questions – where was I from, where was I going, was I married, why was I not married, what did I do – she couldn't stop referring to me as lawyer-Mark when she continued to ask me some less usual questions. "So, lawyer-Mark, what do you think of the forthcoming elections in Indonesia; so, lawyer-Mark, what qualifications did you need to become a lawyer; so, lawyer-Mark, are you a Christian?" She herself was Christian, more precisely a Seventh-Day Adventist, hence the reason for her Western name. She talked to me like I was a long-lost friend and soon she too was sharing food and drink with me. She wondered whether I might consider helping to raise funds for the church when I returned to the UK. Rather disingenuously, I said that I would see. Catherine and her family decided that they would walk a little way around the rim of the crater, and so it was with a heavy heart that I said goodbye as they ambled off. I paused to take in the scene for a few moments more before heading down the steps and out onto the sand plain. I spent another three or four hours wandering, mooching around the Pura Luhur Poten temple, walking around the base of Gunung Batok and criss-crossing the sand plain back and forth between Bromo and the outer edge of the caldera.

I was due to leave Java tomorrow, catching a bus from Probolinggo at 10.30 in the morning to travel to Bali, but I loved my time so much today that, before I headed off tomorrow, I was determined to visit a much-vaunted viewpoint from Gunung Penanjakan, a mountain laying outside the caldera, from where I was promised stunning shots of Bromo and Semeru.

The significance of Catherine's question about my religion only became clear to me much later. Before embarking on my trip, my friend Will had informed me that he had read about there being pockets of unrest and violence in Indonesia. Upon checking with the Foreign Office, I discovered that there were indeed problems but these seemed to be mostly in areas of Indonesia well away from the places I was planning to visit, so I paid little attention at that time to the names of those places. Whilst travelling through South-East Asia I had again heard about further problems in Indonesia when listening to the BBC World Service. It turned out that Ambon was the epicentre of one of those conflicts.

Some of the problems can be attributed to the general feeling of instability pervading the country, partly because of the recent fall from power of President Suharto who had held the post from 1967 until his eventual ousting in January 1998 – the elections that would follow later in my trip would occur as a consequence – and partly as a result of a deep and damaging economic crisis in South-East Asia in 1997. Although there had been one or two earlier problems in Ambon, it is thought that the conflict began, and took on a religious context, on the 19th January 1999, less than four months prior to the events that I have described here. It was considered that the initial confrontation that sparked the conflict was between a Christian minibus driver and either some Bugis youths, or a Muslim conductor, near to a bus terminal on the island. It is generally agreed that thereafter a mob of about 600 Muslim residents, driven on by incorrect rumours that the local mosque had been torched, gathered and marched upon some Christian areas, where they torched numerous houses and businesses. After hearing about this, local Christian residents reacted by launching a counter-offensive. In an all-too-familiar vicious cycle, each chapter of accusations and violence ushered in another round of counter-accusations and recriminations that would be of at least an equal if not greater violence. The upheaval extended to neighbouring areas and I would later learn, for example, that one month earlier, in April 1999, all the Christian residents of the nearby Banda Islands had been expelled, leading to a growing refugee crisis. The violence would continue for another three years, would cost the lives of approximately 5,000 people and would result in the displacement of 700,000 people. Looking back on my meeting with Catherine, her smiling happy disposition disguised the reality of what was happening back home. She never once mentioned about the problems occurring in Ambon.

Before we went our separate ways, Catherine and I had exchanged addresses. Although I noticed the anomaly immediately, I did not query it when the address she wrote down was in nearby Surabaya in East Java, not in far off Ambon, and I didn't give it any more thought. Although I never knew it at the time, and it is only now when I look back that I am convinced of the notion, Catherine and her family were almost certainly refugees themselves from that crisis. A number of things that she had said now make more sense, but the main clue lies in the address that she gave, because why else would she give a Javanese address, if it was only a temporary or holiday address, and conversely, why would she say that her and her family were from Ambon if she had been living in Surabaya? Although her upheaval was inflicted by man rather than nature, Catherine was a supreme example of the indefatigable spirit of the Indonesians, a people who continue to smile in adversity. I feel very moved when I think back to my meeting with the sweet-natured, generous-hearted, laughing, ever-smiling Catherine.

Reckoned I walked about 20 plus miles — very long day especially because of the early start. Had a Javanese massage in the evening — old lady — very good but quite painful.

Friday 14th May – Bromo Again

It was hard work but last night I eventually arranged a trip for this morning to an area known as the Penanjakan Viewpoint (17,500 Rp), from where I was told I would see the best panoramic view of Bromo and the other volcanoes. Up again at 3.00 am — with four others in a jeep — and initially followed the route that I walked yesterday. We were at the Viewpoint by 4.30 am — plenty of time. Could see regular thick smoke and vapour trail going off into the distance from Bromo and also the regular — every 20 minutes — puffs of thick smoke from the equally impressive Gunung Semeru. Great views as sun rose. Event (only slightly) marred by my itchy-arsed group members wanting to move on quickly. I wanted to wait to see the sunrise. I dug my heels in. I was rewarded with spectacular views. Several hijab-wearing Muslim girls insisted on having me in their photos. Then went back with the group in the jeep down across the crater floor to Bromo itself. The party left me and I hung around and did my own thing — again great views — before going back to the hotel, where I arrived with just enough time to pack and leave. I hurriedly packed, had a quick breakfast – then took a bemo (local equivalent to a mini-bus) *to Probolinggo – arrived there at dead on 10.30 am with the bus due to leave at 10.30 am so it was a close shave. Although I was just in time for the bus, I got ripped off (three times). 1. Although I had been told the fare would be 47,500 Rp, I had to pay 57,500 Rp. 2. Then they didn't give me the 2,500 Rp change from the 60,000 Rp that I had paid. 3. Then at Bali, despite receiving assurances to the contrary, the bus went directly off to Denpasar, without going via Lovina and I had to get the bus to stop; they refused my requests for a refund, meaning I had to pay additionally for my onward journey.*

Lovina, sometimes called Lovina Beach, is the name given to a village, or more particularly a collection of villages, and its beach situated on the North coast of Bali, and I had some good friends there, whom I had met on my previous trips to Bali. Back then in 1984, prior to arriving in Bali a friend by the name of Ruth – a mutual friend of Will and I in Australia – recommended that I should head to the North side of the island, and specifically to Lovina, which would be well away from the tourist trap hell-hole that is Kuta. Although Bali is not inordinately large, the hilly terrain created by a ridge of volcanoes that run through the centre of Bali, and the relatively poor roads, mean that the tourist enclave is thankfully mainly concentrated around a fairly small area on the Southern tip of the island in and around Kuta and you do not need to travel too far away from it before you find yourself in real Bali. I fell in love with Bali instantly, with its stunning temples located in the most picturesque of places – invariably atop a mountain, on an island in a lake or on a cliff edge beside the sea, its multi-coloured ceremonies (at least one of which seems to occur somewhere on the island every day), its emerald green lattice-work rice fields and, above all else, its friendly, happy people.

My love affair with Bali was mirrored by Lawrence and Lorne Blair, as described in their book, 'Ring of Fire'. They described their reticence at coming to Bali, believing it to be unduly manicured by tourism, but very soon after succumbing to the temptation to visit the island, they made the pleasant discovery that away from the Southern tip, indigenous Bali is so rich in culture, art and a supremely satisfying and soul-enriching way of life that they set up home there. Indeed, the thought has occurred to me since that they might even have been living there close to where I stayed – my pianola theory coming in to play – when I first travelled to Bali in 1984:

"...for years we had studiously avoided visiting the island of Bali on the quite false assumption that its international airport and beach hotels placed it beyond our professional interest. But when curiosity got the

> better of us we found ourselves almost immediately drawn to a highland community. The Balinese are remarkable in that they give but half their time to the chores of food and shelter; the rest is devoted simply to the celebration of life. The festival days, the sacred plays and dance, the processions that move jangling through the villages at night quicken us to the hidden rhythms by which the island lives. Time belongs to the gods, not to the clocks of the linear West. The Hindu-Balinese calendar is annually calibrated by the astronomer-priests according to lunar and stellar relationships, so that the rites of fasting and planting, rejoicing and reaping, weeping and cremating are synchronised with the actual bio-rhythmic pulse of the island."

Their book wasn't published until some four years after my first visit, and, whereas they had travelled to Indonesia in search of adventure, I had stumbled into Bali almost by chance. However, the Blair brothers were describing the Bali I had fallen in love with, were formulating my hitherto jumble of incoherent thoughts into some sort of meaningful understanding and were expressing this in a far more eloquent way than I could ever hope to do.

On my first visit to Lovina I became friends with a man called Parma. Having decamped in a homestay called Purnama, meaning 'full moon', I went walking along the road that runs parallel to the sea and I came across Parma, who had a homestay right beside the beach, working on his 'Welcome to Parma Homestay' sign beside the road. He asked me where I was staying, where I was from and where I was going. Despite the fact that I had confessed that I was staying in a different homestay to his further up the road, he was happy to engage me in conversation. I was impressed at how friendly he was and how much free information he was prepared to give to me, even though he knew I would not be staying with him. He was a Hindu but he even told me about a Muslim wedding that was due to take place in the village a couple of days later and suggested that I should attend. I became friends with Parma, and on every visit to Bali thereafter I stayed at his homestay. By my second or third visit he was clearly doing well because his homestay had burgeoned into a series of 12 neat and comfortable bungalows, each equipped with a rudimentary but pleasant bathroom and a small veranda, every one looking out at the beach only yards away and set in gardens filled with beautiful shocking-pink bougainvillea and fragrant frangipani. I would again be heading to Parma's on this trip.

On my second trip to Bali and Lovina in 1988 I made friends with a motley crew of sellers of t-shirts, fresh pineapple, coconuts and trinkets, as well as massage ladies. I became especially good friends with four of them who worked on the beach. There was a young married couple by the name of Wayan and Ketut. Wayan sold coral shell necklaces, pendants, bracelets and other assorted jewellery, whilst his wife, Ketut, sold sarongs, t-shirts and other clothing. I also met for the first time Naicah, a tiny old lady, with a beaming smile, and kindly crow's-feet eyes. Her deceptive grandmotherly demeanour belied the fact that she was a strong masseuse. Finally, I became friends with a pretty girl called Komang, who also sold t-shirts and clothing on the beach. Komang spoke a reasonable amount of English, more than the others. We spent a bit of time together, and I accompanied her on one occasion to the nearest town where we bought food, drink and a kamus (an Indonesian dictionary). Talking with the aid of the kamus, our conversations were laboriously slow, but I enjoyed her company and we covered a varied range of topics. I found Komang very attractive and could easily have slipped into having some kind of relationship with her. However, she gave the impression that she preferred to be friends only and despite the fact – or maybe because of the fact – that time was short for us, I never tried to push it, and it never went further than us talking, not even holding hands. She seemed so sweet and innocent and frankly it was very pleasant to simply have her as a friend, so it was to my immense surprise that she was bawling her eyes out when I left at the end of the week. She had seemingly assumed a deeper meaning to our relationship than I had thought.

When I returned in 1990 Komang, Naicah, and Ketut were all still there on the beach doing the same thing, whilst Wayan was mixing his beach-selling work with help as a tour guide. Komang had recently married. They were all pleased to see me, and our friendship deepened. By the time of my fourth trip in 1995 Ketut and Wayan had moved into a shop further into the village of Lovina Beach. They had had two children by then, two sweet photogenic girls. With Wayan's tour guide work picking up, they seemed to be doing well. Komang was not doing so well. She was still selling sarongs and t-shirts and she too had moved away from the beach, but in her case, it was to a road leading to a hot volcanic spring at a place called Banjar. Unfortunately, it had not been a good move because she had too much competition from other sellers along the same stretch of road and her business was slow. Additionally, her husband's work as a builder's labourer hovered between being very poorly paid and non-existent. She had had two children. The sparkle that I had seen in Komang's eyes before had lost some of its lustre. Naicah was still providing massage on the beach.

It was with this background that on this trip I made my way to Lovina in Bali intending to visit my old friends.

As I described in my diary, having descended from Bromo on the morning of my second visit to it, I had made my way back to the main road and the small town of Probolinggo. There I had arranged to pick up a bus, heading to Denpasar, the capital of Bali located towards the South of the island. The bus had originated in Surabaya and was going via Lovina on its way to Denpasar, or so I thought. It was a route I had taken before. Buses, and indeed most public transport in Indonesia are not known for their punctuality, so, although I knew that my bemo was descending painfully slowly from the plateau at Bromo to Probolinggo, such that I knew I would be arriving at or around the due time of 10.30 am, I trusted that I would still have plenty of time believing that the bus would be late. For once it was on time, which was almost my downfall. As I was descending from my bemo, I could see the bus about 30 yards away and it seemed like it was about to move off. As I ran towards it, I waved to ask it to stop and the driver obligingly did so. I clambered on, whereupon the driver's navvy grabbed my large rucksack, took it down the back of the bus and unceremoniously dumped it on top of a pile of other bags and rucksacks on a seat at the back. Flustered and hot, I squeezed into a seat two-thirds of the way back.

Four hours later, we arrived at the Javanese port of Banyuwangi, where after a sweaty two-hour wait in the heat of the afternoon, the bus eventually trundled its way onto a ferry boat, and parked up in one of the lower decks. Most people on the bus descended and headed up some nearby stairs to an upper deck. I followed suit. It was good to stretch my legs and get some fresh air. I went back down to the bus shortly before it docked and I grabbed a guidebook from my large rucksack on the back seat. As I did so, I noticed one of the straps was undone on the rucksack. Fastening it up, I assumed that I had forgotten to do up the strap when I hurriedly jumped on the bus back at Probolinggo.

The crossing was quick, since the straits here are very narrow, and as soon as the bus had manoeuvred onto the gangway in Gilimanuk, a ferry port in the North-Western corner of Bali, it promptly sped off apparently intent on catching up time. It was a good job that I knew this route well, because three miles beyond the port there is a point where the road forks, with the left fork turning East and running along the North coast of Bali towards Lovina, and the right fork heading South. The bus went South. I called out to the half-asleep driver's mate, who jumped up from his seat and made his way to me. When I said that I wanted to go to Lovina, he shouted out to the driver to stop. Having hurriedly grabbed my rucksack from the back seat, I descended from the bus. It was about half a mile back to the fork in the road, so I put my guidebook back into my larger rucksack. When I did so, I noticed that a couple of boxes, in which I had kept my first aid kit, Swiss army knife and other useful tools, had become dislodged within my rucksack. Thinking no more about it, I tied it back up, swung the rucksack onto my back and trudged back up the road. Twenty minutes later

I was on a bemo heading to Lovina.

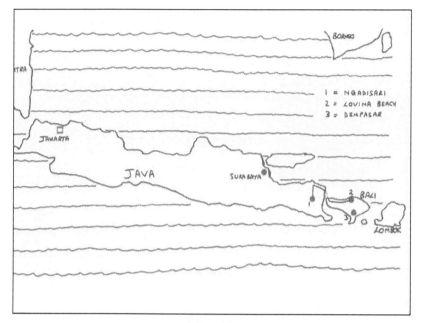

Map 22

The light was fading fast as the bus approached Lovina, but the closer we got, the more landmarks I recognised, and was thus able to ensure that the bemo stopped exactly outside Parma's. When I walked into the open-air courtyard which serves as the dining area, Parma's wife was sitting there stitching, head bowed close to the fabric she was working on, as if she was straining to see under the poor light emanating from the weak paraffin lamps. Maybe she was short-sighted. Nobody was dining tonight, so she was on her own. When she looked up she instantly recognised me and called out to Parma to come outside. A bare-chested, skinny-framed Parma stepped outside. He had aged quite a bit since I had last seen him four years previously, and looked tired and drawn. Both Parma and his wife were pleased to see me. It seemed as though nothing much had changed since my last visit – literally – since much of the décor appeared frayed and worn, just like Parma himself, and it dawned on me that business had probably not been very good. After saying hello, Parma went back inside his house and his wife showed me to the chalets. Since they had very few visitors, I could pretty much choose whichever one I wanted. Frankly there wasn't much difference between them, but I chose number 7, where I had stayed before.

Parma's wife went off whilst I started to unpack, and she returned a short while later with a slightly threadbare, but clean, towel and a small bar of soap. It was by now dark. As had become my habit, I first took out the photograph of my nan from a side pocket and placed it strategically on a table beside my bed. I went to open the main body of my rucksack and as I looked inside a shiver ran down my spine. I knew instantly that somebody had been inside my rucksack. I hurriedly dug inside my rucksack and removed all my belongings from within to check to see if anything was missing and I soon realised that a number of items had indeed been taken. Missing were the short-wave radio that Will had loaned me, the flash unit that I used on my Fujica camera, the zoom lens for my Canon camera and my alarm clock. Curiously, though thankfully, the Canon camera itself, bequeathed to me by my late great uncle, had not been taken, despite it having been situated close to the top of the rucksack, next to the boxes. I wondered why they hadn't taken that as well. Although I checked and double-checked, I could find nothing else missing, but a sixth sense made me worry that something else had been taken that I was not yet able to identify. I felt sick in the pit of my stomach, not least because I felt a sense of betrayal by the people I had learnt to love and trust so much.

Went to Johni's in the evening. Had chicken satay. Mrs Johni was still there – very friendly. Talked about the election. Very interesting. In total, the journey from Ngadisari (beside Bromo) to Lovina was ten hours.

Saturday 15th May – Naicah

A good day which would have been brilliant except that last night I had probably the worst experience of my trip so far.

There had, of course, been two warning signs that I had ignored, the first being when I spotted that the strap was undone on my rucksack when I climbed back on the bus after crossing the straits between Java and Bali. The second was when I noticed the dislodged boxes inside my rucksack when I was dropped off by the bus on the side of the road on the North-Western corner of Bali. I had readily dismissed them from my mind, perhaps considering them to be inconsequential, perhaps thinking that both could have happened when I had packed in a hurry in the morning or when my rucksack was chucked on the back seat of the bus. I now knew different. In fact, when I began to think about it, the only time when I had left my rucksack unguarded was for the 20 or 30 minutes when I had gone up on deck on the ferry.

Last night I couldn't sleep well because I was so upset. However, today I have tried to put it behind me and get on with things. Upsetting and inconvenient but nothing I can't replace.

Had banana pancake for breakfast. Sunbathed for 45 minutes. Went for walk to try and find my friends. Talked to many people, including a number of pretty girls. Bali is not known for its bread but I had a surprisingly good sandwich, and orange juice, for lunch. Saw women in the moneychanger who recognised me straight away from meeting them before. Saw Ketut. Gave her a photograph of her daughter (that I had taken on my previous trip). Will see Wayan later. Saw Kadek. Tried to find Komang's house. I believe that I found it, but not in. Went back to Parma. Saw Naicah. She was overwhelmed to see me, and when she saw me walking towards her along the beach she ran up to me and flung her arms around me. Brilliant moment. Had massage – I could name my own price – chose 20,000 (standard price). Met her daughter – Nur – and the way Naicah smiled when she introduced me hinted at a bit of matchmaking. I am invited to dinner at Naicah's house tomorrow. In the evening had good taco meal. Then tried again to find Komang and this time I found her. She was happy to see me. She said she dreamt about me a night or two ago so she knew I was coming (which is exactly what she claimed had happened last time I visited). Lovely to see her and her family. She now has four children. She said she'd written to me. I told her that I had not received her letter. She said she will have a party for me later.

Sunday 16th May – Meeting Nur

Great day. Almost perfect – only one step down from being an "I've died and gone to heaven" day. I found a cockroach in my bed the other day – horrible things. Very lazy day – intentionally so. Had breakfast of banana pancake and hot Javanese coffee. Walked the 20 yards from my cottage to the beach – had a little sunbathe, had a swim and later had my now daily massage with Naicah.

Yesterday, Naicah had invited me to go to hers for dinner tonight. I had never been to her home before and was looking forward to it. Naicah spoke virtually no English. The word 'yes' was the word she knew best, and she often used the word even when it didn't apply. If I asked her to give me a thousand pounds, she would say, "Yes," and if I asked where I could buy fresh fish, she would again say, "yes." It didn't matter too much because she would usually flash a beaming disarming smile as she said so, which I found very endearing. In the afternoon Nur, Naicah's daughter, came to the beach again. She was slim and petite, at around 5' 2" tall, and she was to these English eyes very pretty. She had high cheekbones, short black hair, deep dark eyes, full lips and a strong jaw-line. She also had smooth, perfectly unblemished, golden-tanned skin, from her brow down her long neck to her toned shoulders and arms, which were amplified by the white singlet top that she was wearing. I cannot deny that I found Nur attractive and, from her demeanour and body language, it was not entirely out of the question that she might be quite keen on me. Although I had known Naicah since 1988, I had never met Nur before. Nur, like her mother, also only spoke a little English, so we communicated partly through my rudimentary, pigeon-version, but slowly improving Indonesian, but mainly via one of Nur's friends, a plump girl called Wayan. Names in Indonesia are interchangeable between the sexes, so that the name Wayan not only applied to the husband of the couple who I had made friends with in 1988, but also to Nur's female friend. After Naicah and Nur had left I was looking forward to this evening even more.

I continued to have a very relaxing afternoon, occasionally reading, occasionally swimming and sometimes dozing, but most of the time I was idly taking in the scene. Lovina has black sand, deposited after a major eruption of the island's highest and most dangerous volcano, Gunung Agung, in 1963. Consequently, it is not quite as picture perfect as the white-sanded beaches that are found in the South and East of the island, but, despite its blackness, it is generally perfectly clean. Lovina has a long sweeping bay, fringed by palm trees and the sunsets are almost always spectacular. The silhouetted mountains of East Java can clearly be seen over 50 kilometres away in the West. The water is calm, with little surf, protected by a reef a mile or two out to sea.

Parma's homestay, and the stretch of beach in front of it, lies towards the Western edge of Lovina and the main area of tourist development, containing bars and shops (Wayan and Ketut's shop being one of them) lies about a mile away in the East. In the 15 years since I had first visited Lovina, it had become an increasingly popular tourist destination, but thankfully it remained generally low key and was certainly nothing like the tourist traps around Kuta. Of course, visitors are hassled by people trying to sell dolphin trips, costume jewellery, coconuts, clothing and massage, but the selling is normally much less intense and usually good-natured. One of the main attractions for coming to Lovina are the dolphin-spotting trips that embark early each morning and on most trips dozens of dolphins can be relied on to be seen, the locals knowing that early in the morning on most days the dolphins come to an area about a mile or so off the coast to feed. I had been on these trips before but I was looking forward to going again tomorrow. In the main tourist area further East, a 24-foot concrete statue of a dolphin had been erected in their honour. The trips weren't around when I first visited in 1984, or at least I wasn't aware of them.

Traditional rural village life goes on amongst and around the tourist areas beside the beach and, in particular, between Parma's homestay and the area around the dolphin statue is the fishing village of Kalibukbuk. Most of the fishing takes place at night-time and during the day the men can be seen cleaning their boats or mending their nets. Although most of the boats are equipped with an outboard motor, they are all traditionally made of wood and carry sails. Kalibukbuk is also home to a sizeable Muslim community and 100 yards back from the beach, beside the main road that runs parallel to the coast, a small mosque regularly calls out to its devotees. Both Naicah and Nur were Muslims. It was in Kalibukbuk back in 1984 that I was invited to the Muslim wedding, attended by Muslims, Hindus, Christians and nosey travellers alike. It was also where I would be going tonight as Naicah lived there. Although I had never been to her house before, I knew roughly where it was located.

As I contemplated the evening's events, and as the sun turned the sky into a sea of scarlet, children were playing at the water's edge, fishermen were setting off in their boats and a lecherous male dog was chasing, and occasionally humping, a bitch dog, who, although yelping occasionally, seemed to be feigning coyness, since she was clearly allowing the male dog to catch up with her. As the vermilion sky evolved into a darker crimson, the lamplights on the fishing boats, bobbing gently out at sea, became brighter, looking like twinkling stars.

Naicah had said that she would come to collect me at 8 o'clock but she called for me at 7.25, whilst I was still in the shower. I heard a knocking at the door and just as I was coming into the main room to see who was there, she walked into the room, seeing me butt naked. She smiled her disarming crow's-feet smile, said, "Yes," and then turned to exit the room to wait on the veranda. After I had finished the shower and got dressed, I went with her.

Her house was simple, set back approximately 20 yards from the road and I had passed by it dozens of times over the years without realising that she lived there. It was single storey, with breeze blocks for walls, window frames made of wood with gauze over the windows and a corrugated tin roof. Three wooden wind chimes hung close by the doorway. Of course, the shoes had to come off as soon as we went into the house. I was shown into the main room, where there were cushions placed on a thin rug on the floor. I was ushered to sit. There were five of us in the room for most of the time, myself, Naicah, Nur, Wayan and a young girl who I believed to be Nur's cousin, but other family and friends seemed to come and go all night.

Only Wayan, Nur's fat friend, spoke English. Two whole fish, which I was told were surgeonfish, were produced together with salad, rice and gado gado, an Indonesian speciality made of steamed bean sprouts, vegetables and a spicy peanut sauce. The fish had been grilled or barbecued and were delicious, with succulent white meat. Wayan informed me that Nur had cooked all or most of it herself. I had taken drink with me comprising a large bottle of Coke and a bottle of beer. Afterwards we just sat and talked. Nur had sat me next to her and she put food on my plate and poured beer into my glass like I was her husband. Wayan informed me that Nur was pleased to meet me. I learnt that Nur was 29 years old. As the night wore on, Nur sat closer and closer until our shoulders were almost touching. Although my confidence was buoyed by the encounters I had already had in South-East Asia, I have always been rather poor at reading the body language of the opposite sex. However, even to my untrained eye Nur's behaviour and signals were obvious and I was disinclined to reject her advances. We arranged to meet up tomorrow.

As the evening wore on, I learnt that larger than life Wayan – larger than life in all senses of the word – was not present solely because she was the interpreter but also because she was Nur's best friend. Although into her 30s, she was single, which I found a little bit surprising, since she had a friendly and bubbly personality. It occurred to me that being a single 30-something girl in Bali was rather sad, but, Wayan, seemingly resigned to her lot in life, was totally oblivious of this. She clearly liked her food, which was obvious not just because of her size, but also because she had several servings and, despite the fact that the rest of us had finished eating, she continued to devour everything on her own plate, before promptly finishing off the food on everybody else's. About 30 seconds after finishing the last plate, she spotted a piece of bread on a dish across the room and, as she reached over to get it, she farted long and loud. It was hilariously funny, made even funnier by the fact that nobody else batted an eyelid.

Monday 17th May – Dolphins

I am now not in any doubt that I have died and gone to heaven. Two anecdotes first.

I love Komang because when she saw me she said that I was skinny – thinking about it, I do believe that I have lost quite a bit of weight since coming on this trip.

In Singaraja today there was some TV news from Jakarta – there were technical problems – and for about half an hour the camera stayed on a newsreader who kept looking to the side for help. There was no attempt to, for example, cut for commercials. In the end, with the camera still on him, he turned round to his news team, pulled his tie off, said the Indonesian equivalent of "Bugger this for a laugh," and walked off set. It was very funny.

I saw dolphins this morning – brilliant – best ever. Many jumping – some all at once – very near the boat too. Then met Nur and Wayan and went to Singaraja. From the off Nur took me by the arm – very touching. I bought a new alarm clock (25,000 Rp) plus incense plus mangoes (4000 Rp for 1 kilogram) plus a Fat Boy Slim cassette (19,000) for Nur and some clothing. Then we went back to Wayan's house and we relaxed on her porch – felt very good. Then had a massage with Naicah.

I had the evening to myself and later I met up with Wayan and Ketut and their children again. The children are very attractive. I also went to meet Komang at her house; we were talking in English and she had just started telling me that she dreamt about me last night for four and a half hours – she had just got to the point when she said that in her dream we were "sleeping together" – when at that moment her husband walked into the room where we were talking. Although he cannot speak a word of English, all the same we felt embarrassed to continue talking.

Tuesday 18th May – Hot Springs

Got up – good sleep – rested more on the beach. Nur came over at around 11.20. A short while later two of her sisters-in-law came and all four of us went to Banjar.

Banjar lies approximately three miles West of Lovina and two miles inland and comprises a village, a Buddhist Monastery and holy hot springs. It was the springs that had particularly drawn me to them on every one of my visits to Bali, and I had sometimes visited them more than once on each trip. The attraction was partly the springs themselves and partly the location. The hot springs are set in lush tropical jungle, and on previous trips I had seen all manner of birds, insects and wild animals, including butterflies, humming birds, green and red parrots, lizards, and macaque monkeys. The ambience in and around the three man-made stone pools, all fed by naturally-hot sulphurous water, is further enhanced by the hum of cicadas. Two of the pools are directly connected to each other. The upper of these two pools is fed with water naturally-heated only feet down inside the earth's crust, which are drawn along pipes and then channelled to pour out of the mouths of eight carved stone dragons. Water in the upper pool, which is the smaller of the two, in turn overflows and cascades through the mouths of five other dragons into the larger pool below. A third pool is situated a little off from the other two and has steaming hot water shooting along four bamboo channels descending into a pool 12 feet below.

Positioning various parts of your body underneath the tumbling hot water, very quickly you feel as though your body has been pummelled into a soft blubbery mass (well maybe that's just my body). I never tired of visiting the hot pools of Banjar. I wanted to visit Banjar again on this trip and when I mentioned this to Nur yesterday, and wondered if she would like to go with me, she agreed.

We initially took a bemo to the village below Banjar on the main road and then we took a pony and trap up to the hot springs itself. From what Komang had said yesterday I thought it had changed but it hasn't. It is true that there are many more stalls on the side of the road, Komang's clothes stall included, but the springs themselves seemed to me to be the same as before. Whatever, still very good all the same. Even better going there with Nur. Nur swam with me in all the hot pools but her two sisters-in-law stayed out. Her older sister-in-law is a girl called Jum who is aged 25, is married and has one child, but her husband is working in the USA for 12 months. He had so far been away for seven months. I don't know whether it's a product of an over-fertile or over-confident imagination, but she seemed to be flirting with me. Good swim. Good lunch. Then we swam again. We then went back to Lovina beach and watched the sunset.

Very frustrating evening. After we had seen the sunset Nur went home but she came back and met me at 7.45 together with Wayan. We had a meal at Superman's. I didn't mind Wayan being with us at first, but when Nur and I went back to my homestay Wayan came back there too. I really wanted to have some private time with Nur and despite my heavy hints to Wayan I couldn't make her understand (unless she didn't want to).

Wednesday 19th May – Chilli Supper

Went to see dolphins this morning with Nur. She had never seen them and I persuaded her that she should see them and I said that I would go with her. Not as many dolphins as on Monday but I may have up to five photographs of them jumping near the boat. Hope so. Some of them were travelling very quickly and flying through the air.

In relation to what happened last night, with Wayan interpreting for Nur at a time when I wanted to be alone with Nur, an episode of Blackadder with the Spanish Infanta comes to mind (for those who are not familiar with the mostly-fictional quasi-historical BBC comedy series, in the scene that came to my mind, the Spanish Infanta is betrothed to Edmund Blackadder, the son of Richard IV; unfortunately, the Spanish Infanta speaks no English and her interpreter follows her everywhere, even into the bedroom, where in the darkness of the room he translates even the coital mumbling and moanings).

Before coming to Lovina, I had only intended to hang around for a day or two to see my friends, but I was enjoying the relaxation, I was adjusting to the way of life and, more particularly, I was relishing spending time with Nur. Each day we did something different. This morning I went with Nur to see the dolphins, this evening I planned to return the favour to Naicah and cook for her, and tomorrow I planned to rent a motorcycle and go with Nur to explore an area of central Bali that I had not seen before.

Nur had breakfast with me this morning after seeing the dolphins and then we retired to my room and snogged and cuddled for ages. We managed to give Wayan the slip.

Had arranged to cook for Nur, Naicah and family today. Decided to cook chilli con carne as it is very easy to do and most of the ingredients are readily available – gave Wayan 30,000 Rp to get beef.

Later went with Nur to Singaraja to the outdoor market and then to the mini supermarket. Bought tomatoes, chillies, garlic, onions, which were all fresh ingredients, and then tomato paste, kidney beans, oil, corn chips and Coca Cola. Also purchased a kamus for Nur. When I met up with Wayan later, she said the beef was 25,000 Rp plus it was 1,000 Rp for the Bemo and 4,000 Rp for her breakfast (cheeky cow). In addition, somebody else told me that the beef should have been 20,000, so she probably kept a bit back for her troubles. Prepared the meal in advance in a big pot, on an open fire set in a small hearth, situated in the dried-earth back yard of Naicah's house; then left it to cool down and infuse; finished off cooking it later in the evening. Compared to the version of the meal that I would usually cook back home it was quite a good one and most people liked it. Everybody seemed happy and pleased seeing me with Nur and she's obviously gaining lots of confidence herself. Talking of confidence, I need to be careful that I don't become too cocky myself – Komang said to me the other day that her friend (also good looking) liked me. She described her friend as a playgirl, which she clearly meant disparagingly, though for me there was much to commend it. My ears pricked up when she said it, and I tried to sound casual as I tut-tutted.

Thursday 20th May

Good meal last night. Everybody shares. People usually eat food with their hands. The pots are old and basic – we sit on the floor and eat. Water's drawn from a well. There were only two large chopping knives. But it all came out well in the end and everybody seemed happy.

Komang came round this morning with her two youngest children. She's still got a cold – I think I've caught it, though I don't feel too bad. I told Komang that I would like to buy some clothing from her before I leave.

Went to a homestay nearby where I made several telephone calls – (this particular homestay was near to my own, and seemed to double up as a travel agent, as I had seen a variety of signs outside advertising travel; today I went there hoping to get some information regarding my planned onward travel to Sulawesi) – *seems as though there are no planes between Lombok and Sulawesi and the boat between the two doesn't leave until the 3rd June, which is too long to wait. Therefore, I must either head East and island hop to Komodo and Flores first before trying to find a way to get to Sulawesi later or else I must fly directly from Bali to Sulawesi.*

It turned out that it was not exactly a difficult decision to make, since I had been contemplating travelling to Lombok with Nur, taking four days out to go and bringing her back. When I invited her and she agreed to go, I knew that on returning to Bali I would have to fly to Sulawesi.

Loose stool today and I couldn't get back to my cottage in time so I went in the sea (twice).

Did not have my massage today. In the evening, I went to Johni's with Nur. She looked great as usual. We then went back to my room at the homestay, this time without Wayan and we had a very heavy petting session. The trousers were left on though – she was reluctant to take things too far because of her religion. That's cool. She didn't stay – saying that she had to leave because Naicah would object.

Friday 21st May – Motorcycle Accident

Up early – 7.20 – Nur arrived just as I was getting up. We had breakfast together. We then went to rent a motorcycle.

I had made what was for me quite a brave decision to rent a motorcycle today – brave because I was a very infrequent and, therefore, nervous user of a motorcycle, and had not ridden one since my last trip to Bali four years previously. My reason for renting was because I wanted to travel to Batukau Temple and Mountain, located in central Bali. At 2,276m Gunung Batukau was described as the third of Bali's three major volcanic mountains and I had never been before, primarily because there is virtually no public transport to it, which also means it is seldom visited by tourists. I was not intending to climb to the top of the mountain, but instead simply wanted to visit the temple, a nearby hot spring and explore the area around it. I had read that the journey to it was interesting in itself, because across the central plains I would see some of man's more creative contributions to nature in the form of architectural rice terraces that had been carved into the landscape over centuries, and spice farms and coffee plantations, set amongst a backdrop of natural flora including tall, leaning, coconut palms, large-leafed banana plants and bright pink and purple bougainvillea. Nur had agreed to come with me. By now Nur and I were becoming better able to communicate with each other, partly because my Indonesian was improving, and partly with the aid of the kamus that I had purchased second-hand at a stall in Singaraja.

We set off just after breakfast. Indonesians are not known for their strict observance of road rules. They are *supposed* to drive on the left, but my first tentative yards made me doubt myself as vehicles seemed to approach from all directions. I was a little nervous at first but I soon got the hang of it. With the wind in my face and Nur clinging tightly on the pillion behind me, I felt like Marlon Brando and his 'doll' in The Wild One, or Thelma and Louise on their road trip, but the cinematic notion of romantic adventure was exaggerated and existed solely in my mind, because in all honesty the motorbike was only slightly more powerful than a moped and our helmets were the kind that looked like hairdryers in a beauty salon.

I was familiar with the first half of the route that I had planned. We rode East to Singaraja before heading due South along the road that cuts through the heart of Bali to Denpasar. We were climbing up the road beyond Singaraja into the mountains and were three miles beyond the village of Gitgit, which has the island's highest waterfall, when the motorbike picked up a puncture. Thankfully, the road between Singaraja and Denpasar is very busy and several people in a couple of different cars stopped to help us. Between them, they took me and Nur in one car, deposited the motorcycle in the back of the other and took us back to Gitgit. They never once asked for money. In the village, after our rescuers had asked questions of some wizened old men who were sitting on a rickety bench beside the road, we were directed to a straw hut further along the road, which looked like every other straw hut in the village, except that there we found a man who just happened to have spare tyres. The motorbike was repaired.

Delayed, though not daunted, we resumed our journey. Climbing back up to the ridge in the high country above Gitgit, we passed through a forest teeming with monkeys and as we were descending into the valley beyond it, the scenery opening out was extensive and breathtaking, with beautiful blue Lake Buyan below, beyond it a patchwork quilt of paddy fields and lowland crops, in the distance white clouds swirled around the dark mountains of central Bali, and all this set against the backdrop of a clear turquoise sky. A short while later we arrived at the village of Candikuning beside Lake Bratan. Although I had visited numerous times before, it was one of many sights in Bali that I never tired of seeing, so we stopped to look around. We passed by a large banyan tree at the entrance to ornamental gardens, before arriving at a Hindu/Buddhist temple, known as Pura Ulun Danau, which protrudes into the lake. It has pagodas made of thatch, and has stunning views across the lake to Gunung Catur. The area was a little more touristy from how I remembered it, but it was still as beautiful as ever.

After a short break, back in the saddle, we headed South to the small town of Pacung, which was the end of that part of our journey with which I was familiar. When we turned off right to head West into the countryside, we were now entering virgin territory not just for me, but, as I learnt, for Nur too. Very soon we passed through coffee plantations with beans drying on sheets of plastic or coarse muslin sacking, where the aroma of coffee was intoxicating. Gentle plains soon gave way to rolling hills, where, it seemed, every slope had been turned over to rice fields that had been moulded around the natural contours of the countryside. We stopped at a very good viewpoint atop a hill looking into a valley to stretch our legs and take in the scene. We hugged and kissed. We were about to move off when eagle-eyed Nur spotted a roadside stall, which looked like any other bamboo-walled and banana-leaf-roofed house to me, but where she correctly identified that we could buy and eat fried banana and fresh mango. We then rode on.

The road was becoming more of a dirt track, with deep pot-holes, and many twists and turns. I was cutting backwards and forwards across the road to avoid the pot-holes, and, as I was coming round a bend at about 15 mph, I found myself in the middle of the track. A little ahead of me coming round the bend in the opposite direction was another motorcyclist, who was also in the middle of the road. At the point when he first saw me, he must have deduced from my position in the road that I was cutting across the road, because instead of going to his left, the correct side of the road, he went to his right. However, at the point where I had first seen him, I had deduced that he *would* return to the correct side of the road on his left, so I went to my left to try to avoid him. Seeing that we were now heading towards each other, he corrected himself and went to his left side, but I, thinking exactly the same thing at exactly the same time, moved to my right to try to avoid him. With the distance between us fast diminishing, it was too late for either of us to stop or take avoiding action and we cannoned into each other to the sound of metal crunching against metal. Thankfully, the bends in the road and the pot-holes had dictated that neither of us had been going particularly fast. However, the combined speeds meant that the impact was strong enough to leave me with lacerations to my left hand, a swollen and bruised left eye, a fat lip, and a bruised foot. I was also a little concussed. Nur was shaken but otherwise okay. The other rider, a young lad, only had a minor cut to his leg. Damage to his motorbike consisted of a broken front lamp, a bent gear lever and a flat tyre. Thankfully, my motorbike only had broken fenders, which meant that we could still use it.

Although my instinctive natural response was to apologise to the lad, it was clear that it had simply been an unfortunate accident, with neither of us to blame. However, the other lad seemed determined to accept responsibility because he repeatedly apologised to me. He told us that he lived with his parents only half a mile back along the road and he invited us to go to his house. The lad had to push his bike back, and, although we could have ridden our motorbike, in an act of solidarity I pushed our motorbike there too. His parents were in when we arrived. Nur immediately started fussing over my hand and had evidently asked for some water and tissue, because when they were produced by the parents, she set about cleaning my hand. The parents provided us all with hot, strong, sweet coffee, which was delicious and very welcome. With the shock of the incident slowly abating, Nur and I considered what to do and, although we were only three miles from the temple and hot spring, we decided to go back. After the combined incidents with the flat tyre and the subsequent collision, we did not want to push our luck any further, and, in any case, the day's events had made our progress very slow and it was already the middle of the afternoon. I preferred to get back in daylight. Not surprisingly, I was quite nervous on the return journey, but we made it back safely.

I had seen Komang in the morning when I was with Nur. She had stopped off on the way to her stall at Banjar, and looked a little taken aback when she saw Nur sitting on a seat on my porch waiting for me. The result was that, although they spoke civilly to each other, they were clearly also quite jealous of each other. Komang is an old friend and I don't want to hurt her, but she is, after all, now married with children. Nevertheless, I will have to move quite tactfully. I suggested to Komang that I could visit her tomorrow to buy the clothing that I had promised to get from her. She agreed. Nur is still in discussions with her mum about whether it's okay for her to come with me to Lombok. She will talk to her mum again tonight.

Saturday 22ⁿᵈ May – Watching the FA Cup Final with Strangers

Nur arrived in good time this morning. Her mum has decided that she cannot go to Lombok. I had already by now pretty much come to the conclusion that I should fly to Sulawesi, but this confirmed it. We went to pay for the damage to the motorbike – 100,000 rupiah (£9.00). We went back to the homestay. Once there, Nur was talking to a girl on the beach. She spoke too quickly for me to understand what was being discussed and it was only when they went into my room that I realised that she had arranged for the girl, a pretty beach masseuse, to give her a massage. Nur disrobed and was naked except for her knickers. I was allowed to stay and watch (in fact both Nur and the masseuse insisted – honest!), for which I confess there were no objections on my part and which I cannot deny was a delightful voyeuristic treat, that is until Komang arrived halfway through (bad timing in more ways than one). I went outside and talked to Komang on the verandah. She said that the night before last she had had a bad dream about me, so when I told her about the accident yesterday she wasn't surprised. A short while later, a fully-clothed Nur emerged from the room and asked me to pay for the massage – which I thought was a bit cheeky since she hadn't asked me beforehand. When I later explained to her why I wasn't very happy, she understood.

I went with Komang on her motorbike to Banjar where I bought one pair of long trousers and one pair of shorts. She gave me an extra pair as a present. On the journey saw many women of all ages breastfeeding – some were young but some, with their creased faces and sagging breasts seemed too old to be mums. Komang stayed at the shop, so I went back to Lovina on my own. I was again loose.

I later went with Nur to purchase my ticket to Sulawesi. I decided to fly out on Tuesday – (a) to give me two more days with Nur, (b) to give more time for my bowels to recover from my looseness and (c) for me to ensure I had fully recovered from my motorcycle accident. Nur was very pleased that I am staying a little longer. I may have to go to Kuta one night. Nur might join me. I had a massage with Naicah. I met a very friendly Indian backpacker bloke in the evening – he was a real character. His name is Joe. Nur and I went to Johni's in the evening and again it was very good food. After walking Nur back home to Kalibukbuk, I stayed in the village to try find a friend by the name of Mak, a Balinese lad who I had met a few days before, because he had told me about his interest in English football and when we talked about the upcoming FA Cup Final, he had invited me to come to his house to watch it. I couldn't find his house but, as I was wandering amongst the houses in the village, a group of lads, who I had never met before, saw me and, when I told them that I was trying to find a friend to watch the FA Cup Final, they invited me in. They were already watching the match live from England. They gave me coffee and peanuts and rice crackers. They were very friendly and we had some good banter. Manchester United beat Newcastle United 2-0.

Sunday 23rd May – Passion

I've got a real cracking shiner to my left eye. It was a lazy day – Nur didn't come over in the morning – so I lazed on the beach, did a couple of postcards and read my book and read my Indonesian Lonely Planet book (which I bought second-hand in a shop in Lovina). I realised today what I had been dreading from the moment that I knew I had stuff nicked. I discovered something else missing – my binoculars.

Later saw Nur – she said that she can come to Kuta tomorrow. Therefore, we decided to leave Lovina beach tomorrow. Naicah talked again today – she confirmed that she is happy for Nur to come with me. Naicah also asked me if I would return. I said that I would try but I couldn't promise – which is genuinely my position. I do want to come back and see Nur (very much) but equally the constraints which are time and money (spoken) and my fear of getting too attached (unspoken) apply. Naicah shared coffee and nuts and fruit with me. I shared my mango with her and I bought a round of soft drinks. I had my last massage with Naicah.

Several interesting people have arrived at the homestay in the last day or so. One was a New Zealand girl called Sindy, who I discovered was here in Bali in September 1990 at around the same time as me and, again like me, stayed at Parma's homestay. I had mentioned earlier in this diary that I had met a funny Indian guy called Joe, who's living in the United States. I also met a good looking (and he knew it) but very likeable French guy. In the evening, I went to collect my ticket to Sulawesi – then had a meal with Nur at a warung (locals' eatery) *which comprised nasi campur, water biscuits, large prawn crackers, a beer and some tea – all for 14,000 Rp (80p). Nur came back to my room and things became very passionate, but, although I was very horny, I respected Nur's religious position and it did not go any further than touching.*

Monday 24th May – Shared Time with Nur

Sindy stubbed her toe last night and believes that she has broken it. I Reikied her toe for her. She was comfortable with me doing so because she had heard about Reiki in New Zealand.

Nur came today at 8.30 in the morning. We had breakfast together. Naicah came to say goodbye yet again. It was all very sad. She is obviously perfectly happy about Nur coming away with me to Kuta.

I had booked a flight to leave Bali tomorrow morning to fly to Ujung Pandang in Sulawesi. I would have been in Bali for near enough 11 days by the time I left, several days longer than I had intended, and I needed to move on. However, it was going to be very difficult to do so because Nur had penetrated deep into my psyche, to the extent that I was starting to fall in love with her. As difficult as it already was, I knew that it would become increasingly harder the longer that I left it. My emotions were a jumble. My heart was telling me not to give up hope and that it might just be possible to somehow find a way to be together, and, for that reason I genuinely wanted to keep in touch. My head reminded me that the logistics were so insurmountable that it was difficult to imagine any real future for us. Another factor, which when I now look back in hindsight seems pretty obvious, was my desire to travel further and continue with the adventure, which I can now see was stronger than my desire to remain. However, it was only fractionally so, and it was only just managing to lure me away. Had I left it another week or so, I probably would never have wanted to leave. As a psychological sop to my emotions, I kept telling myself that it was highly likely that I would see Nur again later during this trip, since I had already worked out that my exit out of Indonesia and on to Australia would almost certainly have to be out of Bali.

The flight out of Bali tomorrow morning would leave early from Denpasar airport on the South of the island, which meant that, as there were no buses from Lovina to get me to the airport that time in the morning, I would need to travel South today and stay one night in Kuta. Naicah had agreed to let Nur come with me. Even though Nur was 29 years old, it was very endearing that she had still sought her mum's permission to come and stay with me. It was perhaps even more endearing that mum had agreed.

The very long bus journey across the centre of the island went via Kintamani and Ubud. The journey was made uncomfortable by the twisting and turning of the bus as it climbed up through a series of S-bends to reach the central mountains. The discomfort was worth it, as, once the height had been reached, the views were stunning as the bus travelled along the outer ridge of a deep and wide caldera, inside of which, stood Gunung Batur and Lake Batur. Gunung Abang loomed beyond it. I had visited the lake and climbed the volcano at Batur with my friend, Wayan, in 1990. The journey on this occasion was made even more enjoyable by being in the company of Nur.

It was as we were heading South, having descended past rice fields, through the cultural centre of Bali that is Ubud and the monkey forest around it, and emerging into the busy urban sprawl towards Denpasar and Kuta, that I half-witnessed a terrifying motor accident. I had been browsing through my kamus, when out of the corner of my eye I saw a motorcyclist, travelling in the opposite direction to us, seemingly misjudge the upcoming 90-degree corner badly and, with him going far too fast, he skidded off. When I turned, all I saw was the bike smashing violently into a brick wall, a thick cloud of dust, but no sign of any rider. A bloke behind me kept saying, "Oh my god, oh my god."

Arrived at Kuta – it was very busy as usual. The bus drove along a road beside the sea and we saw very heavy surf coming in. Found a hotel (80,000 Rp) – Nur happy with it. We later walked along the beach and sat arm in arm on the sand and watched a gorgeous sunset. Very romantic. Had a very poor meal in the evening – the restaurant even ran out of rice!! It was great to finally get to share a bed with Nur. We kissed and cuddled, but it never went further than that. It was nice to simply go to sleep wrapped in each other's arms.

Tuesday 25th May – Leaving Nur

Truly the saddest moment of my trip so far. We got up at a reasonable time. We had been cuddling for about 20 minutes or so. Had breakfast and then went to the airport.

Having checked in and sorted out the baggage, for the next 50 minutes Nur and I sat in almost complete silence, holding each other tightly and with Nur's head nestling deep in the nape of my neck, dreading the moment when we would have to separate. With the few words that I spoke, I tried to exert some mind control over the emotional situation by saying words to her like, "We'll try... it will be very difficult and we must be realistic... who knows what will happen but we must realise that we live a long distance apart... we will see." However, in the end I think I was more choked than Nur. Nur's last words were that she would always be waiting for me. I was very tearful and so was Nur who kept her feelings in until the end. One part of my brain kept reminding me that I couldn't really return in three or four weeks' time because it wouldn't work out logistically and, in any event, it would be too painful to go through the process again – but the other part of my brain considered that perhaps I should not be so pessimistic and perhaps I should trust in fate and just wait and see. I don't think I spotted an ounce of badness in all the time I spent with Nur. She was such a wonderful human being and I had pretty much fallen for her. Just before we separated, I gave Nur some money to get the bus back to Lovina, to buy a new and bigger kamus and to help her attend classes to learn English. I also said that I would try and help her out in the future. It sounds very generous, but a little goes a long way in Indonesia. She waved at me through the window as I walked away.

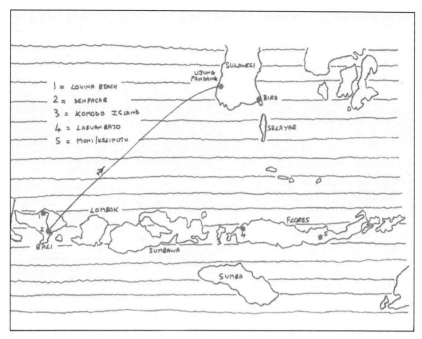

Map 23

I have no memory of walking across the tarmac, of climbing the steps up to the aeroplane or of taking my seat and I must have been sitting there for a good 30 minutes, feeling all wistful and sorry for myself, when I noticed that I was sat at the end of a set of three seats, and beside me were two young, lithesome, fresh-faced Belgian twin sisters who were most definitely not unattractive. What do they say? "As soon as one door closes another two open!" I had already been on an exhilarating rollercoaster ride of extreme emotions during my journey through Asia thus far, but I was not even halfway through.

Wednesday 26th May – Catherine and Valerie

On the plane yesterday, I soon got talking to the girls, Catherine and Valerie. They were very friendly, very chatty and very nice. Once we got to Ujung Pandang we decided to share our resources and, having recruited a tuk-tuk driver, we went in search of a hotel together. The first one that we saw was terrible, with dirty linen, sunken beds and the distant unmistakable high-pitched squeaks of rodents lurking behind the walls. The second was even worse. The third and final one that we saw, the Pondoc Rannu

185

Homestay, was much better and had rooms for all of us. It was not in Lonely Planet but it had been recommended to us by a couple of locals; the people here are clearly just as friendly as in the rest of Indonesia.

Meeting Catherine and Valerie, twin sisters from Belgium, was a breath of fresh air and the timing was perfect in the way that it has very quickly helped me to get into a different gear on my travels after leaving Nur. I ate on my own last night – but when I returned to the homestay there was a note on my door from the girls inviting me to join them later. It was a bit late to go out and they weren't in their room but I stayed out on the veranda and waited a while. When they came back we talked for what seemed like a couple of hours or more. We got on very well. They spoke very good English. They are going to Tanatoraja as well and they invited me to join them. What an invitation! However, they plan to leave today and the timing does not quite suit. I need to sort out a few things here tomorrow, so I might need to hang around for a day or two longer. Also, they wanted to use a guide and I didn't want to go with a guide. The girls were very friendly and seemed to be very happy to be in my company, but I did not take it as an indication that they would want to take matters any further. In any event, I feel as though I need a little bit of breathing space after my time with Nur. I have to say, though, that despite not knowing for sure how far the invitation extended, the slight but distinct and cheeky inflection in Valerie's voice when she asked me to accompany them was promising.

Valerie has been in Bali for eight months on an Indonesian language course (good idea – why didn't I think of that!?). Catherine's a nurse. Both are aged 24 being born on 23rd November 1974. They left today to head up to Tanatoraja and I was sad to say goodbye to them despite having only known them for a relatively short period of time. They certainly seemed genuinely sad to leave me.

Two hours have passed since my last entry and as I resume writing this, I now know that I will, in fact, almost certainly see them again at some point, because later today I made the decision to head up to Tanatoraja tomorrow. They were intending to head up to the small Torajan town of Rantepao, where I too planned to stay. I will use public transport to get there.

I later went wandering around Ujung Pandang and made several enquiries regarding flights to Tanatoraja and other places in Sulawesi. Discovered a boat that goes to Flores on the 19th June and will cost US$200 and takes three nights. It is going my way, it is about the right sort of time, and it is a reasonable price. It seems ideal save that because of the lack of time (I only have a visa for two months) it seems to be pointing to me not going back to see Nur in Bali. We'll see.

As I wandered, it became apparent that the inhabitants of Sulawesi, more than on any other island I had visited thus far, had seemingly fully embraced the upcoming election, because I saw several rallies passing through the city. The first was for *Partai Persatuan Pembangunan* (PPP), party number 9 out of the 48 taking part, sometimes translated as the

Development Unity Party. The predominant party colour was green. The second rally, this one clad mainly in red, with a black bull scored on the party posters and flags, was for the *Partai Demokrasi Indonesia Perjuangan* (PDI), party number 11, otherwise known as the Indonesian Democratic Party of Struggle. Both rallies were busy, noisy, boisterous affairs, comprising mainly young men and women of student age, riding motorcycles and driving trucks and cars, with passengers and pillions waving party flags, hollering slogans and tooting horns. The second rally was louder, longer and vastly more populous than the earlier one. Driving along the city roads without stopping, this form of electioneering seemed to allow no time for political debate and discussion. I did wonder what might happen if the two groups were to meet up, but both groups seemed happy simply to embrace the spirit of democracy. In fact, in all my time in Indonesia I never once saw or heard about any violence directly linked to the election. Most people were smiling and cheering, and giving victory V hand gestures when they saw my camera. The opportunity to vote freely in an election was available for the first time in most of these people's lives and they were clearly keen to embrace it.

I headed North to Paotere harbour. Ujung Pandang, once known as Makassar, has for centuries been the gateway to Eastern Indonesia and the Spice Islands. The Dutch, who arrived in Indonesia at the very end of the 16th Century, appreciated the strategic importance not only of the port, but also of the Bugis who had controlled the trade from here for many centuries before their arrival. Striking up a natural though sometimes uneasy alliance, which was in the main mutually beneficial for each side, the Dutch utilised the skills and know-how of the Bugis, and allowed the Bugis in turn to continue trading too, which they did for many centuries thereafter. After all, the master seafarers of all Indonesia knew how to locate the best trading routes, where to find the islands providing the highest quality produce, how to navigate the hidden reefs and wavering currents, and when to take to the sea in order to make the most of the seasonal fluctuations in wind and weather, particularly around monsoon season. Sometimes, when their fancy took them, they utilised their knowledge of when and where unwary foreign ships unguardedly plied their trade, allowing them to sneak in, jackdaw-like (or sometimes bludgeon in raging bull-like) to plunder their cargo. It is not for nothing that the infamy of the Bugis pirates has given rise to the term 'bogeyman' in Western culture. However, this piratical image of them belies their own deep culture and civilisation, as Lawrence and Lorne Blair observed in their book, 'Ring of Fire':

"The Bugis were amongst the great seafaring tribes of South East Asia. Mentioned by Melville and Conrad, they were the scourge of the East Indiamen seeking the treasures of the Moluccas archipelago. They were the bejewelled and silken-turbaned villains who coloured the pirate archetype of our Western imaginations, wielding their blades and their sea-skills like demons, and bequeathing us their name for our nightmares. Yet, long before we clashed, the Bugis had possessed a highly complex written language, in which every letter looks rather like the cross-section of a different but closely related spiral seashell. They also had tales which recounted the trials and explorations of their Sea Prince heroes who, through numerous incarnations, led their tribal fleets through unknown waters and kingdoms of dragons and witches, whirlpools and man-eating birds, and forests of half-beasts and half-men. In length and breadth these sagas belittle our Iliads and Odysseys, yet few scholars understand them and few have ever been translated."

The skills and hardiness of the Bugis led to Makassar, and Paotere Harbour, becoming a trading hub for the produce of Eastern Indonesia, where goods passing through included pepper, nutmeg, cloves, mace, ginger, galangal, cinnamon, copra, rattan, pearls, trepan, sandalwood and an oil made from bado nuts used by women in Europe as hair dressing (giving rise to the term, antimacassars, which are, of course, the protective embroidered cloths placed on the head rests of upholstered chairs). The Bugis even have a history of trade and cultural links with the Aborigines of Northern Australia.

The Bugis were also especially well-known for their construction of magnificent sailing ships, known as pinisis, famously made without any form of nails, that traded extensively throughout the Indonesian archipelago. Almost all modern trade is still conducted using a pinisi, and I had read that many pinisis still trade out of Paotere Harbour, hence the reason for my heading there.

I was not to be disappointed. Scattered around the wooden jetties were dozens of high-prowed sailing ships, their bows seemingly beached on the wooden gang planks. The upper halves of the hulls of most ships, from the stern to the bow, were painted gleaming white, whilst the lower halves were painted in bright primary colours. Some were painted green, others yellow or blue, and occasionally a combination of two or more of these colours was used. They were a beautiful sight, especially with their oily kaleidoscopic colours reflected off the becalmed late afternoon waters in the harbour. Save for the fact that most craft seemed to possess motors, all the ships retained their traditional pinisi-style characteristics, with long slender, arcing hulls, high, pointed prows and distinctive main sails constructed at the tip of the prow. Most of the ships lay dormant and unoccupied, but close by three or four of them dozens of men were scurrying around like ants. They were diminutive in height but clearly as strong as the proverbial ox, from their necks, through their upper arms and torso down to their muscled legs. For here there were no cranes or other lifting equipment. All cargo was loaded on by hand. At one ship, I saw the men loading large sacks of rice, and one man, who from the rumpled countenance on his brow could have been my grandfather's age, was loading the sacks onto the ships two at a time. By my reckoning, each sack would have weighed 100 lbs, (or 50 kgs).

One or two of the younger ones stopped to speak to me, on the face of it fascinated by my interest in them, although from the frowns on the faces of some of their older colleagues, perhaps they were simply using the opportunity to skive. The word that keeps recurring in my mind when attempting to describe them is 'strong'. They had strong facial features, with high cheekbones, chiselled jaws, and dark hair matching their dark brooding eyes. As already noted, they were, of course, strong of physique. And, they seemed strong in character, being more than just friendly, such that they were confident and self-assured. Instead of me asking questions about them, they were the ones interrogating me. They spoke virtually no English, and, whilst my Indonesian was improving only very slowly, I knew enough to understand that they wanted to know where I was from, whether I was married and, most importantly of all, which football team I supported in England. One group of eight lads had been playing with a much-deflated – and thus very heavy – football on the jetty. When I announced to them that my team was Manchester United, it was greeted with equal amounts of applause and derision. I did at least glean that they were heading off to Surabaya in East Java in a few days' time. Although I personally never once had any cause for concern, I knew that I would not like to cross them or meet them in a dark alley late at night. Even as I was thinking this, the rational side of my brain reminded me that my biased thoughts were heavily influenced by my preconceived notions, having read extensively about the Bugis before travelling here. However, my thoughts turned out to be not entirely without merit, because I learnt a day later that only a few days earlier in a Bugis village not far from this harbour, there had been a real-life knife fight between two of their own resulting in one of them being fatally wounded.

I later met an English chap called Chris, who is the chief marine scientist working on a marine expedition in Indonesia called Operation Wallasee. When he heard that I was planning to go to Pulau Buton he fully agreed that I should. I was very loose again today. Unfortunately, I shit the bed with a wet fart.

Thursday 27th May – Meeting up again with Catherine and Valerie

Left the Pondoc Rannu Homestay today. A little sad to leave because the people are amazingly friendly. The landlord yesterday went out on his motorcycle to get me a bus ticket and today he went out and bought me some more Imodium tablets. Great place – definitely would recommend it. I even had a television in my room, which I hadn't used, except that it came in handy this morning, because I had set my alarm for 3.15 am to see if Manchester United, who were playing Bayern Munich in the European Cup Final, were live on television. They were. The match was already 25 minutes old when I started watching – United were 1-0 down – they seemed to have quite a bit of possession but had little penetration up front and were making mistakes at the back. The clock had just ticked past 90 minutes, with United still 1-0 down, when Teddy Sheringham scored an equaliser. Two minutes later, with the game now deep into injury time, Ole Gunnar Solskjaer scored the winner for United to make it 2-1. Brilliant. Although it was a cruel way for Bayern Munich to lose it, and their players were obviously very upset, I have to say it made it even better – purely and simply because the Germans have got the better of English teams too often and it was nice to see the tables turned for once. I was pretty exhausted and it was not even 5 o'clock, but try as I might it was difficult to go back to sleep afterwards. I got the bus to Rantepao. Pretty uneventful journey. However, there were beautiful views along the way and the scenery became greener and hillier the further North that we went.

We arrived in Rantepao and at the first homestay that I looked at all appeared to be well so I decided to stay. I then went to find the girls, Catherine and Valerie, and I found them fairly quickly at a neighbouring homestay. I had only met them two days ago, and we had separated only yesterday, but it was like meeting long-lost friends. I told them where I was staying which we discovered was not too far from theirs. I arranged for them to come over afterwards. They both seemed pleased to see me. The local people here are very friendly – Indonesians never disappoint me – and I met a lad called Anton who told me about a major funeral ceremony that had already started but which is continuing tomorrow. He told me the location and said that he would arrange for someone to take me – for a fee, of course! When I mentioned this to Catherine and Valerie, they said that it was almost certainly the one that they had been to today (it lasts three to four days) and they later confirmed that tomorrow is the main day. Catherine and Valerie – especially Valerie – described how they were both pretty upset at seeing the ritual sacrifice of animals at today's ceremony. When we changed topics, they told me that they are not very happy with the contract for their guide: (a) he's expensive; (b) although the trip includes food, he's taken them to eat at some pretty poor places; (c) they still have to pay accommodation on top and, conversely, here in Rantepao he has taken them to an expensive place. Their room costs 95,000, as compared to mine, which costs 25,000, and when I showed them my room they stated that it was no different to theirs. I took them to speak to the manager of my homestay to see if there were any free rooms. There probably are. The girls will talk to their guide later.

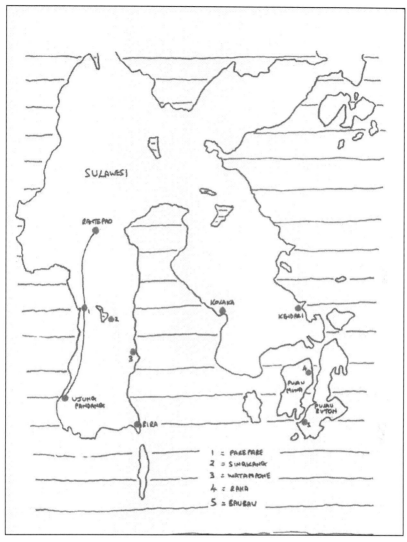

Map 24

Friday 28th May – Funeral Ceremony

Had planned to go to a funeral ceremony today. I had arranged to go there by bemo but the lad that I talked to yesterday, Anton, turned up and said that he had arranged for two other people to join us on the trip and so we would need to share a jeep. Though they largely kept themselves to themselves, and they turned out to be quite a nice couple, I was a bit miffed at first, as I thought I would be travelling solo. I renegotiated my fee with him and I agreed to go. I had dressed in my good event gear, comprising my one decent shirt with long sleeves, my one reasonable pair of long black trousers and my soft shoes, and, as advised, I had purchased a bag of sugar as a present to take with us.

It took us two hours scrambling and buffeting over terrain that at times was very rough to get to the village, along dusty, sometimes muddy dirt tracks, bypassing several rural villages, each of which allowed a tantalising glimpse of the indigenous peoples within, crossing shallow but broad fast-running streams swollen by recent rains and past ubiquitous luculent green paddy fields sculpted around the contours of the undulating landscape. Although I was deposited off the bus yesterday, only now did I feel that I had truly arrived in the beautiful lush Torajaland described by Lawrence and Lorne Blair in their book, 'Ring of Fire':

> "It was here that the Toraja believed their first ancestors had descended from the Pleiades in starships to populate the verdant valleys into which we now descended. It was indeed another world from the coast. Misty green valleys, shot through with rushing vodka-clear rivers; emerald rice-paddies fringed with golden stands of bamboo, and primary forest towered over by soaring escarpments of granite. Through the greens and gold rose the curved and painted outlines of Toraja architecture."

The jeep eventually pulled up at a grassy clearing at the base of a hill and it was with blessed relief that I clambered out. I could just make out the silhouetted shapes of Torajan-style houses at the top of the hill. We were ushered along a wide muddy path heading up the slope towards the houses. There had clearly been heavy rain here only a day or so ago, which the hot baking sun had only partially dried out turning it into a sticky clogging goo, and negotiating it was like wading through treacle. I proceeded slowly, teetering on the brink of going arse over tit. It was early in the day and I wanted to preserve for as long as possible my trousers and my one half-decent pair of shoes. There was a steady stream of humans and animals, some going up the slope, some coming down, passing each other like columns of ants. The animals included buffalo and pigs, the latter portentously squealing as if they understood their fate. The path zigzagged up the slope and as we reached the top we passed half a dozen animal hides ominously stretched out on bamboo canes to dry, before turning a corner and arriving at the village itself. The village was full of houses made in traditional style. I had read that for some of the more important funeral ceremonies whole villages are constructed, and later deconstructed, solely for the purpose of a single funeral ceremony. It was hard to tell if this village had been specially built for the purpose, since the houses here seemed to be made with the same precision and expertise as those that I had seen in Rantepao and in the villages we had passed earlier this morning.

After briefly being allowed the chance to admire the houses, my jaw dropped when we turned into the central square because, although I had been spared the ordeal of watching the ritual slaughter itself, in the middle of a very muddy, blood-drenched, central square men were hacking away at the bodies of half a dozen buffaloes. Although Torajan funerals are famous and I had read plenty about them beforehand, nothing prepared me for this. Maybe I had not expected quite this much gore, but this after all was what I had come to see.

The *tomate*, or funeral, is the most important of all Torajan ceremonies. The Toraja usually have two funerals, the first taking place immediately after death and the second taking place weeks, months, or occasionally even years later. Part of the reason is pragmatic and secular, with the need to prepare, raise the finance, set down a timetable, and organise family members and guests, but the main reason is to wait for as long as is necessary until the spiritual and astronomical indices coincide to be at their most auspicious, thus ensuring the safest possible passage into the afterlife of the deceased. The more important the deceased, the more lavish is the ceremony, the greater the number of buffalo sacrificed and the more vital is the need to ensure that the timing is correct. Lawrence and Lorne Blair described how a king of the Toraja had to wait over four years before the Torajan priests deemed it propitious enough to send him off. The funeral rites are required to be properly observed. If the deceased is given a proper send-off, his spirit can intercede on behalf of the surviving family in its dealings with the gods and creatures in the afterlife, but a failure to do so will result in the spirit of the deceased bringing bad luck to the surviving family. The funeral sacrifices, ceremonies and feasts take place around a central area known as the *rante*, an area of open ground sometimes covered in grass, which is a bit like a market place. Some are extensive and permanent areas, marked with large stone megaliths, and some are specially created as temporary structures for a single funeral, just like the temporary houses and pavilions. The corpse remains in the house where the person has died, preserved either by traditional methods employing embalming herbs, or by chemical injection. Once everything is ready, the body is put in a highly-decorated coffin, which is placed high up in a small tower, specially constructed and positioned at one end of the rante, from where it can preside over the rituals taking place below. The souls of the dead can only pass into the afterlife once the entire funeral ceremony has been completed. It is believed that the souls of animals pass with their masters into the afterlife, and will aid the passage of the soul, hence the requirement for there to be animal sacrifice at funerals. The greater the number of animals slaughtered the easier the journey will be for the deceased. The buffalo is the most important animal at such ceremonies, being a symbol of wealth and power. Accordingly, the more important the deceased, as dictated by age and social status, the stronger the buffaloes have to be and the more of them are required to be sacrificed: one for a commoner, then two, four, eight, twelve and so on, and on very rare occasions the numbers of buffalo sacrificed are measured in their hundreds.

The ceremony that I was attending was probably for somebody of relative importance, because before me lay the carcasses of around eight buffaloes. It was difficult to tell one body from the next, since the rante was one large mass of bloodied flesh and bone. However, the heads and horns of the animals were largely intact, thus meaning that I was able to estimate the number by literally doing a head count. These animals were probably the ones Catherine and Valerie saw dispatched yesterday because the blood had already drained away to mix with the earth. Men and young boys were walking barefoot in the resulting congealing quagmire, some hacking away at the bodies with machetes and some carrying away the spoils. The air was palpably thick with the sickly-sweet smell of fresh blood.

Time seemed to be suspended when I first observed this scene, but very quickly a group of villagers came up to us. They were very welcoming, smiling and shaking hands. Anton, our guide, informed us that he would need to speak to the family elders and left us on the edge of the rante, whilst he went with two of the group to go and talk with the family to seek approval for our visit. He returned smiling only a moment later to confirm that we were indeed welcome and we were taken to meet the family. We learnt that the deceased was a much respected female elder and we were introduced to her widower, a slight, wiry man, wearing gold-rimmed glasses, a slightly crumpled dark brown suit, an open necked light blue shirt and a smart dark brown trilby with a charcoal grey band. With a slightly lazy left eye and an engaging stoic smile, this charismatic gentleman exuded calmness, whilst at the same time maintaining a measure of control and authority that was clearly borne only out of respect. We were invited to sit with him and his immediate family in the pavilion set aside for him and the most important attendees. Very soon one of the younger members brought us coffee and rice biscuits.

As we sat and talked for a while with our new friend, I found it humbling that he should devote so much time to us. I soon exhausted the few topics that I could manage in Indonesian, before Anton took over and translated. I understood that the gentleman's wife had passed away the previous year. He pointed to a small but tall stilted hut, constructed over three floors, located at the edge of the rante. The tower was highly decorated with bands of colourful material around the outside, ornately embroidered predominantly in ruby pink, gold and black, and with the now familiar arced Torajan style roof, made of bamboo. Two storeys up, accessed by a ladder, was his wife's coffin, and I was invited, or more precisely, should I say, encouraged, to later climb the ladder up to the coffin to see for myself and even to take photographs.

A respectful quiet descended and snuffed out our conversation as a gong sounded to announce the arrival of guests from a neighbouring village. The villagers in this group, with every member dressed head to toe in black, walked in single file with the most important family members at the front. The women's heads were covered and many in the group were carrying food. The gong continued to reverberate its repetitive sonorous slow-march chime as the guests solemnly paraded in stately procession around the edge of the rante, passing by the hut containing the coffin. Thereafter, they proceeded to a pavilion which seemed to be a waiting area for guests, where they were eventually received by the family. The gong ceased. Having been formally accepted, the villagers bowed their heads respectfully to our host, who nodded in response, smiling wanly as he did so. They had brought gifts, including food, betel nuts and cigarettes.

A short while later the gong resumed its regular sombre largo-paced requiem and another large group of persons from another neighbouring village arrived. I was surprised to see that all the members in this group were dressed in red tops and black trousers or sarongs. Unlike the first group, none of the women in this group had their heads covered, but they all had their hair tied up into a tight bun at the back. Looking through my Western eyes, and having seen the first group dressed in black, with the women's heads all covered, scenes that I might have found all too familiar at, say, a Catholic funeral in Europe, I had assumed that all attendees would be similarly dressed. However, that was not the case and any uniformity in dress applied only to the members in each individual village group. This group too brought presents, and most of their offerings also seemed to be of food, since their offerings were contained in large bowls covered in white cloth. They too reverentially circumnavigated the rante and passed by the house with the coffin.

Large birds of prey circled over the site, which initially I thought to be falcons, but which on closer inspection turned out to be vultures. No doubt they were hovering, hoping to snatch something from the unwary or waiting to pick up any morsel left behind. I saw a number of live pigs, either trussed up or hemmed inside rudimentary wooden cages, who were squealing as they were led away to presumably be slaughtered. The ceremony certainly had a fascination, but it was definitely not for the faint-hearted.

Our host insisted on us sitting with him as several dishes of food were brought to us, including boiled rice, dried fish, and a vegetable dish containing peanuts, spinach and beansprouts.

At around two o'clock the others in my group, that is Anton and the two Westerners, said they wanted to leave. Feeling disappointed at the prospect of having to leave this mesmerising ceremony, I asked Anton why this was, thinking that we had perhaps outstayed our welcome or that to remain would be impolite, impertinent or impolitic to our host. However, it turned out that my traveller friends simply wanted to visit another site. I was completely absorbed and transfixed by the scene before me, so the idea that somebody would want to leave was beyond my comprehension. I told them that I would prefer to stay as I wanted to continue to soak up the atmosphere, but, as a precaution in order to ensure that I was not imposing, I asked Anton to make sure that our host would have no objection to me staying. The response was a resounding unambiguous declaration that I was very welcome. I had no idea how I would return to Rantepao later. Anton murmured something about there possibly being a bemo that could take me, but frankly I wasn't overly bothered. Although I had no axe to grind with my fellow travellers, and they had been perfectly friendly, I secretly enjoyed seeing them disappear off down the hill back to the jeep and I selfishly relished the fact that I was now the only non-native present.

A short while later, more food was brought to us, including pa'piong, a mixture of minced pork, herbs, spices and a green leafed vegetable similar to spinach. I learnt that it is the Torajan's signature dish and is cooked in long bamboo tubes roasted on open fires. Sometimes chicken or fish is used but on special occasions it is pork. This was evidently one of those special occasions. I couldn't help momentarily contemplating whether I was now about to chomp into one of the squealing mammals I had seen being prodded to get up the slope to the village earlier. However, gluttony won the day since one bite of the exceedingly tasty and moreish food immediately removed all such thoughts from my mind and my voracious appetite quickly erased those initial sensitivities.

To my surprise two members of the family approached me, both of whom spoke very good English. One of them was a grandson of our host, who told me that he had recently returned from working in Jakarta and he explained that his grandfather had been waiting for nearly nine months to bury his wife, and in waiting for the right time, one of the factors had been a need for him – the grandson before me – to finish his secondment in Jakarta. He introduced me to his parents, before inviting me to accompany him around the village, introducing me to more of his relatives. As sombre and respectful occasion as it was, there were smiles all round as I was being introduced and it was great fun.

Eventually we reached the tower at the edge of the rante, which contained his grandmother's coffin. He invited me to go up the ladder on my own to view and pay respects to his grandmother. He insisted that I take my camera with me, and it was with mixed emotions that I climbed up. The coffin was a large cylinder, flat at both ends, which reminded me of the engine on an old steam engine. It was beautifully ornate, coloured predominantly in red, emblazoned variously with black banding, white flowers, a Christian cross, hearts, diamonds, and several cockerels, together with enigmatic geometric patterns that seemed random to me, though they no doubt conveyed some mystical esoteric meaning to my hosts. Many of the features were created using gold leaf. I noted that the position of the tower, and the coffin situated on the third tier of it, had not only a perfect view of the rante and the family and guests sitting in the pavilions surrounding it, but also of a deep and wide valley behind the tower. The old girl certainly had an amazing view. Although there must have been upwards of two hundred people in and around the rante, I had the sensation of being on my own up there. However, far from being eerily uneasy, instead I felt strangely comfortable despite having only for company the for-now nomadic spirit and skeletal remains of an old lady, who I had never met in life. Somehow, I felt as though she welcomed my visit, perhaps appreciating a distraction from the tedium of so much ritual – after all, we were only into the second day and there were at least two more to go – and she did not mind a bit me taking loads of photographs.

Suddenly, and without warning, I started to think of my own grandmother, my recently-deceased nan, and I had a strong sensation that she was up there with me. I wondered what she would have made of so much ritual. She certainly would have appreciated the love of family, the deep warmth held for the elders in this community and the respect for those who have recently departed, but she would not have enjoyed quite so much frippery. I found myself nodding in affirmation when a puff of wind broke the spell and brought me back to the present.

I lingered long into the afternoon, but eventually I knew the light would soon start to fade and even I knew that it was time to go. The grandson said he thought he knew of some guests who were heading back to Rantepao and arranged for them to transport me back. With my head still buzzing from the events of the day, I did not notice in the slightest the equally bumpy ride back to town.

In the evening, I met up with Catherine and Valerie and we swapped stories about our adventures today. They are very funny. Being twins and clearly on the same wavelength, each joke or quip leads to the other being in fits of giggles, which was very infectious despite the fact that their original comments were distinctly unfunny and meant nothing to me. They sorted out the situation with their guide last night to their complete satisfaction – they sacked him! – and they changed accommodation and moved into a room in my homestay today. They told me that they had arranged to go to a wedding tomorrow and asked if I wanted to go. Too right! These days come thick and fast.

Later that night after gazing at my nan's photograph for a while before switching off the light, I would like to be able to say that, as I lay on my bed in the darkness and relative still of my room, listening to the distant chorus of croaking frogs and the hissing of cicadas and pondered the day's events, I was thinking about the widower, the love of family, the food, the architecture or plain old common humanity, but the overriding sensation that suppressed all my thoughts was the vivid smell of blood that lingered long within my nostrils.

Saturday 29th May – Torajan Wedding

I went with Valerie and Catherine to a Torajan wedding today. My good event gear had a second outing. We decided to go by bemo. We gave the guide, Hendrick, 60,000 rupiah to get a present (two photograph albums). He advised that we would find it very difficult to find bemos to take us there but in fact finding a bemo was very easy – getting to the location was a bit more tricky.

When Valerie, Catherine and I met up with our intended guide, Hendrick, in town, he informed us that something had cropped up and he would be unable to accompany us. The wedding was taking place in a small village known as Sangalla, situated 14 miles South of Rantepao, but Hendrick assured us that before he left he would assist us to get there and he also agreed that he would help us buy something suitable to give as a wedding present. I hadn't made the arrangements with Hendrick yesterday – the girls had – and I momentarily wondered if he could be trusted, but Valerie and Catherine seemed happy enough. He suggested that it was possible to get there by public bemo, but advised that we might be better off hiring our own private transport, explaining that public bemos travel very slowly, stop regularly, and only operate when they are full, thus meaning, firstly, that we might struggle to arrive there in good time and, secondly, that it was likely that we would be hemmed inside the bemo like chickens in a battery farm. Catherine and Valerie agreed with me that we should try our luck with a bemo, meaning that not for the first time in my Asian adventure I had to try to explain to a bemused local that we Westerners sometimes preferred to travel like cooped-up hens. Persevering, by trying to explain that our raison d'être was because hiring transport was too clinical and easy, and sharing public transport with locals was part of the fun, did nothing to elucidate him. Luckily, we quickly found one that was almost full and about to depart. Hendrick advised the driver where to drop us off.

After about 45 minutes of a stuttering stop-start journey whilst the bus did indeed stop everywhere to drop off or pick up passengers, the bemo pulled over to the side of the road seemingly in the middle of nowhere, surrounded as we were by open countryside with not a single building in sight. The driver casually waved his arm, nonchalantly pointing to a path running adjacent to the road, seemingly heading into no-man's land across a large paddy field, and he then mumbled something which I was struggling to comprehend. Valerie, however, picked up immediately that he was explaining that the quickest way to get to the village was to trek across the open fields. I was feeling a little perplexed as we three were the only ones to alight from the bus, and as it disappeared off up the road, with neither house nor human in sight, and only the company of birdsong and chirruping crickets around us, I couldn't help wondering if Hendrick had roped in the driver to play some kind of practical joke on us. Maybe Hendrick had not been happy with us declining to use private transport. Maybe he had lost out on commission. Valerie, however, seemed unperturbed, and moments later we knew we were fine when way ahead in the distance we spotted half a dozen people. Able to make out that they were smartly dressed in flamboyant, multi-coloured clothing, and wandering across the same open fields, they clearly were not dressed to work the land and two of them were carrying decorated parasols to shield themselves from the fierce heat of the late morning sun. Although we were able to use the people ahead as a point of reference, working out the route to get to them was still a little tricky as it involved trying to find a way through the maze of raised field-edge banks between wide, swampy or waterlogged rice fields. As we came closer, the half a dozen people up ahead of us soon became a steady procession, and after 20 minutes of criss-crossing between rice and wheat fields, we arrived at a village.

At the entrance to the village, we were met by a group of four people, who turned out to be family members of the wedding party, and who greeted us so enthusiastically that it was apparent that they had been expecting us. "Good old Hendrick," I outwardly voiced to the girls, whilst with my tongue firmly in my cheek, I inwardly berated myself, "I never doubted you for a minute, you old git!" One man in the group introduced us to two other male family members, presumably in the belief that they spoke better English. The way that the face of one of them froze for a split second, displaying an almost imperceptible streak of panic, suggested otherwise and was akin to the man having been given the assignment of spending all day looking after the family nut job, but his unease quickly turned to relief when Valerie spoke to him fluently in Indonesian. We gave our carrier bag containing the photograph frames to one of the two gentlemen, who agreed to hand them to the bride and groom later. In the meantime, the other gentleman beckoned for us to follow him and he led us to an area in the centre of the village where the main events of the wedding would be taking place. This open space was much like the rante I had seen yesterday, except that here there was parched yellowing dried grass in place of blood-spattered mud. We were treated like honoured guests as we were introduced to one and all, and everybody seemed genuinely happy for us to be there. It turned out that we were the only non-native people present.

Although I had done my best by wearing my 'good event gear', I felt distinctly underdressed. Many people had clearly gone to a lot of trouble to dress up and there were some stunning traditional outfits on show. Many men wore sarongs, brightly-coloured batik shirts, and a *peci* (a traditional Indonesian hat, looking much like a fez, which is often made with black felt), and many women wore the Torajan version of the *kebaya*, a beautiful, figure-hugging embroidered blouse-dress worn with a bright coloured batik sarong, dyed with flower motifs. Many women had their hair tied into a bun, and some attached hair clips, styled like butterflies or flowers. The outfits were a mix of traditional and modern, and there were one or two more conventional Western styles on show, with one gentleman, who turned out to be an uncle of the bride, dressed in a navy-blue suit, white shirt and a flowery-patterned red and black tie. One man, who was an apparently important family member in view of the fact that he performed the role of a compere, wore on his upper half a peci and a smart Western-style fawn-coloured jacket over a long-sleeved open neck shirt, whilst incongruously on his lower half he wore a pink and green flowery sarong and flip-flop shoes. Six young girls wore such ornate outfits and were being fussed over by older attendants to such a degree that it was evident they would be performing an important function at the wedding. They each wore either a burgundy red or a shocking pink kebaya, underneath a shawl adorned with abstract geometrical patterns brightly-coloured in gold, pink, black and white, and a type of waistband or overskirt with different coloured tassels hanging down to the knees. Their hair was tied tightly into a bun behind a glinting gold and red headband.

In front of traditional Torajan houses incongruously bedecked with satellite dishes, pavilions had been set up around the central area to provide shade to all the guests to protect them from the baking sun, and the backdrop was a stunning clear turquoise blue sky. Although the events of today were very light in stark contrast to the intensity of yesterday's funeral, what followed was a heady, enthralling very pleasant day. Having been shown to our places in one of the pavilions, we sat back and watched as the groom arrived with a small entourage and go to a house in the village where his bride-to-be was waiting within. Having collected his bride and her own much larger entourage, the two groups exited the village heading out to the church. I was aware that one of the mysteries surrounding the Torajans is the fact that they are Christians – albeit their brand of Christianity has a uniquely Indonesian twist to it, being fused with traditional beliefs – and many anthropologists have long debated how such people ended up living in a forest, surrounded by Muslims, in the middle of Sulawesi. I had hoped that we would be allowed to go to the church, and I asked one of our English-speaking chaperones if we could do so, but, whilst he stated that we could, his understanding of English seemed so ambiguous and unreliable that we were unconvinced. Consequently, though I would have loved to have seen the ceremony itself, we decided not to chance it, not wanting to run the risk of causing offence.

Whilst we were waiting for the marriage party to return, so many people made themselves known to us, from young girls in pretty white frocks to grandmothers chewing betel nuts, that it seemed as though we were the half-time entertainment. We were made to feel extraordinarily welcome. Most of the people approaching us made some attempt to talk to us, but some simply stood and stared, including one old lady who seemed so mesmerised by us that she stopped chewing on her betel nuts, resulting in the red spittle that had been foaming in her mouth running down her chin. Very soon young men started dishing out the palm wine.

Eventually the bride and the groom returned. Earlier I had not been able to see them very clearly since they had both been surrounded by their families, but on returning they stood out at the head of the procession and looked stunning. The bride wore a brilliant white kebaya, edged in intricately woven golden brocade. Though heavily made up, she was very beautiful, with high cheekbones, porcelain white skin, claret-red lips, jet black hair, a wide golden headband, and sparkling gold jewellery hung from her ears and hair like baubles on a Christmas tree. With the gold glinting in the sun, I imagined that Cleopatra might have looked something like this.

The bride seemed to be constantly smiling, whilst in contrast the groom held a permanently stern expression. Neither couple seemed to open their mouths, not even to talk. This went on for so long that I wondered if the couple's expressions were some kind of tradition, and part of the ritual. I inwardly laughed as I said to myself that his frowning could not possibly have had anything to do with me staring too long at his beautiful bride. The groom wore a claret-red long-sleeve chemise, buttoned up to his neck, a gold and red peci and a lemon-yellow satin sarong. Having made their way across the central square, they sat obediently and solemnly on chairs on an ornately-decorated dais. For most of the time, each of them held a kris, sheathed inside a gilded scabbard. For Indonesians, the kris is less a weapon and more of a spiritual object, which is often considered to have an essence or presence, and can possess magical powers, or bring good luck. They continued to sit in reverential silence for the duration of the party that ensued, their designated expressions set like stone, without seemingly eating, drinking or even conversing with the guests.

A number of speeches on microphones then followed from the priest, the chief of the village, and other male and female contributors, whilst the rice wine continued to flow. At one point the village chief turned to look at us, and, speaking firstly in Indonesian and then in English, he thanked the three of us for coming. It was extremely humbling. My god, it was us who should be thanking them.

Then the central square cleared, a six-piece gamelan orchestra began playing a rhythmic tune and the six young girls in their pink or red kebayas stepped forward to perform traditional dancing. The movements were graceful and sensual, and as they kept rhythm with the pulsing hand drums their movements were so hypnotic that my whole senses seemed to align with the rhythm. Then a middle-aged woman emerged from the crowd, walked slowly in rhythm towards the girls, placed a monetary note in the headband of one of the dancers, and then with equally rhythmical dancing withdrew. Almost by sleight of hand, the dancer, whilst still dancing, then removed the money and placed it in a box. Other people followed suit, one at a time. Without warning, the village chief looked towards me and beckoned for me to go up too. With so many eyes bearing down on me in expectation, I was in no position to decline, and up I went. However, in a moment of stage fright, and like a chump, I simply walked up, unceremoniously put a 10,000 Rp note (worth the princely sum of 56p) directly into the box and then sat back down. The village chief whispered in my ear that I should have danced to the drum beat when I approached the girls, and that I was meant to have put the money in the headband. Emboldened by embarrassment, I immediately decided that I should go up and do it again, but the beaming smile with which he delivered his advice assured me that it was meant as an observation rather than a chastisement, so, considering that no harm had been done, I knew that the embarrassment would abate more quickly if I just sat it out.

Bizarrely, the conclusion of the dancing was followed by an auction off of pig meat. The man with the fawn jacket and flowery sarong conducted the auctioneering. Then the food itself came out, which included sticky rice, vegetable pa-piong, spicy pork pa-piong, mixed vegetables, several chilli sauces of varying degrees of heat and a dish of sweet potato leaves, much like spinach. We ate the delicious food with our hands from a paper plate, which was accompanied by more rice wine.

I took many photographs as the afternoon wore on, including several close-ups of the bride and groom. Bowing and thanking them after I had taken my photographs, the bride's beaming smile was disarmingly trance-like, but when I turned to the groom he looked at me with such disdain that I felt sure I must have done something wrong. Could he really have read my mind, I pondered? Whilst I really didn't think so, I was no longer completely sure that this was part of the ritual. Not only did the girls and I take many photographs of the people, but many of them insisted on taking photographs of us, and asked us for our addresses. At no point did we feel like outsiders.

Valerie and Catherine clearly enjoyed it too. I had almost forgotten that I was with them, not because I had been ignoring them, but simply because I had felt so at ease in their company. Although I had known Valerie and Catherine for several days, today was the first day that I had spent an extensive amount of time with them. I felt very comfortable being in their company, and I sensed that they felt the same way too. I was effortlessly getting to know them and was tuning into their different characters. Maybe it was the wine talking, but, whilst it had not been lost on me from the outset that they were slim, fresh-faced and pretty, they were becoming even more attractive by the minute. Valerie was cheeky and flirty, whilst Catherine was quiet and reflective. Valerie did most of the talking, and was the one I had, therefore, engaged with most in the beginning. However, I felt myself gravitating towards sweet, enigmatic, occasionally blushing Catherine. I still had no idea whether their friendship would extend any further, and I knew that it was unlikely that I would ever find out. I must confess that whilst I genuinely cherished their friendship, I knew full well that if either or, indeed, both of them were to have truly extended – shall we say – an 'invitation' to me, I would have momentarily paused out of politeness to consider their invitation, before a nanosecond later jumping at the chance. However, I did not want to upset this beautiful friendship by doing something silly like asking them. The devil in me, of course, wanted to know what was in their minds, but the angel knew that I wouldn't want to have been disappointed by any sort of negative answer. The angel won. Preferring to remain in ignorance, I felt, as a consequence, that I had no option but to continue to hover in an emotional no man's land, waiting and wondering.

It was late afternoon when the first guests made to leave, and when one did so, they all did so, as if they had all been waiting for the first person to make a move. Valerie, Catherine and I decided that we should leave too. We approached the bride and groom, who were now standing on their dais, to thank them for allowing us to share their day. I first spoke to the ever-smiling silent bride, who half-closed her eyes in an apparent attempt to convey to me that she was genuinely pleased that we had shared the day with them, but when I turned to the ever-frowning silent groom his wide-eyed glare so disconcerted me once more that I almost felt compelled to apologise, though I knew not what for, that is until a nod and a quick half-wink reassured me that all was well.

The day was not yet done with us. As we followed the crowd intending to simply re-trace our steps across the field-edge paths the way that we came, one group of persons invited us to follow them as they said they had something interesting to show us. A ten-minute walk brought us to a grassy clearing beside a rocky outcrop, where up on the cliff were numerous small caves. On the ledges in front of the caves were a number of rickety wooden boxes, and a tingle went down my spine when I quickly realised they were coffins. The eeriness was completed by the coffins being accompanied by several miniature wooden effigies of humans, known as *tau tau*. Being one of the most famous of Tanatoraja's many cultural gems, I had intended to explore some of the tau tau and grave sites over the next couple of days. I had read that one site is so famous that coach loads of tourists often descend on it en masse, but here we were getting a foretaste of what was to come, in the presence of new Torajan friends, who clearly delighted in proudly sharing their heritage with us and without a tour guide in sight.

Having found a bemo back to Rantepao, and having freshened up, Valerie and Catherine joined me on the balcony of our homestay for a drink and to take in the cool night air. They told me that originally they were intending to leave today but they had changed their minds and they will stay at least two more days. Unless it was the after-effects of the day's palm wine talking, they seemed to beam knowingly when they told me so. Interesting!!

Sunday 30th May – Inside a Torajan House

A quiet and relaxing day. Laid in and had a long and lazy breakfast and did some postcards. I caught Catherine and Valerie who were heading out to the village of Batutumonga, where they planned to stay overnight. I had wanted to visit there too, but I preferred not to stay over. I agreed to meet up with them tomorrow. Saw loads of fireflies last night. Saw a white-headed eagle off the balcony. I went for a walk in the afternoon to

Kete Kesu — seven or eight miles in all. I saw great rice field scenery and gorgeous wild flowers, looking just like an old-fashioned meadow in an English summer.

I had read about a village called Kete Kesu, located only four miles South of Rantepao, which contained a large number of typical Torajan houses. I decided to walk there and explore it today. What I hadn't bargained for was that the entire village would be given over to Torajan houses, which were stunningly set amongst leaning palm trees and dark red bougainvilleas, around a central area carpeted with lush green grass, and almost completely surrounded by forest. The downside that I discovered on arrival was that, whilst the houses were authentic, old and original, most of them were no longer inhabited, and the ghost-town village had the sterile atmosphere of an uninspiring museum. Nevertheless, I spent some time wandering around.

I had read plenty about the way Torajan houses are styled and the houses here were exactly as described. Bulky wooden houses are raised up on stilted piles with exaggeratedly elongated arc-shaped rooves tapered at both ends. There are several suggestions for why the rooves rear up at either end. One idea is that the house represents the head of a buffalo, and the roof represents the horns. This idea has considerable merit, considering the reverence with which buffalos are held. Others suggest that the rooves are shaped like boats, and the raised ends represent the bow and the stern. This idea too has merit since the houses are usually laid out with the fronts facing North, which is where scientists believe they came from. Certainly, the Torajan people look ethnically very different when compared to their near-neighbours, the Bugis, and anthropologists have argued that they look more like Cambodians or Siamese, lending weight to their theory that they had migrated to this area from the North. However, it is another idea that is most mysterious and evocative to my mind, since, as Lawrence and Lorne Blair observed in their book, 'Ring of Fire', when the Toraja themselves are asked where they come from, they reply, "Before the dawn of human memory our ancestors descended from the Pleiades in skyships." The rooves, they say, are accordingly shaped like arcs, with the tips pointing up to the sky, in order to launch the souls of the dead back to the cosmos from whence they came.

The houses are built with the main living area five or six feet off the floor and each one sits on a dozen or so thick wooden pillars. As was the case with this village, the rooves of the older houses traditionally use overlapping pieces of bamboo (though modern ones often use corrugated iron) and each gable end is supported by a single pole. The wall panels are dexterously decorated with paintings or carvings, sometimes with symbols of animals, including cockerels and buffalo, and sometimes with intricate geometrical designs, none of which are created purely by chance since they each have an individual name and meaning. I casually noticed that the black buffalo carvings within this village resembled the black bull painted on the party flags of the Indonesian Democratic Party of Struggle that I had seen in Ujung Pandang. The walls are often gilded in different colours, each of which also has a specific meaning. Red symbolises human life, being the colour of blood; white refers to purity, being the colour of flesh and bone; yellow represents God's blessing and power; and black represents death and darkness. The ubiquitous buffalo feature large in the construction of the houses in other ways. The front of most houses is decorated with an accurate, rather than symbolic, carving of a buffalo's head, the pole supporting the gable end at the front of the house being adorned with real buffalo horns – indicative of the wealth of the family, whereby the greater the number of horns, the more wealthy the family. I had read that historically the artisans employed to decorate the houses would themselves be paid in buffalo. Along the sides of some of the houses hung 30 or 40 buffalo jaws. Although I would never claim to have any special knowledge of architectural design – my only memory of woodwork lessons at school being when I sliced open my thumb with a chisel – even to my untrained mind, the intricacies with which the houses were constructed and the knowledge that the beams and supports were so expertly cut that they simply slotted together with no necessity to bind with nails or pegs, was frankly breathtaking.

As I ambled past one of the houses, I saw an old man leaning out of an upstairs window. He beckoned me to join him in his house. I clambered up. He spoke Indonesian sufficiently clearly and slowly to enable me to understand that he was the only remaining person still living permanently in the village, although others, he said, lived there part-time. He showed me the three levels that Torajans typically live in, including the area where the rice and food is kept, the store cupboard, the area set aside for tools and the sleeping area. He told me that virtually everything in the house was exactly as it would have been one hundred years before, but, considering that the only difference between the house then and now was that where there was once a wood burning stove there was now a paraffin-fired one, he could have been telling us that the house was as it would have been five hundred, or, for that matter, one thousand years before. Paraffin was not exactly a modern invention, so the existence of paraffin-fired stoves did nothing to alter its authenticity in my eyes. With his cheery receptiveness and his happy smiling face, yet again I found myself bowled over by the hospitality of the Indonesian people. The village no longer felt like a museum.

Just as I was concluding my visit to the village and was about to head back to the road, the old gentleman I had been speaking to shouted down to a teenage lad who was kicking a football on the lush grass, pointing at me when he did so. Without needing a second prompt, the young lad, speaking in broken English, said he had something to show me. He took me along a path behind the village towards a hill, where on the cliff face were some grave caves and some hanging graves. Some of the minute caves were easily accessed by a zig-zagging path running up the side of the cliff. The lad strode up and beckoned me to follow. Many of the wooden coffins inside the caves had broken open – whether through natural erosion or through the intervention of animals, or humans (possibly in the guise of grave robbers), was impossible to tell. Skulls and piles of other human bones were lying exposed to the elements, although most had at least been laid tidily. In front of one cleft in the cliff face lay a skull and cross-bones. The skull, minus its jaw bone, lay embedded in the earth, just as if the original occupant had been buried up to his jaw, and the cross-bones lay behind him. Still following the young lad, as we rounded the next corner he pointed up to a parade of miniature tau tau, standing on a wooden balcony wedged part way up the cliff. One effigy wore a wooden bandana and pink shirt. Another, looking like Jesus, sported a thick beard and white head band over a turquoise blue chemise. Of the 30 or so tau tau, about six of them mysteriously had black skin, embedded with exaggeratedly white eyes and wore wide-brimmed straw hats, looking like characters straight out of a Mark Twain novel. I wondered if the tau tau represented an ancient link to black ancestry, and, if so, where from. Would they have been from Africa, or maybe from Australasia? The hanging graves were not so much literally hanging as lying two or three at a time across wooden platforms suspended part way up the cliff face, with the platforms held in position by a pair of struts. I shivered. The air seemed chilly beside the cliff, and I sensed it was not entirely due to it being in shadow from the sun. I was rather glad when I eventually returned back to the relative warmth of the road back to town.

Monday 31st May – Hill Views

Got up in good time and went to the village of Batutumonga – which is situated on a ridge on the slopes of Gunung Sesean – to meet up with Catherine and Valerie. I needed two bemos to get there, one from terminal Bolu in Rantepao and the second from the village of Lempo. Having been dropped off on the outskirts, I walked into Batutumonga to try to find the Losmen where the girls were intending to stay when Catherine spotted me from a distance. Her beaming smile when she kissed me on both cheeks suggested that she was genuinely happy to see me. Valerie joined us and we decided to walk along the track to Lokomata and beyond, which followed the contours of a ridge on the slopes of the volcano. Saw green rice field scenery, stunning panoramic vistas, many beautiful road side flowers, several small waterfalls and lots of indigenous people with their children. We also saw many buffalo and birds, including eagles, falcons, blue backed swallows and kingfishers. It was such good fun being with Catherine and Valerie. They are very funny and we got on so well together. We walked back to Batutumonga and, rather than take the bemo all the way, we decided to walk part of the way back to Rantepao by heading South to Tikala via the village of Pana. Met a lad called Rema on the way and he seemed (and initially was) very helpful and friendly – he showed us Torajan houses, rice barns, grave sites, stone graves and both tree graves and baby graves, along what was a very scenic walk. Unfortunately, the lad spoilt it for us at the end by demanding cigarettes or money for being our guide. Maybe we were gullible, but since all three of us had experienced almost universal kindness and hospitality, with only the merest hint of commercialism, in our various Indonesian adventures, it came as quite a shock to us to discover that his friendship came at a price and we felt as though we had been deceived. In any event, the track was very clear and we had known our way back, so if he had ever suggested that he could be our guide, we would probably have declined. We refused to pay him anything. He quickly became upset and shouted at us and when we walked away he followed us still shouting. He continued to follow us for quite some distance and his persistence was worrying but I could also feel myself becoming angry as I became protective towards Catherine and Valerie. Eventually we lost him and walked back all the way to Rantepao. I reckon we walked at least 14 miles but it could have been closer to 17 miles. My legs told me that we had walked quite a distance. Maybe they were tired, or maybe the experience with the lad had taken the shine off the day, but Catherine and Valerie were quieter than usual in the evening.

Tuesday 1st June – PADI Party Meeting

Woke up and was very loose again, but it was not at all painful. After a long, lazy and deliberately light breakfast I went into town with Catherine and Valerie. As soon as I arrived there I felt loose again, and, having diplomatically told the girls I'd left something back in my room, I managed to collar a becak driver to take me back to the homestay as quickly as possible. When I accepted his first price without haggling, he hesitated, and momentarily seemed disorientated, which made me wonder if I wasn't going to find myself in the same impasse as Brian, when confronted by the ex-leper in the Monty Python film, 'Life of Brian'. Thankfully, however, he recovered his composure so quickly and then jumped so excitedly onto his becak that I couldn't help wondering if he had cottoned on to my predicament. Needless to say, I was in no position to stand on ceremony, so back we went, my mentor pedalling like fury, before I did what I had to do and hopped back onto the same becak for a more leisurely ride back into town. I wrote and sent 10 postcards today. Had a lazy wander back to – and then past – the homestay and wandered down to the river, where the scene was idyllic and very pretty.

Saw a hummingbird, herons, eagles with their eaglets, and a tiny lizard with a sapphire-blue fluorescent tail. Also saw chattering women and children washing clothes by the river. Catherine and Valerie are planning to leave tomorrow morning. I will probably leave to go to Sengkang on Thursday. I saw a Partai 41 rally parading through town today with what ominously seemed like army personnel (wearing army fatigues and red berets) also waving the same banner – the army are supposed to remain impartial. Somebody told me that Partai 41 would be in coalition with the Golkar party (the ruling party for the last 26 years) if they win enough seats. But then somebody else told me that they will not. At our hotel, there was a party meeting for PADI (I think Partai 4). I was welcome to observe and somebody happily pointed out that it was the first time that they had ever been able to have such a meeting so freely, explaining that previously they would have had to get permission from – and be heavily supervised by – the police.

Wednesday 2nd June – Tau Tau

Catherine and Valerie left today. Circumstances contrived to mean that the departure wasn't too emotional. Today I had planned to view the famous tau tau at Lemo and I was hoping to get out early but as usual the staff at the homestay were very slow in sorting out breakfast, and new guests arrived which slowed them down even more. Consequently, my mind was distracted at the point when the girls left. In any event the departure was not the same as when Nur and I went our separate ways last week, not just because my relationship with Nur had been different, but also because I am as sure as I can ever be that I will meet up again with the girls somewhere in the future, if not in Indonesia then back in Europe.

I made my way by bemo to Lemo, 8 miles South of Rantepao, where I had a 15-minute walk after being dropped off on the main road.

Tau tau are effigies of the deceased, which are traditionally placed at the entrance to caves in which the dead are deposited within their wooden coffins. I had read somewhere that, although the Torajans' deep convictions regarding funerals and death date back to pre-history, most scholars suggest that tau tau were introduced relatively recently in the 19th Century. Torajans believe that the dead can take their possessions with them to the afterlife, and traditionally the deceased have been entombed with their possessions, with the inevitable consequence that the tombs have been the target for grave robbers. As a result, the custom evolved for coffins to be placed in locations that were difficult to get to, the preferred venue of choice apparently being high, vertical cliff faces. Sometimes, the coffins would be placed in caves hewn out of the rock, with some caves dug deeply to accommodate whole families, whilst others literally hung from the cliff face.

At the same time tau tau were created so as to be strategically placed in front of the caves to provide an extra layer of protection of the tombs and to ward off bandits and chancers. At the time, I couldn't help wondering, however, if the tau tau were counter-productive in that they represented some kind of advertisement for those on the lookout for such tombs, particularly since I also learnt that not only were they once produced mainly for the wealthy, to reflect the status and wealth of the deceased, but that the quality of the tau tau varied according to how wealthy the deceased and his surviving relatives were. My thoughts at the time were that a wandering thief didn't need to look too hard to find potential targets, since the sight of tau tau, and especially well-heeled ones, represented the equivalent of a flashing neon sign. I concede, however, that maybe I was looking through faithless, narrow-minded, Western eyes, since to most Indonesians, the spirits protecting the afterlife are a power not to be meddled with.

Traditionally, the tau tau were simply carved, representing only the gender of the deceased. However, in more recent years they have become more and more elaborate, actually attempting to imitate the likeness of the deceased. Some wear clothing or colours associated with the deceased, or are carved to reflect some physical element, such as wrinkles or scars. The types of wood used for the effigies, and what they are clothed in, also reflect the status and wealth of the deceased. Tau tau of the wealthy would generally be made of wood from the jackfruit tree, whereas the less wealthy would have their tau tau made from bamboo. It was no wonder that the finely decorated, intricately carved tau tau before me were the primary source for so many postcards, because they were very impressive and the quality was clearly very high.

The reason why I had been hoping to arrive early was because I had read that the tau tau at this location are best seen when the morning sun is low and shining directly onto them. Unfortunately, by the time of my arrival it was true that most of them were partially in shade, but, whilst I might have lost the opportunity to capture the perfect photograph, their haunting beauty was in no way diminished. High up on the cliff face were several balconies, with rows of well-kept, well-dressed figures standing and facing out to the valley below, many of them with arms outstretched as if in welcome. Some wore the traditional kepi, most wore gleaming white tunics, and with their jet-black pupils set in broad white eyes, many had a beguiling hypnotic look to them. Beside the balconies small square wooden doors set into the sheer rock face signified that the coffins of the deceased were close by.

It was quiet when I first arrived at Lemo, and it was thankfully still quiet when I left. I had only seen a couple of locals milling around the base of the cliff whilst I was there. However, I had had a close shave because as I headed back along the path and was about halfway to the main road, a whole coach load of garrulous German tourists came marching by.

It was early in the day, so rather than go straight back to Rantepao, I decided to take a bemo to Sanggalla and from there to walk along country roads and tracks via the villages of Randanbatu, Labo, Palatokke and Kete Kesu, back to Rantepao. I was well rewarded.

The scenery was pretty. Within gently rolling hills a smattering of grazing buffalo roamed on emerald green pastures, which were punctuated every mile or so by small traditional Torajan villages. The air was pleasantly warm rather than stifling, and perfect for walking. The people I met were consummately friendly, with virtually every single person smiling and saying hello to me. On no less than three occasions I was offered – and accepted – invitations into family homes, where I was given tea or coffee, was bombarded with questions and where my hosts and I exchanged addresses. One of them even offered to cook me a meal but I politely declined. When I look back on it, a part of me thinks it strange that I should have declined the offer, because the opportunity to dine with a family in their own home would have been wonderful. However, when I think more closely about what was going through my mind at the time, I am reminded that the non-stop hospitality was becoming a bit too overwhelming, and I also considered that there wasn't much that I could offer in return. It wasn't as if I could entertain them with sparkling conversation because, although most of them spoke a little English, our topics of conversation in either language were exhausted within about five minutes. In any event the value lay in the fact they had offered in the first place.

At one of the villages I was taken to see more grave sites, but here the coffins were broken, lying on the ground at the base of cliffs, with the splintered wood of the coffins and the bones of the dead laying scattered all around. On one particular plank of rotting wood, what could have been a football team of 11 human skulls, minus their jaw bones, had been neatly placed in a row, all facing forward, in a kind of macabre beauty parade.

A massive PADI Party rally passed me twice today, firstly near Lemo and secondly as I was walking along the back roads. On both occasions, I was deep in countryside but bizarrely the people within the long convoy were as noisy as if they had been parading in the middle of town. I wondered if the show of exuberance was mainly for my benefit. They were particularly excited on the second occasion, in part I suspect because they recognised me from when they had driven past me before, since they acknowledged and waved at me like a long-lost friend. Although I've seen a wider cross-section of parties other than PADI here in Sulawesi, as compared to Bali or Java where they are dominant, if the size of the rallies is anything to go by PADI are still the most popular and should win by a landslide. We'll see.

Thursday 3rd June – Meeting Married Couple

Had changed my mind and decided to leave tomorrow so today was a lazy day. I gave myself a Reiki in the morning. I then went into town to get a ticket to Pare Pare, to get money and to buy other odds and ends. As I was wandering and ambled into a warung for a spot of nasi goreng, sitting in the same warung was the couple whose wedding I went to last Saturday. They recognised me straight away, as I did them, despite their lack of make-up. Having ordered my meal, they both smiled at me – both! – before they beckoned for me to sit with them whilst I waited for my lunch to arrive. Their names are Agus and Betty. They explained that they both live and work in Jakarta and they would be heading back there soon. However, they had come to Tana Toraja to be with their families and because they wanted to have a traditional Torajan wedding. I thanked them for sharing their special day with me and the girls, and I offered to send them copies of my photographs if any turn out to be okay. They gave me their address.

After my meal, I went for a walk out into the countryside and crossed over the river using a bridge that from a distance looked like it was two bridges. Back at the homestay in the evening I got talking to other people staying there. One was a long-haired bloke from England, whose name is Alex, and he was full of himself. I must confess that his Indonesian seemed to be very good, which I presume is why he thought he should intervene by rudely and arrogantly butting in when I was trying to talk Indonesian to somebody else. I tried to ignore him and just ride above it. I got talking to a couple who had arrived in the homestay a day or two ago, one being a British lad. With his bald, or perhaps shaven, head he appeared to be in his fifties but perhaps looks are deceptive because he was with a gorgeous Javanese girl called Rini, who looked to be around 30. She got talking to me a couple of days ago over breakfast. She is very unhappy because she is very bored.

She described herself as a city girl and – reminding me of (my cousin) _Stephanie – likes music, dancing, singing, drinking and more music. However, her boyfriend is currently contracted, I presumed for work, to stay here in quiet Tana Toraja for two years. I later discovered that they are in fact already married and have only been together for four months. I also later discovered that the lad is only 39. She made quite a fuss of me when in answer to her question I told her that I am a lawyer. At one point, she insisted that her husband should leave the area where we were sitting, in order for her and I to talk on our own in private (strange). He agreed (even stranger). I have the feeling that I haven't heard the last from her._

Friday 4th June – Leaving Tana Toraja

Finally left Rantepao today.

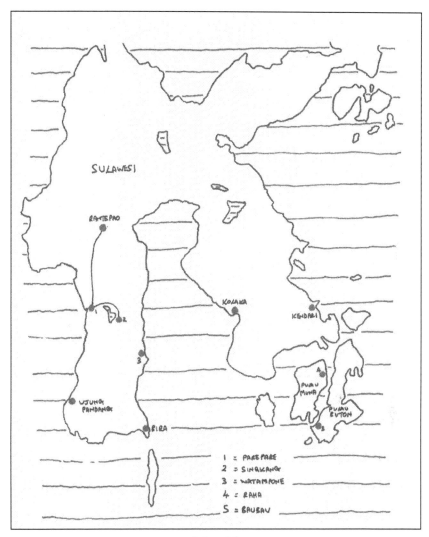

Map 25

There is a really irritating bloke called Alex – I mentioned him yesterday – who's English and so full of himself. He's obviously a seasoned traveller, knows all the guides and all the best places to visit (nothing wrong with that), but he loves people to know it (plenty wrong with that!). The staff were as usual very slow this morning and they were still sorting things out as I went for the bus. I received what at first glance seemed a whopping 700,000-rupiah bill last night. More than I thought. When I checked the figures, though, it turned out that they were accurate (and when I thought about it, it's only around £40 for eight nights' bed, breakfast and several evening meals, so I can't really complain). Got bus to Pare Pare, 5 hours – sat next to, and got friendly with, a German lad called Marko – he's been to Kalimantan (Borneo) and he's now off to Flores. I might see him later. Nice bloke. Then got bus after Pare Pare to Singkang, two hours. I arrived in good time in daylight. I was immediately collared by a guide – which for once I didn't mind because he seemed quite genuine, and since I didn't plan to stay here too long, I considered I could use him to help me quickly get my bearings and to make plans. I later met a New Zealand guy called James. He clearly loved to talk, but he turned out to be a very interesting bloke – has just come from Kalimantan, and has come up through Sulawesi from Ujung Pandang and Bone. I planned to head down to Bone later and got some tips from him. We walked up to the hill behind Sengkang and saw a good sunset and great views across the lake. I had a good meal in the evening. Saw many women wearing very brightly coloured sarongs today. It is possible that there is some sort of ceremony or celebration going on. It turned out that James and I are the only travellers in town. He plans to leave tomorrow morning and when he does so I will be on my own.

Saturday 5th June – Lake Tempe

I got up at a reasonable time and when I looked out of my homestay I saw the guide hanging around outside who had collared me yesterday when I first arrived in Singkang. I guessed he was probably waiting for me, and, true enough, when I popped outside after breakfast he invited me to use him as a guide today. For once I found the persistence of a guide more endearing than annoying and I agreed to use his services getting the price down to 35,000 rupiah. I met up with him about an hour later and we took a boat out onto the lake. We firstly went down the river and I couldn't believe how much flotsam was in the water. It reminded me in a way of the floating debris in the Yangtze but in this instance the rubbish was all natural material washed down by storms and heavy rains from the jungles upstream. The river seemed unusual in that it had a very wide mouth, but yet the flow was out of the lake not into it. We went past numerous stilt houses on the river, where the people are mainly Bugis. My guide informed me that each house has three levels, the upper representing sky, the middle air and the bottom earth. No mention was made of water, but being surrounded by the stuff I guess there was no need. Water in the lake apparently rises and falls regularly by quite a high margin. Saw many birds, including herons, egrets, cormorants, kingfishers and cranes. I saw people fishing, some with hand-nets and some with spears. We then went to the floating village – the bamboo houses really do float and I must admit that it seems to be quite a pleasant idea to live in a place that rocks very gently. I was introduced to a family in one of the houses who gave us lunch. We ate with our hands, the food comprising rice, fish, curry sauce, chilli sauce and fish eggs. It is a pity I am not a huge fan of fish!! Their cupboard-love cat snuggled up to my feet whilst I sat cross-legged on the floor of the floating house eating my fish. Evidently, he was a bigger fan of fish than me! In the evening, I wandered around the *small town, visited the impressive mosque and I went up the hill again to see the sunset, which was good. On reading one of my guidebooks, I realised that my Aussie visa must be used with a recognised airline which Merpati isn't so I may need to change my plans for how to get there.*

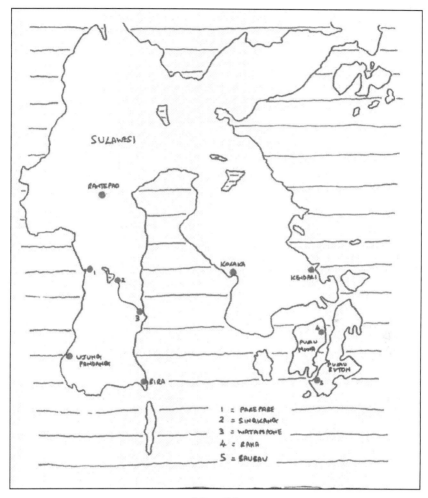

Map 26

Sunday 6th June – Meeting Four Bone Girls

Long wait for bemo, but eventually left Singkang today. Yesterday was overcast and pleasantly cooler. Today was back to normal and roastingly hot. Very rough road on journey to Bone (pronounced Bone-ay), also known as Watampone. After checking into a small but clean hotel, costing 30,000 Rp per night, I went for a wander. Found the statue of King Arung Palakka, which Kiwi James had said was quite good, but which, to my mind, was nothing to write home about. I then wandered the streets of Bone. The people are as friendly here as elsewhere in Indonesia, but very few can speak English. I decided to wander back to the main square, intending to grab a cooling beer and to sit back and have a read, when four girls started talking to me. Before too long we were surrounded by 15 kids. One of the girls invited me back to her house to meet her family, and to have coffee. I accepted. To be honest only one of them was really good looking (and she was the one that was least interested in talking to me) but in my heightened horny state I was flattered by the interest. As the four girls and I walked along the road back to her house, with the 15 kids in tow, it seemed as if everyone was hanging out of their houses and catcalling to the girls as we walked along. There is absolutely no chance of me staying in the background in this part of Indonesia. Back in the house, one of the girls kept saying that she loved me. (So soon!) Another young girl, probably about 20, who was a member of the household, was sitting on a chair openly breast feeding and the sight of her full and very gorgeous breasts, wasn't exactly helping. Having eventually extricated myself from the situation (by agreeing to meet up with them later) I later met and spoke to several police officers, who were very open and friendly. I was aware that tomorrow would be Election Day and when I mentioned this to them and wondered what they thought of it, they invited me to meet back up with them tomorrow when they proposed to talk more. I harboured hopes that I might be allowed to accompany them on Election Day.

<u>Monday 7th June – Election Day</u>

I am going through a phase in my travels where I am not getting much inspiration. In fact, a part of me is looking forward to getting to Australia, which is a bad sign because I don't want to waste my time in Indonesia. I think I will speed things up in Sulawesi and move on, possibly going back to Bali early if all else fails.

All I can say in hindsight is that I should have been careful about what I wished for. At the time, I perceived that the sights were getting less interesting, and that I hadn't had a really great day since the Torajan wedding, nine days previously. Looking back, it seems obvious to me now that I had been spoilt by so many interesting cultural experiences in Tana Toraja, so much so that anything thereafter was bound to be an anti-climax. However, it was also the case that, by travelling to areas less visited by travellers and tourists, I was more of a novelty for the indigenous population and virtually everyone noticed me. It also seemed to me that fewer people spoke English and, I suspected, were not fully literate, because when I produced a kamus they didn't seem to be able to use it which meant that each conversation consisted of the same basic questions. Additionally, the conversations were mostly one way because when I asked them a question they invariably were unable to reply and so I had the same question and answer session with each person over and over again. It's not that I didn't want to engage with everybody that I met – they were all so friendly and so well-meaning, and I was determined to show my appreciation – but 15 or 20 encounters each day going over the same questions was pretty draining.

I had been looking forward to this day, being election day, but it turned out to be a bit flat. The fact that it was made a national holiday did not help, because it meant that the roads were quiet and most places were shut. Additionally, I couldn't find the police officers that I had spoken to yesterday, so my self-delusional thinking that I could roam around with them like Alan Whicker, as if I was some kind of roving political analyst, did not come to fruition. To give myself the best possible chance of engaging with the voters, I wandered around the town, trying to find the voting areas, and in the course of the morning I found three. At each one of them I shyly didn't want to enter uninvited, so I hung around outside hoping somebody would engage with me. Despite the fact that most voting booths were very busy, nobody accosted me, and this was the case at all three areas. Typical, I thought, that no-one talks to you when you want them to do so. I went back and lazed around the hotel for an hour or so trying to find inspiration, but in the end, I decided that there was no point in hanging on just for the sake of it, so I decided to leave. I found a bemo to take me the short distance to Bajoe on the coast and from there I bought a ferry ticket to the port of Kolaka, situated on the West coast of the South-East tentacle of spider-shaped Sulawesi. I had read that ferries ran regularly from Bajoe, and, true enough, when I arrived at the terminal a boat was just about to depart. Having hurriedly purchased my ticket for the boat ride, and emerged the other side of the ticket booth, a young lad pointed to the boat, which was a tiny speck in the distance, with a three-kilometre-long jetty between me and it. Smoke coming from one of its funnels suggested it was ready to depart. There was no chance of catching it, at least that is what I thought, until another young lad beside me tugged on my rucksack and pointed to his motorbike. A perilous rickety bone-jangling journey then ensued, along narrow gang planks that felt like they would give way any moment, with me riding helmetless and pillion behind the lad, and laden with two rucksacks on a motorcycle that felt like it was running on airless tyres. It was lucky for the lad that I had tipped him before I got on the bike because I was in no state to think about it afterwards, when, with my teeth rattling in my brain, I just managed to clamber aboard the boat at the other end as it was about to cast off. Thankfully, it was a quiet boat trip and I arrived in Kolaka in the early hours of the morning.

Tuesday 8th June – Kendari Bay

Arrived in Kendari at about 7.15 in the morning after a very bumpy and uncomfortable bemo ride from Kolaka – had arrived there at around 2.10 am.

I was stuck in the back with my knees embedded in the front seat, and with my feet turned in pigeon toed and unable to move. I was tired, but I had nowhere to lean my head to try to get some sleep, whilst the man to my right was able to sleep and he was constantly falling against me throughout the journey. Found a hotel (33,000 Rp), and grabbed some sleep. Wandered later. Kendari Bay or harbour is quite attractive with the odd pinisi schooner dotted around. Kendari is known for not being discovered by the Dutch until some 200-odd years into their occupation because there is an island shielding it from view. The harbour area is quite extensive and I couldn't see out to open sea. It looked like the harbour was wholly enclosed. There were the usual smelly drains and constant shouts of, "Hello Mister," from kids, but I didn't have a decent conversation with anyone all day.

On the way back from the harbour I got talking to one girl who offered me a massage – she smokes, wears heavyish makeup and has scars on her face, but not entirely unattractive! I think the type of massage on offer was the more risky type, so it was easy to resist. Later telephoned the Australian Consulate in Bali, where they confirmed that Merpati airlines are definitely not on the ET & A Register and without a full visa I cannot enter via Kupang on Timor Island. Therefore, I must either go to Bali to get a visa or to fly from there to Australia. We'll see.

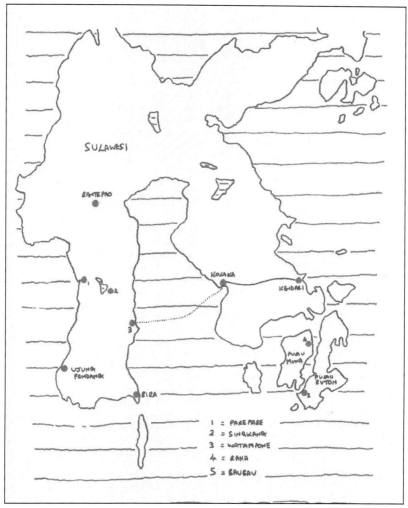

Map 27

Wednesday 9ᵗʰ June – Pushing Boat

Today was much more like it. After a slightly later start than planned I went first to the tourist office. They were quite helpful in confirming one or two details. Last night I had an accident through not quite getting to the toilet in time – luckily the bathroom floor was tiled! I don't feel ill, just loose and very quick.

Decided to go to Batu Gong Beach today. A brochure that I picked up described it as a silver white sand beach – on arrival it looked more like a dark grey or brown, but it *was still attractive nonetheless. Very quiet, very few people around – no tourists or travellers. A couple of young lads joined me, and one of them cracked open a fresh coconut – we drank the milk and then devoured the flesh. I was not sure if I should offer to pay for the coconut, but when I tried to do so he brusquely declined. Having thanked him, I walked barefoot along the beach, with the warm water lapping against my feet. I was joined by initially a few youngsters, but, like a pied piper, the crowd grew in size as I made my way along. I saw – and was able to observe close up – a group of thirty people from a nearby village trail fishing just offshore by dragging the nets along and onto the beach. Having sorted out the catch, one of them then invited me to sit in a canoe, whilst one of his colleagues paddled it. The canoe was fairly unstable, and I nearly capsized it with my lumbering weight as I clambered aboard. I then noticed that I had left my shoes on the beach but one of the villagers on shore had spotted them before I had a chance to say anything and, having picked them up, waded out into the water to bring them to me on the boat. We paddled along the edge of the beach for a couple of hundred yards and the lad pulled into a beach close to a village, where he dropped me off. Very soon I was surrounded by, I guess, 40 or 50 people, mostly kids, who had already been chattering away to me nineteen to the dozen, but when I pulled out my camera to take photographs they went absolutely mad. I got chatting to a mother and her two daughters and within minutes of speaking to her, two bananas and fresh drinking water had been produced for me. I made my way back along the beach and it started raining. A wiry middle-aged man, who had been pushing his bicycle along the beach, beckoned for me to join him. I followed him, not sure what to expect, but it turned out his intention was only to take some shelter under a tarpaulin tied up against a tree, and to invite me to shelter there with him. I had nothing that I needed specially to keep dry, the rain was warm and not particularly heavy, and my camera was stashed away protected deep inside my daypack. However, I was touched by this small but deeply thoughtful act of kindness shown to me, a total stranger. I felt especially pleased that I was able to return the favour, when a short while later he needed to bring his boat up from the beach further onto dry land. When he went out to collect his boat I joined in to help push it, as did a couple of other locals when they saw what we were trying to do. My help seemed to aid them a lot and their gratitude was very heart warming. They spoke no English. It was simply their smiles that told me all I needed to know. The man who had given me shelter then walked with me to the village to show me where to get the bus back to Kendari. He didn't once ask me for money or anything else.*

I should mention that not one person asked me for money today, from the man with the coconut, the lad paddling the canoe, the lad who collected my shoes from the shore, the mother with the bananas and water, to the man who sheltered me from the rain. Great day.

Thursday 10th June – Hit-and-Run Accident

A fantastic day that ended very unfortunately. Received a telephone call last night to my hotel room after I had gone to bed from an evidently gay man who offered to give me a good time! I had no idea who he was and found it disconcerting that he should know that I was staying here alone. I could only guess that someone in reception had passed on the fact that I was staying here.

I arrived early at the harbour in Kendari and searched for a boat to charter for the day and, having checked with a couple of boat owners, I arranged to charter one for 70,000 Rp. I had been spending relatively little and budgeting well, particularly in areas in Indonesia well away from the tourists. I had become used to local prices and 70,000 Rp seemed a lot of money at the time, but it's a mark of how cheap it was at the time to travel around Indonesia since it was still less than £5.00. I clearly wasn't doing too badly. The boat was a dual-armed outrigger, with one long narrow canoe, balanced by two bamboo arms and powered either by sail or by motor depending on the prevailing weather conditions. My 'crew' consisted of two lads, one of whom was in his early 20s who spoke only a little English but who was full of chat, who compensated for the other lad who was slightly older, definitely deaf and probably mute.

Using the motor, and having navigated beyond the straits between Kendari and the island sheltering it, the crew headed South on a two-hour ride across open sea to an area called Lapuko Bay, which sported a beautiful white sand beach and crystal-clear water. They dropped me off on the beach and I went off on my own to wander around nearby Lapuko village, which itself was very interesting, but I had read about an impressive 100-metre-tall waterfall just inland from the village, which I thought would be good to visit and I understood that I would be able to find transport within the village to get to it. However, by the time of my arrival at around midday I discovered that there were no more bemos and I would have had to have chartered my own transport to get there and back. Although it would have been nice to have seen it I wasn't overly bothered and I headed back to meet up again with my crew. I suggested to them that we should return to Kendari via Pulau Hari, reputed to be a beautiful uninhabited island. My crew agreed.

Pulau Hari turned out to be a tiny speck of an island, measuring only 50 metres across, and the epitome of tropical paradise, with its untrodden bleach-white sand, lop-sided palm trees lolling obliquely over the beach and fronted by a mirror-like turquoise-blue lagoon. The scene was complete when a couple of raucous red and blue macaws flew out from the palm trees. The island was protected by a coral reef offshore producing glassy, clear, calm water within the lagoon between the beach and the reef edge. The lads stayed on the boat whilst I hopped off and wandered around the island imagining that I was Robinson Crusoe. The only footprints that I discovered on this island turned out to be my own. I have no doubt that the primary reason why I found the notion of remaining on this island to be so idyllic and paradisiacal was because, subconsciously, I knew that I had a boat waiting to take me back to (relative) civilisation. Had I been completely stranded on the island it would have been a very different story.

The lads took me back to Kendari and, having thanked them for their help and paid them a small tip, I took the opportunity to make enquiries at the harbour about onward boats heading South along the coast. I discovered that tomorrow there would be a boat heading to Pulau Buton, my intended next destination. It seemed ideal. I then ambled back to my hotel. It was dusk, with the tropical sun fading fast, and my mind was distracted by idyllic images of the tropical island paradise, by thoughts about leaving tomorrow, and by what I would have for tea, when I was suddenly struck from behind. A vehicle hit me so violently to my lower back that I was sent flying along the road. I had been walking on the gravelly, dusty area off to the side of the road, well away from any danger, or so I thought, and as I was shunted forward I put out my right hand instinctively to break my fall. The result was that I effectively slid five or six feet along the gravel on my hands, elbows and knees. In that instant, the shock dulled any pain and when I looked up to see what had hit me I saw that a pick-up truck had stopped ten yards up the road as if to check to see what had happened. As I gingerly got up, however, the driver of the truck clearly had second thoughts about remaining any longer, because he took off up the road, accelerating fast. Instinctively, and illogically, I jumped up and ran off up the road after the truck, but the realisation that I was never going to catch it kicked in a split second later and I stopped. The moment I did so was when the pain truly kicked in. As various parts of my body had been scraped along the gravelly road, flesh had been removed from my left hand, my right elbow, both knees and my right ankle, leaving bleeding open wounds. The skin, pock-marked with gravel and covered with dust, was in places literally hanging off and the exposed areas were starting to bleed profusely.

Straight away half a dozen people came over to attend to me. A couple of men who were talking to each other were animatedly pointing up the road towards the pick-up truck that was now in the distance. Then a middle-aged man and a young woman, who I took to be father and daughter, took me by the arm and led me across the road to a seat in front of their vegetable stall where they could assess the damage. Everybody seemed genuinely shocked at what had happened and all were concerned and very supportive. Having sat me down to look at my wounds one of them gestured to another man who was leaning on his bicycle trishaw, whereupon they led me to the bicycle and, before I knew it, the man was cycling up the road with me. My driver took me to a police station and there a police officer in a khaki uniform seemed to take control of the situation and, having seen my injuries, and having peremptorily said the single word, "Come," to me, he took me across the road from the station to a nearby medical centre. There the police officer spoke to a member of staff and then turned to me and said in English that I should return to the station and speak to him later once I had been cleaned up. At the medical centre up to four members of staff attended to me. I was taken to a bed where a couple of nurses started to clean the wounds by removing the grit and stone with tweezers before using sterilised pads to deep clean. The wounds stung with high-intensity pain as the antiseptic was being applied but it was the sort of pain that made me instinctively believe that it must be doing me a power of good. They decided against using stitches, relying only on steri-strips to be applied to the worst places. I was then given an anti-tetanus injection. I advised one of the nurses that I had already received the usual precautionary jabs back in the UK, which had included tetanus, but the nurse advised that I should have it again just in case.

It turned out that, although they looked very nasty, and were extremely sore, my wounds were relatively superficial and something for which a few days' rest wouldn't do any harm. It could so easily have been far more serious. The real danger, however, lay in the fact that the wounds were deep and raw and in this tropical, dusty, insect-rich climate they had the potential for becoming infected.

I then went back over the road to the police station where I met up with the policeman and I gave him my account of the incident. He advised me that there was little chance of finding the pick-up truck, which was no more than I had expected, but he promised that he would do what he could. The police station was only half a mile away from my hotel but the police officer offered to drive me to it. I declined, telling him that he had been too kind already, and advising him that the walk to stretch my legs and get them moving would probably do me some good.

Back at the hotel I carefully showered myself before applying more of the iodine solution, which the medical staff had given to me, to my wounds. As I laid back on my bed to Reiki myself I considered the day's events and two things struck me. The first was that, in effect, I had two memories of the incident, the original one where I was taken completely by surprise by being struck from behind and the other where my subconscious looked round and saw the pick-up truck about to hit me immediately before the collision. Remembering how I had responded, I realised that my subconscious memory had instinctively reacted a split second before the collision occurred, leading me to use my left hand to cling tightly onto my rucksack and allowing me to immediately put out my right hand to break my fall.

The second thought that occurred to me was how caring and friendly the people had been today in the aftermath of the accident, from the eyewitnesses to the accident, to the rickshaw driver, to the police officer and to the nurses at the medical centre. Needless to say, at the time I had thanked all of them for their help, but the more I thought about it the more I considered that mere words could not express sufficiently the depth of my gratitude. Perversely their kindness and hospitality had been so overwhelming that it turned an adverse experience into a truly positive one.

Friday 11th June – Speaking to Girls on Bus

Very sore in the morning – had four main injuries – cut to arm and cut to my knee, both of which appear OK, but there are two separate cuts to my right ankle which I had covered and which looked very pussy. Overnight I had left the two lesser injuries open but covered the other two. Those two looked worst. I thought about yesterday's events and my first thought when I was struck was that it had been a deliberate act – that was my first instinct – and in fact for the last split second before it struck me I have a memory of it coming towards me. However, looking back on it I'm not so sure now that it was deliberate and it could possibly have been an accident. In the driver's defence, I was wearing a dark blue t-shirt at a time when it was already well into dusk and, as is common with most places in Indonesia, there are no street lights, and as is equally common (and as my second memory of the incident attested) the truck might not have had its lights on.

Not liking the look of my right ankle in particular, I decided that I should take myself back to the hospital to have the wounds checked just to be on the safe side. The nurse looked at my ankle and cleaned them up again just to be sure but she said that they should be fine. It was then that I spotted a fellow patient sitting in a chair counting out money, and it suddenly dawned on me that, of course, I should have paid for the medical expenses and treatment that I received the previous day. Coming from the UK, it hadn't even crossed my mind. I went to the reception desk to enquire about it, fully intending to pay, but when I asked the middle-aged woman sitting there how much I needed to pay for my treatment on both days, she smiled and informed me that the police officer had paid for all my medical expenses the previous day. To say that I was dumbstruck is an understatement, and I have to confess that I was very moved. His kindness and generosity was overwhelming, not least because I knew that the average Indonesian's wages were very low, and I could not imagine a police officer's salary being any different. It also struck me that nobody had told me, and, but for my last-minute conversion, I might never have known. Indeed, in a society where medical treatment is never free, I wondered what the officer must have thought of me when I hadn't even mentioned it to him back at the station. I immediately went to the police station to search out my benefactor and I soon found him. I thanked him profusely and tried to persuade him to let me pay him back, but he was not open to persuasion. Some consolation was gained, because the beaming smile on his face, when I shook his hand and said goodbye, suggested that his real reward was simply to have received some recognition.

In addition to the four main injuries I also have a bruised backside, have scraped my left arm and have bad grazes on my left shin. However, on balance, I reckon my body's in pretty good shape to have survived how I did with relatively so little injury. I was in shock yesterday for a while whilst the adrenalin kicked in. Seeing the vehicle bear down on me in the course of my second memory of the incident is a recurring nightmare. Decided the wisest thing would be to stay put today. Did several Reikis to myself, both local to injuries and full body. Seemed to help. Decided to take my mind off things by going on the bus around Kendari Bay to West Kendari and I got chatting to two very beautiful girls on the bus who, just before they got off, invited me to meet up with them later outside the tourist information office. I had a feeling that they wouldn't show and, once I had wandered around the market and mosque and made my way back, they indeed did not turn up.

Saturday 12th June – Meeting Fitria

The pendulum's swinging again and today has been a busy 'happening' sort of day. Although they contained all the colours in the rainbow the scars on my ankle looked much better today – they seemed to have dried out and scabbed up nicely. Got up in good time, had a quick piece of breakfast and headed out to the harbour to get a ticket for the boat. I wanted to go to Pulau Buton and decided that I would take the fast boat. When I turned up I was pleasantly surprised that the staff had reserved a ticket in my name. I had, of course, made enquiries two days ago about leaving, so whether the ticket had always been an open one, or whether the staff had somehow been told about my accident on Thursday and had made some allowance for my situation, I would probably never know.

I discovered that the boat would first visit the island of Pulau Muna, a sister island to Pulau Buton, and I made the last-minute decision to stay for at least one night in the town of Raha on Pulau Muna, before later moving on to Buton. The fast boat turned out to be a jet boat and did indeed move very quickly, the only disappointment being that it was not possible to go outside, since the roof was closed up. However, I could still just about see through the thick tinted glass and the entire coast of South East Sulawesi seemed to be one long stream of banana plants, palm trees, rocky outcrops and white sanded beaches. At Raha I made my way to Hotel Ilham where the room was 25,000 Rp without aircon. I then wandered around the town to get my bearings and as I did so I was as usual accosted by several indigenous people including one gorgeous girl, with an hourglass figure, who went by the name of Fitria. She told me that it was her birthday today and she invited me to come to her party this evening. I readily agreed, not expecting the invitation to be honoured. In the afternoon, I took a bemo out to visit the lagoons of Napabale and Motonunu. Both are inlets from the sea with only a very narrow channel separating them from the open sea.

Consequently, the water inside the lagoons is very calm, warm, very clear and amazingly blue. Having been dropped off by the bemo and as I was heading towards one of the lagoons four middle aged ladies were chatting away drinking beer under the shade of a shack. They didn't seem too interested in my arrival but as I was about to go past them one of them abruptly said to me, "You want boat?" Turning on my heels, I agreed to hire a boat – a skipper and his son came with it – and for about an hour I was kayaked round the interlinked lagoons and then out through the narrow channel to the open sea.

When I came back I was debating whether to risk it by going for a swim in the water, because I was concerned about whether immersing my open wounds in the water so soon after the accident was a good idea. However, I decided that the salty water was bound to do them good and, in any event, the water was simply too inviting to ignore. When I came out of the water the wounds on my right ankle seemed to be worse at first but once they dried out they looked a lot better. As I made my way back past the four still-chatting ladies and on through the village to find a bemo, several people, mainly children, started to follow me until at one point there must have been up to 30 people following me.

In the evening, I made my way to the street where Fitria had said that she lived, and to my surprise there waiting for me was Fitria. She seemed very pleased to see me. She took me to her house, which was nearby. Several of Fitria's friends and family were present too, but the get together was not really a party, at least not to these European eyes. There was no drinking or music or food, just a group of people sitting around chatting. She spoke a little English and the kamus helped us further. Fitria was clearly very literate. We were chatting away and were having a good in-depth conversation and I cannot deny that I was warming to her, when all of a sudden she declared that she loved me and wanted to be my girlfriend. I was deeply flattered, and, despite the impetuosity of her pronouncement, I was very tempted to change my travel plans. She was after all very beautiful. I hadn't given much thought to her age, and, if I had have done, I would have placed her at mid-20s, but at one stage, however, she told me that she was 17, whereupon I told her that I was 28 (oops!). Although I was still deeply flattered that a sweet 17-year-old should show any attention towards me, the knowledge that she was less than half my age was probably the wake-up call that I needed to tread a little more warily and not commit to any alternate plans just yet. When I tried to take some photographs of her she seemed to shy away.

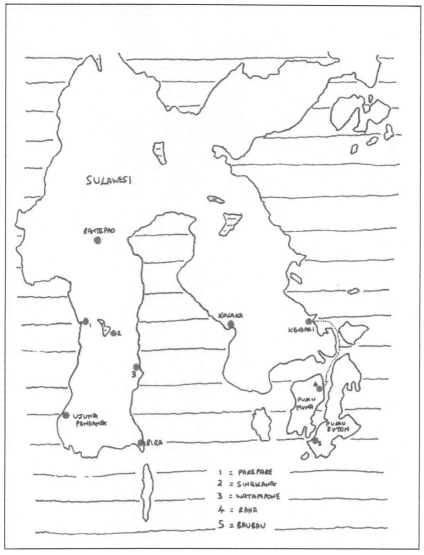

Map 28

A little while later, when I pointed out to her that with my visa running out I would have to leave the island fairly soon, to my amazement she started crying. If I needed any more reminding about how young and immature she was then that was it. I cannot deny that I was very attracted to her, with her beaming smile, her beautiful dark brown eyes and with her very full figure, but I considered that the two or three hours that I would spend talking with her this evening were likely to be the sum total of our 'relationship'.

Later when I was about to leave I motioned to kiss Fitria on her cheek but she pulled away saying that she could only do so if and when we were married. Before I left she asked me to promise to meet up with her tomorrow evening. She told me that she had work to do during the daytime but would like to see me at least one more time before I leave. Although I didn't say so to Fitria, I had intended to move on to Pulau Buton tomorrow. I will postpone it for one day but I will definitely leave on Monday.

Sunday 13th June – Meeting Aba

I hadn't been able to find any postcards so I couldn't send any to Robbyne. On the whole, my injuries seemed a lot better including those around my right ankle but the wound still occasionally weeps, which is a bit worrying. Good day. Pulau Muna is famous for its horse fighting and yesterday I was advised that there would be horse fighting taking place today in the nearby village of Masalili. The village was tricky to get to, and when I arrived it turned out that the information that I received yesterday was false and I would not see any horse fighting. In one way I was mightily relieved, since although I thought that I ought to see it, I had read that the 'sport' can be rather cruel. Went wandering through and then beyond Masalili. It didn't take long for me to be surrounded by large groups of people (I counted at one stage 35). You certainly cannot afford to be shy in Indonesia. Several kind people showed me the way to the top of a high hill where there were great views down to the lagoons at Napabale, where I had swum yesterday, and across the narrow straits separating Pulau Muna from Pulau Buton. I effectively passed through the village of Masalili twice today. When I passed through it the first time I got talking to a pretty girl who said that she hoped to see me later. When I returned to Masalili I met up with her again. She introduced herself as Aba, so I gave her my name and we sat down on a rickety wooden bench outside her house to talk.

Aba's English was reasonable, so with the combination of her English and my Indonesian we had a decent conversation that went well beyond the usual: "Hello, mister. Where are you from? Are you married?" In the course of the conversation, I told her about my encounter with the pick-up truck two days previously and showed her my battle scars, whereupon she told me that she too had recently had a bad accident. In her case she had come off a motorbike and hurt her leg. When she rolled up her trousers and showed me the injury on her leg I couldn't prevent myself from gasping. There was a large hole in her calf – big enough to be able to insert a golf ball – that seemed to be oozing yellow pus. When I asked her if she had been to see a doctor she said that she hadn't. She blanked the question when I asked her why not, but when I persevered and asked her a second time she said that it was because she had no money. I was shocked. Normally, I would diplomatically shy away from any demonstration of my relative wealth, but this time I was determined to right an injustice, and, perceiving that Aba would be too embarrassed to actively aid me to help her, I suggested that she should wait there. I made my way to the heart of the village and engaged in conversation with a middle-aged couple who, in answer to my question, advised me that there *was* a doctor in the village and they pointed to where I should go. I went back to Aba and offered to take her. She initially declined looking obviously embarrassed, but I insisted and she eventually agreed. When we arrived at the surgery – a ramshackled hut – the doctor wasn't present, so we waited outside. However, in the time that I was there, he didn't turn up and time was fast approaching when I would have to leave to catch my connections back to Raha. Consequently, I asked Aba how much she anticipated it would cost and she advised me that it would be 5,000 Rp, whereupon I gave her 10,000 Rp to cover the expenses just in case. She was very pleased, and clearly very touched, as tears welled up in her eyes. To her 10,000 Rp was clearly a small fortune, but it represented less than 60 pence in English money. Although I was pleased that I had made somebody very happy, I was all too aware that for me the sum represented about three per cent of my daily budget, and I couldn't help feeling a little fraudulent.

In the evening, I met up as arranged with Fitria and, if anything, we got on even better than we did the previous night. Fitria wore a miniskirt revealing athletic, bronzed, shapely legs. She might have been only 17, but she had the fully developed body of a girl ten years her senior. I knew full well, though, that unless or until we were married the goods on show were only for window shopping. We ate out at a local warung. Part way through, she said she would like to go the local *Toko* (shop) where she hoped that I would buy her a present. I had no problem buying her something as a memento but, as we wandered around the Toko I became concerned at the prices of the items that she was looking at. With the intention of putting a realistic limit on her spending, I decided that I would offer to give her 50,000 Rp, thinking that was generous enough, so that she could use it to buy what she wanted. Although she thanked me, it was pretty half-hearted and she pointed to a pair of shoes that she wanted, where the label read 88,000 Rp. I tried to explain to her that unfortunately my budget could not stretch that far, but she didn't seem overly pleased, even when I handed over the 50,000 Rp in cash to her. She put the money in her bag, and we left the Toko empty handed. As I walked her back to her house in stony silence, it did not go unnoticed that I had given her five times more money than I had given to Aba. The lukewarm response from Fitria in relation to her desire to purchase a pair of shoes was in stark contrast to the joyous reaction from Aba much earlier in the day, when I had practically forced her to obtain the medical treatment that she so clearly had needed.

Monday 14th June – Meeting Neny and Family

Left Raha in the morning. Fitria had said last night that she'd meet me today. I expected her to come to my hotel but she did not turn up. As I was about to board my boat in the harbour, the thought did cross my mind that I might have been mistaken and that she might have expected me to go to hers. I am quite sure that wasn't the arrangement, but either way we didn't meet up. Maybe it was better this way. Leg better in the morning.

Went by fast boat to Bau Bau in Pulau Buton. Got to Bau Bau at 12.30 pm and tried three hotels; the third was the best. Then went wandering. Got ticket for the Pelni ferry ship leaving on Wednesday at around 4.00 pm from Bau Bau to Ujung Pandang (despite several people assuring me that there was no such boat). Found the Kantor Pos (the Indonesian Post Office) but they had no postcards. Walked to Fort Keraton with the intention of visiting the Wolio Museum – which is the location of the palace in the book 'Ring of Fire.' On my way up to the fort I stopped and spoke to a girl called Neny, who's aged 19 and is very beautiful (it is becoming very repetitive but she really is). She spoke reasonable English and was very friendly. I said my goodbye and continued to the fort on my own. I was a bit too late to go into the museum so I decided to return and try again tomorrow. Having left the Fort, I retraced my steps to head back into town and on the way discovered Neny who was waiting for me where she had left me. She offered to walk with me back into town. She invited me back to her house to meet her family and I readily agreed. There I did indeed meet her family – all 12 of them – and they gave me tea, coconut biscuits and homemade popcorn. They were very nice and a lovely family. Arranged to meet up with Neny again tomorrow. In the evening, I talked to many people at a warung. Again, got talking to several beautiful girls.

Tuesday 15th June – Meeting Neny Again

Had nasi goreng for breakfast – very good. Managed to buy a couple of postcards at the Fort yesterday so I went into town and posted a card to Robbyne. Then made my way back to the Wolio Museum – popping into Neny's house on the way. Nobody was in.

I carried on to the museum, which was so-so – good collection of photographs, some swords, emblems, garments and what looked like long jousting poles. I left the museum and was wandering back into town when I saw a familiar figure in the distance who turned out to be Neny. It was such a huge thrill that she had taken the time to come and find me.

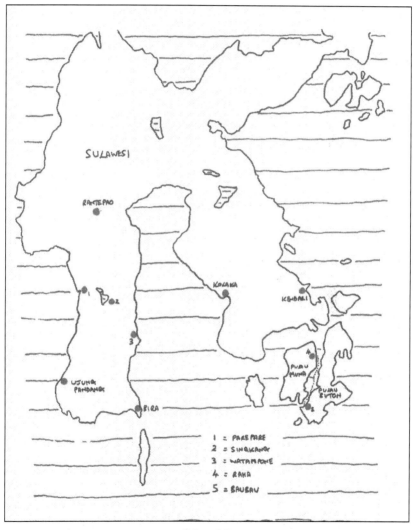

Map 29

I had already observed in my diary that just about every girl that I had met in this part of the world was beautiful, but it was absolutely true, from the flirty girls on the bus in Kendari, to gorgeous Fitria (who in her mind I was to all intents and purposes probably already engaged to), to pretty Aba, and to the cheeky girls who I had spoken to in the warung last night. Neny was no exception. She was fresh-faced, with an engaging, beaming smile, revealing perfect white teeth, and possessed high cheekbones and dark attentive eyes. When I first met her, she was wearing a crisp, clean, white t-shirt with a 'USA' emblem printed on it, the whiteness accentuating the golden-brown soft skin of her smooth neck and arms. There was never ever any hint of romance – Neny had mentioned early on that she had a boyfriend in the army – but the warmth of her welcome and the sincerity behind her smile were engaging and endearing. Having been bombarded in recent days by one beautiful girl after another, I was beginning to understand the warning given to Lorne and Lawrence Blair prior to their arrival in this very town, as described in 'Ring of Fire' (part of which I quoted earlier, but which is worth repeating here):

"...our crewmates warned us about the Butonese girls' reputation as practitioners of a dangerous form of magic which could trap a man on their island for ever; then they disappeared ashore into the backstreets. Going ashore ourselves, we soon realised that the girls' magic was of a straightforward kind. Almost without exception, they were breathtakingly beautiful."

The Blair brothers had also talked about the extremely hospitable treatment shown to them by their hosts here in Bau Bau:

"...our arrival was cause for celebration, and on the very first afternoon we were whisked away ... to stay in the comfort of the sultan's guesthouse; [we were told that], "everyone in Buton has noticed your arrival – since World War Two only four other Westerners have been here before you." Over the days that followed their hospitality knew no bounds. They drove us as far as the mud roads would allow in the royal land-rover, and down to the bay where a pearl-oyster hatchery was being tried for the first time; and at night there were more festivities, and endless delectable maidens vying for our attentions. On the fourth day, they took us up to Wolio, the old fortress that sprawled across two hill-tops overlooking Bau Bau. We had often seen its crumbling ramparts from a distance, and had assumed it was Dutch, but now learnt that it had been built by the islanders, long before the Europeans."

232

I had no doubt that since the Blair brothers' visit 20 or so years previously, there had probably been a few more Western visitors to this island over and above the original six referred to, but in many ways very little had changed. The fort was still crumbling away, the girls were still very beautiful and alluring, and the people were very hospitable. Indeed, the hospitality shown by Neny's family to me was only just beginning.

We went back to Neny's house, arriving at just after 12. I had read about a picturesque beach just a little South of Bau Bau, called Nirwana – pronounced Nirvana – Bay, which I wanted to visit and when I mentioned this to Neny and her family they said they had coincidentally been planning to go there today. Nirwana Bay was clearly the go-to place for people living in Bau Bau, so I wondered whether this bay was the location of the pearl-oyster hatchery described by the Blair brothers. Neny's father said that they were planning to leave at around 2.00 pm. It wasn't explicit in their conversation that I was welcome to join them, but when I tactically suggested going on my own and meeting up with them later, they soon made it clear that their plans had included me. They informed me that they had already prepared a picnic lunch and had taken it as practically a given that I would join them. I had no intention of disappointing them. I had taken with me the photograph of my nan, and, whilst we were waiting I showed it to Neny and her family. Neny's gran in particular was pleasantly surprised to learn that we in the West are capable of having a deep attachment to our grandparents too.

Indonesian rubber time kicked in and we eventually left at around 3.25 pm. All the family came too, including mum, dad, gran, sister, a niece, a nephew and half a dozen cousins and we all piled into a single bemo. When Neny's older sister – aged 34, mother of two, and also very good looking (no surprise there, considering the extensive genepool of talent in this corner of Indonesia) – talked to me, she did so with a cheeky broad smile and such a twinkle in her eye that I was convinced she was flirting with me. Certainly, the father of the two appeared not to be on the scene! Nirwana Beach lived up to its name and was indeed very beautiful, with soft white sand, and ubiquitous leaning palm trees, but it started to cloud over just as we arrived. Nevertheless, it remained pleasantly warm, and my swim in the sea did my injuries the world of good. On the previous day, I had told Neny about my accident, but I hadn't mentioned this to her family and it became clear that neither had she, because when I emerged from the sea and they saw my injuries, they were clearly very shocked. Neny's mum, in particular, made quite a fuss of me, and I have to confess that – mothering me like a poor little soldier – I did not find the attention unwelcome, and I shamelessly lapped it up.

The lunch (or rather supper, by the time we ate it) included several fish dishes, which, despite my relative aversion to fish, were extraordinarily tasty. Between us thereafter we devoured several pomelos, which were delicious and very juicy. The younger members of Neny's family had seemed rather star-struck in my presence when they had first met me, but as the afternoon wore on they clearly relaxed and there was much singing and joking throughout the entire return journey. Having arrived back in town with her family, Neny asked to see me again the next day before I was due to leave on the late afternoon ferry.

I was on such a high at the way in which I had been accepted into Neny's family, and having had such an enjoyable day, I wasn't ready to retire back to my hotel just yet. My meander around town did nothing to help because, as I did so, I met and engaged in conversation with so many more ultra-friendly Butonese people that by the time I arrived back at my hotel my head was still buzzing and it was quite a while before I could fall sleep.

Wednesday 16th June – Meeting Rahma and Others

Today is my mum's 60th birthday. Having packed up most of my things I had several hours to kill until my boat was due to leave later on in the afternoon. I went into town to meet up with Neny as arranged. We then went down to the harbour as Neny said she had heard that "some big fish" had earlier been sighted there. Unfortunately, we saw nothing. When Neny asked around to try to find out what sort of fish had been seen, we discovered that the animals were whale sharks no less – only the biggest fish on the planet – and there were up to five of them in the harbour not a day or two before.

The jetties and foreshore around the harbour were very busy, so Neny and I left to find some privacy. We had a good chat, and later we had some lunch. Despite the age difference Neny and I had got on very well from the first time that we had met and, although she was very pretty and bubbly, I had only ever thought of her as a friend. She told me over lunch that she is hoping to see her boyfriend this coming Friday. It was very sad when we eventually had to say goodbye. I agreed to send her some of my photographs when I get back to the UK. She hugged and held me tight for a few seconds before pulling away. Just before leaving, a tear started to run down her face as she then affectionately kissed me on the cheek. It was hard for me not to do the same.

Having returned to the hotel to take a shower and collect my things I went back down to the harbour at around 3 o'clock to wait, with the boat due at around 4 o'clock. However, it didn't show until 6.30. In the meantime, several more people came and talked to me. At one point, I was talking and joking with five young girls – all good fun. At least it was fun to begin with but I was soon surrounded by a large crowd of people, many of them children, who all wanted to talk to me and pretty much all at the same time. Not wanting to offend anybody, I politely responded to every question put to me, but it was actually becoming quite tiring and the five girls could see what was happening and were laughing at my predicament and teasing me. Having exhausted their repertoire of questions, I managed to shake off most of the kids and the group left, leaving me to talk to the five girls, whose names were Yuli, Rahma, Rima, Yana and Mila. We chatted for two or three hours. At one point 23-year-old Rahma declared that she loved me. Although Rahma was attractive and I had great fun doing my share of teasing and flirting back to her, I think, however, that I got on best with the youngest and smallest girl, Yana, because she was so funny and always laughing and just so sweet. I learnt that all five girls are Muslim refugees from Ambon. I had met many other refugees in Bau Bau, who are Muslims, and who have left the Moluccas because of the troubles. The girls stayed behind at the harbour to wave me off on the boat.

On getting on to the boat I met up with some English people, Olga, Susannah and Martin who are living and working in Indonesia with Operation Wallasee, the marine expedition (of course, I had mentioned earlier meeting the organiser, Chris, in Ujung Pandang). *I had planned to sleep on deck and, following the drill of all the other locals who were doing the same, I had purchased a hessian mat. One of the English travellers offered to lend me a roll up mat to put over the top of it – which I accepted. I then found my own personal space on the deck. The combination of mats had very little give in them, meaning that it was going to be only fractionally better than sleeping on the hard wooden boards of the deck itself. The English group had their own cabin, with bunks, mattresses and bedding. I wasn't a bit jealous (yeah, right!). A near neighbour on the deck was yet another attractive girl who was single and aged 29. She spoke very good English and was clearly well educated. When she quickly guessed that I was a lawyer, I jokingly suggested that she must be a practitioner of witchcraft, and I then reciprocated by guessing – correctly – that she is a Gemini.*

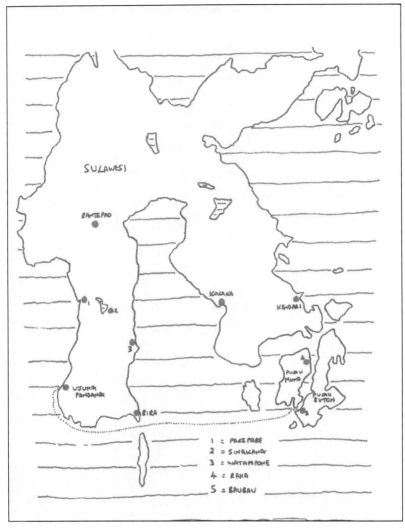

Map 30

<u>*Thursday 17th June – Sleeping on Deck*</u>

I forgot to mention that, when I was flirting with Rahma yesterday, and she said that she loved me, I made a joke of offering to kiss her, to which she said that she wasn't able to because of her religion, mirroring what Fitria had told me. I learnt that the friendly girl on the boat is called Tientien. The journey to Ujung Pandang took 12 hours and I must have slept for no more than one hour in total on deck. It was a very hard surface to sleep on. *A very kind girl from Irian Jaya had yesterday warned me to be very careful of thieves. I kept a good eye on all my belongings and made sure that I slept with the straps of both rucksacks tucked through my arms.*

Once back in Ujung Pandang I went back and thankfully found a room at Pondok Rannu (the homestay where I had stayed before) *and I grabbed a couple of hours' kip. Instead of making me feel less tired the sleep actually made me feel worse. Got talking to a chap who said that he knew of a schooner that would be heading down to the island of Flores. He advised me that the cost is normally $200 (USD) per person, but there needs to be a minimum of two paying passengers; he added that the ship would still go if I was the only one to use it but I would have to pay double, that is $400. I told him that I would let him know. I later made enquiries around the docks to see if there are any Pelni passenger ships between Sulawesi and Flores and there are none. On the basis that I am determined to visit Flores next, that then leaves me with four options – to go to Flores by schooner for $400, or to fly from Sulawesi to Flores using connecting flights via Denpasar (Bali) for £130, or take a ferry to Surabaya and then fly to Flores, or hunt around Paotere harbour to find a trade ship. Although the latter option sounds great – not least because it was precisely what the Blair brothers did – I was advised that, even if I were able to find such a boat, the journey time is usually a week which would not give me much time to get from Flores back to Bali.*

Whilst sitting in a becak today another becak careered straight into us. Although physically I was totally unscathed it's made me a nervous wreck. So far on this trip I've had accidents with a bus, a car, a motorbike and now a becak (I need to avoid boats and planes!). In the evening, I managed to bump into some of the Indonesian friends that I had met on the ferry ship last night, and I spent some time chatting to them. As I was later wandering around on my own and heading in a general direction back to my hotel, I made the mistake of going through a park, where I was accosted by several prostitutes. Scary. A fat one grabbed my cock and placed my hand on her tits. Scarier. She was then joined by a friend who I initially thought was drop-dead gorgeous, that is, until 'he' spoke. Scariest. Later I met up again with the lad who is trying to organise the schooner trip to Flores, who told me his name is Lola. He told me that he had spoken to the skipper of the boat, who had confirmed his intention to sail to Flores in the near future and suggested that we speak again soon. In the course of my conversation with Lola, he told me that he is the grandson of the last King of Makassar. He said it with such a straight face that it was hard not to believe him.

Friday 18th June – Booked Trips

Went to a doctor in Ujung Pandang yesterday to have my leg checked just to be on the safe side – the doctor was a little worried about my ankle but he said it should be okay and all the other wounds were healing nicely. When I went to pay him, he refused to let me pay anything. I just cannot get over how kind and generous the Indonesian people are. The doctor weighed me and I discovered that I am now 11 stone 13lbs (I've lost two stone).

Today was a good 'sorting out' day. I decided that the notion of sailing to Flores is too good an opportunity to miss and the idea of chartering a boat on my own is also not such an unattractive idea. After all, $400 for chartering my own boat to take me to Flores is really very cheap, especially when I factor in that it includes three or four days of bed and board. I decided that I would have to pay for half of it by card. In the morning, I spoke to the grandson of the last King of Makassar and informed him of my decision. He telephoned his contact in Bira and discovered that his contact is already here in Ujung Pandang. The grandson of the last King of Makassar told me that he would speak to his friend and come back and see me later. I posted a card to Nur. Eventually found a reasonably priced money changer. Then booked and paid (by card) for my flight to Australia. I fly out on the 4th July. Cost $371 (approximately £260). Sent a postcard to Steve (my friend in Australia), *to advise him of the flight details in the hope he might be able to meet me at Brisbane airport. Then decided to go to Bantimurung to see the waterfalls. With all the fart-arsing around with becak, bus and bemo connections, by the time that I got there I only had about 25 minutes to explore. The waterfalls were attractive and I would like to have explored more but I don't especially feel that I've lost out too much. As I walked along the riverside I met a family who were picnicking by the river. They gave me a homemade coconut-flavoured sweet which was very tasty. I met a girl on the bus – Riana – who was a scarf-wearing Muslim. She was very helpful and spoke quite good English. In the evening, I met up again with the grandson of the last King of Makassar and he advised that they had now found other passengers who wanted to go to Flores and I would therefore only have to pay $200. Job done. The boat would leave Bira on Sunday and we would therefore have to leave Ujung Pandang and make our way to Bira tomorrow. In the evening, I had a good curry and discovered – too late – an authentic massage for 20,000 Rp.*

Saturday 19th June – Lola

Had long chat with the grandson of Last King of Makassar in the morning. He talked about the Makassarese attitude to life and how protective he is personally of family and friends. He confirmed when I asked him that he is the oldest in his family. He told me how he had killed someone who had stolen from one of his father's friends. He also described a mafia-style killing for which his friend, who took part in the attack, is in prison. With the only thing that I needed to kill being time, I went wandering to see the Mandala tower – quite impressive – and to the Al Markas mosque, both of which are relatively new buildings. Caught my ankle as I was getting out of a becak, and ripped open the wound. Very painful. Also got film for my camera and other bits and pieces.

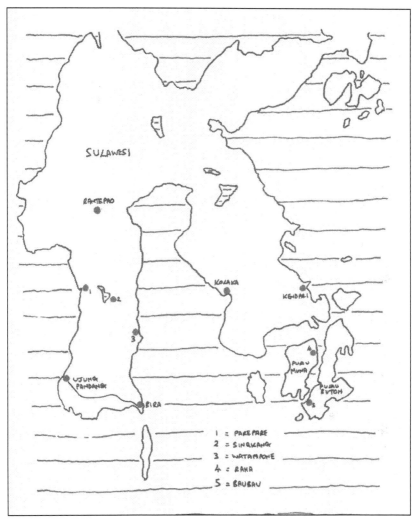

Map 31

Met the grandson of Last King of Makassar back at my hotel and said goodbye for the second time to my amazing hosts. We then left to meet up with Robin, who would be the skipper of the boat, who is an American guy in his 50s. Also with him was his fiancée, a pretty young girl from Jakarta, who I guessed was in her teens. Journeyed to Bira.

Bira was the destination for Lorne and Lawrence Blair, after they had been searching for, and found, a boat to sail East through the Banda Sea to the Moluccas, and more specifically to the Aru Islands in search of the Bird of Paradise. Having failed to pick up a boat at Paotere Harbour in Ujung Pandang, they were advised to head out to Bira, where they had learnt that the Biranese were master boat-builders:

"[Bira and Kasuso] proved to be the isolated buccaneer haunts we were looking for, and the hidden source of most of the nation's sailing prahus (pinisis) and their mariners... in the coconut groves by the beach, scores of men were building prahus from scratch, some over 150 feet long. Their only tools from the outside world were the 'parang', the broad-bladed machete of the East, and a hand-drill representing an over-sized corkscrew, with which they could make all the other tools they required to produce these spectacular Noah's Arks. Prahu-building is ruled by ancient deities, mediated by specialised shamans who choose their timbers by 'calling' to the trees and cutting only those which 'reply'. The boats thus grew from no clear design – but emerged organically, with asymmetrical spars, as if barely freed from the forms of the forest. Precisely chiselled pegs of a different wood from the rest of the ship, which swelled and secured the timbers once they were immersed in the water, were used instead of nails or screws. At night, the beaches flamed with bonfires lit to extract lime from the coral, which was then mixed with coconut oil to form the white cement with which the hulls were caulked."

I was thrilled to be almost literally following in the footsteps of the Blair brothers, even to the description of the very journey I was now about to make from Ujung Pandang to Bira as, "a good seven-hour jeep-lurch."

On way to Bira we encountered heavy rain. At Bira, or more precisely at a village a few miles before Bira, we stopped. I had presumed that we would be staying in a losmen for the night before setting sail in the morning, but we went straight to the boat in order to sleep there. Most of the others on the boat are English, plus one Dane, one Swiss or Austrian (I'd better get that right), plus Robin, his fiancée and three Indonesian crew. Washing and defecating is out the back in a toilet/washroom – a small wooden shack with a corrugated iron roof, jutting out behind the stern – where everything drops straight to the sea. Wouldn't you just know it, but the first time I christened the 'poop' deck one of the girls came walking by. I'll just have to get used to it. Saw male boatbuilders carrying very heavy non-floating ironwood out of the water. I was informed that the Blair brothers got their boat very near to here. Saw tuna jumping out of the water.

Gunung Bromo, Java

Circumnavigating Mt. Bromo

Inhabitant of Ngadisari village, near Mt. Bromo

Lovina Beach, Bali

Candikuning, Bali

Kids playing at Lovina Beach, Bali

Bugis football team, Ujung Pandang

Paotere harbour, Ujung Pandang

Election Rally, Ujung Pandang

Torajan village

Torajan funeral, Sulawesi

Widower at Torajan funeral

Tau tau, Tana Toraja, Sulawesi

Team of skulls, Tana Toraja, Sulawesi

Dancers at a Torajan wedding

Sunday 20th June – Setting Sail

Didn't sleep too well last night. Not used to sleeping on a boat. The boat is not the classic Pinisi type which I'd hoped that it would be but it is still attractive for all that. Went ashore to Bira with a lad from the boat called Joe, where there was yet more rain. Bira has a wide beach but otherwise was quite disappointing. Although we passed a couple of interesting villages on the way, including one where many women wearing bright sarongs were seemingly heading to a party or festival, Bira itself was quite disappointing and seemed to lack character. Made our way back to the boat and eventually set sail – the boat is well stocked with beer – five x 24 size crates. Posted card to Robbyne in nearby village.

My home for the next four or five days would be a 60-foot schooner, which was not a true pinisi, but which nevertheless had many of its features. The ship was fitted with two masts, and three sails, they being a foresail, a triangular mainsail and a square mainsail. Further power was provided by a motor which was intended to supplement, or occasionally replace, wind-power.

The Indonesian crew comprised three men of the Bugis tribe that were straight out of Treasure Island. One of them was a middle-aged man, who was nominally second in command behind Robin, but who clearly knew this ship far better than the skipper. He was constantly by Robin's side guiding him on the rigging, the currents and the sea-charts. He had a weathered copper-tanned complexion, evidently from years spent at sea, sported a grizzled Fu Manchu moustache, wore a gold-coloured bandana and was constantly smoking kretek cigarettes, which he smoked out of the corner of his mouth. These cigarettes are special to Indonesia, and are part tobacco and part cloves, and the scent given off is sweet and aromatic and not entirely unpleasant, even to a non-smoker like me.

The second member of the crew was a young lad, with Frank Zappa style facial hair. When relaxing, he would be found sunning himself on deck, showing off his tanned, toned body, naked save for his bright yellow briefs, matching yellow turban and shades. However, he was a very hard worker and the times when he would be relaxing were few and far between, because he would just as often be found breaking out the rigging, cleaning the deck or shinning up the masts like a marmoset.

Completing the triumvirate of workaholic buccaneers was a wiry, older, clean-shaven man, who was the main chef, bottle-washer, deck hand and general gopher. His switch was either fully on or fully off, in that he seemed to be either busy on the go, never seeming to stop, or conversely completely zonked out – which was the only time I ever saw him not working. It was clear that when he did stop, he must have been so worn out that he could have slept on the proverbial bed of nails. Indeed, in the course of this voyage, I would stumble upon him asleep in several different areas of the boat, including in the middle of the rock-hard deck or lying across the mass of twisted ropes that comprised the rigging. None of our in-house pirates spoke any English.

With 11 of us on this ship, space was at a premium and I soon learnt that social norms and etiquette that would ordinarily apply on dry land go out of the window at sea, as amply demonstrated by my early introduction to the processing of ablutions. The cabin was narrow, as was my bunk therein, my bunk being the bottom of two. A thin mattress provided a limited degree of comfort. There were three rows of double bunks, one up and one down, either side of the central aisle. Each group of four bunks was separated from the other by only a flimsy curtain, affording the two girls on this boat minimal privacy. I was told very early on that it was suspected that there was a mouse on the boat, which had apparently been there a few weeks. Although nobody had yet seen it, it had reputedly left its 'presence' and had so far managed to evade all attempts to trap it.

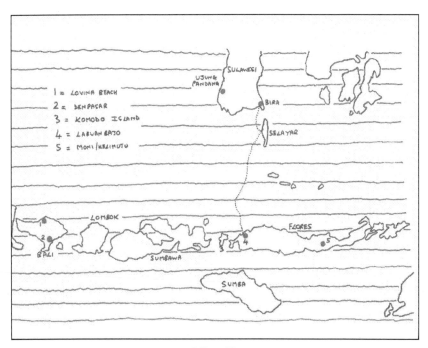

Map 32

When I later also saw a cockroach scuttle across the cabin floor I was reminded of a memorable passage in Lorne and Lawrence Blairs' book, 'Ring of Fire': -

"From Lorne's diary: our cabin is barely large enough to accommodate both us and our equipment. We cannot fully stretch out in it, nor sit upright without cracking our heads on the decking above. It is four feet six inches wide, extending to a princely six feet six, but the forward end is so packed with our gear that there is barely enough room for our legs. We share it with an unwelcome assortment of fellow travellers. Some are there to suck our blood, while others are content to compete with us for our meagre stash of private food. This morning a rat poked his nose in, but they usually seem to prefer the main hold. It's the insects that enjoy travelling cabin class. We don't see much of them in the daytime, but at night the bedbugs crawl out from under our mats, and we listen to the cockroaches munching away merrily in the food-basket between our heads and the brittle scrabbling of their feet on the ceiling a couple of feet above us. They haven't found their sea legs yet, and a sudden lurch can bring several of them raining down on our faces. It's hard to sleep with a panic-stricken cockroach clawing its way out of one's eye-socket."

The environment in my relatively modern ship was far less rudimentary than the setting on theirs, and I had so far only seen just the one 'roach, but this was one part of their adventure I would be happy not to emulate.

The sails were up and we used the motor too, as we chugged along all day at a steady four to six knots. Although the pace is only slightly faster than a brisk walk it was surprising how quickly the miles had piled up some 12 hours later. The boat comprises me, Martin from Switzerland (definitely Switzerland – paying – lived in Thailand for two years), Robin (the skipper), Rima (his girlfriend), Joe (chief dive master – English), Viv (younger brother of Joe – also paying and learning to dive, also English), Ann (Danish – dive master – girlfriend of Viv), Ben (English from Gloucester – very funny) and three Indonesian crew. Agreed deal with Joe to pay him £100 to try to complete the dive course whilst on this boating trip – I will send him a cheque for £100 payable at the best exchange rate in Australian dollars when I get to my friend's, Steve's, place in Australia. Excitement when we saw a large school of dolphins near the boat. Superb stars at night.

Monday 21ˢᵗ June – First Dive

Read up first two modules (of five) of the diving manual yesterday. Talked it through with Joe and did the first two tests; 10 out of 10 score in each. We'd moored off an island called Tambolongang. Went ashore to do my first stages of diving. Equipped with mask, tank, vest, regulator, pressure gauge, and buoyancy equipment. Having got a basic grounding of all the instruments around me we went down and we went through a whole series of tests, including loss of regulator (breathing device), loss of mask and out of air. The scariest was when I had to remove the entire mask and then replace it and blow out all the water. But I did it. We were at a depth of perhaps 8 to 12 feet. I was down there for about two hours – time flew by. Saw two manta rays but not a great deal else. After the dive, we went ashore to the island of Tambolongang – absolutely gorgeous island – superb, perfect, almost untouched white sand beach – I reckon stretching for two miles. Small village with amazing people – lots of perfect palm trees and small hills just behind it. It was the sort of place I'd like to stay at for a while. Back on boat I cleaned up my leg using the iodine solution – it seems to be generally okay except I am still concerned about the two areas on my foot. Although I'm happy that they are certainly very clean now, they are not scabbing as well as I would have liked. Saw another big school of dolphins – many jumping – five in unison.

Tuesday 22ⁿᵈ June – Rough Night

Late yesterday afternoon we had arrived at a beautiful coral atoll. The late afternoon sun lit up the inviting beach bordering the nearby micro island, and as it slowly sank over the horizon the sun kaleidoscopically turned the pure white sand from bleach-blond white to autumn-leaf gold to claret-wine crimson. We had anchored up in the lee of the island in a lagoon protected by the outer reef, thinking we had perfect shelter. We were planning to dive early in the morning today. It had been a still, cloudless evening and, as dusk quickly turned to dark, a myriad of stars in the Milky Way and a crescent waning moon lit up the heavens and bathed our ship in ambient light. All seemed well. Fu Manchu, though, appeared restless. Like a dog looking for a gap in a hedge, he was pacing up and down the port side of our boat looking at cauliflower-shaped clouds ballooning up into the sky on the far horizon. I didn't give it much more thought at the time, since Frank Zappa and our chef weren't overly bothered and the clouds seemed so far away. However, as the evening wore on the wind started to pick up and the sky began to darken. At first there was just the occasional gust of wind, as if Zephyrus was exercising his lungs in readiness for the full orchestral performance later, but the gusts quickly turned into a stiff breeze and then to a howling gale in a matter of moments, followed by deep guttural rumbles of thunder that became progressively louder as dark clouds edged closer to us. Soon the latent moon and the twinkling stars were completely masked and the sky turned ominously black. Rain began to fall, initially as large singular globules but this quickly became a torrent. It was mid evening and a little early for bed, but Robin, on advice from Fu Manchu, suggested we should retire to our cabins as it looked like the storm was set in for a while. All of us, save for Robin, and our three Bugis friends, duly obliged. Just before I descended I observed that Fu Manchu was recommending to Robin that we should up one of the anchors and then turn the ship, I presumed so that it faced into the wind rather than side on, though, of course, I was no expert.

Making my way to my cabin was like performing the cakewalk, as the ship lurched from one side to the other, but I clung on tightly to posts and banisters. Having manoeuvred my way to my bunk, I just about managed to remove my contact lenses in the poor light, kissed the photograph of my nan and hunkered down. Trying to get to sleep proved impossible, with my body clock complaining that it was still early evening and with the ship rolling from side to side. Outwardly at least, nobody else seemed unduly perturbed by the situation. Indeed, Robin and the crew appeared to be fully in control. However, although I am not a worrier by nature, I couldn't shake off the sinister feeling that something was not quite right. It was partly the fact that the people around me were a bit too quiet – nobody was saying anything, not even Ben, the ship's resident comedian – but partly also because I knew we were vulnerable, being exposed on this relatively small boat, in the middle of a huge ocean, miles from the nearest land proper, and completely defenceless to the elements.

A little while later the lolling from side to side became less pronounced – I presumed because they had managed to turn the boat – and I started to relax. I even began to drift off to sleep. However, I woke with a start when I heard panicked shouting from Robin above, who required everybody save for me and the other paying guest, Martin, to get back up on deck. I was now convinced that something serious was up. The boat had resumed its exaggerated rocking, which was even more pronounced than before, lurching so steeply from one side to the other that it was a struggle not to fall out of bed. I felt completely useless being there down below in the cabin, since my instinct was to get up and try to help, but I knew that if I did so I would be far more of a hindrance than a help. From the occasional flash of torchlight, I could see that portentously there was a lot of water sloshing around the cabin floor. The wind was literally howling, as it streamed across the deck above me, whistling between the masts and rigging, and the boat creaked as if it was being stretched to breaking point with each lurch from side to side. I was awake for what seemed like hours, as the storm showed no signs of abating. However, I must have eventually dozed off at some point, because, when I did wake up, it was to bright sunlight and with the boat becalmed. A gentle swaying motion told me that we were moving. I lay there in semi-slumber for a while, lapping up the fact that all now seemed well and considered that I had overplayed the danger that I thought we were in last night. When I eventually made my way up onto deck, there was Robin at the tiller, bare-chested, showing off his mound of curly black chest hair, as laid back and as cool as ever. Nobody else was up. "Sleep well?" he airily asked, in his lazy North American drawl, a lop-sided cheeky grin escaping from the corner of his mouth.

"Like a log going over Niagara," I replied, when I had eventually found an apt analogy.

He continued. "We decided last night that it would be better if we took the boat out and away from the island," he nonchalantly informed me. "We were like a sitting duck back there." As we sat at the helm together, with us remaining the only two persons up for the best part of two hours, the coffee that morning tasted particularly good.

Robin never said anything else at the time about the previous night's shenanigans. It was almost as though the storm had never happened. Two days later, however, when we were safely moored up at Flores, he casually revealed over dinner that he had thought we were going to lose the boat on the night of the storm and he also disclosed that we had come within five metres of being grounded on a reef and shipwrecked. Although Robin attempted to deliver his pronouncement in the same casual, laid-back manner as normal, there was enough of an inflection in the way that he said it to send a frisson running down my spine at the realisation that this habitually super-confident, cool, laissez-faire guy was being deadly serious.

I had cooked a Mexican style rice dish yesterday. Today I cooked lunch and I made a barbecue type sauce, with plain rice (fluffy), spinach and cooked chicken. It was good (if I say so myself). Washed up using seawater. Made a stock by boiling up the chicken bones for use later (Nan would have been proud of me). Also went through modules 3 and 4 of the diving manual, and almost completed both with Joe. The intention is to complete the diving course at an island just before we get to Flores. Saw several — what I believe to be — storm petrels and also saw another large school of dolphins — one seemed to be swimming sideways and flapping its fin, just as if it was waving at us. Three other dolphins floated up to the surface in unison with all their noses pointed up just like a team of synchronised swimmers. Unfortunately, they were too far away to photograph.

Wednesday 23rd June – Marlin Jumping

A rocky night at the beginning but it improved and I slept a bit better. There had been some water on my bedding last night which I was slightly surprised about because I thought it had been dry during the day – I assumed that I must either have been wrong and it did rain or else there must be a leak somewhere. However, I woke to discover that there was a small hole in my contact lens solution container. Deducing that this must have been the source of the water, it then dawned on me that it might have been the work of the dreaded mouse on the boat and the cheeky little bugger had got a thirst for my contact lens solution. When I mentioned this to the others, I discovered that my supposition was correct since I wasn't the only victim. Ben discovered that a small pack of peanuts of his had been torn open. I woke to find we were in an amazing area surrounded by idyllic islands and beaches with Flores one way and the shadow of the island of Komodo, home of the dragon, further away. Early in the morning I saw a marlin jumping out of the water. We eventually went out to do a dive. Although I was struggling a little with the buoyancy it seemed better because I was a little less apprehensive. Saw a turtle. On the way back, we saw tuna jumping out of the water. Only when I was back on the boat waiting to go back out again did Joe point out that we might not have enough time to finish the diving course by tomorrow. We concluded we had no option but to see how we do. The boat continued into Labuanbajo harbour. Very pretty. Joe then declared that there was not enough time to go out again today, which in turn meant that, having given it more thought, he was now certain that if I have to leave to go on with my journey tomorrow, I definitely would not complete the course. We agreed that I could get up to the point where I had completed all the academic steps, which would leave me with three lots of open water dives to do. Saw an osprey and several gannets. Went up to a hill behind Labuanbajo where I could look back across the harbour to see our boat and had a great view of a lovely sunset.

Thursday 24th June – I Can Dive

I learnt over dinner last night that Robin was concerned that we were going to lose the boat on the night of the storm. Surprisingly he's not the most confident of guys despite his outward demeanour. Also learnt that we had come within five metres of being grounded on a reef. Today I learnt that Rima is aged 19 and Robin is aged 55 (dirty bugger – or do I mean lucky bugger?) – roughly what I'd thought except that Rima actually looks and acts even younger (I'd guessed she must have been slightly older than her looks).

We cruised into a beautiful large sweeping bay late yesterday afternoon where we moored up. We had arrived at Labuanbajo, the main town at the

Western end of the island of Flores. At this point the coastline arcs round to create the bay, providing natural shelter for the many small fishing boats that I could see idly bobbing within it. Picturesque Labuanbajo, and the coastline around it, is surrounded by rugged green hills, and the bay and the sea a little beyond it is peppered with tiny islands, most of which – I was told – are uninhabited. With this part of the coast facing in a West/North-Westerly direction, we were treated last night to a glorious golden sunset that lit up the water to furnish us with yet another master class in impressionist painting.

Having decided a few days earlier to take the scuba diving course, I had been hoping to complete it to enable me to receive my Open Water PADI Certificate, but with the storm two nights ago washing out one day, time was now getting tight. I was due to fly out of Bali in ten days' time on the 4th July. Between now and then, I wanted to spend some time in Flores, and in particular I wanted to visit the spectacular crater lakes of Keli Mutu in East Flores; I hoped to visit Komodo, in the hope of spotting the eponymous dragon; I needed to hop back across the chain of pearl necklace islands that make up Nusa Tenggara between Flores and Bali; and I still harboured hopes of getting back to Bali with enough time to spend a day or two with Nur. I had a dilemma, because Joe had made it clear that if I decided to leave today I would not have enough time to complete the course. As tempting as it was to stay, it was more tempting to try not to miss the main sights I had been planning to see. I decided to leave. A little bit of reassurance mitigated the position when Joe suggested that it might be possible for him to give me a referral form confirming the steps I had completed thus far for the PADI certificate, so that if I was able to find a dive school in either Bali or Australia, then perhaps I could complete the course there.

I had gone on shore yesterday, where I had located a bus that would be leaving this evening and heading East to Ende in Eastern Flores, which in turn meant that I had some spare time for the rest of today. Even if I could not finish the course, I was still keen to have another go at diving. When I returned, I asked Joe if we could go out and he readily agreed, saying we should think of it as my first pleasure dive, as opposed to an educational one. At the harbour in Labuanbajo Joe chartered a small boat to take us to one of the outlying islands. We moored up 100 metres off-shore, we kitted up and over we went, with my first proper legs-astride jump into the water. We swam down to about ten metres. Initially I still could not quite get the hang of trying to control my buoyancy, but all of a sudden, the penny dropped and I could sense that I had managed to find perfect equilibrium, in that I had locked into being able to control the buoyancy with my breathing. As I breathed in I floated up, and as I breathed out I floated down. The feeling was exhilarating, and was as if before this point everything had been a blur, whereas now that I had been provided with the scuba diver's equivalent of a perfect pair of spectacles, I had 20/20 vision. Having acquired this element of control, I was much more confident to go on and explore my surroundings, although, like an adolescent that can't quite break completely free from its parent's apron strings, I still wanted to make sure that I kept Joe in sight. Swimming out a little deeper, I glided over and around beautiful forests of coral, and swam with fish of every spectral hue that were lit up like many coloured jewels by the refracted bright light that penetrated the crystal-clear water. Amongst the numerous marine creatures that we were able to identify were angel fish, butterfly fish, a sea cucumber and a highly venomous scorpion fish. Time flew by underwater and I was down for nearly two hours. Joe gave the underwater signal for us to finish and we swam to a beautiful white-sanded beach on the nearby island where we decamped, and were welcomed by a shrill chorus of shrieking monkeys.

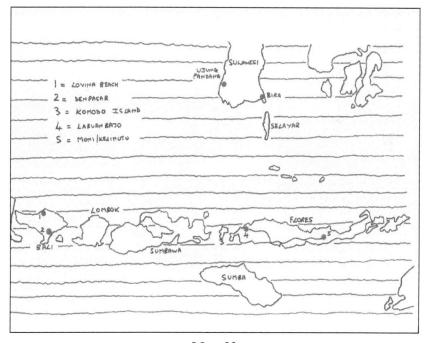

Map 33

Went back to the boat, changed, said my goodbyes and then left. Although I didn't get that close to them all, I had been with them for nearly five days and it was sad to go.

257

Got bus to Ende. A long trip ahead. May complete the diving course in Bali.

Friday 25th June – Trip to Ende

I made the very rough, very long and very uncomfortable bus journey from Labuanbajo to Ende today/last night. Took 14 ½ hours – I was cramped, and my feet could hardly move. During the journey, I had some water leak out onto me and onto my bag, but because I was hemmed in I couldn't do anything to prevent it. It was not an easy journey. From what I have seen, I like Flores already. I had thought it would be dry and arid, but in fact it seems very green and lush and the banana leaves seem so much bigger here than anywhere I've seen before. It really is a fabulous place. The road I was on was described as the trans-Flores highway, but it was full of twists and turns and pot-holed, reminding me of the roads in Laos. Maybe the inability to travel quickly is what helps to ensure that the island remains remote and untouched. We passed several volcanoes, most of which were out of the window to my right, the South. They seem to be mostly either out to sea or bordering the coast right beside the sea. The people don't seem so instantly friendly – perhaps more shy or more tourist-wary – but maybe it is because, compared to most places that I have been to in Indonesia so far, it's quite out of the way and not on the regular tourist or backpacker circuit. Also, there are many people with a Polynesian or Melanesian appearance – blacker, fatter or broader, and mops of dark curly hair. At Ende managed to get the connecting bus almost immediately to take me to Moni, the nearest settlement to Keli Mutu. Checked into Losmen Friendly, which was right on the edge of the village – 15,000 Rp. including breakfast and tax. Had coffee and nasi goreng – very good – and had about an hour's sleep. It was very overcast and raining heavily, so prospects for seeing Keli Mutu tomorrow are not good. We'll see. Village seems very pretty. Saw a dead snake on the road. Arranged to join up with a bemo heading up to Keli Mutu at 4 in the morning tomorrow.

Saturday 26th June – Keli Mutu

Made a series of bad decisions today. First – I relaxed and did not get straight up when my alarm went off at 3.15 this morning. Result. Knock on the door at 10 minutes to 4 and I kept everyone waiting. Second – poor choice of losmen, because, being so remote at the edge of the village, at 4 in the morning it was pitch black when I was going out to the bemo. Result. I slipped over and tumbled part way into a muddy ditch. Clumsy git. As it was, I hurt my ankle again, removing part of the scab and it was agony. I also hurt my thumb and had mud everywhere. I had no choice but to go back and clean myself up as much as I could in the little time that I had.

"Of all the sights in Nusa Tenggara, the coloured lakes of Keli Mutu are the most singularly spectacular." I had heard many good things from word of mouth about Keli Mutu, and the above description from my Lonely Planet guidebook only enhanced that view. There were several places that I was still hoping to visit in Indonesia, and this included spending time exploring the island of Flores. However, with me due to fly out tomorrow week, time was getting short, so I concluded as a consequence that I had no alternative but to limit myself to the main highlights. Keli Mutu was a must-see and was the furthest East that I would travel within Indonesia, so I had decided to head straight there, and then see how much time I had left when returning West. Despite the very lengthy bum-numbing bus journey to get here, and despite my shenanigans in the morning, it had all been worth it and I was well rewarded, albeit for an all too brief 45 minutes or so. Keli Mutu itself is a volcano, but it contains within its structure three different-coloured crater lakes.

I had mentioned in my diary that it had been cloudy and rainy yesterday and prospects for seeing the lakes today were not promising, but locals advised that the best chance to see them was to arrive early, hence my decision to join others in hiring a bemo. The road up the volcano conveniently took us most of the way to a ridge near to the top, from where we could look down upon the lakes. We were there by 5.30 am, leaving plenty of time before sunrise. When we first arrived, it was still very murky and misty, but just as the first splintered rays of the sun filtered over the horizon the mist lifted to reveal the lakes in all their glory. One was a light turquoise, another was olive green and the third a little further away was an ominous black. I later read that the lakes are of enormous interest to geologists because of the very fact that three differently coloured lakes should be part of the same volcano, and also because the colours change over time. Previously they were blue, maroon and black and before that they were blue, red-brown and the colour of milky coffee. Nobody, it seems, has been able to satisfactorily explain how the colours change or why they are always different to each other. Although no extensive scientific survey has ever been undertaken below the surface of the lakes, it is thought that the colours emanate from minerals within the water, which change as a result of chemical reactions triggered by volcanic gas activity. The theory is that underwater fumaroles discharge gas and steam, mixed with sulphur dioxide, hydrogen chloride, hydrogen sulphide as well as carbon dioxide, creating an upwelling which drives denser nutrient-rich water upwards to the surface (quote/unquote). It sounded plausible. They were certainly spectacular, with each of the lakes sided by steep rugged walls. Local folklore suggests that the lakes change colour according to the mood of the spirit, and that the souls of the dead depart the material world through these lakes. Translated from its local name, the usually blue lake is called Lake of Old People and the usually green lake is called the Lake of Young Men and Maidens. Murderers and thieves have the misfortune to end up in the currently black Bewitched Lake. Quite where the souls of semi-virtuous middle-aged farts like me are meant to go is unclear.

By 6.45 am the clouds had rolled back in and all three lakes were lost from view. I counted only ten people, who had made the early morning trek to look down on the lakes up here on the high slopes of Keli Mutu. They included the six with whom I had shared a bemo. The other three had come up together in a jeep. As I gazed down on the spectacular volcanic scene before me, I mused that I was fortunate that this place was so remote and wondered how long it would be before developers moved in to build an international airport to exploit the volcano, the people and the beaches nearby; but for now the sparsity of my fellow human beings this morning was a blessing since it meant that the atmosphere was tranquil and respectful, if not downright reverential, and the haunting heady ambience of this other-worldly place was in no way diminished.

When the bemo was about to head back down the volcano, I decided that I would walk back to the village. Bad decision number three. The bemo drove on leaving me there. Result. It began pouring with rain soon after I started out – with no place to shelter I got very wet. I had no option but to carry on walking. It eased off after a while and I dried out a bit – I walked in all for 3 ½ hours, about 9 miles. There were great views when the mists cleared, but being shrouded in cloud had its attraction, since the mist created its own brooding atmosphere. Halfway down I saw a tree laden with juicy looking mandarins, so I shook the tree to try to loosen them. Bad decision. Result. A partially dried out yours truly got soaked again as I brought down all the water hanging in the tree. Laurel and Hardy, eat your heart out! Met several very interesting people as I trudged down the volcano, most of whom were working on the land. I was about to photograph one photogenic old woman who had not seen me approaching, and because I wanted to get the perfect picture I paused to adjust the shutter speed. Another bad decision. Result. The woman spotted me trying to photograph her, whereupon she stood up, and smiled, revealing a miserly three stained brown teeth in the whole of her head, and she spat – none too successfully – causing phlegm to hang from her mouth. I gestured to the now-not-quite-so-photogenic woman that it was too cloudy and dark to be able to photograph her, and strategically withdrew. Saw a foot and a half long worm today. Once back at the village I left my homestay and got a bus back to Ende – where I stayed at Wisata.

Sunday 27ᵗʰ June

Got up in good time in order to have brekkie and to catch the bus back to Labuanbajo, except that when I arrived I discovered there were no direct buses running today. Although today was a Sunday I hadn't noticed before in any part of Asia that the indigenous population treated this day so much differently to any other day. I met up with a Scottish couple who also wanted to catch a bus to Labuanbajo. After a quick conflab, we decided that we might as well get the bus to Ruteng (which would take us eighty per cent of the way) and if needs be we would share the cost and charter transport thereafter. Their names were Mark and Nicola and they were really nice people – they have just spent a year in Australia and now have six weeks in Indonesia. The bus trip was no better going back than it was coming out – not that I expected it would be – and was very painful on the arse, but the scenery was superb. Saw numerous volcanoes and gorges and rivers and villages and lots of ikat weaving and women pounding rice and grain. Great stuff. Our bus driver was mad and we nearly had an accident on at least four occasions. Got to Ruteng and luckily, we were able to change and get an onward bus to Labuanbajo very quickly. Another journey from hell. Shared bus with live strung-up chickens inside the bus and a live strung-up goat on top of the bus. We had left Ende at 7 in the morning, and we got to Labuanbajo at 9.15 pm – long day. Had trouble getting a room because my first two choices were full up – stayed at Mitra – 25,000 Rp.

It had been a very long and tiring 14 ½ hour bus journey to Labuanbajo, not arriving back, as I had stated, until 9.15 pm. I was tired and I was hungry, and lugging my rucksacks between the various hotels was no fun, particularly when I discovered that the first two losmen that I tried were full up. It was approaching 10.15 pm by the time I had finally found somewhere to stay, decamped and was eventually ready to go out to explore. There was no time to shower, or to eat – those little luxuries would have to wait until later – since I needed to make some quick decisions, and the first priority was to check the ferry times for onward travel, especially since I had no time to waste if I wanted to visit Komodo before going back to Bali. I discovered that there were one or two organised trips to Komodo, including one that would leave tomorrow, but they all would return to Flores. Since Komodo lay to the West of Flores I had hoped that it might be possible to go to the island under my own steam and then to continue travelling further West to the next island in the Nusa Tenggara archipelago, and my next destination, Sumbawa, rather than waste time coming back. Unfortunately, independent travel to Komodo was not possible. I then also discovered that the ferries between Flores and Sumbawa are irregular. There would be a ferry leaving early tomorrow, but then nothing again until Wednesday. The onward journey via connecting buses or bemos from

Sumbawa would take the best part of two days. So, if I left on Wednesday, that in turn would mean that I might not arrive at Lovina in Northern Bali until Friday, or possibly even Saturday, and, of course, I would be leaving from Denpasar airport in Southern Bali late on the Sunday evening. I then enquired with a couple of tour operators to see if there were any planes leaving late tomorrow or Tuesday, but they too were notoriously unreliable and, in any event, there were definitely no planes either tomorrow or Tuesday. I had no alternative but to leave for Sumbawa early tomorrow morning and I would have to miss Komodo. Although I didn't want to eat too much too late, I was nevertheless still hungry and managed to find somewhere, where they could muster me up some mi goreng (fried noodles). As I sat there contemplating my fate, my initial frustration very soon abated as I reminded myself that I had actually been very lucky with the places I had been to, the people I had met and the sights I had seen, and the only reason why I had left myself so little time for Flores and Komodo was because I had had such a good time in Java, Bali and Sulawesi. I also knew that for so long as I lived and breathed I would never tire of returning to Indonesia, not least because I still had another 12,980 of the 13,000 Indonesian islands left to visit!

Monday 28th June – Meeting Selfy

Got up in good time but I was very loose again and spent too long on the khazi, which left me short of time. In the circumstances, I thought it would be wise to skip breakfast. I also feel achy today, like flu but without any symptoms in my head, save for a slight headache. Boat to Sumbawa left at 8.30 in the morning.

The boat pulled out into the bay, and once it had manoeuvred past the headland into open sea, I went wandering around the boat, partly in order to see what facilities there were and, being armed with my camera, partly to see if I could grab some cool photographs. The boat was large and very busy, and I spotted a Western couple, to whom I nodded and said hello. They didn't seem to be in too much of a hurry to make conversation, so I moved on. It looked as though everybody else on the boat were Indonesians. Shortly after I had begun walking along the starboard side of the boat I bumped into a pretty, petite young Indonesian girl in dark sunglasses, wearing a bright red jumper, who was leaning with her back against the side rail, arms outstretched, facing upwards to catch the early morning sun, and who greeted me with a disarming ear to ear smile when she breathily addressed me and said, "Selamat pagi" (good morning).

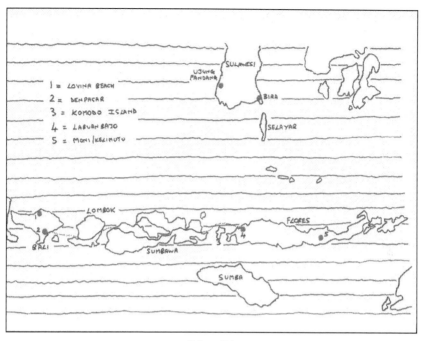

Map 34

Repeating back to her, "Selamat pagi," I stopped to talk to her.

As she pushed back her shades to sit on top of her head, in her broken English she introduced herself as Selfy and told me she was aged 19. Reminding me of Dao, she was very chatty and very forward, and the main clue confirming that she was very keen to spend some time with me, were I to have fully taken it on board at the time, came when she suggested we go up onto the virtually deserted top deck to talk and take photographs. Naively, I agreed. The only persons up there on the top deck when we arrived were a couple of crew members, who smiled knowingly when they saw us and then quickly disappeared, leaving me with the disconcerting impression that they and Selfy knew each other. As soon as they disappeared she gestured for me to stand down one rung on the stairs, which I obligingly obeyed not realising that she simply wanted to equalise our height difference. The next thing I knew was that she flung her arms around my neck and planted a robust kiss on my lips. I was shocked, though I cannot claim to have struggled a great deal. The kiss was long and passionate, but not sloppy, there being no visitation by tongues. One long passionate kiss was quickly followed by a second, long passionate kiss.

When she pulled away she smiled again with that same broad beaming ear-to-ear smile that had first greeted me. We sat on the stairs holding hands and talking. Very soon the conversation turned to her religion, which she stated was Muslim, and when I asked her – tactfully, I thought – how strict was her religion, she instantly, loudly – and proudly – declared, "I'm not a virgin." I glanced around thinking the whole ship might have heard her pronouncement, but thankfully we were still alone. I steered clear of asking her how many encounters she had had. She also then informed me that she was heading to Kuta Beach in Southern Bali and suggested that I should stay a night with her in Kuta before I move on. Talk about handing it to me on a plate. I did wonder what exactly a single, pretty, ex-virgin like Selfy was going to Kuta for, but I didn't dare ask. Although she was pretty, the fact she was so keen and so forward was counter-intuitively unattractive and the initial thrill lost a little of its lustre.

I was tired and wanted to have a nap, and said this to Selfy, so we made our way back down to the lower decks, where Selfy said she would sit and talk to her friends. I found a single spare seat a little way off from her where I could grab some sleep. When I woke up a short while later, Selfy was still sat across with her friends. Although she smiled at me when I looked across, it lacked the enthusiasm shown earlier and she quickly turned away to resume talking to her friends. It occurred to me that my one and only opportunity to deflower Selfy would have been an hour or so ago on the top deck. To be honest, I wasn't overly bothered by her apparent new coolness towards me, though I did chuckle to myself when it suddenly dawned on me that today was my birthday and I had effectively thrown away what would have been a rather interesting and unexpected birthday present.

Twice played chess twice today and twice I lost. It must be because I'm unwell! Arrived at Sape at the Eastern end of Sumbawa, and from there we were loaded onto a bus for the rest of the journey all the way to Bali via Lombok. Stopped for a bite to eat at Bima.

Today had been my 39th birthday, but I made no mention of it in my diary. The fact that, save for one brief moment, I had just completely forgotten all about it tells me all I need to know about how unimportant it was in the grand scheme of things – if I'd been in England, supposedly well-meaning friends and family would have been sending cards and ringing me up, inadvertently, or occasionally downright openly, reminding me that I, a single man, was spinning headfast towards officially being middle-aged.

Tuesday 29th June

Another long day on the road. I cannot say much about Sumbawa, as most of my time there was spent travelling at night. Got to the Western end of Sumbawa in the early hours of the morning. I was seated next to an English girl called Debbie, who grew on me as the day wore on until I really fancied her. We were slow to get talking, mainly on my part because I was knackered and unwell, but when we did we seemed to click, and she was chatty and friendly (you see, once you break through that good old English reserve, we are just as friendly as the natives). She's 25 and she is working in Australia for a year. She's taking a short break in Indonesia. She told me that she'd been on a ship that had been cruising from Lombok to Labuanbajo on Flores, via Sumbawa and Komodo, and then back again, when her boat hit very bad weather and was rammed by another boat. It started to take on water and they had to abandon ship. Scary. It is only now as I am writing in this diary and comparing probable dates that I have realised that the storm that her ship encountered was highly likely to have been the same one in which our schooner was nearly shipwrecked. I shuddered at the recollection, and reinforcement, of Robin's words about how close we had come to disaster. Debbie also told me that she's recently completed a very strenuous two-day trek to the top of Gunung Rinjani. The volcano is located in Lombok and is the second highest mountain in Indonesia outside Irian Jaya. It was clear to me that Debbie is fit in all senses of the word. After crossing on the ferry the short distance between Sumbawa and Lombok, the bus traversed Lombok – the road was well maintained and smooth, the scenery was green, beautiful and lush, and I saw many Muslim women in colourful hijabs. Then the bus hopped onto the ferry between Lombok and Bali, and moving onwards it eventually stooped on the outskirts of Denpasar. Debbie was heading South to Kuta, whilst I was heading North through Denpasar and back to Lovina, and somehow Debbie and I missed each other at the terminus – it might be that she was whisked away on a connecting bus – and we never properly said goodbye. Got to Ubung station on the Northern edge of Denpasar late in the afternoon, still hoping that there would be a bemo or bus going North. I found a bemo and waited for it to leave, but, as is the case with Asian buses which only leave when they are full, it continued to wait for more passengers. However, the new passengers were arriving very infrequently in ones and twos, and by 8.30 it was still only half full. I was getting anxious, because I didn't want to arrive too late, particularly since the bus was only going to Singaraja and I would still need a connecting bemo for the onward leg from Singaraja to Lovina. In a final attempt to get things moving, I decided to call the driver's bluff by pretending to walk away, but the driver did not bat an eyelid and refused to take the bait. Rather than accept defeat to the driver I thought, "Stuff it," and I decided to go back into central Denpasar to find somewhere to stay the night. Found a room at Nakula Familiar – good, 30,000 Rp.

Wednesday 30th June – Meeting Nur Again

At breakfast, I met a very nice girl from Switzerland called Beatrice. She's just arrived in Bali, this being her gateway into Indonesia and she was looking for information. I was happy to give it and I gave as much as I could. We chatted for quite a while and got on very well. The time just flew by and when I let it slip out that I was heading off to Lovina Beach later today she was debating whether to come with me. As nice as she was, and despite the hint that my rich vein of form with the opposite sex could be continuing, I didn't really want to have the complications of explaining to Beatrice my situation with Nur. In the end, I just about managed to persuade her not to follow immediately, (but she may travel up there very soon). I had read on a poster yesterday about the nearby Taman Budaya Art Centre, which advertised traditional Indonesian dancing. As I was talking to Beatrice about it, she recognised the name Taman Budaya, having already been there and had understood that there would be more dancing today. Having packed my rucksack ready to nip off quickly later, I went to the Arts Centre on the off chance to see what was on. On arrival, I recognised it to be somewhere that I had been to before on one of my previous trips. I thought I was in luck because the Arts Festival was indeed continuing today, but it did not include either Kecak dancing or any of the other types of traditional dances that I had wanted to see. I didn't hang around, so I popped back to the hotel, reported my findings to Beatrice, said goodbye and then left to go back to Ubung station and on to Lovina. This time there was no delay, and the bus I took first went West via Pupua, which, although longer in distance, was more convenient and probably shorter in journey time not least because it went directly to Lovina before looping back to Singaraja. It was also just as cheap (5,000 Rp) and involved less hassle.

Got back to Parma's homestay at just after 6 pm.

I quickly checked into a beach cottage at Parma's and raced onto the beach hoping to catch Nur, but she was not there. A little further along the beach I spotted some of Nur's friends, who were still milling around, so I walked towards them. As I approached them, they instantly recognised me, and, before I had a chance to say anything, they announced that Nur had acquired a new job selling sarongs on the beach, and informed me that she'd already left to go home. I went back to my room, grabbed a quick shower and shave and went up the road to Nur's house. Maybe it was a sixth sense that brought Nur out of her house, because just as I was about to turn in off the road and head up the dusty path to her house, she came out of her door, glanced my way, and then seemed to freeze for a split second before running towards me, jumping up at me and clinging on. We silently held each other tightly. You could say that she was pleased to see me – very pleased – but I was just as pleased to see her. It made me feel very humble and, to an extent, very guilty, because by coming back I knew that I would be putting Nur and I through an emotional wringer one more time when it came for me to say goodbye for the final time. But for now, for this beautiful precious moment, it was all worth it.

We went for a meal to a warung in Kalibukbuk, where I told Nur all (well, almost all!) about my travels and travails through Sulawesi and I showed her my battle scars. Nur confirmed that she'd started selling sarongs on the beach, and she'd managed it by using as capital the little bit of money I'd left her with. She also told me that she'd already written to me, and that there would be letters waiting for me at my pal's in Australia. Nur came back to my room at Parma's, where we cuddled up to each other, clinging tightly, and our rapprochement became steadily more steamy and passionate, even to the extent that Nur declared that she was ready for us to make love. My conscience got the better of me, because, despite my strong feelings for her (and even stronger carnal desires), I still harboured serious doubts about how we were going to make our relationship work, and, not wanting her to waste her purity on a passing gad-about like me, I succeeded in persuading her to think about it first. Nevertheless, she stayed all night and we fell into a glorious deep sleep wrapped in each other's arms.

Thursday 1st July – Kecak Dancing

Nur stayed the night and left at around 5.15 am – but not until we'd had another heavy petting session. Nur said last night that I looked skinny. Consequently, when I had breakfast this morning, this was the excuse I needed to have a bigger breakfast. Come to think of it someone else last night had also observed that I'd lost weight – I can't remember who. I haven't been described as skinny for a good 15 years, so it was another nice massage of my ego (as if I really needed it). Saw Nur later when she came to do my washing – she insisted (honest!!). After another snog, I gave Nur a full Reiki, and then she left. Later had a haircut with a Mad Max, the butcher of Bali. I'd asked for a very light trim and what I got was a very severe short back and sides – no kidding. I can't deny that he did a good job and I couldn't fault it other than it wasn't remotely what I'd asked for. Still it looks a lot tidier. I went round to Nur's house later and had lunch, which Nur prepared in the style of a nasi campur – comprising a scoop of nasi putih (white rice) accompanied by small portions of a number of other dishes, including meat, vegetables, peanuts, boiled egg and krupuk (fried shrimp) – which was delicious. Nur told me today that her age is 27 (not the 29 which I had previously thought) and her birthday is the 22nd August (which by my calculations would make her a Leo). Had a very productive afternoon – funny how one day is an enormous struggle and you cannot do a single thing, whilst the next day life seems so easy and you get so much done. I made enquiries about completing my diving training and it will take too long to complete in the short time that I have, and it is very expensive too, so that idea was kiboshed. I then enquired about hiring a car on Saturday as I wanted to explore several areas with Nur and hiring a car seemed like the best way to do it. In particular, I wanted to go back and complete the journey to Batukau, which Nur and I couldn't complete because of the motorbike accident. Discovered the cost would be 70,000 Rp all inclusive (just over £4, so I can just about afford it). I also heard that there is kecak dancing in Lovina village tonight. I confirmed my ticket to Australia. I bought some good postcards. I met up with Kadek and I bought two wind chimes, one for me and one for my friend Steve, and two brightly coloured large mobiles for Steve's children, one of fish and one of stars. Went back to Parma's and had massage. Gave a girl who had a headache a head Reiki. It worked. Had shower and went round to Nur's. She turned up just as I arrived, in her Muslim dress – very attractive.

Nur and I walked deep into Lovina village to an open-air mini theatre, where earlier today I had seen a hand-painted advertisement for a performance this evening of the dance known as Kecak. It was a dance that I had always wanted to see, my first recollection of having seen it being in the televised version of 'Ring of Fire'. In that programme, aerial shots were taken from directly above and looking down on the arm-waving, swaying, very large body of men below made one imagine one was looking down on a human eye, with the empty centre of the group representing the pupil, and the circles of men around it representing a dilating and moving iris. Others have likened the movement to a living, moving mandala, a spiritual and ritual geometrically patterned <u>symbol</u>, representing the <u>universe</u>, much used in <u>Indian religions</u>, including Hinduism and Buddhism. I had never seen it during any of my previous visits to Bali.

My expectations tonight were low, because I was anticipating that it would be an uninspiring touristy affair. I was to be very much mistaken. Later that night I wrote the following in my diary, *"I got the feeling that I was seeing the pub band equivalent of Kecak, rather than Oasis, but many pub bands are brilliant."* Tonight's performance was indeed brilliant. It was true that there were several tourists among the audience, but, if anything, they were slightly outnumbered by Balinese, and I recognised several people from the local village. The Kecak is performed almost entirely by men, with usually only one exception, and with no gamelan orchestra to accompany them. The musical aspect is provided by the main body of men, who sit in a series of complete concentric circles facing into the middle of the circle and who chant a repetitive, rhythmical 'chak-a-chak-a-chak' sound. The Kecak portrays the Ramayana, a story about Prince Rama, who is an incarnation of the Hindu God Vishnu, and his fight against the evil king Rawana. Rawana abducts Rama's beautiful wife, Sita, so Rama goes after Rawana and with the help of the monkey god, Hanuman, and the monkey king, Sugriwa, he eventually engages Rawana in battle, defeats him, and rescues Sita. Two concentric circles of bare-chested men, wearing black and white checked sarongs around their waist, sat around the central stage and they represented the monkey army, swaying from side to side in unison, waving their hands above their heads, and chanting non-stop their chak-a-chak vibrato. The trance-inducing chorus of chak-a-chak rose and fell, becoming steadily more hypnotic and beguiling over time. In the middle of the circle, performers in brilliantly coloured costumes portrayed the central characters in the Ramayana story. Their performances were part dance and part mime, with the only sound emanating from them being the occasional over-the-top bellowing or theatrical cursing. The only females present were beautiful Sita, clothed in a gold and maroon coloured kebaya, and her attendant handmaidens. With the monkey god, Hanuman, looking suitably grotesque in a mask that looked like a cross between a pig and a dragon, and with the sword-carrying evil Rawana sporting a villainous moustache and black-painted elongated eyebrows and cheeks, the performance reminded me very much of pantomime. With the archetypal pantomime villain in Rawana playing up to the audience, the story was surprisingly very funny. Nur loved it too. Indeed, Nur's reaction capped a perfect evening by provided authenticity to the occasion, and reassuring me that I was seeing real Kecak.

Friday 2nd July – a bit of this, that and the other

Nur stayed again last night and again left at 5.00 am. I was knackered this morning, because we talked about sex until quite late last night. Nur is very keen to have sex, but being acutely conscious of the restrictions placed on her by her religion, I managed to persuade her – again – that we should not have full sexual intercourse. How ironic, after all my exploits in Asia, that I should be trying to persuade someone NOT to make love with me! However, I did suggest that we could still pleasure each other and she agreed. I did her, but I'm not sure how much success I had. She then did me, but she tired very easily. In the end, we both gave up. Later in the morning, I lazed on the beach, and wrote out a few postcards. Then went into Singaraja with Nur and had another productive day. I bought two gamelan tapes. I bought more, and better, incense. I bought coffee for me and coffee for Steve in Australia. I bought some stamps, and I bought four cheapish films for my camera. Nur and I had bakso (meatball soup) for lunch – quite good. Made some more enquiries about renting a car on Saturday and then realised that I would have a problem, because I don't have my driving licence with me. I was advised that it would cost me 95,000 Rp plus petrol with a driver. Later one of Nur's relatives offered to take us for 100,000 Rp including petrol. I was tempted, but I did some counting and realised that I would not have enough money left to see out my trip in Indonesia, at least not if I wanted to help out Nur. Many tourists seemed to arrive today – I think there are at least 14 more. The beach workers were suddenly pouncing. I saw one fat American man being quite rude and brusque to a young girl selling t-shirts – there was no need to behave that way, because she was not being pushy and a polite but firm "no" would have been enough to do the trick. I must say, though, that the way some of the sarong sellers spread out their sarongs reminds me of Dracula spreading out his wings to ensnare young virgins. Same thing really! Of course, I was caught out once (come to think of it, more than once). Nur had a massage with a friend of Naicah's in my room – but the friend did not want Naicah to know – all curious and silly. In the evening, Nur and I had another go at pleasuring each other and this time was much better. Nur seemed much more relaxed when I did it to her. I then showed her what to do to me, and this time she was spot on and took great satisfaction and delight at seeing me come. We then went to Mrs Johni's restaurant, where the meal that night of chicken satay was especially tasty. We met a couple from Taiwan who were also eating there and had a good conversation, particularly about their desire for independence from China.

Saturday 3rd July – Legong

Made the final decision that I couldn't afford to hire a car and go to Batukau today – too much. Nur stayed last night and again left at 5.00 am. I've been a little concerned that I might have typhoid. I had noticed that I have pink spots on my face. I checked in the Lonely Planet guidebook health section, and amongst the many symptoms for typhoid are pink spots (I have), a cold (I have), and constipation (I have). Although I had received an anti-typhoid jab before leaving the UK, I also read that it doesn't completely prevent you from getting it. BUT, I haven't had too many of the other symptoms. One of the main ones is a fever, and, although I did have a slight temperature when I first noticed the spots a couple of days ago, it hasn't persisted or progressed into anything worse. Also, since I know that it is a serious, potentially fatal, disease, I believe that I should be a lot more ill than I am. Maybe I've caught it, but my relatively strong and healthy constitution and the anti-bodies created when I had my anti-typhoid injection are managing just about to successfully fight it. Still, it's something I need to keep an eye on. Bought a whole pineapple from a young boy on the beach, which he expertly then pared, by first cutting off the green spiky top, then carefully cutting off the rind as close to the edge of the pineapple skin as he could, knowing that the sweetest and juiciest parts of the pineapple were usually right at the very edge, and then carefully cutting away at the now exposed brown eyes, forming V-shaped trenches as he moved around the pineapple to remove them. Fascinating to watch, delicious to eat. I shared this with my beach-seller friends. I went over to Banjar in the afternoon to meet up with Komang in order to say goodbye. I bought from her a shirt for Steve and shorts for Nur. Earlier in the day, I'd met and got talking to a sweet girl who was trying – unsuccessfully – to find customers upon whom she could massage. I cannot deny that she was attractive, but my motivation was in genuinely wanting to help her and, being the good-hearted chap that I am, I suggested that she come to my room in the early evening at a time when both Nur and

Naicah would be busy showering and feeding the extended family. I didn't want to cause any offence to them and accordingly hadn't mentioned it. The girl came to my room at a little after 6.00 pm, with me thinking that I probably would not see Nur for a good hour and a half or more, and knowing that the massage would last about 40 minutes. Although I thought I had plenty of time, I locked the door as a precaution. She was actually very good, and had done my back and was working on my calves and feet when Nur knocked on the door. I felt like I had been caught in flagrante delicto. I felt a moment of shock and panic and was momentarily tempted not to answer it, but knowing that in truth I had done nothing wrong, I decided to front it out. I opened the door. Nur initially seemed perplexed, but I told her about my wanting to help out the girl and my not wanting Nur's mum to know, so as not to offend her. To my intense relief and surprise Nur said that she entirely understood. With the moment having now passed, I had no desire to continue with the massage, but I paid the girl in full. After she had gone Nur was a little quiet, but she chirped up soon afterwards. We went back to the dance venue this evening and this time we saw Legong dancing. I had seen it numerous times before, but it was as beautiful as ever and was made even more enjoyable by being able to share the experience with somebody in Nur who understood each twist and nuance of the young dance-girls' movements.

I learnt that the votes had finally been counted in the Indonesian legislative election, with the result that the party with the largest number of votes was *Partai Demokrasi Indonesia Perjuangan (PDI)*, the Indonesian Democratic Party of Struggle, the ones with the red flags with an ominous black bull in the centre. However, they had no overall majority and initially less than half the parties accepted the results, a seemingly unfortunate common trait with losing parties in emerging democracies across the world. On the plus side, the differences were being discussed without much bloodshed or violence, though there was still to come the thorny issue of who would be the next president. Megawati Sukarnoputri, the leader of PDI, seemed to polarise opinions.

Sunday 4th July – Déjà Vu

Another sad day. Nur stayed again last night. But again she left at 5.00 am. She came back a little later because she had been to a Muslim circumcision party – poor little sod. I'm still rather constipated but I had a little success. On its own it would be OK, but I have a lot to catch up. This trip is crazy, one day I'm loose, next day I can't go at all. Said goodbye to several people. Saw the girl who came to give me a massage last night and assured her that Nur was OK about everything. Saw a little girl – Kadek – who offered to get me a mango: I agreed but she couldn't find any. Nur and I went for a little walk along the beach.

She wanted to swim in the sea, so we both swam, which was great — she absolutely loves being with me and I don't deserve even an inch of her love. I had a final massage with Naicah. Then I changed money. I was running out and although I had tried to budget to avoid having to change more money, I wouldn't have been able to give much money to Nur — maybe only 10,000 Rp. Nur stayed with me when I went back to my room and packed and eventually the time came when I had to leave, but not before there were floods of tears from Nur. And from me. We'd agreed that she wouldn't come to the airport with me this time, so she said goodbye to me at the gate to Parma's homestay.

It was a very sad day. In the afternoon, I headed South and found a restaurant in Kuta, which was close to the airport, where I was able to kill time before catching the evening flight to Australia. I had left Nur behind in Lovina this time, because we both agreed that it would be better this way. As sad as it was when it had come for me to leave Nur, in a way it felt different compared to the previous time. It felt as though the last occasion was the time when we spiritually and emotionally went our separate ways, and the last four days had been a bonus. It was also a very poignant day in the sense that I would be saying goodbye to Bali, to Indonesia, and indeed to Asia, after an action-packed four months full of memories and not a little intrigue. Although geographically I would be heading further East, in a sense I would be heading West, in that I would be heading back to the relative familiarity of Western civilisation, and, as a result, I felt a strong sense of anti-climax, thinking that this would be the end of the adventure. How wrong would I be!

CHAPTER 7

Australia

<u>*Monday 5th July – Meeting Steve and Family*</u>

After a quiet and reasonably punctual flight to Australia – 6-hour journey, 2-hour time difference – arrived in Brisbane in the early hours of the morning. Steve wasn't there to meet me.

I was aware that the Aussies are strict about bringing fauna or flora into the country (or out, for that matter), so I decided I should probably declare my wooden objects, (being the two wind chimes and the two mobiles – flying fish and stars) *that I had got for the children. Unfortunately, one of the wind chimes was infected by some type of woodworm. I was told that I could have it treated, but it would cost A\$30 to A\$40 (£15 to £20), and I would have to leave it and then come back to collect it. As it only cost me a little over £1 in the first place I had no realistic option but to ditch it. It was taking up too much room anyway. Found a bus heading South to the Gold Coast, which left almost immediately, and after one quick change at Southport, I was able to hop off right outside the front door to Steve's house. I arrived at 7.45 am, and when I knocked on the door Steve was clearly shocked to see me standing there looking like a waif and stray. Luckily Steve had been up a short while, as had the two children, whilst* *his wife, Sonya, was still in bed. Steve informed me that he had not received my postcard from Indonesia, which was why he wasn't there to meet me at the airport. After the initial shock, he seemed really pleased to see me.*

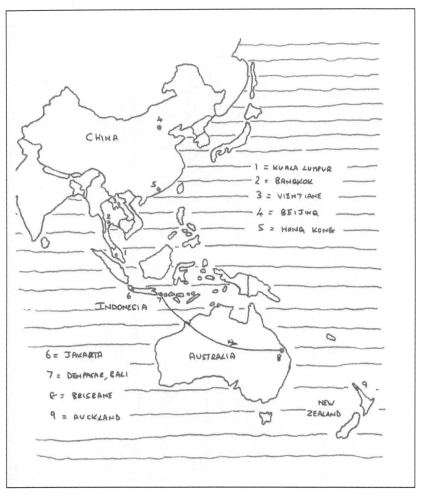

Map 35

And so it was that I had kept to the promise that I had made to Steve five years previously to visit him in Australia in 1999. I had known Steve for about 28 years. Although we went to different schools, we were brought up on the same estate and he lived a couple of doors down from another best friend of mine. Football was our main passion and along with other mates from the same estate we would grab every available opportunity, after school and weekends, come rain and shine, to go over the playing fields, armed with jumpers for goalposts and play until it was either time for tea, or until it was too dark to play (whichever was the later). We were exactly the same age, with only 11 days separating us and in 1978 at the age of 18 we had a combined coming of age fancy-dress birthday party. We were also part of a larger group of friends who referred to ourselves as the Barn Gang. This was not the sort of gang that these days would carry with it sinister connotations. Instead, we were simply a group that had a pal whose parents had an old barn or stable out the back of their house that we were allowed to use as a type of social club. We would play music, drink beer and brag about the sexual conquests that we (claimed to have) had in the mythical upstairs room to the barn. Being lads, we would not have openly confessed to such unmasculine emotions, but Steve and I were close. So it was with a great deal of disappointment that Steve announced in 1985 that he was planning to emigrate to Australia. His father had died when Steve was young and his mum had brought up Steve and his only sibling, an older sister, on her own. His sister had emigrated out to Australia several years earlier, moving to live on the Gold Coast in Southern Queensland and when Steve went out to visit her he fell in love with the place. In particular, Steve was attracted by the warmer climate, and the guarantee of summer sunshine, so maybe those years playing football in the mud through the English winter in wind, rain and snow had taken its toll after all. It was also a fact that Steve is a butcher by trade, and he had learnt that not only were prospects very good for obtaining work, but that it was also pretty certain that he would receive far better pay in Australia, with its meat-rich diet, than he ever would have done in the UK. Consequently, the venture to Australia was almost risk-free, and the promise of a much higher salary, together with a way of life that guaranteed regular summer weather, was for him a heady mix. Steve emigrated in 1988. Subsequent to his emigration, he had returned to the UK to visit his mum, and to catch up with us, on a regular basis, but this became less regular with his marriage to a girl called Sonya and the subsequent birth of his son Kyle in 1995 and his daughter Haylee in 1996. I had never met Haylee but I had met Sonya and baby Kyle when they had last come over to the UK with Steve in 1995.

Upon being ushered into the house, the biggest shock on meeting Steve's family was the discovery that his daughter, Haylee, has Down's Syndrome. In all his letters and Christmas cards and in all my communications with his mum there had never been any mention of it. I guess it wasn't exactly something to shout about but equally I was surprised that he had kept it secret. Haylee was almost three years old. It is no exaggeration to say, though, that I fell in love with Haylee very quickly. As is often the case with persons with Down's, she was sweet-natured, playful, loving and always smiling and very quickly felt comfortable enough to sit on my lap and to allow me to feed her. I learnt that Haylee's disability is not as pronounced or severe as others with Down's Syndrome. In fact, she was quite bright, so much so that, to compensate for a defect in her speech that specialists had said would improve only very slowly, she had quickly learnt to use sign language. It was very endearing to see her 'talk' through her hands to Sonya, Steve and even four-year-old Kyle, all of whom were also learning sign language so as to be able to communicate with her. My initial shock at the discovery soon disappeared and, save for the reminders that came when Haylee was whisked away to visit her therapist, the notion that she had a disability was soon forgotten. I settled into the routine at Steve's very quickly.

Chucked my rucksacks into the room laid out for me, considered whether to quickly bung all my clothes in the wash but decided to leave it until later, set up the photograph of Nan on the bedside cabinet, pondered on whether Nan had ever met Steve, but decided it was unlikely, went back out to have a cup of tea (a proper English cup of tea with milk and sugar), and toast with Vegemite and then I had a shower before retiring for 2 hours or so to grab some sleep. Steve's children seemed to take to me – Kyle's 4, but is clearly a handful, and Haylee's nearly 3. Although Haylee has Down's Syndrome, she seems so full of life. Steve and Sonya clearly love her to bits. The children loved the mobiles, and Steve and Sonya were grateful for the coffee and wind chime, though they weren't so enamoured by the incense; reminding me of Life of Brian' – (in the scene, Brian's mother Mandy is thanking the three wise men for coming to visit baby Brian, who they mistook for baby Jesus, "If you're dropping by again do pop in, and thanks a lot for the gold and frankincense but don't worry too much about the myrrh next time)." *Sonya was very friendly and made me feel welcome immediately. Went into town to do some shopping and get some money. I needed to get myself checked out medically. Found a Medicare office* (the Australian equivalent of the Department for Health), *went in to make some enquiries, and discovered that they can help me for free as the Australian and British governments have reciprocal arrangements. I then went to the doctors' surgery used by Steve's family in the evening and showed him my leg wounds and my pink spots. He was happy that my leg wounds are healing nicely, and, in relation to the pink spots, he does not believe that I have anything seriously wrong (certainly not typhoid), but he took some blood tests just in case, and he said that he would speak to an expert in tropical diseases tomorrow. Had a fat, juicy Aussie steak in the evening. Lovely.*

Tuesday, 6th July – Photograph with Meter Maids

Difficult getting up – the 2 hours time difference does make a difference. Had eggs and bacon for breakfast. Sonya had gone out in the morning to take Haylee to physiotherapy. When she eventually came back we all went swimming to the local pool. We literally had the whole pool to ourselves. I swam 48 lengths and felt good afterwards. We then went to the local RSL Club (technically a club for ex-servicemen, but anyone can go along), where we had a good meal for A$3.50. Later we all drove into Surfers Paradise in search of Mr. Oilman.

One of the most vivid memories from my trip to Australia in 1984 was of a man who became a folk hero (to me at least). He worked on the main beach at Surfers Paradise and his job was to apply sun tan lotion to those who needed or desired it, and he did it without touching. He was a bronzed, muscular, Adonis of a man, in his mid to late forties, wearing only a sun visor and boxer-style swimming trunks, with a full head of black hair, a trimmed nest of chest hair, and sporting the sort of bushy black moustache that seemed to be all the rage with Aussie cricketers at the time. The area of the beach that he patrolled was clean, backed by cultivated palm trees and, with a jetty full of gleaming white yachts anchored just under half a mile away, was seemingly the preserve of the jet set, this Aussie equivalent replicating, and maybe even rivalling, that of a St. Tropez, a Barbados or a Copacabana. My cousin Mark had recommended we go there to take in the 'scenery'. Mr. Oilman was sitting in the middle of the beach on a deckchair shaded by a parasol. With me suitably kitted out with my voyeur's armoury of a sunhat, bottle of water and zoom lens ready fixed to my camera, my cousin suggested we take up a perch on the low wall at the back of the beach to wait for the action to start. We did not have to wait too long before a gorgeous leggy girl, wearing a loose-fitting singlet top and close-fitting high-legged thong bikini bottoms, elegantly sashayed from the promenade onto the sand. She was sinuously tall, being just a little short of six feet, with long, natural-looking, mousey blonde hair topped off by a straw hat, she wore expensive-looking sunglasses, carried a small, chic, straw beach bag and sported a curvy lightly-tanned figure. The way her singlet billowed and bounced when she walked her catwalk walk across the sand tantalisingly hinted at the possibility of there being an absence of a bikini top underneath. She walked over to Mr. Oilman, leant over to suggestively whisper something in his ear, which seemed to stir him into action, and then carried on walking past him a little way to find her territory on the beach. She put down her bag, took out from within it a sarong and spread it out on the sand. She then stood up and glanced expectantly at Mr.

Oilman – no words were spoken – whereupon Mr. Oilman seemingly on cue walked up to her armed with a type of spray gun that looked like he was about to do serious damage to some flies. The girl took off her hat and sunglasses, placed them on the sarong, then stood back up and with her right hand crossing over to her left side and with her left hand crossing over to her right side – such expertise leaving little doubt that this was not the first time she had performed to the gallery – she took hold of the bottom edges of her singlet and provocatively slowly peeled it over her head, confirming in the process the absence of a bra or top underneath. As the singlet slipped over her pert breasts, they jiggled momentarily before quickly finding their equilibrium. Her nipples were small and erect. She leant over to place the singlet on the sarong and then stood invitingly in front of Mr. Oilman with arms outstretched above her head and her bare breasts projected in his direction. Mr. Oilman then went about his work, moving steadily around her body, pumping and squirting his golden liquid over her apricot-tinted torso whilst she stood patiently. I was salivating.

Cousin Mark, who was sat beside me, broke the spell by proudly announcing, "Strewth, cuz, she's a beaut and no mistake, told you it'd be good." Only then, as I turned to glance at Mark sat beside me, did I notice a dozen other young men sitting silently along the same stretch of wall staring trance-like, mouths-agape, in the direction of Mr. Oilman and the model. This was obviously top box office stuff. The audience sat silently, affording the performance the sort of stoic reverence normally reserved for an English classical concert. Certainly, it was quite a show and gained a place in the annals of this human's history as amongst the best jobs in the world. On my return to Australia this time, a visit to Mr. Oilman was on my 'to do' list and when I suggested it to Steve, he was keen to go. Sonya, who turned her nose up in distaste at such boorish crassness, was not so keen, but she was content to indulge these boys in their little fantasy – for now. Steve said he had a vague recollection that Mr. Oilman was still there, though, of course, the older female models had been replaced by younger versions. He was not confident, however, that we would see much today, with it being the relative cool of a mid-winter's day in Australia. His nonchalant delivery did not fool me. It was abundantly clear that the bugger knew full well that Mr. Oilman was still plying his trade, and he probably also knew Mr. Oilman's seasonal movements like a fisherman knows his tide timetables. And I guessed that Sonya could see through the camouflage too, but if she did, she did not let on.

We found him, an ever-so-slightly arthritic, sallow, and slack-muscled shadow of his former self (but enough about me), though for a man who must have been in his sixties Mr. Oilman wasn't doing at all badly. Unfortunately, the beach was very quiet and there would be no oiling up of any models today.

I got chatting to one girl on the beach, who had been sunbathing, and who was not unattractive – nothing came of it. We mooched around the shops backing onto the beach at Surfers Paradise and bumped into two Meter Maids, who are gorgeous girls, who go wandering around giving out cents to help people whose meters on their cars have run out. In their tight-fitting crop tops, denim jeans and stetsons they were sexy, if not a bit too dolled up. But like any good tourist I had to have my photograph taken with them. Then we went to an arcade, where the intention had been to find Steve's children some amusements, but where the bemused kids, together with Sonya, had to wait and watch whilst Steve and I raced against each other on a horse racing simulation machine. Great fun. Then had an enormous ice cream. Went back to Steve's via a bottle shop, where we bought beer and wine for this evening. In the evening two of Steve's friends, John (Kiwi) and Susie (brassy) came round. We had a barbecue and in the course of the evening drank beer, port and a butterscotch liqueur.

Wednesday 7th July – Scored a Goal

Again, I was a bit tired in the morning. Missing Nur. I've been told that we are going out on Saturday and I've got a date with a girl called Linda. She looks OK on the photo.

Finished reading my book. Had rice and meatballs for lunch. Then me, Steve and Kyle went out. We went to Burleigh Heads, (a promontory on the Gold Coast, which separates Broadbeach from Palm Beach, the latter being the place where I stayed with my cousin, Mark, for 8 weeks in 1984). *We had great views along the beach both heading South towards Palm Beach, and North back to Surfers Paradise. Walked down the hill to Tallebudgera Creek and walked around to Palm Beach itself and dipped a toe in the water. Went back to Steve's and in the evening, I went out with him to play football. There was no guarantee of me getting a game, but I put my name down on a list, and eventually I got a game. The match started before I was kitted up ready and I went on 5 minutes in. It was really tough going and I found it very hard to get in the game. Even though I had lost quite a bit of weight on this trip and felt generally fit, it was a different thing to be running around on a football pitch. I have never exactly been the quickest on the pitch and I had a totally crap first half, like a lunatic chasing after but never quite catching the ball. I had a better start to the second half and I had a few good touches. Then we had a free kick, so I went up into the box, and as the ball came over into a melee, I stooped to dive in and head a goal. Great. Substituted immediately thereafter, though, which was disappointing. Good day.*

Thursday 8th July

Had breakfast on the patio – lovely and warm in the sun. The children were dropped off at kindergarten early today, and Sonya was working, so Steve and I went to play tennis, where Steve beat me. It was hot work. After I'd had a shower, we then went to play pool, where I beat him. Apparently, there is horse racing on Saturday on the Gold Coast. Steve is keen to go. Returned home via a supermarket to get a couple of items, as I had volunteered to cook. Decided to do roast pork, which later at Steve's went down well, despite me mucking up the timings so that the meat took a long while in the oven. Later in the evening we watched a video – The Siege – quite good. On the whole, despite all the sports and the good food, and spending quality time with one of my oldest friends, I am feeling a little down. I am really missing the buzz of being around new or different people, and living on my wits in Indonesia. I'm missing Nur and the way of life and I'm feeling really rather nostalgic. I'm even now trying to think of a way to go back out there again. Apparently, Sonya's friend, Kitty, is coming for breakfast on Sunday morning.

Friday, 9th July

A miserable wet drizzly day. And Steve's birthday. I gave him my present, a t-shirt from Bali. In the post he received several cards, together with my postcard from Indonesia, inviting him to come and pick me up at the airport. Better late than never? Not in this instance. Sonya went off to work. The kids went off to kindergarten. Me and Steve had to find things to do. I went swimming on my own. When I came back we went into town, where I sorted out my onward ticket for New Zealand – I depart on the evening of the 21st July – and took out some money. I also arranged to send money to Joe for the diving course. Steve and I then had a game of snooker – I won. Headed back and discovered Sonya at home. Although she thought she needed to work today, she was told that she was not required, but it was too late to organise a babysitter. I cooked a chilli con carne, and we watched a video – 'Very Bad Things' – quite good, though a bit gory. Will rang tonight, so I told him my flight plans and we made some provisional arrangements for when we meet up in New Zealand. He's suggesting we trek right up to the Northern-most part of North Island and the Northern Coast of South Island. We'll see.

Saturday, 10th July – Horse Racing

Today is Al's (my brother's) birthday. He'll be 36. A bit better day, because we actually did something. Good breakfast. Met Sonya's mum and dad. They bought Steve a wall cabinet for his birthday – weird or what! Then met two of Steve's friends. Then *went racing to the Gold Coast Turf Club at Surfers Paradise. We arrived too late to see the first race, but there were 8 races left. I had 3 winners, all in consecutive races. Steve had no winners, but was very unlucky since he had a placed horse in every single race. Taking into account the stake, entrance fee, price of the programme and food I was still only A$3.50 up on the day. But I can't complain. Got back to Steve's, and Sonya was in a snot. I stayed out of the way. I had my bath and got ready to go out. Sonya went off in one car, whilst Steve and I went out in the other – went to the pub first, and then to the restaurant, where we found Sonya and her friend – my date – Linda at a table for two. Sonya and Steve exchanged verbal blows, so Linda and I went to the bar to get a drink and to let them get on with it. Eventually Steve and Sonya forged an uneasy truce. Had a good meal – snapper, with chunky, white meat – then went to several bars and clubs in Surfers. Thought I was onto a promise when Steve and Sonya said they needed to get home to which Linda suggested that I stay at hers and kip on the couch (oh yeah!). I stayed, but, although Linda was perfectly attractive, we didn't have a lot in common, and, as the conversation petered out to nought, it all ended in a damp squib, with me getting a A$25 taxi fare to get back to Steve's.*

Sunday, 11th July – Meeting Kitty

Good day. After a late night last night, I was knackered this morning. I could hear Sonya talking to her friend, who had already arrived. Had shower and then went through to meet her. Although I didn't take to her immediately, she seemed nice enough. She is into Feng Shui (which she insisted is pronounced fong shoy), and she was striding round their house, discussing the finer elements with Sonya, and pointing out what needed to be done to improve the home's karma. After last night's shenanigans between Steve and Sonya the atmosphere was much improved today, but I guess Sonya is keen to do whatever she can to lessen the chances of a repeat. The girls went out and brought back a Chinese takeaway for lunch.

We sat around the table, picking from the takeaway containers and after lunch Kitty hung around. The conversation began as a free-for-all, with me occasionally joining in, but it evolved into Kitty and I talking more directly with each other. Kitty was keen to know about my travels and my back story, whilst I was just as keen to know more about her. Kitty was born and brought up in Australia, and she talked with a typically broad Aussie twang. Indeed, when I had heard her voice from my bedroom earlier on I would not have been surprised if she had Aussie roots going back several generations. However, she was ethnically Chinese, her parents having migrated here shortly before she was born. Kitty held a high-powered position at an investment bank, based in Brisbane, and was clearly a talented, ambitious and modern city girl. She still lived at home with her parents. This situation owed as much to her ethnicity – in so much as the Chinese are culturally more comfortable about living with their elder generations than those in the West – as to the probability that she had been so busy forging a career that relationships had presumably been an afterthought. As the afternoon wore on I was talking to Kitty more and more, the conversation was sparkling and we were getting on so well that she was becoming more attractive by the second. It was the polar opposite of my experience with Linda the previous night.

Part way through the afternoon Kitty told me that her parents were planning to enter into a new business contract, but were wondering if the terms of the contract allowed for them to be able to get an extension. Kitty had been planning to take the contract to her bank the next day to hopefully get one of her colleagues in the legal department to take a look at it, but on hearing that I was a solicitor she wondered if I would mind having a look. I am often being asked by friends and family to provide legal advice about areas of law that have nothing to do with my specialisation in crime, and I am always very wary of giving such advice. At the same time, however, I try not to be churlish and I am usually keen to try to help, so, having given Kitty the usual caveats, I agreed to take a look. Sometimes, all it takes is for someone to break through the jargonise and, thankfully, that was the case with Kitty's parents' contract, because it was quite easy to read. I advised that it did not seem that it was possible to get an extension to the contract, at least not based on the terms contained therein. The fact that I had been prepared to take a look at the contract did nothing to lessen Kitty's apparent growing interest in me.

Steve and Sonya had been planning for the family and I to go round to a friend's house for a barbecue in the evening. Sonya was very keen for Kitty to join us, but when she put this to her, Kitty was reticent, pointing out that she didn't know the other friends too well, and felt like she would be intruding. However, when I chipped in and reminded her that I was in the same position, if not worse, in view of the fact that I had *never* met them, and suggested she could come along to give me moral support, she readily changed her mind. It was a good evening. Steve and Sonya's friends were very accommodating, the conversation flowed and Kitty and I continued to get on very well. Driving to the friends' house, Kitty had taken Sonya in her car, whilst I went with Steve and the children. However, when it was time to return later in the evening, I asked Kitty if she would mind taking me back. She agreed. I hadn't taken much notice of her car earlier, but it turned out to be a sporty number with a personalised number plate starting with the letters KIT, which Kitty proudly announced was a Honda NSX, but which frankly meant nothing to me. As we pulled up outside Steve's house,

I asked Kitty if she fancied going out during the week. When she declined, I thought that I had either blown it or misread the signals, but reassurance came with her explanation that she works long hours during the working week, not to mention her lengthy commute into and out of Brisbane and she suggested we go out instead on Friday. I readily agreed.

Steve's friends seemed really friendly, and the barbecue was great. Feel good. Had a good chat with Sonya back in the house later, who commented on how well me and Kitty were getting on. I was still hyper after my day spent chatting to Kitty, and I went to bed late tonight, feeling tired but satisfied. I pondered on how I had been so confident in asking Kitty out for a date at the end of the evening, just like it was the most natural thing to do, whereas the me who had started out on this adventure over 4 months ago would have fretted and ruminated on the situation for ages before eventually – or probably not even at all – plucking up the courage to do so.

Monday, 12th July – Minjungbal Aboriginal Centre

I woke up in the after-glow of my meeting with Kitty yesterday. I considered how ironic it was that, having thought that I had left Asia behind, the first girl that I should gravitate towards in Australia should be of Asian origins. It was clear that whatever her roots, Kitty had fully embraced the West in that she was an ambitious, dynamic, and very modern career girl. I had already guessed that the main reason why Kitty was still single was probably because her career was her priority, because there could be no other earthly reason why Kitty should be so. She was beautiful, with a full and sexy figure, she was both fun to be with and downright funny, with a wickedly dry sense of humour, she had a beaming inviting smile and she was interesting to talk to. In the short time that I had been with her it was apparent that she had an interest in the world around her, be it nature or politics or social affairs. My mind was buzzing.

Sonya went off to work. After getting the kids ready, we took them to the Minjungbal Aboriginal Cultural Centre. There was a museum, which was reasonably interesting and an exhibition of aboriginal art and artefacts. A number of musical instruments were demonstrated being played by aborigines, including didgeridoos, bullroarers – which are sacred objects used in aboriginal religious ceremonies, consisting of a piece of wood attached to a string, whirled round to produce a roaring noise – and music sticks – which are sticks that are knocked together repeatedly to make resinous noises. The very fact that these instruments were played gave them a context and a meaning and they were, therefore, interesting, but the other objects on display were dry and disappointing. Saw a Bora circle — an initiation area — and then walked around the reasonably attractive nature reserve grounds, which contained mangrove swamps, and were full of birds. Went to a scenic outlook point at Tweed Heads/Coolangatta. Came back. Had a swim. Sonya had lots of left-overs that needed to be binned or eaten — including pork, rice, chilli con carne, bubble and squeak, mushrooms and an avocado. I made them into a veggie bake, with garlic mushrooms, Chinese style pork and rice, and had them with baked potatoes. My improvisation was actually quite good (if I say so myself). Sonya later told me that Kitty had rung this morning to speak to Sonya at work, because she thought that she might be upset about us going out on Friday. Sonya reassured Kitty, telling her that she was very happy for us both.

Tuesday, 13th July – Springbrook

Sonya wasn't working today, there were no therapy sessions for Haylee, and no kindergarten for either Kyle or Haylee, so we all went swimming first thing and we then drove out to an area known as Springbrook. Steve and Sonya pointed out their old house which we passed on the way. We hadn't got far out of the city before we were in attractive rolling countryside. We visited several great spots for panoramic views where down in the valleys we could see waterfalls and fast-flowing streams. The area that we were looking at was once a huge volcano, which over millions of years has eroded away. Much of the valley was covered in verdant rainforest. At a couple of places Steve and I hopped out for a little walk, and one of the best places we visited was an aptly named viewpoint called 'Best of all Lookout.' Sonya had brought a picnic, which was great, and many birds, including magpies, rosellas, crows, and mynah birds (according to Steve, but I had my doubts), were attracted by the bread, which the kids had thrown for them. We had a cup of tea at a supposedly authentic English country garden tea shop — tea seemed authentic, but garden not so. We later saw some rock wallabies. Sonya went out with a girl called Annette in the evening, and Kitty was due to catch up with them later, leaving Steve and I to have a quiet night in watching Cleopatra, a heap-of-shit-of-a-crap-acting-supposed-blockbuster.

Wednesday, 14th July – Long Telephone Call

Sonya took Haylee to therapy in the morning, so Steve and I took Kyle to a playground beside the coast at Southport, and later went out to a spit of land opposite Southport, where Kyle and Steve (and later I) tried to fly a kite. It was quite tricky not least because it was a bit too windy. I then treated us all to some fish and chips, and we found a bench where we could eat them and look back across the bay. On doing so, we found ourselves entertained by three blokes struggling to get both them and their surfboards across the narrow inlet, where they were determinedly fighting against fast-flowing tidal water and the wind. They didn't quite make it and one bloke had to be rescued. I nearly choked on my chips. Went back to the house and I went for a swim whilst Steve went to the dentist. Did 48 lengths – feel that I am getting stronger. We had arranged that Steve would come and pick me up when he was done, but that I would start walking back if he wasn't there when I had finished. I started walking and never stopped – a 50-minute journey. In the evening Steve and Sonya went to the pictures as I had offered to babysit. I made a home-made soup for tea. I telephoned Kitty later to make arrangements for Friday – rang at 8.55 pm and finished at 10.45 pm. In the course of our chat Kitty went into her bedroom whilst at one stage I got in the bath. The conversation was very intimate and involved – she even suggested coming over to the UK to visit me at Christmas and wondered if I would mind having a flatmate for a while. Did I object? – Did I hell! We came to a compromise about Friday. She agreed to drive over to Steve's house and I would drive thereafter. Not sure which bit is the compromise, but maybe I will find out. Steve and Sonya's film was rubbish. Glad that at least one of us had a good night.

Thursday, 15th July – Sexy Smile

Woke up thinking of Kitty. Yesterday on the coast saw a sulphur-crested cockatoo and pelicans. Last night Steve and I had a long heart-to-heart about Haylee and her Down's Syndrome. He confessed that when she was born he could not cope or face up to the situation, not least because it came as a shock, since they didn't find out until after she was born. That was one of the reasons why he hadn't told any of his mates back home in the UK, because he was struggling to come to terms with it himself. He is much stronger now and appreciates Haylee for the amazing character that she is rather than dwells on what might have been (or on what Haylee might be missing out on). I told him about both my Great Uncle Durrant and Nan Thompson passing away shortly before I came out. He has a vague recollection of meeting Nan at some point. Today we set off to climb Mt. Warning. I prepared sandwiches and we stopped to get water and other provisions on the way. We'd seen quite a bit of rain which all looked very ominous and, true enough, when we got to the car park at the base the mountain was shrouded in cloud and there was intermittent rain. Steve had also developed a headache. It might have been psychosomatic, or tactical, but genuine or not, I was not complaining at the exit strategy it potentially offered. In addition, by the time we had arrived at the start of the walk it was 12.15 pm and we had noticed warning signs at the entrance to the road coming into the reserve advising against commencing any trekking after 12. We looked at each other, with Steve frowning pleadingly, and I nodding in acquiescence and, without a word being spoken we dived into our sandwiches. As we sat there, we saw numerous brush turkeys. On the way back, we drove along the coast via Kingscliffe, which true to its name has a cliff, from which we saw extensive views of waves crashing in along a wide sweeping bay.

We parked up and when I went to the machine to purchase a parking ticket a spectacularly gorgeous blonde girl in tight denim jeans smiled at me as I passed by. Back at Steve's, Sonya advised me on options for restaurants for my date with Kitty tomorrow night and she helped me to book a table at the Paragon restaurant in Surfers Paradise.

Friday, 16th July – Date with Kitty

What a superb day (and a half). Steve took the kids to kindergarten and then came back and we went to play golf – he thrashed me by 14 shots over 12 holes. Good fun, though. Went to Robina shopping centre afterwards, where I bought flowers for tonight. Steve asked me to pick up the kids from kindy (jeez, I'm starting to talk like an Aussie), and when Haylee saw me she ran up to me excitedly, arms raised imparting that I should lift her up. It did not go unnoticed that there were a lot of good-looking young mums waiting outside kindy, including one who appeared to give me a second look. In years to come when I read this diary, I might sound smug, but I seem to have found and mined a rich vein of golden confidence and I am open to every little ego-boosting nuance. Came home and got ready and Kitty arrived at 7.15 pm.

Kitty looked the proverbial million dollars in a navy-blue jacket and skirt, cut just above the knee, with a blue-grey figure-hugging woollen top underneath. She was grimacing as she came into the house, though, as she had a headache. I offered to Reiki her and she did not hesitate at the chance, treating it as though it was the most normal thing in the world. She sat on a high chair in the dining room and I stood behind her and placed my hands on her head, one on the top of her forehead and the other at the back of her crown. She asked what Reiki is exactly and I explained to her that Reiki is a natural healing energy that exists both within the human body and the wider universe. In the course of my recitation, she observed that there is at least one common theme connecting Reiki and Feng Shui, in that both work along or relate to lines or fields of energy, save that we agreed that one important difference is that with Feng Shui some areas of a house have positive energy and some have negative energy, whereas Reiki is always a positive energy. The fact that we both had an interest in a world beyond the material one gave us yet another connection. Once Kitty and I had exhausted the finer points of our respective ethereal worlds, a bored-looking Sonya returned the conversation to more mundane matters by asking Kitty where she had had her nails done. Sonya and Kitty, and occasionally Steve, chatted away whilst I continued applying Reiki for 20 minutes, and by the end Kitty said that her headache, though not completely cured, was much improved.

We headed out to the restaurant, with me driving as agreed, and arrived a little after 8. For the main course Kitty ordered spaghetti carbonara and I ordered barramundi, and we agreed to share a Greek salad as a starter. For drink, she had vodka, lime and soda, whilst I had a glass of red wine. It is fair to say, though, that throughout the evening we were focussed more on each other than we were on our food and drink. We ate our salad very slowly because we couldn't stop talking, so much so that when the main courses came they seemed a little dry as if they had been kept warm for a while. The barramundi momentarily distracted me, as the fish was very meaty and tasty. We chatted over our main course so long that, by the time we had finished, it had gone 10 o'clock and it was too late to order a dessert, since the restaurant had stopped serving. Indeed, with the disappearance of one other couple who had been sitting in the far corner of the restaurant, we became the only persons left in the whole place. It all seemed rather bizarre for a supposed top restaurant to finish so relatively early on a Friday night, but we had been completely oblivious of our surroundings.

We went back to Steve's, arriving at a little after 11, with Steve and all the family safely tucked up in bed and the house hushly quiet. Kitty's headache had returned, so I Reikied her again and on this occasion very soon after doing so the headache disappeared completely. We sat on the sofa and continued talking for well over two hours, when I could contain myself no longer and leaned across to kiss her, a light peck on her cheek. The conversation stopped, she looked into my eyes and we leaned in together for a lingering, passionate, lips-locking kiss. Once we had started there was no stopping us and we were all over each other. The kissing was turning me on like crazy and, like a probe sent on a reconnaissance mission to test for any resistance, my right hand migrated over the undulating contours of her body. There was no resistance. Over her clothing, I stroked her curvy backside, whilst she pressed her body up against mine. I could sense that she was manoeuvring her body to search for, feel and then enjoy the full hardness of my bulging erection against her midriff. I moved my hand round to squeeze her breasts. We were still on the couch, but we soon retired to my bedroom, where Kitty removed her jacket and skirt in quick succession, and then expertly removed her bra from underneath her top, leaving her wearing only her lacy white knickers and woollen top. With her large breasts amplified by her tight-fitting jumper, I was completely turned on, and it didn't take long before her knickers came off too. I laid back on the bed, she climbed on top and we made love. It was difficult to be quiet, since we were both so horny, but we managed – just about – to keep a lid on our love-making. I came to a shuddering climax only moments after she had orgasmed, whereupon we remained locked together in our warm embrace whilst we simmered down. Kitty smelt lovely.

A great day topped off by a superb night. Kitty eventually left at 3.45 in the morning, not before we made arrangements to meet up again.

Saturday, 17ᵗʰ July – Shopping with Kitty

Was woken up by everyone banging and shouting. I got up at 9 – very tired. Had the Spanish Inquisition from Steve and Sonya. Kitty had said that I could tell them anything and everything so I did. Kitty rang to make arrangements. She will come round for tea later today and take me to Mt. Tambourine tomorrow. Lounged around in the garden – played football with Kyle, had good talk with Sonya, and cuddled Haylee. Annette – friend of Sonya and Steve's, not unattractive – came round. Whilst still outside, Kyle and Sonya ganged up to take me on in a water fight – later I gained some recompense by spraying them with shaving foam. Later played tennis with Steve, and lost. Came back and got ready for Kitty. She looked scrummy in her jeans. We went shopping together for the ingredients that I need for tomorrow evening – I plan to cook chimichangas – and had the odd snog along the way. Kitty had to leave early. It was a good, though quiet evening thereafter, with me constantly yawning my head off. I retired early and when my head hit the pillow I was out like a light.

Sunday, 18ᵗʰ July – Enjoying the Great Outdoors

Kitty arrived early today. I wasn't feeling too good, so perhaps I am coming down with something. Kitty and I then left – just the two of us – and headed out to Mt. Tambourine, which is a ridge from where hang-gliders and paragliders take off. It was a beautiful clear day and to see so much brightly-coloured stretch nylon disappearing kamikaze-style over the ridge was a spectacular sight – reminding me of scenes from Mam Tor in Derbyshire back home. From the ridge were extensive, stunning views looking both inland and out towards Surfers Paradise and the sea.

You could say that Kitty and I were loved up. We held hands, took loads of photographs and went for short strolls, stopping every now and again for a little snog. We stopped at an inviting organic farm café, where we had pumpkin soup and a seeded granary roll for lunch. We then drove to a picnic area, intending to park up and go for a walk, but where ours turned out to be the only car in the car park. No words were necessary, because the moment Kitty stopped the car and looked over to me expectantly, I leant over and started kissing her. We became extremely passionate extremely quickly, with my hands wandering from her breasts to her buttocks and with Kitty's hand gripped vice-like onto the taut crotch of my jeans. I slid my fingers through the top of her jeans and inside her knickers. She was very wet. I asked her how adventurous she felt. "Very," she gushed breathily. I slid my seat back as far as it could go, and I turned to kneel in the footwell whilst she climbed over to sit in the passenger seat. Leaving our tops on, I quickly pulled my jeans down, she tugged her trousers down and she pulled her knickers to one side whereupon I deftly slipped inside her. As I did so a car pulled into the car park and, despite it being a very large empty car park, wouldn't you know it but the bugger parked only 25 yards away. We froze and lay there, still coupled, pretending that we were asleep. Another car came into the car park, parking a little further away. Nobody exited their cars – a small blessing. We stayed huddled together – bum naked – for several minutes, but eventually both cars left and we tried again, this time with Kitty on top of me. I entered Kitty again and we were going great guns when, just as Kitty was about to climax, another car came into the car park. That put paid to that. She rolled over and we assumed our 'sleeping' position once again. This time the car parked up well away from our car, but a couple of nosey young kids, each licking ice lollies, got out and came wandering over seemingly intent on looking into our car. Whether they were attracted by Kitty's sports car, or whether they were curious to see why the windows in our car were so steamed up, we did not hang around to find out, because Kitty had had enough. She clambered over into the driver's seat, fired up the engine and, still de-trousered wearing only her knickers, sped off as expertly as if she'd been on a Grand Prix starting grid.

As we drove we came across a pretty mill, converted into a quaint café, where we decided to pop in. Whilst I had a cup of tea, a now fully clothed but slightly dishevelled Kitty found a bathroom where she could sort herself out. On her return, I reminded Kitty that I was due to leave on Wednesday. She sighed, saying that she was only too aware and didn't need reminding. I asked Kitty if she fancied joining me for a couple of days in New Zealand. Kitty said that she would love to, but doubted if it would be possible, agreeing, however, to at least check out air fares.

Went back and I cooked my chimichangas – not too bad. Then we all – kids included – played board games in the evening. Kitty left me another contract to look at (cor blimey, I'm meant to be on holiday!). Great day.

Monday, 19ᵗʰ July – Currumbin Sanctuary

Good day. Got up – feeling better than yesterday, but still a little tightness in the throat. I was told that Kitty had telephoned at 5 to 9, just before I got up. Steve and I decided to go to Currumbin Sanctuary. It was a really great place and I think because the kids enjoyed themselves so much it was probably the best family day out yet. Saw snakes, koalas, kangaroos, pelicans, crocodiles, emus, kookaburras and many other birds, some wild, and some in captivity – I hate to see birds in cages, but these enclosures were large and not too restrictive. Saw a snake show and saw aborigines dancing. Kyle was fascinated by the huge boa constrictors, whilst Haylee found her rhythm and danced to the sound of didgeridoos. We rode on the train and saw lorikeets being fed – all very entertaining. The kids loved it and it was a good day out. I paid (in the knowledge, I cannot deny, that the kids went free). Back at the ranch I looked through Kitty's mum's contract. Made a number of points thereon. Kitty rang from her mobile during the day and raised several questions regarding the contract. She said that she had checked air fares to New Zealand and she was quoted A$900. Spoke to Will in the evening – he's OK to meet me at the airport at Auckland on Wednesday. Spoke to cousin Lynette in Adelaide. Then spoke to Kitty on the phone (one and three-quarter hours again). The conversation turned a little fraught because she is doubting that I will wait for her. I reassured her that I would. We arranged to meet tomorrow in Brisbane.

Tuesday, 20ᵗʰ July – Brisbane

Another cold night – but another warm sunny day. After shower and sorting myself out, I went to Brisbane by train. Steve took me to the station. Got to Brisbane with 40 minutes to spare before it was time to meet Kitty. Wandered around Anzac Square, which is a monument to those who died in World War 1 – very evocative. Then spotted a camera shop and decided to get one of my films developed. Saw Kitty.

Earlier in the morning before travelling to Brisbane I telephoned a couple of travel agents, both based in Brisbane, to enquire about flights to New Zealand and at one of them I was quoted A$449, exactly half of that quoted to Kitty. At a little under £170 when converted into sterling, it was much more like it.

I met up with Kitty at Anzac Square in Brisbane, and she took me to a plaza, where there was a range of prepared foods available. Kitty took sushi, whilst I had a cheese salad roll. I told Kitty about my news regarding flights to New Zealand and she informed me that fortuitously the way that her work rota panned out meant that she had a long weekend off work this coming weekend, so in that respect at least the timings could work out well. However, she said that she still needed to think about it. After lunch, we had 15 minutes before Kitty was due back at work, so we strolled arm in arm around Cathedral Square. Kitty told me that she had received some good news today in that she had been informed that a long-awaited attempt at promotion had finally been successful. I congratulated her and we walked back to her office. I had arranged to wait around in Brisbane in order to go back on the train with Kitty after work. Also, with tonight being my last in Australia, Kitty had planned to come over to Steve's in the evening and the four of us would go out for a meal. Kitty was planning to stay over. Before leaving, Kitty gave me a letter which she had handwritten and which she asked me to read after she had gone back to work. After saying goodbye, I found my way to the travel agent that I had telephoned earlier to double-check that the price I'd been quoted was still correct and to see if flights were available. They confirmed the price to be A$449 and there was indeed availability.

I went out and found a seat in a park and thought about the situation. I had wanted to mark the fact that Kitty had got her promotion by buying her a little memento and the more I thought about it, the more attractive became the idea that the perfect present would be a ticket to Auckland. I considered that it was a little bit generous for somebody I'd only recently met, and £170 was outside my budget, plus, of course, I would have to spend a little bit more on a slightly more fancy hotel in Auckland than the sort of backpacker's haunt that my budget dictated that I would normally have had to make do with. However, the opportunity seemed too good to miss, and I decided that a little bit extra on my debit card was worth it. I went back to the travel agent and explained my situation and asked if they could hold open a booking for me pending a final decision. They agreed, giving me 24 hours to cancel or confirm and they gave me a provisional booking on their letterhead.

I collected my film, and went back to the park where I looked at my photographs. I was pleased with them. I then read Kitty's letter. It was very touching, telling me how much Kitty cared about me and how much she hoped that despite us living on the opposite side of the world from each other that we should not give up hope that there might be some way for us to make our relationship work. I wandered around the riverside, took a ride on the ferry and criss-crossed some of the bridges over the river. It was a lovely warm sunny day.

At the due time, I went back to meet up with Kitty. As we walked to the station, we passed by another small park and I invited Kitty to sit with me for a minute, and when she did so, without saying anything, I gave her the booking form from the travel agent. Her reaction was completely unexpected. I had been imagining her to be happy and overjoyed at seeing what I had done, but she was the complete opposite, looking clearly very shocked and after a minute or two of cold silence, she said that she felt pressurised by what I had done and that I shouldn't have done it without consulting her. I was stunned. I felt aggrieved not least because I believed that I had indeed consulted her, but I never said this to her. Instead, I tried to explain why I had done it this way. I said that I had meant well and had intended it to be a nice surprise, I pointed out that it was only a provisional booking, so if she did not want to go then I could cancel it and I also explained that it was intended in part as a reward for her promotion. She thanked me – half-heartedly – and said that nevertheless it should have been her decision and hers alone to make. I cannot deny that I was a little put out by her reaction and the journey back to the Gold Coast was spent in awkward silence. Kitty picked up her car from the station and drove me back to Steve's and after a quick peremptory kiss on the cheek, she said that she would see me later.

When Kitty returned, the four of us went out for dinner at Conrad's Hotel, Steve's place of work. I was sulkily quiet at first, but as the conversation – and the wine – flowed, I mellowed out and in the end, we had an enjoyable evening. However, there was no more discussion about New Zealand.

Back at Steve's, I said my goodbyes to Sonya, as I anticipated that I might not see her the next day, since she needed to get off to work early and I thought that by the time she returned home in the evening I would be on my way to the airport. I had been genuinely touched by how welcoming Sonya had been to me, despite me being an almost complete stranger, and how I had felt totally relaxed in her home, and I told her so. I had grown quite close to Sonya. Kitty and I then retired to my room, where we kissed, cuddled, made love and eventually fell asleep.

Wednesday, 21ˢᵗ July – Leaving Australia

Got up very early and very tired – I didn't sleep too much last night – and once Kitty was ready we went to drop her off at the station. Steve drove, whilst Kitty and I sat in the back and on the way, she informed me that she had decided to come to New Zealand this weekend. I squeezed her hand. She said that she'd slept quite well in bed. I said that I hadn't. Came back and Sonya was still there and after having breakfast and saying goodbye to her for the second and what I thought would be the final time, Steve and I went with Kyle and Haylee to Playgroup. There we saw Linda with her son, Jordan. A lot had happened since I last saw her. I was slightly embarrassed to see her – I don't know why I should have felt that way — but we had a good chat. Came back and had lunch and then went to Haylee's therapy class in the afternoon. Her attention span was very short and the staff were struggling to get her motivated. I was very touched to be later told that Haylee's behaviour was probably because she knew that I would be leaving today. Came back and I had a call from the travel agency to say that my flight tonight would be delayed and would leave at 10.20 pm. Earlier in the day I had telephoned the travel agency to confirm Kitty's booking for New Zealand. I rang Will and told him about my change of plans and the slight delay to tonight's flight. He said he would still be able to pick me up. Had steak with Steve in the evening and said my third and very final farewell to Sonya, as well as to the children. I telephoned Kitty and confirmed the booking for Friday and gave her all the details. Steve then took me to the airport. Sad farewell after a great and successful two and a bit weeks.

As we headed up into the night sky and I looked down on the extensive strip of orange lights below me on the Gold Coast, I pondered on the ironies emanating from the Australian leg of my journey. My plan to travel to Australia and to keep my promise to visit Steve had been the first and main motivation for me deciding to take a break between jobs. Although it was quite a bit later that my ideas developed into making it such a long and extended trip, Australia had been the catalyst. However, once I had made my plans to travel through exotic-sounding places like Laos, China and New Zealand, it seemed to me that Australia would be the least inspiring of all the places that I intended to visit. Although I had genuinely been looking forward to spending some extended quality time with one of my best friends, I had considered that this leg of my trip would represent a lull in proceedings, partly because I knew that I would be based primarily around the cosmopolitan area of the Gold Coast, which, of course, I had been to before, and partly because I would be going back to a Western-style civilisation. For pity's sake, I would even be talking English (or at least a slightly more acerbic version thereof) with just about everyone. I never would have thought that I would be coming away with my head buzzing, chock full of memories of a whirlwind romance with somebody who, if all the cards played out right, could even turn out to be my life partner. It occurred to me that we had clicked from the moment we met: Kitty was beautiful; Kitty was interesting to talk to; Kitty was fun to be with; Kitty was a bloody good shag! I smiled at my self-indulgent levity, but as I was thinking all this, I reminded myself that I had history for falling for someone too quickly and I knew that it was way too early to be seriously thinking that far ahead. Not for the first time on this trip did I ask myself how on earth I was going to be able to conduct a relationship with somebody on the opposite side of the world; and again not for the first time on this trip did I tell myself that what will be will be and that I should concentrate on the immediate future, which was not to be sniffed at since, of course, it was about to involve a lovely long weekend with Kitty.

It also occurred to me that I had stopped thinking about Nur and I instantly felt a pang of guilt. I reminded myself – perhaps kidded myself – that Nur and I had both been adults who knew full well the limitations of our relationship, that I had after all behaved quite honourably towards her, that I would still treasure both the moments we had spent together and our friendship, and, in any event, perhaps I should not dismiss so readily the possibility of it being us who would ultimately get together, since who knows how things might work out. One of the ironies that struck me was that even though Nur lived almost 3,000 miles closer to me in England than Kitty, the very fact that Kitty lived in a Western culture meant that prospects for Kitty becoming my life partner were far higher than those of Nur. Although I genuinely had not thought about it before, the fact that Kitty probably earnt very good money at her investment bank was not a complete irrelevance either. Again, I told myself not to get carried away.

It was fast approaching midnight – two o'clock in the morning New Zealand time – when the stewardesses insisted on bringing me a meal (although in truth I accept I wasn't exactly force-fed).

I then pondered on the sheer physicality of my carnal relationship with Kitty. One factor was that I was fitter and much more confident than I had been when I touched down in Malaysia. One other factor was that, despite all the near misses and attention shown to me by various girls, in particular throughout Indonesia, not to mention the dalliances with Nur, I hadn't enjoyed complete coitus since my nightmare experience in Xian (which, when I checked in my diary, was exactly three months ago to the day). I concluded that my not insignificant contribution to our shared Epicurean acrobatics was precisely *because* I had had all those near misses, been showered with all that attention and been teased by my close encounters with Nur. I was practically fit to bursting. And in a couple of days' time I had a full four-day weekend's worth of licentiousness to come. With my stomach gurgling away ten to the dozen complaining at the ignominy of eating so late, and looking back down at Australia through squinting eyes as the last remnants of the twinkling lights on the Gold Coast disappeared into black oblivion, the stewardesses were probably wondering why I appeared to be staring out of the window and grinning like the proverbial Cheshire Cat when my eyes fluttered and I drifted off to sleep.

CHAPTER 8

New Zealand

Good flight. Talked to nice Kiwi girl sat next to me. Arrived in Auckland in good time.

Will was there to meet me. I'd only had half an hour's sleep on the plane and I'd not had much the previous night, so I was pretty knackered when we arrived – but I had such an adrenalin rush that I was soon wide awake again. It was good to see him.

Will was, and still is, one of my best friends. He was born in the UK to an English mother and a New Zealander father. His father had migrated to live in the UK, where he met Will's mother and had five children in all. Will was the youngest by a mile, and had been a happy final hoorah to his father's enduring fertility. With the death at an early age of his mother, and with his much older siblings having dispatched themselves to various parts of the globe, Will was left at home with his dad. At some point, shortly after Will's mum's passing, his father, who had long had a hankering to return to his roots, upped ship and returned to New Zealand taking Will with him. He bought a sheep farm 15 or so miles West of Hamilton, located on North Island, and Will and his dad lived out an idyllic rural lifestyle. We met in 1984. Will was supposed to be travelling the world but had not got very far when he holed up on tropical Hayman Island, part of the Whitsunday Islands in Northern Queensland, Australia. Will's gregariousness is very natural, which can sometimes be irritating to those of us who envy his talents and have to work at it, and he had already cheerily introduced himself, as was his wont, shortly after my arrival on Hayman Island. However, it was on the third night of my stay that we properly forged an alliance.

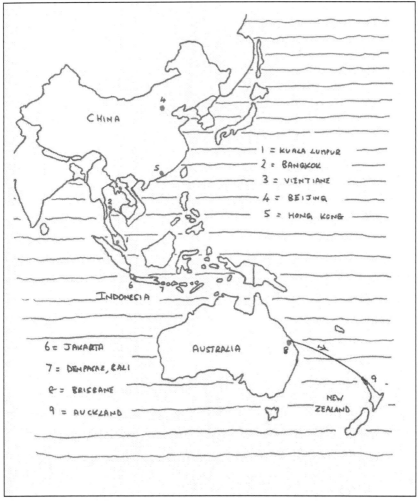

Map 36

I had managed to obtain a job as a drinks waiter cum cocktail barman at the five-star hotel on the island. I had obtained the position by going through a recruiting agency whilst staying with my cousin Mark some 750 miles further South on the Gold Coast. I had needed to work at a couple of local bars on the Gold Coast to prove my credentials, paid the bus fare for the exceedingly long journey from the Gold Coast up to Hayman Island, as well as paying for the boat transfer out to the island, bought my own barman's kit of two white shirts, a pair of smart white shorts, a pair of long black trousers, a dicky bow, a cummerbund, long white socks, short white socks, black shoes, white shoes, a corkscrew and a bottle opener (let it not be forgotten that I was backpacking on a shoestring budget at the time), when on my third day in the job I was sacked, "Through lack of experience." It turned out that the hotel was particularly fussy about bar and drink waiting etiquette – my deportment was wrong, in that I didn't hold myself the correct way when serving a customer at a table, I was not learning the constituent ingredients of the cocktails fast enough, and my attempts to balance the drinks tray were so inept and precarious that, try as they might, customers could not avoid anxiously watching me, wondering if I was about to empty the contents – liquid, ice, umbrellas and all – into some poor sod's lap. The hotel on the tiny island was the only human habitation and had to provide its own staff with facilities, including a staff bar, and I was in there on that third night, drowning my sorrows, contemplating the cost of my failed venture – although the kit had mostly come from charity shops, I had still spent the best part of A$200 in total – when Will came up to me with a ludicrously jaunty, "What's up, mate?"

Not needing a second invitation, I explained all to him, ten minutes later concluding with the postscript, "Well you did ask!"

"No worries," he replied, "I'm sure I can fix you up with a job with me in the pantry; there's my boss over there, I'll talk to him," at which Will pointed to his boss, Eddie, a well-oiled red-nosed Austrian gentleman seated by the bar a little further along, who was clearly sozzled, and was leaning so heavily over the bar that I thought that any moment he would topple over and hit his rather large Romanesque nose on the counter. I was not reassured. A sixth sense must have aroused Will's boss, because, before Will had approached him, he sat upright, looked across our way, and then smiled through cross-eyed eyes, before assuming his aforementioned hypothenusal position.

Thankfully, I was able to find work in the pantry after I went to visit the assistant manager the following day to explain my position, and to my amazement Eddie had seemingly been more in touch with the real world than his countenance had suggested, because he had passed on the word that he'd agreed to take me on. Essentially, I became a lowly dish washer, but the job was far less stressful and the hourly rate paid was only slightly less than that of a drinks waiter.

Five weeks later, with my travelling funds sufficiently augmented, I left Hayman Island. Will remained on the island for several months thereafter, rising to the rank of official beach raker. We kept in touch.

Will moved to the UK a couple of years later. When they were previously living in England, his father had lived in a large house on the Western fringes of Fareham in Hampshire, but, when he moved to New Zealand, for some reason he did not sell his property. For a decade or more the property had remained abandoned and had become the abode of transients, resulting in the partial destruction of the house by fire through a careless act, probably a discarded cigarette, by one of them. Will moved to the UK in the late 1980s intending to renovate and sell on the property. Our friendship evolved during this time.

Will continued to visit New Zealand, where his father and his two sisters lived, spending several months there each year before returning to the UK. I had made a promise several years before to visit and share time with Will in New Zealand. I was now able to fulfil that promise.

I was due to fly out and return to the UK on Wednesday the 25th August, so I would have near enough five weeks in New Zealand and our plans had originally been that I would spend roughly half of my time backpacking on my own and half of my time travelling with Will. The amount of time I would spend with Will had been slightly curtailed by my impending long weekend with Kitty in Auckland. Will was planning several walks, including two separate three-day-long treks, when it was likely we would have to carry our equipment – tents, water, provisions et al – with us.

Good journey back and I talked quite a lot about my trip. Told Will about Nan – he seems to recall meeting her, but we could not place the context in which he saw her. Arrived at Will's dad's in the early hours and went to bed. Had good sleep. Then I met Will's father. Very nice man and we got on very well. Had several good chats. Looked outside and the farm is in a very pretty setting. Went into town with Will. Later we changed up money and bought food for tonight. Made some plans tomorrow for my return to Auckland. Heard that New Zealand All Blacks are playing Australia in a rugby union test match on Saturday. Might try to go. Looked at hotels in Auckland. Also discussed with Will plans for later. Will suggested that we do Northland and Coromandel as well as Abel Tasman. He's hoping I can afford to fly. I think I'm OK. Came back and made Singapore noodles in evening.

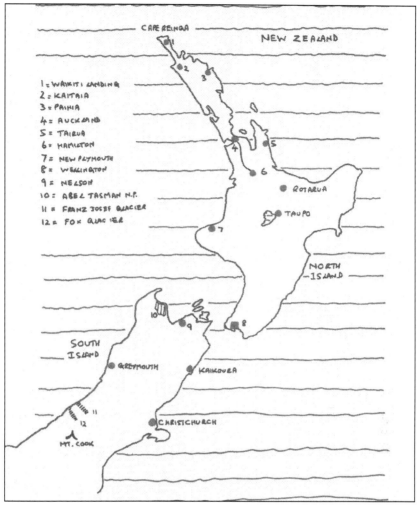

Map 37

Friday 23rd July – The Farm

Will's dad is a great character and very welcoming – much more so than the image I think I had of him beforehand from Will.

Prior to meeting him, the impression that had formed in my mind from everything that Will had mentioned over the years suggested that his dad, Bob, could be patriarchally bossy, sometimes dour, downright curmudgeonly, and rather unemotional, not to mention undemonstrative, parsimonious and reclusive to the extent that he was happy in his own company. Although it was entirely possible that at times Bob could be any or all of these things, he was certainly not unwelcoming, and, in fact, I took to him immediately. As I gradually got to know him, it seemed to me that it was more the case that his gruff outward disposition was borne out of a strong desire to be upfront and direct, to want to get to the point and to not use two words when one will do, whilst at the same time expecting the same from those around him. It was clear that he was someone who would not take fools gladly. Well into his eighties, he was not only very welcoming but downright friendly and seemed genuinely interested to hear about my travels. He had a lovely dry sense of humour and he seemed to particularly enjoy listening to me recount my story about meeting Kitty and my ongoing plans to meet up with her again this coming weekend, which he received with a knowing smile and a twinkle in his eye. I was aware that Will's father had served in the navy, reaching the rank of Commander, and also that he had served as a councillor on the local council back at Fareham. Indeed, I also understood that a certain set of traffic lights, located on the main road heading West out of Fareham, which his dad had tirelessly campaigned for, and which over the years since had help up countless impatient drivers, with steam coming out of their ears, is still sometimes referred to as Commander Allen's revenge. He was an unfussy gentleman, very intelligent, was clearly well-read and it was a testament to his deep stoicism that he made a point of insisting on taking a freezing cold shower every morning; "Gets my blood circulating – you should try it."

Laid in today until 10ish. Had brekkie and then made several calls to try to find a hotel. Very difficult because of the New Zealand/Australia rugby match. Either too expensive, or no en-suite or grotty. Eventually went for a medium expensive one – NZ$135 per night for two nights initially, but with the possibility of staying more nights (the current exchange rate meant that I was paying £43 per night on a £20 per day budget – that's love for you!! – I will have to see if I can get Kitty to help). Also telephoned to see if I could get tickets for the rugby match – no luck as yet. Had a great introductory walk around the farm (despite the rain) and Will's dad's place is fabulous – with a couple of creeks, areas of woodland, fir trees and Will showed me the lambing sheds – most of which were hand-made by his father. Will then took me into Hamilton and I got a bus to Auckland (return fare NZ$29 – £9.35). Luckily and totally coincidentally the bus terminal was only 200 yards from the hotel. The room was quite good, though the hot water was not particularly hot. Sorted myself out and made my way by shuttle bus to the airport. I had to wait 2 hours, but it was fun seeing the smiles and hugs of those who were meeting loved ones in the arrivals lounge.

Saturday 24th July – Auckland Museum

Eventually last night it was my turn to be the one hugging and kissing a loved one in the arrivals lounge. It was great to see Kitty again, who was positively beaming as she spotted me upon exiting the arrivals hall. "I'm sorry for giving you a hard time and I'm so glad you arranged for me to be here," she purred into my ear whilst clinging on to me tightly. We had only been apart for two days, but it seemed like weeks. We didn't venture far or for too long from our hotel room last night.

We got up late this morning. Our hotel room was very good, spacious, tastefully decorated and, with a king-sized bed, bedecked with spotlessly white sheets, let's just say that Kitty and I had already begun to make the most of having a room all to ourselves.

Telephoned several agencies to try to get tickets for the rugby test, but I had no luck. Spoke to Will. It turns out that Kitty has a friend who lives in Auckland, whom she telephoned and arranged to see later. "You don't mind, do you?" she smiled, with the arrangement clearly having already been made. I said that I didn't. We decided to explore Auckland. We went first to the visitor centre to pick up brochures so that we could plan the next few days. Went to the food court in the city centre, which had a large variety of food of different ethnicities and we both chose Greek. We then walked down to the harbour to check on the timings of harbour cruises. We were out of luck to go today and might have to do it tomorrow. We then walked up to the Parnell area, one of the least developed areas of Auckland and home to many craft shops and art galleries. Quite attractive. We had bought a bottle of port to take back to our room, but I dropped and broke it. We then went to the Auckland museum. It was a fabulous museum. Good exhibits, some interactive and well thought out – themes included Maori culture, animal world, war and old Victorian-style shops. We also visited several art galleries – mixed views; we saw a lot of rubbish, but equally there was some great stuff too. Then wandered back to the hotel. We'd hoped to get back in time for a little more intimacy – I mean to say, it had been well over 6 hours since the last – but out of luck as by the time we got back Kitty's friend was due to arrive very soon thereafter to pick us up. Changed. Told to bring swimming trunks, as they were intending to use spa pool later. Kitty's friend, Caroline, picked us up – a Kiwi, not unattractive. Thought I was in for a rum evening when Kitty and Caroline initially talked non-stop without involving me in any of their conversation, but, once the girls had caught up with each other's life stories, they began to engage with the rest of us and it all worked out OK. Caroline's husband James (Taiwanese) was very friendly, as were their friends, Misty and another James. Good evening. Good food. Watched the New Zealand/Australia rugby test on tele, part of the tri-nations series, which New Zealand won 34-15.

Sunday 25th July – One Tree Hill

Got up later than intended (more sex, so I'm not really complaining). We'd planned to change accommodation today as well as do some walking. We packed up and then went and had lunch at the same food plaza as yesterday. Had very good lasagne. Then went back to the hotel – and took a taxi to the B&B. Very good B&B. Then went to start of walk – described as the Coast to Coast Walkway, from Manukau Harbour in the South-West to Waitemata Harbour in the North-East. Had to use taxi again (NZ$15 each time). Start was at Horns reserve at Onehunga Beach, which would have seemed quite quaint but for the fact there was a busy by-pass nearby. Walked through suburban areas to Green Hill, where we saw pretty cottages and bay views. Then on to One Tree Hill. It was very distinctive as we approached, with – you'd never guess – just the one tree atop a hill, and a Concorde-shaped obelisk dedicated to the Maori. It was reputed to be the biggest and most populated Maori pa, (a Maori defensive fortress). Great views from the top of the hill, of terracing, and of an amphitheatre, which is part natural and part Maori-made, and beyond. Then wandered back. It was getting dark by the time we arrived at Mt. Eden – location of the highest volcano in Auckland and another sacred Maori site – and, therefore, did not climb it. We went back to the B&B full of carnal intent, but initially I could not quite perform to the gallery, which upset Kitty, but she performed her snake charmer's magic to get me to rise to the occasion and all was well in the end. Went to a Thai restaurant in the evening – food was very spicy – but on arriving back at the B&B I realised I'd left my rucksack behind.

Monday 26th July – Arguments

Got up at a reasonable time and had breakfast and then had sex (we are certainly making the most of our time together). Having organised ourselves, Kitty and I went into town. We went first to the art galleries – second one was a waste of time. First one contained Warhol's famous Campbell's tomato soup tins. No matter how hard I tried, I didn't like it – seems to me to be a load of pretentious crap – but I guess it was still good to see it. Quite a good exhibition overall. We then went down to the harbour to do the cruise. On the way Kitty became upset because I insisted on going to the Post Office first. Not sure what that was all about. The cruise was a bit of a let-down – some good views, but generally a damp squib. We were allowed only 25 minutes on interesting Taragita Island, which meant we didn't have time to go far. Then went back to Devonport, passed under the bridge, passed the marina where some huge yachts are based and then back to base. I had hoped to go to Kelly Tarlton's Underwater World and Antarctic Encounter, but Kitty wanted to wander around the shops, which I agreed to but I soon got bored and my inability to not let *it show led to upset number two for Kitty. In fact, she became very tearful. We made up. Later, for dinner, we both had great steaks and then went back to the B&B, where we had bust-up number three, which started from something very trivial, so trivial that as I write this I cannot think what it was about, but I got upset too. However, we managed to make up again completely and we both fell asleep feeling fully reassured.*

Tuesday 27th July – Leaving Kitty

Got up at 3.30 in the morning to go with Kitty to the airport. Took shuttle at 4, arrived at airport at 4.15 – very early – very few people about. Soon checked in and then sat around and waited. Kitty left to go through departures at 5.15. Very sad. Watched her from the viewing gallery for a while. We left on very good terms.

Not for the first time on this trip was I saying goodbye to someone I had fallen for, the main difference this time being that it was the girl who was flying off and leaving *me* behind. It also felt very different in another way, because I knew that as much as it was humanly possible to predict and to physically engineer, we would definitely be seeing each other again. Nevertheless, it was still very sad to cling on to Kitty one last time and kiss her before she made her way into the departure lounge (it has always struck me how these stuffy departure lounges or arrivals halls, in habitually-characterless airports are paradoxically chock-full of poignancy no matter whether people are leaving, staying, or arriving). I stayed to watch Kitty slowly make her way through the various check-points in the departure lounge, wearing the same blue-grey figure-hugging woollen top that she'd worn on our first proper date. We had got on so well most of the time we had been together and there was no aftermath from yesterday's little spats. I considered that in any event those incidents had proved to be productive, since, it seemed to me that, if anything, today, when we were sitting just outside the departures lounge, we both felt even closer to each other, not despite those arguments but because of them. Like two fully-formed aging tectonic plates coming together, there is bound to be a little friction before the two can find equilibrium. Not only were the arguments an indelible part of getting to know each other, but they were also a sign of how close we were becoming, with us both on edge and knowing full well that yesterday would be our last full day together for some time. Although the future prospects for us were very bright and very real, not least because we had already made plans for the future, I am sure that Kitty recognised the possibility as much as I did that if the fates conspired against us our intended-to-be temporary separation could still turn out to be rather more permanent. Late last night we had talked about Kitty coming over to visit me in England either later this year or early next year, when she would try to stay over for three weeks. After squinting to try to keep sight of her in departures as she manoeuvred past pillars, conveyor belts and other machinery, eventually Kitty disappeared behind the last screen, having turned to give me a final wave before she did so. I cannot deny that I had to wipe away a tear as she slipped from my view.

My meeting with Kitty had taken this adventure in an entirely unexpected direction. We felt so comfortable being in each other's company, we felt so connected and we were already falling deeply in love. I had to pinch myself to remind me that we had met only 16 days ago, and had had our first proper date only 11 days ago. I hadn't set out on this adventure to find a life partner, but circumstances had contrived to make this a very real possibility. Not only did I have the security of a job to return to in England in just over a month's time, but I also had the satisfaction that upon my return I could properly make plans for me and Kitty. I knew full well that at least one, if not both, of us would have to make some difficult decisions at some point, and the problems of trying to maintain a relationship with somebody on the opposite side of the globe could turn out to be insurmountable, but for the moment I could bathe in the warm afterglow of having spent some quality time with Kitty. I had always intended to enjoy my stint in New Zealand but the prospects for ensuring that I would do so were substantially increased, because I could now do so in the knowledge that there would be someone waiting for me at the end.

Went back to hotel. Had a little sleep, then enjoyed a good breakfast. Arrived at bus station in good time for the coach return to Hamilton. Will was not at the bus station in Hamilton to meet me when I arrived, but he came along later – his dad was in town and we went to collect him before doing a few jobs. His dad's a real character – very interesting and full of life with a beautiful wry sense of humour. Bought stuff for two meals – roast lamb tonight and moussaka tomorrow. Will told me that Kitty had telephoned to say that she had safely arrived and would ring me later. Very tired and had kip in car whilst I was waiting for Will at the shop. Drive back was glorious. Great countryside. Fantastic. During the bus journey to Hamilton, studied my lonely planet and planned my trip from here on. Kitty rang in the evening and we had a good chat. She's missing me already and she's half planning to come to the UK early. She may write to me at Will's.

Wednesday 28th July – Will's Dad's Farm

Great day. Yesterday I saw – and regretted not photographing – a pukeko, a bird which is known elsewhere as the purple swamphen. Amongst the numerous birds I saw today were kingfishers (yellow body and blue/black head and wings), a rock pigeon, white-backed magpies, a New Zealand harrier, a paradise duck, fantails and welcome swallows. Today was the day for me and Will to finally start doing some walking. First – after an early rise – I helped Will by cleaning the work surfaces in the shed that Will was working to repair. We had lunch and then went walking.

The land area of New Zealand is slightly larger than that of the UK, but its population at the time of my visit, at 3.5 million, was around 5% of that in the UK, with approximately 70% of those reputed to be living in the five major cities. Accordingly, New Zealand has a lot of open space and Will's dad's farm was located in a lot of open space. Bob still lived in the same farm that he bought when he first migrated back to New Zealand, located 15 or so miles West of Hamilton. Hamilton itself is not overly large, though with a little over 110,000 people it was still described at the time as the largest inland city in New Zealand, but as you head West, you quickly reach open countryside and the topography becomes more rugged and more rolling the further West that you go, so that very soon the gap between one house or farmstead and the next one is measured in miles rather than metres. As the terrain is sometimes scrubby, rough-hewn and more undulating than flat, sheep or cattle farming was the norm. Although rugged, I noticed that the countryside is vibrantly bedecked with varying shades of green; with whole fields of grass the colour of limes or shamrocks, small clumps of conifer trees the colour of basil or pine, and patches here and there of ferns the colour of olives, pistachio or mint. Small streams cut through this landscape. A mile or two out of Hamilton there are no street lights, and consequently no light pollution. It is the sort of place where neighbours could live tens of miles away from each other but yet know the intimate details of what each other was doing (when, with what and to whom!).

It had been a very cold night last night and, with me billeted on a sofa-bed in the living room, once the dying embers from a log fire had finally died out to grey cinders, it became very cold inside Bob's house too. The house clearly had electricity running to it, so I could not quite make up my mind whether the absence of central heating was through a combination of sheer bad luck, poor design, and/or tightness on the part of the management, or was part of Bob's grand masterplan to make men out of all of us. Although I had been given plenty of thick blankets to anchor me down on the sofa-bed, which meant that I was as warm as toast inside my bed, it was bitingly freezing outside. I tried to keep my outer extremities tucked inside the covers, but I knew that at some point I would have no option but to make the perilous journey – tackling cold and unadulterated darkness – to the loo. And, as is the nature of these things, in view of my in-vain struggle not to think about it, maybe I would have to go even more than once.

At some God-awful time in the morning, I heard Bob take his cold shower and I considered that maybe, in comparison to the icy cold of the house, the water in the shower for *him* was positively balmy – relatively-speaking; but even just thinking about it made *me* shiver profusely. Peeking out from under the covers, I glanced at Nan's photograph, which I had strategically placed on the mantelpiece above the fireplace and we exchanged a smile. I sensed that she knew what I was thinking. Once I had eventually plucked up the courage to extricate myself from my warm bed, it was good to make myself busy, and working with Will in the shed was one way to warm up.

Today was a beautiful, sunny, crisp, clear day, and being July, we were in the middle of the New Zealand winter. Its latitude South of the equator at 40 degrees being roughly equivalent to that of the Mediterranean Sea 40 degrees North of the equator, meant that nights could be bitterly cold, but the sun would have a degree of intensity to it when it shone. Today was just such a day and would be a good day for walking. After lunch, we made our way along the track leading from the house down to the main road. As we did so we passed Will's dad, with sleeves rolled up, and strands of his long silvery-white hair falling loosely across his face, who was beavering away mending a gate. A barely audible grunt was all that greeted Will, but, when he caught sight of me walking a step or two behind, I was positively lauded with a quick smile and a cheery nod. But no words, though. After leaving the farm, and after walking about 50 yards along the road, we turned left to go into a pasture, crossed a bridge over a stream and then made our way through a meadow heading up towards a ridge that formed the edge of a range of hills that ran to the North of the farm. We were in open countryside, with no visible footpath and only the company of cattle and sheep. We were greeted by the sounds of birds and livestock, including the occasional guttural bellowing sound of testosterone-fuelled bulls (I know how they feel) echoing across the valleys. Some of the land was like moorland, being very boggy and muddy in parts. Of course, where there were cattle and sheep there was plenty of cattle and sheep shit to negotiate too. The landscape seemed to me to be a mixture of the familiar and the exotic: familiar with its rolling limestone hills, craggy ridges, sweeping green valleys and sparsely dotted with trees, reminiscent of uplands in England, such as Derbyshire; and exotic because the wide variety of tree ferns, some giant, some feathered and some with long curly tongues, could have come straight out of a tropical rain forest. Once we had reached the top of the ridge, we were afforded fabulous views looking back down. Will advised that the distance of rolling landscape heading South that was visible to us probably stretched for 50 miles or more, and we had a perfect panoramic view of Bob's farm, which looked to be in a picture postcard setting, idyllically nestled between low lying hillocks and bordered by a stream. We turned to walk West, and when the ridge turned to head in a Northerly direction, as it looped back alongside a valley spur, we continued along it heading North. When, after half a mile or so, we dropped down from the ridge into a glaciated valley where there was a shallow but fast-flowing stream leading from a tarn, we could have been walking in Scotland or Wales. Having reached the stream we turned left and South to walk along its bank downstream until eventually our small stream joined a larger stream which we continued to follow. I soon realised that this was the stream bordering Bob's property, which we had crossed over earlier and which I had seen from the ridge. We hadn't walked any great distance, but it had been a truly wonderful walk, with us having the first real chance to stretch our legs, open up our lungs and take in a snapshot of the best of Kiwi countryside. Will and I both agreed that the other sights in New Zealand would have to go a long way to equal, let alone beat, today's walk and views.

Cooked moussaka in the evening. Not bad.

Thursday 29th July – Thermals and the Scary Maori

Had breakfast and Will took me in to Hamilton. We both commented that we would have to go some to beat yesterday's walk. Finally bought a bulb for my torch. Lovely scenery all the way – bus nearly conked out. Arrived at Rotorua and after collecting brochures and maps I went to the Hot Rock Backpackers, where I obtained a bed in a room for 4 – NZ$18. Good value and clean. Then went walkabout – first to Kuirau Park, saw lots of steam and mud pools and great gardens. Then wandered down to the Maori village known as Ohinemutu – saw great church and sombre but beautiful cemetery, and meeting house and kingfishers and black swans. Wandered along the edge of Lake Rotorua and everywhere that I went there seemed to be sulphurous steam coming out of every orifice. Really uncanny. Saw large colonies of gulls and a picturesque museum (the Rotorua Museum of Art and History) – which was formerly a bath-house (might go there tomorrow). Came across a Polynesian spa (might go there Saturday). Very sunny until very late in the day.

At dusk, I was walking along a path when I saw a Maori man striding towards me.

Rotorua is a wonderful place, famous for its geysers, hot springs, bubbling mud pools and shimmering lakes, but for me on this day there occurred a series of small events that on their own would have been relatively insignificant, but taken together gave the place an other-worldly eerie feel to it. Rotorua town is a reasonable size, with over 60,000 inhabitants, and as you wander through it, as I had observed in my diary, steam seems to be emerging from every nook and cranny and in places a sulphurous mist wafts along the streets, like special effects in an over-the-top Hammer horror film.

In addition, Rotorua is a highly significant spiritual place for the Maoris and I had spent some time wandering around Ohinemutu, a lakeside Maori village, where I had found the Anglican Church and the nearby cemetery to be particularly atmospheric. Inside the church, as recommended by Lonely Planet, I located the window into which the image of Christ wearing a Maori cloak is etched, and which is positioned looking out at Lake Rotorua in such a way that it appears as though Christ is walking on water. It was uncannily realistic. I later went to the cemetery which I found to be particularly moving with its respectful fusion of Christian and Maori symbolism; but it also took on a sinister twist when spectral wisps of mist emerged from the ground besides some of the graves to blow macabrely across the graveyard.

An illustration of how my imagination was working overtime came a short while later, when I came across a very large colony of gulls, with some individual birds so large and raucous that an image of Hitchcock's film, The Birds, came into my mind. Moments later I saw a bevy of black swans. I had always been fascinated by the fact that antipodean swans are pure black as opposed to their European counterparts being pure white, and today their brilliantine blackness seemed to befit the sombre mood.

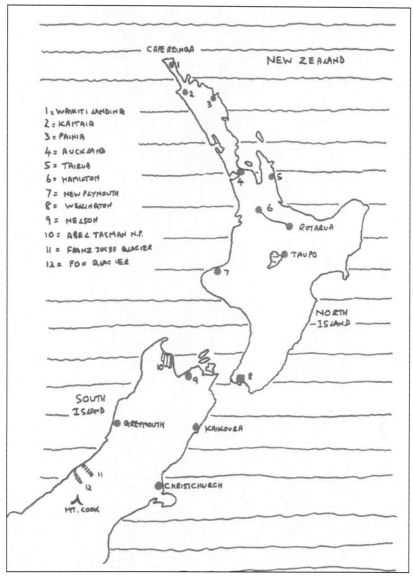

Map 38

Later in the afternoon I found myself walking along a path beside the lake, heading out of town into open countryside. I was on my own and the sun was low in the sky over my left shoulder. Here and there sulphurous smoke continued to appear mysteriously out of the ground. At one point, as I turned to look behind me, thinking I should perhaps head back into town,

I saw the shape of a huge silhouetted man emerge out of a cloud of mist, striding purposefully towards me. He looked to be over six feet four inches tall, with broad strong shoulders, and an equally strong six-pack torso beneath his tight t-shirt to match it. As his features came into view I could see he was a stern-looking black-haired Maori, and with both arms swinging purposefully beside him he was making giant strides coming towards me along the same path that I was on. Although I tried to rationalise what I was seeing I couldn't help but feel very spooked. I froze. Thinking that to carry on walking would take me further away from the safety of town, whilst to turn back to walk towards him might seem confrontational, I decided that I should stand where I was and make out to be taking in the scenery by looking out across the lake beside me, and hope that any intent on the part of the Maori man would be friendly. The never-smiling Maori walked so quickly that he was upon me in moments but though I felt the spine-tingling sensation of his aura merging with mine as he passed behind my back, he mercifully carried on striding his giant strides past and beyond me. The immediate feeling was one of relief, but it was followed very quickly thereafter by a feeling of stupidity for letting such irrational thoughts get the better of me. Curiosity, though, took over and I wondered where the Maori could be going, so I decided to follow him, continuing along the path but keeping a discreet and safe distance away from him. Moments later I discovered where he was going, and a feeling of stupidity came upon me a second time, since the clues had been there all along for any fool to put together if he had logically thought it through properly. This tall, thickset, muscular, giant of a Maori man, striding quickly and purposefully out of town just as dusk was about to fall on this Thursday evening, was simply heading out to join his mates for rugby training.

Had Mexican meal in the evening.

Friday 30th July – Maori Haka

Good day. In a four-man room – with Dan from the US and Gino from London. Decent guys. Went to communal breakfast and then made tracks. Went to Te Whakarewarewa. Walked the 3 km from my hostel. Bought deodorant and took out money on the way. Running short of money. Saw lots of thermal activity, some similar to yesterday but some different. Saw boiling mud and mists wafting across the water which was very atmospheric. Went to see geysers at Whakarewarewa – discovered too late that there are two areas with the same name (one a village and the other a forest park) and I was in the wrong one. I managed to get back to the correct one, but although I arrived in *good time and stayed for a good two and a half hours, I didn't see a single eruption from the two major geysers, despite the fact there is meant to be on average one every hour. Saw lots of little ones which were still quite spectacular. Made friends with a girl called Tomoko from Japan. Lovely. Walked back to town and I went to the Museum. A hurried trip but it was worthwhile and a great video show in the museum. In one of the interactive exhibits, the seats move to simulate the effects of an earthquake. In the evening, I went to a Maori concert and Hangi (where the food is cooked in an earth oven). Cost NZ$52. Made friends with Brian (Scot) and Oonagh (Irish) and I may go with them when they head South on Sunday. Saw Maoris dancing and singing and demonstrating their weapons. The food was excellent. Saw several hakas – great. They made us interact – shouting, "Huh," and rubbing noses. A bit touristy, but great fun and definitely worth it.*

Saturday 31st July – Mount Tarawera

Great day and one which went exactly according to plan. I had intended to explore Mount Tarawera today. Got up in good time and set off at 8.35. Checked that I didn't need permission to enter the park at Mt. Tarawera (which is Maori land). Was told that a warden would be around at one of the entrances to collect NZ$2 from me. As I walked along the path recommended by the map in the Track shop, more steam and sulphurous smoke was coming up from various holes in the ground.

I planned to visit Mt. Tarawera today, but there was no public transport to take me there. Despite being over 30 kilometres from Rotorua, I was determined to take my chance. I had read that there were two main routes up to the mountain, one on the Western side leading up from Lake Tarawera and the other heading up from a car park on the South-Eastern side. I chose West. I decided that I would traverse the lake, head up along the footpath leading from the West to the top of the volcano, loop along the ridge and then drop back down to the car park on the other side, hoping that I would find some way to transport myself back to town. I was planning to hitch-hike. Mt. Tarawera and its lake were drawing me in not only because of the promise of spectacular scenery, but also because of a famous legend that emerged at the time of its last major eruption, which I had heard a great deal about at the museum yesterday. The story was also narrated in my Lonely Planet guidebook, which is worth repeating here:

"In the 19th Century, Lake Tarawera was a major tourist attraction. It brought visitors from around the world to visit its pink and white terraces: large and beautiful terraces of multi-levelled pools, formed by silica deposits from thermal waters, which had trickled over them for centuries. The Maori village of Te Wairoa, on the shores of the lake, was New Zealand's principal tourist resort. From here Sophia, a Maori guide, took visitors on boat trips over the lake to view the terraces, which were regarded as one of the Seven Wonders of the World. Mt. Tarawera towered silently over the lake, although the Maori believed that a powerful fire spirit lived inside it. One day in June 1886, Sophia took a party out on to the lake as usual, to go to see the terraces. As they were on the lake, they suddenly saw a phantom Maori war canoe gliding across the water, the Maori boatmen inside it paddling rapidly. It was an ancient war canoe of a kind which had never existed on this lake. It was seen by all the people in the boat, both Maori and Pakeha [*a Maori language term for New Zealanders who are white and of European descent*]. To Maori people, the appearance of a phantom Maori war canoe is an omen of impending disaster. Back at Te Wairoa, an old tohunga [*a Maori wiseman*] ... said the sighting of the canoe foretold disaster. He predicted that the village would be "overwhelmed." Four days later, on 10th June 1886, in the middle of the night, there were earthquakes and loud sounds and the eruption of Mt. Tarawera suddenly lit up the sky, with fire exploding from several places along the top of the mountain. By the time it was finished, six hours later, over 8,000 sq km had been buried in ash, lava and mud, the Maori village of Te Wairoa was obliterated, the pink and white terraces were destroyed, 153 people were killed, Mt. Tarawera was sliced and opened along its length as if hit with a huge cleaver, and Lake Rotomahana was formed ... The guide Sophia became a heroine because she saved many people's lives, giving them shelter in her house. The old tohunga, however, was not so fortunate. His house was buried in volcanic ash, and he was trapped inside ... Finally, after four days had passed, he was dug out alive by Europeans, who took him to be cared for in Rotorua. He died a week later, aged around 104."

I headed out of town, walking along the road in the direction of Lake Tarawera and I started hitchhiking. It was a clear, sunny day with barely a cloud in the sky. I didn't have to wait too long before a young lad in a pick-up truck, with his pit-bull dog sat on the bench seat beside him, stopped to give me a lift. It turned out that he wasn't going as far as Lake Tarawera but he generously offered to take me all the way there nevertheless, pointing out that he was not especially busy on this day. It was obvious that the lad appreciated the company because he was continuously jabbering all the way. His dog, on the other hand, with his tongue lolling out, and panting rapidly, sat quietly beside him, his eyes fixed steadfastly looking out through the windscreen and concentrating on the road ahead, which was perhaps rather astute, since it was a great deal more than could be said of the driver. After a mercifully short journey, I alighted at the shores of Lake Tarawera. In the relative cool of the breathless early morning a gentle ripple wafted over the flat, calm surface of the lake. I found a small kiosk where I was able to get a cup of tea whilst I was waiting for the boat, where a young lad who worked there alarmed me by saying that the walk up to Mt. Tarawera from the lakeside would take me the best part of one day and one night. He also said that even the usual route to climb up from the car park on the other side, which was the shorter route, takes at least four hours. This advice went against the information contained in my Lonely Planet guidebook and against the advice given to me by staff back at the Tourist Information Centre, so, although I often take heed of advice given by locals, who I usually judge are likely to be 'in the know' by virtue of them being up to date and better informed than guidebooks, I rather recklessly decided to press ahead nonetheless. A short while later the skipper turned up and I purchased a ticket for the boat crossing of the lake. We left at 10.30.

There were only three of us on the small boat, the skipper, myself and one other passenger. However, the skipper, who was Scottish, clearly took his tour guide role seriously, since he insisted on talking through his microphone, even though we two paying customers were standing directly behind him inside his cabin. The skipper relayed the story of the Maori war canoe emerging from the mists, reminding me of my own encounter with the Maori rugby player who himself had appeared out of the mist just two days ago. Ahead of us the shadowy outline of Mt. Tarawera was less the classical conical shape of your archetypal volcano and instead looked more like a deflated soufflé, but that was probably to be expected after its earth-shattering volcanic eruption.

On arriving on the other side of the lake, my fellow passenger hopped off to walk along the shore, whilst I headed past the cluster of half a dozen houses to locate the indistinct path that went through a belt of dry scrubby trees before very quickly taking me in a trajectory straight up the side of the volcano. I spotted a single wallaby go bounding away. Halfway up, the path disappeared and the going became extremely tough, as I began wading through scree and crumbling volcanic scoria, with the result that I was finding it increasingly difficult to find traction underfoot and I could feel the ground constantly giving way. With me sliding back down with each step, it felt as though I was having to take the equivalent of four steps for every one that I might have made on a stable surface and the going was resultingly slow. However, I managed to get from the boat to the top in two and a half hours, reassuringly much quicker than predicted by the lad back at the kiosk, and I had even managed to take a breather on the way too.

Having gained most of the height, the rest of the walk along the rim was undulating but relatively easy. The views were certainly very spectacular. Behind me I had a perfect panoramic view of the azure-blue waters of Lake Tarawera and a little further South of the century-old Lake Rotomahana. Looking even further South, in the distance I could see ice-capped mountains. Looking in a North or North-Westerly direction I could see sunlight glinting off the sea in the Bay of Plenty, and a little further out at sea I could clearly see smoking away the extremely volatile island volcano known as Whakaari, or White Island. However, as I made my way along the ridge up to the highest point of the volcano I was on, my eyes were drawn to the even more spectacular colours, shapes and contours below me. The eruption of 1886 had cleaved open a schism, five kilometres long and half a kilometre wide, to push up and reveal multi-coloured layers of strata, the base a chalky white, the mid-section the colour of copper-red and the top a layer of pumice-stone grey. Vegetation had managed to take hold in the odd place, to provide patches of bright green. Here and there, nature had clearly taken its toll on the brittle upper layer of grey rock – whether through wind, rain, frosts, earthquakes or a combination thereof – to send sections of it tumbling down into the well of the volcano, scoring through the middle red layer to leave a dried up dirty avalanche of red and grey stone trailing through the otherwise crisp, clean layer of white chalk. It occurred to me that these layers of rock replicated the famous, long-since vanished and much-vaunted pink and white terraces, though the geological or chemical forces that created the rocks before me were probably entirely different to those that created the pink and white terraces. I must have wandered around the ridge for a good three hours or more and by mid-afternoon, the sinking sun was creating dark, crisply-lined shadows along the Northern edge, the part that I was on.

After leaving the boat back at the lake I had not seen a single soul – save for the wallaby – until I bumped into a lone, 20-something, lanky American close to the highest point of the volcano. Whilst the drama of the scenery all around me was enough to satisfy *me*, it was clearly not enough for *him*, who, like a junkie seeking his next fix, was in a desperate search for an additional adrenalin rush. Barely registering my presence, he trotted along the edge peering down into the abyss, examining the red-sand slopes for the best spot to dive into the cleft whilst declaring, "I gotta get down there, man." I could clearly see the barren, dry bottom, where I could even make out the indistinct lines of a footpath. The American lad was looking for the best way to 'ski' slide down the side to the bottom. Suddenly, without warning or fanfare, over he went, disappearing down the slope to shrieks of delight. At first, I smugly turned up my nose at such boorish behaviour, but when I peered over the edge to watch him go, I confess that I was sorely tempted. Then, as I looked across, I could just about make out the tiny figures of a group of three people walking along the Southern ridge, and I then spotted the outline of a path leading up diagonally from the belly of the volcano to this Southern ridge. I guessed that the route down to the car park on the other side of the volcano must be somewhere between the two. So, with the excuse that I needed and without further ado, over I went too, surfing down the powdery scree on the steep slope all the way to the bottom. I cannot deny that it was great fun, although it left me filthy, covered by a film of ochre red dust.

I made my way up the path to the other side and found the route from the ridge to the car park, which took me an hour and forty minutes (not the four hours as advised back at the kiosk). However, there were no cars in the car park when I arrived and I had not seen anybody as I had walked down from the mountain to it, not even the three people that had been walking along the Southern ridge, nor did I see any sign of the Yank. The sun was by now low in the sky with probably less than an hour left of full daylight. I walked along a dusty track leading away from the car park and the volcano, which I presumed to be the way out. After half a mile, I reached a single-track tarmac road. Although I was still looking to thumb a lift, I knew that I should start walking, just in case nothing came along and in the hope that I might eventually reach a main road. I chose the direction heading West into the sun, deducing that this was the road that most likely would take me in the general direction of where I wanted to go. Luckily, within a minute of doing so, a dirty-looking cattle truck with an equally dirty-looking driver came up from behind me. On sticking out my thumb, the driver stopped his vehicle immediately and, poking his head out of the cab, charmingly announced, "Yurra lucky bastard!" He looked to be in his late 40s, was unshaven and had a weather-beaten, lined face. He wore a dirty brown trilby, perched slightly askew towards the back of his head revealing a few wisps of black greasy hair, and a dirty charcoal-grey jacket over an open-necked lumberjack-style shirt. I asked if he would at least be able to take me up to the main road. He replied, "I assume you're going to 'Rua, 'cause if y'are and yur'okay to wait a bit I can take you all the way to town." I replied that I did not mind waiting at all and would be very grateful.

As I clambered into the cab, he introduced himself as Slack Bachelor. I momentarily froze, glancing over to him to see if he was ribbing me, or to see if I'd misheard, since it was entirely possible that he might simply have been conveying to me his marital status, but a rigid jaw and a straight face told me he was kosher. He explained that he needed to collect eight bulls from a field which he wanted to transfer to another field before nightfall and he asked me if I could help him. Wondering what I had let myself in for, I said that I could. He assured me that thereafter, he would take me into town. Slack was a colourful character in more ways than one, since his language was awash with the vernacular, with every other word seeming to be either 'cunts' this, or 'pricks' that or 'fucking bastards' the other. He pulled up beside a narrow lane and reversed his truck into the top of it to pull up beside a gate to a field, within which were the eight bulls. "Jump out," he instructed, as he himself jumped out and went to the back of his truck. I followed him to the back, where he dropped down the ramp and set up two cattle gates to block the way beside it. "What I need you to go and fucking do is stand part way down that fucking lane, not too far now, and I'm going to open up that fucking gate and go into that bleeding field to collect those fuckers and I'm going to herd them out through that fucking gate and into the fucking truck, and what I want you to do is be prepared in case any of those cunts tries to go along the road the other way, and if those cunts do try to go your way, you need to fucking stand still and wave your fucking arms; don't worry that they might fucking charge you because they fucking well won't when you wave your fucking arms." Not a little perturbed, I stood as directed and off he went into the field.

The bulls were young but they were still pretty hefty and did not seem to take kindly to Slack's hollering, as, herded together, they moved stubbornly slowly, and reluctantly made their way through the open gate. As anticipated by him, instead of turning left to head towards the back of the truck, the bulls obstinately did indeed turn right and began walking towards me. My instinct was to turn and run rather than stand my ground with several tons of prime rib bearing down on me, but I planted my feet, stood with my legs astride, stretched out my arms and started waving; and to my amazement wouldn't you know it if the fuckers didn't indeed turn around to go back the other way and go walking docilely up the ramp and into the truck. We took the bulls to another field and after I had helped him sort out his cattle, he glanced at his watch before asking me if I would mind it if we went back to his house first, because he had planned to go into Rotorua in the evening and asked if it would be OK if I waited whilst he washed and changed. I readily agreed, the only reservation springing to mind was how I was going to fit so much into my tiny daily diary. We went back to his wood-built farmhouse, where he offered to make me a cup of tea, whilst he went off to have a shower. The cup of tea turned out to be a giant mug of tea, which was strong and refreshing, though the multi-layered permanent brown staining on the inside of the mug, slowly revealing itself to me layer by layer as I drank from it, left a lot to be desired. It was clear that Slack Bachelor lived here alone and I considered that I had never met a man more appropriately named. He then took me into town. Although he was minus his dirty hat and jacket, and his shirt seemed reasonably clean, he could not quite shake off the country in him because his shirt had clearly not been ironed, he had not condescended to shave and on the way he asked if I was looking for a nice New Zealand girl, "Or I can find you a dirty hot fucker if you'd rather," he guffawed. I declined.

Having thanked Slack, I went to the Polynesian spa in the evening. Some of the pools were very hot – one had a maximum temperature of 44 degrees centigrade. Later had an Indian meal. Then met up with Oonagh and Brian to talk about plans. It was a brilliant day all round.

Sunday 1st August – Lady Knox Geyser

Another good day. After breakfast, I went with Oonagh and Brian to Lake Taupo stopping off at Waiotapu on the way.

Oonagh and Brian were a lovely couple. It is difficult to remember how I came to be so friendly with them, since they silently and subtly crept into my consciousness without me realising it, until at some point it suddenly dawned on me that I did indeed get on so well with them. I had met them at the Maori concert two days ago, and I felt totally at ease with them from the outset, despite the fact they were a two and I was a one. Oonagh was from Dublin and I seem to recall Brian saying that he was from Southern Scotland, and although their accents were distinct, they were thankfully not overly strong. In their mid-30s, they had both decided that they needed time out from their jobs and had elected to spend some extended time in New Zealand, travelling around as they were doing in a cheap, aging car that they had purchased solely for this trip upon arriving in the country. Like me, they were intending to head South, initially to Taupo, and then to Wellington, and, like me, they were intending to do so at around the same time. They offered to take me and I readily agreed. We would go our separate ways after Wellington, as I was then planning to cross into South Island, whilst they were intending to explore more of the Southern reaches of North Island.

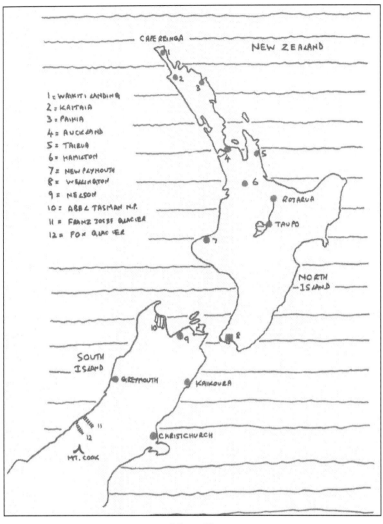

1 = WAIKITI LANDING
2 = KAITAIA
3 = PAIHIA
4 = AUCKLAND
5 = TAIRUA
6 = HAMILTON
7 = NEW PLYMOUTH
8 = WELLINGTON
9 = NELSON
10 = ABEL TASMAN N.P.
11 = FRANZ JOSEF GLACIER
12 = FOX GLACIER

Map 39

We left Rotorua in good time, as we had planned to take in a couple of sights on the way. First stop was Waiotapu, about 20 miles South of Rotorua, described as one of the best thermal sites in the area. The site was home to the famous Lady Knox Geyser, which was guaranteed – not least because it was given a little helping hand – to perform punctually at 10.15 every morning. The geyser did not let us down, blowing off at 10.15 as promised, aided by a park ranger releasing soap powder down into the well from where the water came, the soap supposedly working to reduce the surface tension and thus leading to an upsurge in the water. It was certainly pretty spectacular and, although the fact that it had needed a little encouragement would normally be off-putting, the very act of prompting it by using soap powder is itself a historical act, with the inaugural one reputedly being performed by convicts when they lived in New Zealand over 100 years ago. We then wandered around the rest of the reserve. Clear blue skies provided the perfect light for illuminating the colour and beauty of the attractions within. We saw boiling mud pools, the surface of which seemed to be constantly shifting in a strangely hypnotic slow motion. In some places, air pockets would bubble and rise from within, forming globules that expanded until they burst in miniature explosions, and created expanding concentric rings on the surface of the liquid mud. Elsewhere the mud would froth and steam. Wandering further, all around us ubiquitous mists and steam wafted over the terraces. We made sure that we did not avoid what were reputedly the two most outstanding attractions in the park. One feature is known as the Artist's Palette, a wide acidic pool, which was not only shaped indeed like an artist's palette, but contained pigments of white, yellow, green and orange-coloured sediment underneath the surface of the water to amplify the effect (and justify its title). We also located the Champagne Terrace, so described because bubbles of carbon dioxide gas continuously rise up from deep within the water, which then pop as they reach the surface and are emitted into the atmosphere. Under the water, the centre of the pool was a dark racing green, whilst around the edges was a bright, orange, three-feet wide crust, the colour allegedly deriving from arsenic and antimony sulfide deposits. Waiotapu did not disappoint.

Having left Waiotapu, our second stop on the way was to see the Huka Falls, a series of spectacular rapids, where the continuing strength of the mid-afternoon sun illuminated the vibrant colours in the water, in parts a bright frothy white and elsewhere a fluorescent turquoise.

We first saw the Lady Knox Geyser. Very good. Then to Taupo. The accommodation is excellent being NZ$17. The lake is also very good. Mount Tauhau is nearby and dominates the scenery on one side. There are distant views of snow-capped mountains across the lake. Saw the bizarre sight of a man wearing flippers, a snorkel and goggles, retrieving golf balls out of the lake after a hole in one competition. In the evening, I went to Taupo spa which was very good.

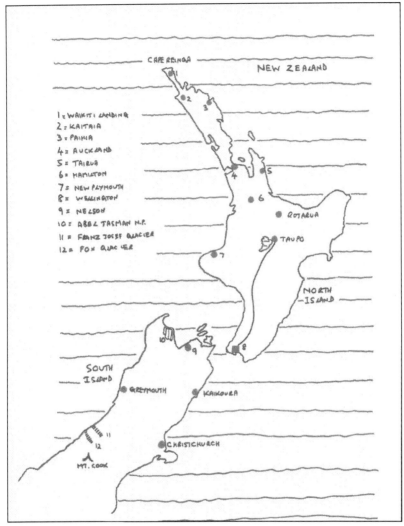

Map 40

<u>Monday 2nd August – Oonagh and Brian</u>

I had already concluded several days ago that Brian and Oonagh were great people. Today totally confirmed it.

Set off from Taupo – brilliant backpackers' place – having posted cards to Robbyne and Kitty. Drove round Taupo lake and past Tongariro National Park with Mounts Tongariro, Ngauruhoe and Ruapehu (which last erupted only two or three years ago) and *then past the Ruahine range and eventually the hills of Tararua National Park. Many mountains were snow-capped. The weather was pleasant but not quite as good as yesterday. We eventually arrived at Wellington, the capital city. An attractive city particularly around the harbour area. Tried the Wellington City Hostel – fairly full – then got to Rowena City Lodge, which didn't seem particularly good but Brian and Oonagh said yes to staying there before I had had a chance to say anything so I felt obliged to stay – only NZ$17 though. In the evening, we went into town and had a Malaysian meal – good – and then went to Kitty O'Shea's Irish Bar. Again good. Oonagh and Brian are great – I get on very well with them and they are such a genuine and lovely couple. Of all the Westerners I have met travelling on this trip, they and the Belgian twins are the ones I have got on best with. Great people.*

Tuesday 3rd August – Wellington Harbour

Reasonable day. Travelling. Got up later than planned. I am pretty sure that the place doubles as a home for transients. It is definitely the worst hostel I have been in whilst in New Zealand and ranks with all the worst ones that I have stayed at in Asia. Although I was planning to move on quickly today in any event, the state of my accommodation did nothing to dissuade me. Said my goodbyes to Oonagh and Brian, who planned to hang around Wellington for a day or two more. Walked up Mount Victoria and had great views of the harbour and back across to the airport and beyond. Although it clouded up later it was a clear and bright start to the day. Then I walked back down into town to check out – grabbed my luggage, and booked it into a locker at the train station. Then went to Te Papa Museum, which is known as the National Museum of New Zealand. At the museum, there was much information about earthquakes and earth facts, futuristic art and Maori exhibitions. I hadn't got much time to dwell so it was a quick flick round. Probably the most interesting part and the one that fascinated me most was when standing in a mock-up house which felt the effects of a simulated earthquake and shook accordingly. It really brought home to me the violence that goes with an earthquake and I would certainly not want to be present during a real one. I went back to the station, grabbed my luggage and then took the ferry to Picton on South Island. On the boat, a rather attractive girl asked me to take a photograph of her. It was a very clean and pleasant ferry. The views back across the harbour and around Marlborough Sound on the other side were spectacular. Arriving at 6.00 pm, immediately got the bus on the other side and went to Kaikoura where I found accommodation in Topspot Backpackers – very good and at NZ$16 excellent value. Had seen lots of dead possums on the side of the road. Also, the roads are very clear of traffic and therefore a pleasure to ride on.

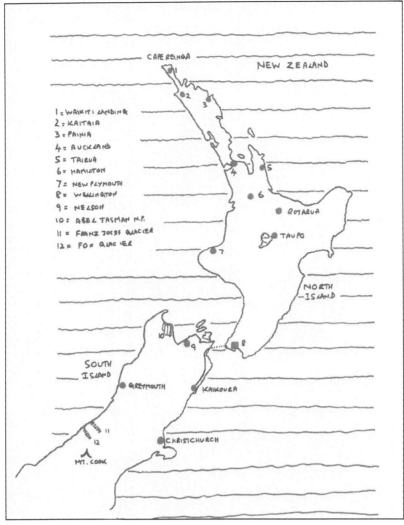

Map 41

Wednesday 4th August – Sperm Whale and Fur Seals

Great day. After breakfast, I telephoned Whalewatch and they had a vacancy at 10. Took it. When I arrived, I was told there was a risk that the boat would not go out because the water was too choppy.

The weather in the morning was misty and murky, and the surf was strong and foamy as huge rollers roared in to pound the shingle beach. Prospects did not look good but, as the morning wore on, the mist lifted, and eventually the skipper of the boat decided that it was fine enough to go.

Yesterday, I had stopped off at the tiny town of Kaikoura, situated on the Northern promontory of Kaikoura peninsular, itself located off the East Coast of South Island. As the guidebook suggested, there would be a very good chance of seeing whales, dolphins and other cetaceans here. Whale-watching trips had become big business, but neither the prospect of sharing a boat with dozens of other tourists, nor the inflated prices (NZ$95), did anything to put me off taking such a trip.

Today's tour was on a fast boat, with 25 or so other paying customers, and I certainly felt the pounding from the waves hitting the boat as we headed out to open sea. As we journeyed out, we spotted common petrels, cape petrels and numerous wandering albatrosses. The guide advised us that these are the albatrosses that have the longest wingspan of any bird on the planet, measuring up to 12 feet, which to my mind doesn't immediately sound a great deal until you remember that 12 feet is more than twice the height of an average human. Some of the facts relayed to us about albatrosses are staggering. Pairs of wandering albatrosses mate for life, and spend most of their life in flight, landing only to breed and feed. Verified statistics about the distances covered by some tracked birds include one that travelled 6,000 km in 12 days, and others that have circumnavigated the Southern Ocean three times, covering 120,000 km in the process.

Most of our views were of wide, empty sea but our boat was fitted with sonar, so the crew members were able to detect that there were several whales nearby but they suspected that the heavy swell was discouraging them from coming to the surface. After a series of near misses – or so we were told – we were finally in luck. The whale in question was a sperm whale and it was only 30 or 40 yards away from the boat, so I could see it very clearly as it crested the surface of the sea and shot water out of its blowhole. After parading before us for about ten minutes, it upended itself, brought its huge tail to wave at us above the water and then dived down to disappear into the depths. It was a thrilling sight. As the boat made its way back to land, I was slightly disappointed that we hadn't seen more whales, but one was better than none, and as we passed close to a bay on the peninsula, the prospect of recompense came when I spotted a seal colony, which I decided that I would attempt to get closer to in the afternoon.

Consequently, after grabbing a cheese sandwich for lunch, I made my way South across the neck of the peninsula, a walk of less than a mile, until I reached the coast, where I turned East to walk in an anti-clockwise direction around Kaikoura Peninsula. The weather was breezy, but bright. The walk along the coast took me initially along rugged cliffs, before quickly dropping down to pass along the shoreline. The stony beach was fringed at the high tide limit with thick, shiny, leathery kelp, and foraging therein were shags and oyster catchers. When the beach became more rocky, it wasn't long before I saw my first fur seal, followed very soon afterwards by many fur seals, lounging on the rocks and lazily lapping up the warmth of the hazy afternoon sun. The males were easily distinguishable from the females, since male fur seals are on average five times the size of females, and can weigh up to a quarter of a ton. I couldn't tell if any of the male fur seals before me weighed quite that much, but what I could say for certain was that there were some huge specimens sprawled across the path in front of me. Trying to circumnavigate them as best as I could, I could not avoid getting perilously close to them – less than six feet at one stage – so close that I occasionally caught a waft of their putrid, fishy breath (I entirely accept the possibility that *they* were not exactly enamoured by *my* cheesy breath). Most of them did not seem overly fussed by my presence, and it was only when I was near what appeared to be young seals that any of them seemed bothered by me, but a quick hiss or a snort from the mums reminded me who was boss and ensured that I kept a safe distance.

I think that in many ways the seals were as fabulous a sight as the sperm whale partly because I was mainly on my own, having seen only one other person during the entire walk around the peninsula, and partly because I was able to get very close. Kaikoura is a lovely wild place.

Thursday 5th August – Notting Hill

A wistful ending to a funny day. Woke up to a lot of rain – the sort of day that spoils a typical English summer. However, as this is the first rain that I have encountered in New Zealand in two weeks – and it is their winter – I can count myself lucky. I had set off in the morning to take a bus for the three-hour journey from Kaikoura to Christchurch, where I purchased a newspaper and went to sit in a café to have a cup of tea and to check through my Lonely Planet guidebook. Although the weather had improved by the time we reached Christchurch it started to worsen again later. When I had eventually decided on accommodation, I had to plump for my second choice hostel as the first one was full. Mine was called Round the World Hostel, and it cost NZ$16 for a twin room where there was already another occupant – a really untidy student, though he seemed pleasant enough. Went into town and made plans: will take a tour to see Mt. Cook and the Southern Alps tomorrow; then I will attend a Maori concert on Saturday evening; on Sunday, I will leave

Christchurch and take the trans alpine train across to Greymouth on the West coast; and then I will get the early bus on Monday to take me from Greymouth and head North along the West Coast to Nelson, where I would meet Will.

Christchurch has a pretty centre to it, described by Lonely Planet as, "The most English of New Zealand's cities; punts glide down the picturesque River Avon, a grand Anglican cathedral dominates the city square and trams rattle past streets with oh-so English names."

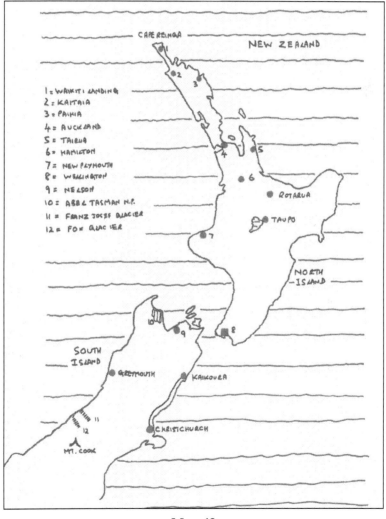

Map 42

There is no doubt that the calm and tranquil waters of the river snaking its way through the city, with a couple of punts braving the elements, the overhanging willows lining the riverbanks and the expansive botanical gardens, the plethora of students and student bicycles, and the quasi Gothic architecture of the Cathedral combined with the faux Tudor architecture of some of the buildings stretching back from the Cathedral Square, give the city a Cambridge-esque feel; and the dreary English-style weather certainly played its part in justifying the description. However, although it was difficult to put my finger on exactly what the difference was, whilst it might have been superficially authentic, something about it did not seem right. Away from the gentrification, Christchurch was a bustling modern city, with an earthy underbelly exemplified by the fact that it had a surprising number of massage parlours (I hasten to add that this time I shied away from verifying their authenticity).

In the evening I ate a cheap, but very cheerful, five-dollar pasta at a five-dollar pasta shop, before heading off to the cinema to watch the film *Notting Hill*, a romantic comedy, whose main characters were played by Hugh Grant and Julia Roberts. To my mind, it was overplayed in parts in the usual Richard Curtis/Four Weddings and a Funeral mould, with the romantic parts being ultra-slushy, whilst the comedy was extremely hilarious, but for all that, it was certainly a great film to watch at the cinema... except that! Part way through the film it occurred to me that the place was full of couples, with everybody in the cinema – literally so far as I could see – being with somebody else and almost all were arm in arm. It seemed like I was the only person in there on my own, and, as I was seated in the centre of the cinema, the paranoia in me sensed that I stood out like a flashing belisha beacon. I thought of Kitty, and though it felt good to be reminded that she was out there waiting for me, I wished that she were with me at this time. In fact, the more I thought about it, the more I was sure that Kitty had previously told me she had been to see – and loved – this film. As a consequence, I was already in a wistful mood when, hands buried deep inside my pockets, at the end I shuffled out of the cinema alongside the crowd of cooing couples. However, the dolefulness deepened as I was walking across the Cathedral Square where the drizzly rain was made visible by the dazzling spotlights illuminating the cathedral. As people were forced to huddle together under umbrellas, a droll down-and-out was busking and playing 'Raindrops Keep Falling on My Head' on a trombone, which echoed around the square to crown the melancholic mood. It felt so surreal that it seemed like it was part of the film. As I exited the Cathedral Square and walked on down the side streets, the echoing sound made by the trombone could still be heard, but it gradually became fainter and fainter like a slow fade on a record. I was deep in thought. I could not help wondering if Kitty had also been on her own when she had seen the film. I thought it unlikely. It was not a thought I wanted to dwell on. I mused that Hugh Grant got his girl, whilst I would have to wait for mine – hopefully. Then, for some reason, an image of my nan came to me, and in my mind's eye I saw her smiling her radiant smile, reassuring me that all would be well, whilst at the same time gently chiding me and wisely reminding me that patience is a virtue.

Bought some provisions at the supermarket.

Friday 6th August – Alpine Flight

Another great day in what is becoming a great last bit of a great trip. Got up in good time and the bus was already waiting to pick me up.

It was a drier day than yesterday but there was still quite a bit of cloud around. However, as the bus drew closer to the Alps the skies cleared until there was hardly a cloud in the sky. On the way out of Christchurch, the bus had picked up the pretty girl who I had seen on the Wellington to Picton Ferry on Tuesday (the one who had asked me to take a photograph of her). She passed by me and sat towards the back of the bus. She was wearing a thick brown coat but I noticed that her left hand poking out of the sleeve was in plaster. The scenery out of the bus was stunning all the way.

The brochure for the coach tour to visit the Southern Alps had promised views of crystal-clear lakes, snow-capped mountains, alpine scenery and the tallest mountain in all of Australasia, Mt. Cook. During the journey, we were further entertained by mouth-watering promotional videos about Mt. Cook flights, where the aerial photography was stunning. Although the videos were clearly designed to whet the appetite, I had no idea at the time of precisely how – or why. When the bus turned inland from the coast road and climbed up West towards Mt. Cook National Park, the scenery quickly became rolling and gradually more spectacular, with snow-capped mountains, that were initially distant, creeping nearer and nearer. After a three-hour journey, the bus stopped beside Lake Tekapo, nominally for passengers to take in refreshments. However, as I was about to clamber off, surprise, surprise, a rep from the Mt. Cook Flights Company climbed aboard. Smartly dressed, with hair slicked back and a clipboard in hand, this young chap clearly meant business. I like to think that I am immune to overt salesmanship, but evidently I was sadly mistaken because I stood no chance with this man. I was easy prey. Subconsciously, I had clearly been softened up so well by the videos that when the rep told us there were only four seats left, and then offered a discounted price of NZ$180 instead of NZ$210, I grabbed the bait hook, line and sinker. With 45 minutes to wait before moving off, I tried to rationalise why I had made the sudden decision to blow my £20 daily budget. I recognised that the weather had played its part, since with it being a crisp, clear, sunny, windless day, I would never get better weather conditions. Also, the price of NZ$180 was only a little over £56, so it wasn't inordinately expensive. After all, I had budgeted very well on this trip up to now, so, with my new job due to start in only a matter of weeks, I considered that a little bit extra on my debit card would do me no harm.

It turned out to be a great decision. I was seated in a small, ten-seater prop plane. As we took off on a very short strip of tarmac beside Lake Tekapo, we were immediately afforded great views as we banked across the azure-blue lake itself. The plane turned towards the mountains, and we headed up the Tasman Glacier. At the head of the glacier was a thick blanket of fresh, clean snow, whilst further down the slope the snow turned to ridges of crumpled ice. As we headed up the glacier and banked West, the classic diamond peak shape of the summit of Mt. Cook came into view. Named after Captain James Cook, I learnt that at 3,755 m. the mountain is not a great deal lower than the highest peak in the European Alps. Crisply-lined, jagged, corniced ridges ran to the North and South of Mt. Cook. As we headed further West, we were met by wave upon wave of rocky buttresses and cliff edges peering above pristine snow, which was glinting and sparkling in the sunshine. Far out to the West, I could see the Tasman Sea, where the sun's rays reflecting off the water created a band of golden light. We passed over New Zealand's two most famous glaciers, the Fox and the Franz-Josef. I was advised that nowhere else in the world do glaciers advance so close to the sea, and the reasons, I was told, are threefold: firstly, the West Coast of New Zealand is bombarded by very moist air blowing from the West; secondly, the mountains of the Southern Alps are very high and very extensive, with the result that there are very heavy deposits of snow and ice; and, finally, the slopes down to the West Coast are very steep, so that the rate of descent of the glaciers is very fast. Indeed, the rate of descent of the Franz Josef Glacier can be an impressive five metres per day, as compared to most of those in the European Alps that move at just under five metres per fortnight. As I looked down, smooth thick layers of pure-white snow crumpled and folded as they headed down the valleys, creating ever more deformed ripples of icy seracs and crevasses. At the very bottom, melt water became a stream that formed a silvery trail snaking across the narrow alluvium floor, looking from up high like a giant snail's trail. As we turned to head back East, we again passed Mt. Cook, where, in an otherwise cloudless sky, a crescent moon-shaped wedge of white cumulus cloud now clung to its South-Eastern face, protecting it like a giant scarf. The plane turned South for a short stretch to give us stunning views of blue mountain lakes, and yet more snow and ice, before turning and heading back to Lake Tekapo. Time had passed very quickly and I had loved every second.

I met up again with the coach a short while later at the same refreshment stop beside Lake Tekapo and this time I made a bee-line for the attractive girl who I had seen on the ferry three days ago. Her name is Claire, aged 25 and she is single. She had had a snowboarding accident yesterday and had broken her wrist. She showed me her plastered arm. She has been sailing for a living for five years. She told me that she was heading further South today to Queenstown, and had asked the bus driver to drop her off when it reached the coast road. She seemed quite keen and disappointed when I told her that I wasn't going on and I was heading back North. She even hinted that I should consider changing my plans. I was sorely tempted, but my conscience got the better of me and I made the excuse that time was now very tight for me, which in fact was not completely untrue. Lovely girl. Shame I hadn't talked to her earlier.

Saturday 7th August – Doing the Haka

Although I did quite a bit today it was still an anti-climax after yesterday. The lad in my room came in pissed (but he was good about it – not making a complete song and dance of it). We were joined by another lad – Welsh. After breakfast, I went along the river Avon – quite pretty – but there were a few ugly modern buildings nearby to spoil the view of the handful of old buildings and the tree lined scenery along the river. Ended up at the cathedral. The cathedral was okay and I saw several excellent mosaics and murals. Then went to the National Marae. The 'meeting house' was explained – it's the National Marae because it joins all the Maori tribes in New Zealand. Then there was a concert. Certainly wasn't as good as the first one I had been to in Rotorua but I was one of four – picked out of a hall of 50 – invited to go up on stage to do the Haka. Good fun. I then went back into town and went to the museum – again very good – the 'history of Israel' room was evocative and informative. Then did some clothes washing back at the hostel. Normally this wouldn't warrant an entry in this diary, but I did wonder whether this might be the last main wash that I would do on this trip. Will see. Then went to the Five Dollar Thai House where I had Tom Yum soup and a curry with rice. Overall, I spent 12 dollars at the Five Dollar Thai House (though at £4.00 I guess it was still good value). I had an apple pie back at the hotel where I met a lad from Fakenham (from my home county of Norfolk in the UK).

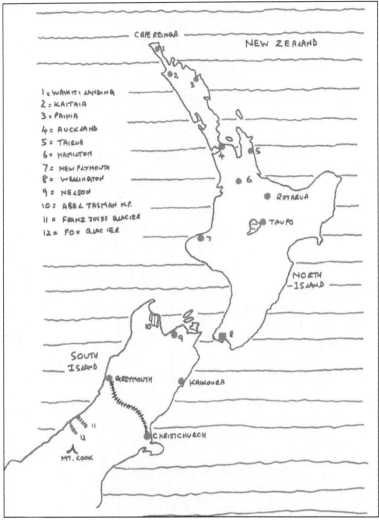

Map 43

<u>*Sunday 8th August – Alpine Train Trip*</u>

   A good day. Got up in plenty of time to catch the free shuttle bus from outside my hostel to the train station, but when I went out to catch it with 5 minutes to spare, I learnt that it had already left, more than five minutes earlier than scheduled. I thought I would not be able to catch the train, but thankfully I managed to get to the station on time – and discovered that the bus had left on time and it was the tourist information office that had given me the wrong timings. Found a good seat on the train opposite two hard-as-nails New Zealand 30-something housewives – evidently, they had stayed up until 5.00 am drinking and watching the South Africa v New Zealand Rugby Union Test (New Zealand won – thankfully!). Shortly after the train had left Christchurch it didn't take long before we were in some truly stunning scenery. The line followed the edge of dried-up riverbeds, with a backdrop of snow-capped mountains and frost and freezing ice clouds and blue skies and lakeland scenery and trees covered in frost. It was great. The middle carriage on the train was an open-air viewing deck. It was very cold but I persevered so I should hopefully have some decent photographs. The train crossed over Arthur's Pass and, having left behind dry scrubby moorland scenery at the entrance to an eight-kilometre long tunnel, it emerged into much greener scenery. Still very attractive but it was too cold to remain out. Arrived at Greymouth and went to Noah's Ark Backpackers – a really good place – with each room named after an animal. I was on my own in the penguin room.

I went for a walk down to the coast and along a jetty jutting out into the sea, where I had a good view looking back towards the town and up towards the plateau heading inland behind it. This is where the River Grey flows down through a narrow cleft at the edge of the plateau, and from where my train had emerged earlier. It was blustery and there were very high waves coming in off the sea, and as I looked out, I saw a seal swimming in the surf. In the evening, I had dinner at a three-dollar barbecue diner, where I had sausages and a salad – good value, because this time I was successful in managing to pay only three dollars.

Late in the evening, I was brushing my teeth in the bathroom, ready to turn in, when I heard the distinctly audible sound of somebody sighing over my right shoulder from the direction of the shower cubicle and I immediately felt a frisson run down my back. I glanced in the mirror, but could see nobody. I quickly turned around, saw nothing and then looked into the bedroom, thinking – perhaps even half hoping – that somebody had come in and was playing a trick on me, but nobody was there. I hurriedly finished brushing my teeth, whilst keeping a constant watch in the mirror. I had been completely spooked. Back in the bedroom, I opened the main door and peered into the corridor, where the lights were shining dimly, but there was no-one about and I could not hear a sound coming from any of the other guest-rooms. As I made myself ready for bed, I tried to think of a rational explanation for what I had heard. I was not inordinately tired. It was not inordinately late. I had not been drinking and had not been on any medication. I had not been feeling any element of stress, and I could not think of anything else that could have made that sound. I looked across at my smiling nan's photograph, perched intact on the bedside table, and felt some semblance of reassurance. When I switched off my light and went to bed, I was too alert to be able to go to sleep. I was at least grateful that enough light from the corridor was able to creep under the doorframe into my room to provide a degree of ambient light, sufficient to faintly illuminate the images of penguins painted on the walls. Looking back on it, although my immediate thought was that I had heard a ghost, I didn't want to contemplate it, let alone admit it, at the time, and so it was a couple of days later, when I had long since departed Greymouth, that I finally acknowledged that possibility by mentioning it in my diary. Much later, after leaving New Zealand, I made a few enquiries about the site, and discovered that the building was once a monastery adjoining a church. Indeed, I remembered that the name of the road where the Noah's Ark Backpackers building is located is Chapel Street. I was unable to discover what happened to both the church and the monastery, but I did find out that the site was regularly used as a place of refuge by local inhabitants when the River Grey flooded.

Monday 9th August – Letters from Kitty

Left Greymouth early in the morning. There was only one other person on the bus all the way from Greymouth to Nelson, a journey of seven hours, taking into account a couple of stops. Although the bus was a regular public bus, the driver stopped at Punakaiki to allow the other passenger and I the opportunity to see the famous Pancake Rocks and Blowholes.

Through a combination of sea, wind and rain, rock has eroded away to leave a series of weathered rock formations structured like pillars, that look like multi-layered pancakes, piled up American style. The softer rock in amongst the harder rock has been worn away to create chimneys, through which at certain tides water is rapidly forced up and spews out of the top, looking just like geysers. We were lucky that at the time we arrived the tide was strong enough to create the blowholes, but although the sight of fountains of frothy water shooting out of the holes was impressive, even more impressive was the thunderous, earth-shaking, almost frightening, sound the pressured water made as it forced its way up through the tubes before disgorging out of the blowholes.

The entire journey was fascinating, as the bus made its way along the Buller Gorge and down the Moutere River to Motueka. This was wine growing country and fruit growing country and there was evidence of it everywhere. We came around the bay into Nelson and the views on arrival were terrific. Nelson instantly seemed an attractive and *inviting place. I arrived at about 2.30 in the afternoon and after booking in my gear at the left luggage section of the Tourist Information office, I went for a walk. I ended up at the cathedral which was completed in the 1960s. It was quite attractive from the outside, and it certainly commanded a great position on a hill, overlooking the city. I went inside. Just before I left I saw a couple of teenage girls laughing as they ran out of the cathedral – it turned out that they had defaced the Visitors Books with obscene graffiti.*

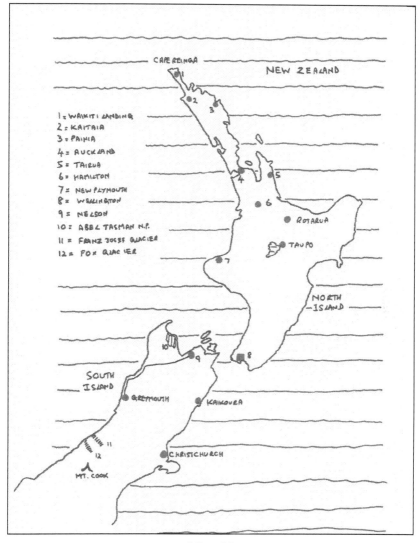

Map 44

Met up with Will a short while later. Good to see him. Then we met Karen, an old friend of his, with whom we were going to stay the night. Will gave me a pile of letters from Kitty. Wading through them it was evident that she had missed me, as indeed had I missed her, though I felt rather guilty, both at having had so much fun without her and, save for a couple of cards, of not putting pen to paper to her.

Tuesday 10ᵗʰ August – Wading Barefoot

Karen's very friendly and obviously has Will well sussed. Had a great Thai meal in the evening last night which Will paid for (I suspect it wasn't me he was trying to impress). Got up in good time in the morning and Karen took us to catch the 7.30 bus, which went via Motueka to Kaiteriteri where we transferred to a boat. It was a glorious day – sunshine all the way (and later I realised I had caught the sun). We sailed in and out of several bays and saw lots of shags and gulls and an Australasian gannet – I heard it splash as it dived into the water nearby and then saw it emerge out of the water and fly off. I couldn't tell if it had caught the fish that it was after. We were dropped off at Totaranui.

We had planned to walk three days along the Abel Tasman Coastal Track, which was described by Lonely Planet as, "One of the most beautiful in the country, passing through pleasant bush overlooking beaches of golden sand lapped by bright blue water; the numerous bays, small and large, make it like a travel brochure come to life." The Abel Tasman National Park lies at the Northern end of a range of hills and occupies a peninsula on the Northern coast of South Island abutting the sea. There are several trails through the park, but the most popular is the coastal trail. Although the area is very popular for visitors, and hundreds of walkers can be walking in high summer at any one time, the peninsula is largely inaccessible by road, which as a consequence helps to ensure that it remains relatively remote. We anticipated that there would be very few hikers walking at this time, this being the New Zealand winter. We carried with us almost everything that we would need, including clothes, food, water, and sleeping bags. One item that we did not need was a tent, as the path was served by a series of wooden shacks that would provide shelter.

Access to the park was by boat, which in the morning ran from Kaiteriteri at the Southern end of the coast to Totaranui at the Northern end. On arrival at Totaranui the boat anchored 50 yards out from the shore, where we transferred to a small dinghy that dropped us off on the 400-yard-long golden-sand beach. Nobody else alighted from the boat, so we had the entire beach and the nearby campsite to ourselves. Not a single solitary footprint marred the sand, that is until Will and I, like excited overgrown schoolchildren in our size 9 ½s, trampled all over it, walking backwards, hopping sidewards and walking in each other's footprints in circles in an attempt to confuse the enemy.

Although Totaranui was the Northernmost point for boat drops, it was not the Northernmost point of the walk itself, so Will and I spent the first two hours trekking North to beautiful Anatakapau Bay and Mutton Cove, before returning back to have lunch where we started at Totaranui. We then tramped South to Awaroa Bay. Although the route mainly comprised two types of walking experience, a series of grassy tracks weaving through bush inland, followed intermittently by treks on sand along beaches or coves, this is not to say that the walk was monotonous – far from it. The tableau along the inland paths was constantly changing, with them bordered by ancient trees, spreading palms, tall tussocky grasses, New Zealand ferns of varying shapes and sizes and a surprising number of flowers – including snowdrops, hellebores and primroses, whilst the bays were invariably lined with pristine beaches of clean ochre sand, backed by lush green overhanging trees and shrubs, and an azure blue sea. Birds, butterflies and insects danced with each other in and out of the forest lining the coastal path. Apart from when Will and I did some yakking – which was seldom – the only sounds came from the singing birds, the whistling, buzzing, humming or chirruping insects or the gentle swish of the sea lapping against the shore. The winter air was clean, cool and very fresh. Padding through the canopy was easy underfoot but exhilarating as the path snaked between tree and bush, each twist or bend tantalisingly masking what was around the corner beyond it. Occasionally, we would stumble upon a bird in the middle of the path which would hurriedly scurry away into the undergrowth.

After two hours walking through bush and along beach, we arrived at an inlet, where we had to take our boots off to wade across the shallow waters of the Awaroa River estuary. Large orange triangular signs ear-marked the route of the coastal path, with a straight line between the two representing the safest point to cross the inlet. The water was cool and refreshing, but the shallow river bed was thickly matted with cockles and broken cockle shells which made walking hard for my tender feet. Around us, oyster catchers and herons darted up and down the estuary, foraging for food, oblivious to the sight of two large non-aquatic mammals lumbering unceremoniously through the water. On the other side, we arrived at Awaroa Hut, a walkers' lodge, where we had planned to stay the night and after a quick de-camp we ravenously dived into our food. We had arrived in good time to make the most of the late afternoon sun, which was just as well since there were no lights in the cabin. Facilities did, however, extend to mattresses, toilets and a wood store. Two other lads were already at the hut, intending to stay the night. They seemed pleasant enough, but Will's persistent inquisitions drew unenthusiastic monosyllabic replies. Realising that trying to make conversation with our companions was like wading through treacle, even Will eventually gave up, so we walked out to the water's edge, where we watched the strangely hypnotic ebb and flow – though mainly flow – of the tide as it swept in at break-neck speed to rapidly cover the shallow beach.

Wednesday 11th August – Drying Feet in the Rain

There were mice in the hut last night. We saw them on our bunks in the sleeping area. They seemed to stop bothering us when we went to bed and instead could be heard running around the kitchen/food area. We retired at around 8.15 pm. We virtually slept round the clock, getting up at ten past eight – I thought that it was much earlier. There were perfect blue skies at sunset last night, but when we emerged from the hut there was pouring rain and it was very overcast. We eventually set off at five to ten, when the rain had abated. It was a hard slog because the high tide meant that, instead of following the beach, we had to cut slightly inland and my trousers quickly became uncomfortably wet as we waded through the saturated long grass. Then it started to chuck it down. I attempted to provide some protection by stretching a bin liner over the top of both me and my rucksack but whether I did too little, or simply left it too late, it didn't seem to work. Despite the poor weather, the scenery was still stunning – lots of small isolated clouds of mist emerged from the trees, looking like steam evaporating out of a jungle – great vistas from the tops of rocky promontories – beautiful perfect white beaches along bays and coves – and blue water, even in the cloudy conditions. We had to wade knee deep across one creek, so I had no choice but to take off my trousers, socks and boots. As it was still pouring with rain, re-dressing in wringing wet clothes was difficult. As if to match the weather, Will seemed to be in a cantankerous mood, just as if a black dog of depression had descended on him. He said that he was not, and my questions only seemed to irritate him even more. We met four English people on the way including one girl by the name of Lookey, who reminded me of Peggy in Hi-de-Hi – scatty. Had to wade across Torrent Bay at the end. Met a nice New Zealand couple at the next hut, who shared their wine with us. The girl had brought four bottles.

Thursday 12th August – Completing Walk

Yesterday we saw a pair of yellowhammers. Today we saw a bellbird, a silver-eye, a southern black backed gull (the gull had a broken leg), three wekas and Canada geese. The weather today was much better than yesterday. I slept well. The Kiwi couple had already left by the time we got up to go and, like a scene from the Rise and Fall of Reginald Perrin, Will took the opportunity to run screaming out of the hut to take a skinny dip in the sea. I sat on the veranda, sipping my hot steaming tea, watching the lunatic on show and thinking, "He gets that from his father." We set off at a reasonable pace and again passed and stopped at some amazing bays and beaches. We had a long lunch stop, which is where we saw the poor gull with the broken leg. I fed it scraps of apple and biscuit and bread. I then went dyking – something I hadn't done since a child – digging a channel between two parts of the beach. It was Will's turn to sit back drinking tea, shaking his head and watching in silent bewilderment at me. We arrived at the terminus of the walk at Marahau, 15 minutes before the 3.30 bus back to Kaiteriteri, which was good timing in one sense, though I would have liked to have hung around a bit at the end. We met up with Lookey, who was also waiting for the bus. We learnt that she had walked all the way from Bark Bay in a single tramp. I worked out that over the three days we had walked in all between 56 and 60 kilometres (between 35 and 37½ miles). On the bus from Kaiteriteri back to Nelson the bus driver gave a great running commentary; one of the best quips was when he referred to the numerous dead possums on the road as being food for birds of prey, and suggested they were, "Meals from wheels." Great character. Met up with Karen back in Nelson, where in evening we had a delicious chicken meal with wine. She's a lovely girl as is her house friend, Fiona.

Friday 13th August – Flying out of Nelson

Got up at a reasonable time. Packed. Talked a little to both Karen and Fiona. Nice girls. Karen took me and Will to the airport. Tiny airport but nice. Small plane – 12-seater. Clear weather and therefore great views looking over Nelson and the Marlborough Sound but also back at Abel Tasman, where I could plainly see Awaroa Bay and the very long spit of sand that is Farewell Spit.

As we passed over the West coast of North Island I looked out for, but could not properly see, Mt. Taranaki, as it was shrouded in cloud. Touched down at New Plymouth before taking off again. Although it was cloudier and a little showery on North Island, the weather still wasn't too bad.

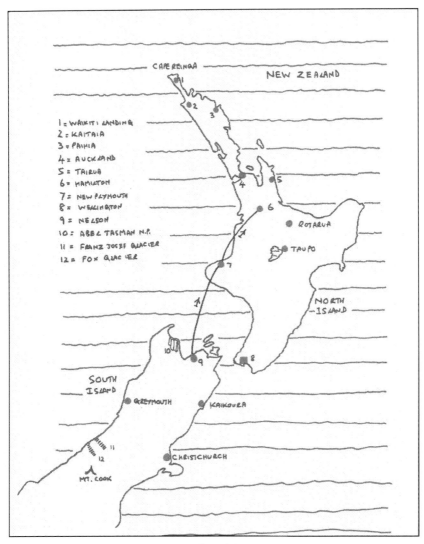

Map 45

1 = WAIKITI LANDING
2 = KAITAIA
3 = PAIHIA
4 = AUCKLAND
5 = TAIRUA
6 = HAMILTON
7 = NEW PLYMOUTH
8 = WELLINGTON
9 = NELSON
10 = ABEL TASMAN N.P.
11 = FRANZ JOSEF GLACIER
12 = FOX GLACIER

CAPE REINGA

NEW ZEALAND

ROTARUA

TAUPO

NORTH ISLAND

SOUTH ISLAND

GREYMOUTH

KAIKOURA

CHRISTCHURCH

MT. COOK

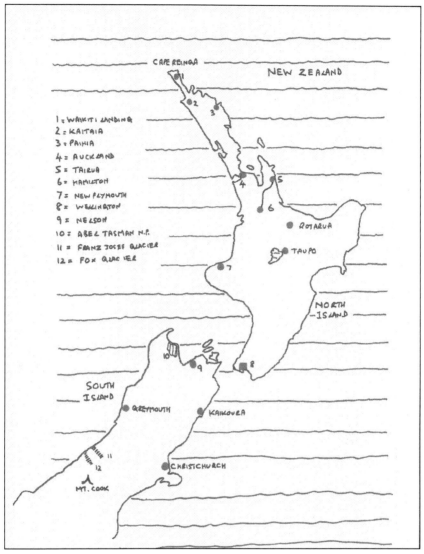

1 = WAIKITI LANDING
2 = KAITAIA
3 = PAIHIA
4 = AUCKLAND
5 = TAIRUA
6 = HAMILTON
7 = NEW PLYMOUTH
8 = WELLINGTON
9 = NELSON
10 = ABEL TASMAN N.P.
11 = FRANZ JOSEF GLACIER
12 = FOX GLACIER

NEW ZEALAND

CAPE REINGA

ROTARUA

TAUPO

NORTH ISLAND

SOUTH ISLAND

GREYMOUTH

KAIKOURA

CHRISTCHURCH

MT. COOK

Map 46

Will's dad was there to meet us at Hamilton Airport. Not much was said, but he seemed glad to see us and was in good spirits. He told Will that he was a little concerned about the car yesterday but today it appears to be running okay. We went back to Will's dad's farm, where we had a light lunch and then set off again. We viewed the completed house before I left. Very good. Popped into Hamilton to see Will's sister, Jane. She wasn't in, but her husband, Barry, was, and he seemed a nice chap. I took out NZ$300, which I hope to see me through, made up partly from using the last of my travellers

339

cheques and partly by debit card. I know that I am approaching the end. I am behind on my budget but not by too much. We did some food shopping and we set off in the car. It was dark all the way. I drove a good part of it. We arrived at Tairua on the Coromandel Peninsula, close to where Will's other sister, Liz, lives, where we grabbed some fish and chips before we retired back to her house. Whilst Will knew that Liz would be away, her stepson, Peter, was expected to be about, but nobody was at home. I did some more washing (it was fast becoming necessary).

Saturday 14th August – Slideshow/Kauaeranga

Last Monday Will had brought with him stuff that Kitty had sent to me – apparently whilst I was away she had rung six times and had spoken with both Will and his dad (I'd like to have been a fly on the wall in that conversation). She had sent me three letters, a card, five photographs of her, and a t-shirt for my niece, Robbyne. Lovely girl. I am very lucky. Today I felt a bit down, particularly in the morning. Will had got to me but I couldn't quite put my finger on why or how. We left latish and we headed to Kauaeranga Valley in the Coromandel Forest Park, where we went to the visitor centre first. The visitor centres throughout New Zealand are fantastic – informative, interesting and entertaining. There was a free slide show which demonstrated the logging trade that went on in the park. It was surprisingly moving and nostalgic and very well done. We then had lunch before heading off for our walk, an 8 ½ miles trek through the valley to an area known as the Pinnacles, a jagged limestone outcrop. We were advised that it would take 4 to 5 hours but we did it in 3 hours and 20 minutes in total. It was a steep and sometimes very arduous walk in parts but also very rewarding with some great views. We were walking along stretches that we had just seen in the slide show which gave the show a real and proper context, and which was a little bit eerie because of that. We went back to Will's sister's, where there was still no sign of the stepson, and had steak for tea and then we watched a great Harrison Ford film.

Sunday 15th August – Railway Line

Good day. Cloudy, greyish start to the day but it promised to be better later. Drove up to Coromandel town – 1 ½ hours – intending to ride on the Driving Creek Railway, but we arrived too late for the morning departure. Decided to go back later. Then we drove round Coromandel Peninsula – good views. Saw several New Zealand dotterel – a rare kiwi bird – when we stopped and went for a walk along one of the East coast beaches. Returned to Coromandel town.

We managed to get back in time to catch a ride on the small private railway known as Driving Creek Railway. The man who owns and constructed it, Barry Brickell, built it initially to carry clay, which he uses to make pottery, from one end of the line on top of a hill to the other end in the valley near his home. The narrow-gauge line, which stretches 3 ½ kilometres in total, switches back several times as it rises steeply 100 metres from its base to its highest point. Now the train doubles up as a tourist attraction in its own right.

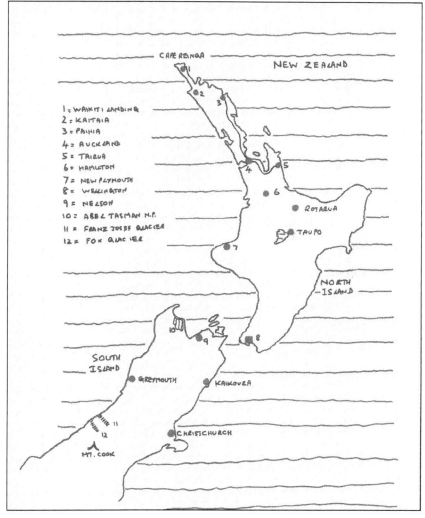

Map 47

Barry Brickell was present today to personally drive the train and give a guided commentary. Dressed in a mustard-coloured jumper, brown slacks and open-toed sandals – no socks – he was clearly a lovable eccentric.

Visit to the railway was brilliant. On drive back, we stopped at a Kauri grove. The Kauri trees were huge despite being some of the younger variety – the oldest was a mere 600 years old. Then we went to a place known as hot water beach, where literally hot water bubbles up from underground onto the beach. Unfortunately, it was raining quite heavily. We debated whether or not to go, but in the end, we decided to go – bad move. We had hoped to be able to dig a hole to allow the hot water to seep up but we couldn't manage it, because every time we removed one lot of sand, water would flood back in bringing other sand with it – Will thought it was because the tide was too high. Then the rain started to bucket down even more heavily. We both got soaked. Big lesson learnt, never ever to be repeated (until tomorrow). Had chilli con carne in the evening. Liz's stepson, Steve, finally turned up but he was very unsociable, greeting us with a cursory grunt before disappearing into his room – he seemed to resent us being there.

Monday 16th August – Miranda Beach

I have had a really sore nose all day. It is like I've got itchy spots on the inside of my nose and it is very painful and swollen. Left Will's sister's place at Tairua in reasonable time (having made some sandwiches for lunch) and we first went to the summit at Paku where there were spectacular views down towards Tairua and Pauanui and towards the bay, the sea and the coast all around. Great. Then went to Will's sister's second house (smaller than the first) where a short distance away we had even better views than the ones we'd seen earlier. We then made tracks, travelling around the coast and along a relatively quiet back road to Auckland known as the East Coast Pacific Highway.

How do you convey to those who are not there 'in the moment' why something, which at any other time and to any other person in any other circumstance, would seem petty or trivial or innocuous, but which to us should be so hilariously funny? Will and I had a real giggling fit today over something which was so comical that it continued to tickle our funny bones every day throughout the rest of our time together in New Zealand. One moment, there would be silence, the next moment one of us would start chuckling, which would set off the other, without a word being exchanged. Even now, as I write this, I cannot stop smiling. The dark, depressive cloud that had been hanging over Will for a day or two had lifted and he was in a much better mood this morning, as we made our way around the

Coromandel coast and headed North to Auckland and the peninsula beyond. It was a clear, bright, dry day marked by hazy high-level cloud. After the best part of two hours, we decided that we should look for a place to stop for lunch this side of Auckland. We turned off the highway and headed along a sandy track to the edge of a beach. This was Miranda Beach and it was a beautiful arc of empty, isolated, grey-white sand, backed by a turquoise sea, with the phantasmagorical silhouette of the hills on the Coromandel Peninsula stretching out across the bay, the Firth of Thames. The sun was just about filtering through and it was a warm afternoon, so we wound down our windows whilst eating our sandwiches. A gentle breeze wafted ozone-rich, clean, fresh air into the car, and a couple of insects buzzed and danced on the windscreen. The shoreline turned out to be an ornithologist's paradise and I tried to show off my tiny bit of knowledge to Will by naming those birds that I claimed to have recognised, including knots, bar-tailed godwits and red billed gulls. A taciturn Will seemed less than interested. I know that he wouldn't have been able to correct me if my identification of the birds had been wrong, and I don't think that he would have registered what I was saying even if I'd told him I'd spotted naked dancing girls. With a vacant, expressionless look on his face, he gluttonously chomped down on his sandwich whilst staring out to sea. I said no more. After about ten minutes, our attention was drawn to the low earth-vibrating rumbling noise of a vehicle turning off the main road, which, when we turned around, turned out to be a huge transporter, laden with a couple of caterpillar diggers on its back. We watched in reverential silence as the truck came down the same sandy track that we had travelled down, passed behind our car and continued further along the track beside the beach before stopping 50 yards or so beyond us. We were watching transfixed as a ramp dropped down to let the caterpillar diggers drive off the back and onto the beach, when Will laconically quipped, "There's something here for everyone." The light aside was delivered with such perfect comic timing that it quickly turned two grown men into quivering jellies. We were soon in fits of laughter, with tears rolling down our eyes. I don't really recall thereafter what happened to the diggers, the knots, the godwits, and the gulls, and I haven't a clue how or when we managed to finish our lunch. As I say, you had to be there.

After lunch, we carried on heading North, passing through some very scenic countryside before driving across Auckland Harbour Bridge. We paused at Whangarei to have a meal and then continued on to Paihia where we found a small hotel to stay the night. Very good and only NZ$45 for the room. Had a beer in the bar later where we got talking to two Finnish girls, Paula and Katja. Both were attractive – one extremely so. Although we had a very pleasant chat there was clearly no mileage there.

Tuesday 17th August – Treaty House

As had become customary, we got up later than planned. My painful nose looked even worse and I was becoming concerned. I went to a chemist and they said there was nothing they could give me without a prescription. I asked if there were any local doctors and they pointed one out to me. I managed to get in virtually immediately – but it cost me NZ$40. The doctor checked me over and said it was cellulitis – a bacterial infection of the mucous membrane – for which he prescribed antibiotics. I am glad that I went. We drove to the Treaty House located at the neighbouring town of Waitangi which is the site of the historic signing of the Treaty between the Maori people and the representatives of Queen Victoria's government in 1840. We saw a video show, where we were given much more information about the Treaty of Waitangi itself. The meeting house and the war canoes were especially evocative. On the lawn outside, Will and I re-enacted the historic signing for a self-made photograph, with white-skinned Will representing the Queen and a still-very-tanned yours truly representing the Maoris. We had intended to visit the tiny town of Russell, but we were running out of time so we headed on up North.

Shortly after leaving Paihia, we came up to a T-junction where our intended route took us left, but on the corner of the road was a solitary, stunning, 20-something blonde goddess of a girl trying to thumb a lift in the opposite direction. Will gave a polite, apologetic wave as we passed, but as we accelerated up the road we glanced at each other enquiringly – the silence spoke volumes. Although it was all 'boys' talk', it cannot be denied that in the ensuing conversation we both claimed to be tempted to turn back and chance our arm in the opposite direction. After all, it's easy to be brazen when you are heading in the opposite direction. Although neither of us ever had any real intention of doing so, the salacious talk of what each one of us would have liked to have done with that dreamy vision of Venus kept these two quasi-teenagers occupied for miles. It is entirely likely that the girl we had passed was sensibly dressed in jacket and long-legged jeans, but by the end of our journey our memory of her was permanently embellished with her wearing hot pants and a tight, white, figure-hugging t-shirt.

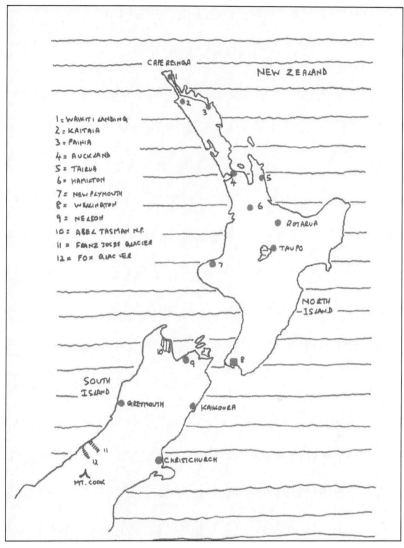

Map 48

Although this last bit of the journey to the Northernmost tip of North Island was not too long, a couple of times towards the end, Will and I were a bit fractious with each other and started bickering like an old married couple. When planning anything, one of the dynamics is that I am perhaps a bit too fussy about details whilst Will to my mind is not fussy enough. We arrived at Waikiti Landing, a very small village and our staging post, where we booked into a guest house and finalised plans for our three-day walking trip starting tomorrow. I am looking forward to it.

Wednesday 18th August – "Oh My God."

I started on my antibiotics yesterday and I gave myself a full Reiki last night. This morning I seemed a lot worse, so much so that my left eye was really puffed up. Will had got up to take a shower and I went to have a wash in the basin in the same bathroom. Will asked how I was and poked his head around the shower curtain and when he saw me exclaimed in a theatrically loud, but deadly serious, voice, "Oh my god!!" It was very funny. After finishing packing, and a quick breakfast, the girl who runs the place drove us to the beginning of the walk for an early start. Right at the outset I had to get my boots off to walk across a shallow stream. Will, as usual, went marching off ahead. We had to cross huge sand dunes – the biggest I've ever seen – looking like a real desert scene.

The North tip of North Island stretches out into the ocean like an index finger at the end of an outstretched giant arm, and right at the Northernmost tip of the Aupouri Peninsula is Cape Reinga. Will had never been this far North and was very keen to see it and explore it. We had planned a three-day trek, and this time we would have to take *all* our provisions with us, including a tent, which we had borrowed, sleeping bags, cooking equipment, food and water. Cape Reinga, whose full name is Cape Reinga Te Rerenga Wairua, is wild and remote and lies more than 100 km North of the nearest town and at the time access to it for the last 19 km was along an unsealed gravel track. The 'Te Rerenga Wairua' component of the name in Maori language means the 'leaping-off place of spirits', whilst the 'Reinga' part of the name is the Maori word for underworld. Both refer to the Maori belief that the cape is the point where the spirits of the dead enter the underworld. According to <u>mythology</u>, such spirits travel from their last resting place within New Zealand to Cape Reinga on their journey to the afterlife. At Cape Reinga they depart the mainland, by leaping off the headland, descending to the underworld through the roots of an 800-year-old pohutukawa tree (which still exists and which we would later see), turning briefly at a set of <u>islands</u> just off-shore for one last look back towards the mainland, and then completing their journey to their traditional homeland by using the Te Ara Wairua, the 'Spirits' pathway'. Modern anthropological science tells us that the Maoris originally came to the land we now know as New Zealand from Polynesia, which lies to the North in the Pacific Ocean, so it seems natural, if not logical, that that this should be the place from where they return to their ancestors. It is fair to say that some of the gaps in my knowledge were only filled when, with my imagination fired up, I carried out some research later, but I had learnt enough beforehand to know that it was indeed a sacred place. For me, with only a week to go before I returned home, the walk represented the last main adventure of my six-month trip, the final leg of my own personal odyssey, which was especially poignant with it taking place on the very furthest extremity of the furthest nation on earth from home. Little did I know that it would turn out to be probably the most memorable walking trek I have ever made.

The start to the walk was only a couple of miles West of Waikiti Landing, where the 4x4 dropped us off beside a stream, that was reasonably shallow, but deep enough in parts to require us to take off our boots. The slow start was exacerbated since for the next hour or so, weighed down with our rucksacks at their heaviest, we clambered along and over huge sand dunes, where the going underfoot was tricky and arduous, with the powdery sand making it difficult to gain traction. It was also very deep, meaning that it was impossible to get any kind of pace or rhythm going. Will appeared to be making lighter work of it than me, and he was scampering away. A strong breeze didn't help, though it did provide a little impish satisfaction to me by forcing him to slow down when it blew Will's hat off and he had to abandon his rucksack and go haring after it like a lunatic. Although it was windy, it was bright and sunny.

We eventually emerged onto a huge expanse of flat sandy beach. We had arrived at the top end of Ninety Mile Beach. Neither when traversing the sand dunes, nor when arriving at the beach, did we see any footprints or other evidence of humans. It was clear that we were the first people to pass this way for several weeks at least. The tide was out but the wind was very strong, whipping up waves to crash land onto the beach. It was very dramatic. We turned to head North. Not for the first time on this walk – and certainly not the last – the wind again blew Will's hat off and sent it spinning back along the beach from whence he had come.

Shortly thereafter, we came across a young seal pup on the beach which appeared to have got lost. He – I believed it was a he – seemed to be in good health, and unharmed, but he was clearly distressed and was seemingly crying out for his mother. Unfortunately, the cries were lost in the wind. He didn't seem disturbed by our presence and, in fact, if anything, it was possibly the contrary as he fixed his eyes on us when crying out his lament as if to beg us to help him. I was very concerned, because to me he looked young enough to still require weaning, and if his mother never found him he would surely perish. It was distressing to know that we could do nothing to help him, and it was heart-wrenching to walk away and abandon him to fate, with him still crying after us, and staring at us pleadingly with his sad, doleful eyes.

We soon left the beach and walked along spectacular coastal scenery, around one headland after another, with a mixture of dramatic cliffs, beautiful sheltered coves, stretches of longer beaches and views of wave after wave of striated foamy, frothing, white horses racing towards land across a baby blue sea. Some of the walk took us along paths through parched scrubland, but much of it was on firm, flat sand. Late in the afternoon, we stopped and camped on a grassy ridge overlooking a bay. It was idyllic, particularly when the wind dropped to allow other sounds to fill the air. From the shrill call of oyster catchers, and the raucous squawking of gulls, to waves washing over the sand, this surround-sound of ambient acoustics made us feel completely at one with nature. Supper that night tasted particularly sweet.

Total walking time today was 6 hours and 15 minutes which equates to 15 ¼ miles or 25 kilometres.

<u>Thursday 19th August – Dolphins at Tapotupotu Bay</u>

Great day; up early but took us quite a while to break camp.

We had found a brilliant camping spot, and, with the wind having completely abated, we awoke to a dawn chorus of oyster catchers, whose excited, high-pitched calls to each other echoed around the beach. The rest of the day was equally idyllic. It was a bright, clear day, with hardly a cloud in the sky. We strode down to and then along the beach we had camped beside with an extra spring in our step, not least because our rucksacks were lighter by one day's worth of water and food. At the far end of the beach we climbed up to the headland at Cape Reinga itself and followed the path round to the lighthouse. Here we encountered the only humans that we would see on our entire walk, a party of four, who had driven along a track to get to it. I cannot deny that I felt a little smugly superior, having arrived here the hard way, but we condescended to be friendly to the natives by nodding and saying hello. From the lighthouse itself, where a sign informed me that I was 10,499 nautical miles from London, there were fabulous views along 180 degrees of coastline. A path led on down from the lighthouse to a series of rocks at the water's edge, and here we saw the tree at the end of the cape which is sacred to Maoris, and which was leafless and so small and wiry that it was hard to believe it was 800 years old. We could also clearly see a maelstrom in the water, where the Tasman Sea and the Pacific Ocean supposedly meet. We had hoped to top up our water supplies from a stream at the cape, but a sign warned against drinking the water, so, erring on the side of caution, we were persuaded not to take any.

We continued East, where the coastline on this side of the cape was much greener and less rugged than on the Western side, but it was no less beautiful for it. This stretch of the walk beyond Cape Reinga was a gentle roller-coaster of a ride, rising and falling along cushion-soft, grassy paths between a succession of beautiful white-sanded coves, with the colour of the water therein evolving from a stunning turquoise close in by the beaches to a sapphire-blue further out. It was when we had stopped for lunch on the crest of a hill looking down into the next beautiful cove that I had such an experience that it was nothing short of an epiphany. I wrote about it in my diary immediately.

I am writing this diary halfway through the day whilst I am sitting on top of a hill looking down on a beautiful beautiful bay – Tapotupotu Bay – with white sand and a beautiful stream running into it and a rocky bluff and cliffs and a path leading up a hill beyond which we're going to have to climb later and the waters are turquoise blue and the sun's beating down and we can see Spirits Bay at the end of our journey about 20 kilometres in the distance and we have just seen a pod of twenty or so dolphins which we first sighted jumping out of the water in the cove right below us and then followed them splashing and playing and jumping out of the water the entire length of the coast as far as we could see.

I can count the number of times when I have had such an experience on one hand, but they almost always occur when I am walking. It is as if I am completely at one with my surroundings and with nature. It is a sublimely spiritual experience and above all else I feel so ecstatically happy. Will had felt it too, and shrugged off his normal impatience to move on. We lingered long at our lunch spot today.

Later we had to cross a stream which was wide and waist high at its deepest. Will had stripped off and was crossing over the creek butt naked before you could blink an eye. I was a little more hesitant but I soon followed suit. Very funny. We continued along the coast and negotiated several steep climbs up to the cliffs along the coast edge before we eventually descended to Spirits Bay. Set up camp in a very pretty spot on the Western edge of Spirits Bay and made a fire. Today we walked for 6 hours and 40 minutes equating to 16 and 2/3 of a mile or 27 kilometres.

Friday 20th August – Ghost of Will

We got up at dawn and saw a lovely sunrise. I was a little tetchy with Will because I'd intended to make breakfast but he was his usual impatient self and got on with it before I had a chance to do it. I felt quite achy and very sore after being so cold in bed last night. Feel like I might have a cold coming on. We broke camp.

Last night had been an uncomfortable one. The sun seemed to set very quickly and once it had done so the night became very dark, so dark that we could not see much beyond our camp. During the previous night we had had the sounds of nature to entertain and comfort us. Last night was, in contrast, a brooding eerie silence. Even the camp fire could not do much to raise the mood. By necessity, it was normal for us to do our ablutions away from the area of the tent, but last night I made sure that I did not stray too far, returning as quickly as possible to the psychological protection afforded by the fire. Will retired early as usual, leaving me outside on my own, but for once I found his familiar swine-like snuffling and snoring quite comforting. At some point, however, he must have turned onto his side because he became silent, which coincided with me noticing that the fire had subsided to glowing embers. The silence around me acquired such a malevolence that, despite me urging myself not to be so stupid, I could not shake off the notion that somebody was sitting in the tall grass nearby watching us. I did not hang around outside too long, and I confess that before retiring I made no attempt to take my last piss away from the campsite. Inside the tent I tried as best as I could to go to sleep, but it was far too early for me and I was far too hyped up. Needless to say, the more I tried not to think about it, the more I wanted to go again, and what I thought had been my final piss turned out to be my penultimate one and I had to go outside one last time. Again, I went beside the tent and again I did not stay out long. Back inside, I struggled once more to go to sleep, but at some point, Will must have turned onto his back, because he started snoring again. It is entirely possible that the noise would have been loud enough to keep the devil at bay, but I must have found the snoring comforting because it was the very last memory I had before going to sleep.

When I woke up in the morning, the earth was still spinning on its axis, I was living and breathing and Will was still snuffling away, so I dismissed whatever had been going on last night as just my fired-up imagination. Today's walk would be solely around the long, sweeping, concave arc of the beach at Spirits Bay. The beach was flat and wide, and seven miles long, backed by a continuous series of dunes, and although it was quite pretty, it was not as spectacular as some of the scenery we had seen in previous days.

In the morning, the sky was filled with dappled clouds and hazy sunshine, but it became more dull and more cloudy as the day wore on. The day was largely uneventful and I might even have used the word 'monotonous' to describe the walk, except that it was punctuated by a truly bizarre occurrence.

Immediately after breaking camp in the morning we had descended onto the Western edge of the beach and had stuck close to the water's edge, walking in an Easterly direction with the sea to our left. However, halfway along Spirits Bay we decided to split up. Will said that he wanted to walk up between the dunes to find a footpath, which he believed existed and which he thought would be quicker. I wanted to continue walking along the beach at the water's edge, because I was equally sure that my way would be quicker and so in a show of petulance I said to him, "Well, you go your way then and I will go mine." I was convinced that my way would be quicker and, as I strode on, I was self-certifying my stance by chewing over in my mind the various reasons that would support my position. Firstly, the beach was arcing away to our left, so in effect I would be taking the inside line. Secondly, in view of the fact that he had to walk at least 50 yards to reach any path, he was in effect giving me a head start. Thirdly, I was walking on flat, hard sand and could keep up a steady pace, something he might struggle to do if he had to walk through soft sand, or there were undulations, or he had dune grass to negotiate, or maybe even if there was no path at all. Finally, my route was relatively direct, whilst his could well be winding in and out of dunes. Even though I had convinced myself of the science, I was so determined to prove my point and ensure that I arrived at the far the end of the bay before him that I speeded up my pace and strode quickly along the water's edge (you wouldn't believe that I had turned 39 this year!).

Once Will had gone his merry way, I saw no more of him along the entire length of the beach, presumably because the dunes between me and any parallel path that Will would be walking along were sufficiently tall to hide him from view. Just before the end of the beach, I turned right to walk inland off the beach, and go through the dunes to try to locate the path running behind them. I was absolutely sure that there was no way that Will could have arrived there before me – I'd made sure of it – but when I reached the path on the other side of the dunes and turned to my right, to look back along Will's path to see if I could see him, there was no sign of him. However, when I turned to look left I saw Will a good hundred yards ahead of me further along the path walking up to the top of a high sand dune before disappearing over the other side down into a hollow or valley behind it. I couldn't understand how he had got there so quickly. Disappointed that the bugger had beaten me, I trudged on after him. I didn't see him reappear out of the valley beyond the dune, despite the fact that I was walking on a high path and the contours were such that I ought to have seen him emerge. After a couple of minutes, I arrived at the top of the same high dune where I had last seen him, but when I looked into the valley beyond it I couldn't see him anywhere. Stopping to wonder where he could be, I suddenly heard someone shout my name and when I looked back along the path from where I had come, Will was there behind me. In fact, he was just over a hundred yards back and was in exactly the same spot where I myself had walked up from the beach to connect up with his path and from where I had seen him – or had believed that I had seen him – disappear over the dune in front of me. It was really bizarre and very puzzling. I tried to rationalise what I had seen. If I had simply been mistaken and it had been somebody else walking along the path instead of Will, I would definitely have seen that other person again, either in the same hollow or emerging out of the other side of it. In fact, we hadn't seen a single other person all day. I also considered whether Will was deliberately winding me up, but it wouldn't have been physically possible for Will to have played a trick on me, because he would have had to cover over two hundred yards in near record pace circumventing around to avoid being seen, whilst still carrying his rucksack. There was, and still is, no doubt in my mind that the person that I had seen up ahead of me was Will. In my mind – even to this day – I can vividly see him, wearing the same red-peaked cap atop wispy blond hair, carrying a large rucksack and with his whole deportment in walking being that of Will. How I could have seen Will both ahead of me and behind me is a complete mystery. I waited at the top of the dune for Will to catch up and when he did so, I told him what I had seen. Will could see that I was shaken and, to his credit, did not try to make light of it. He was as perplexed as me and could not offer an explanation for what had occurred – at least not at first. I had been half-hoping that Will *had* indeed somehow managed to play a trick on me, but he was adamant that he had not. We walked on in silence.

On leaving the sand dunes we found ourselves in a broad grassy clearing, where a track led away from it, which we realised was the park where our lift would pick us up. As we waited there, half exhausted, Will broke the silence by turning to me and saying, "Mark, don't forget that the name of this place is Spirits Bay." I hadn't really connected the phenomenon I'd experienced with this fact until then. Much later, when back in England, I carried out some research on Spirits Bay and learnt that it is as deeply sacred for the Maoris as is Cape Reinga, because it is at Spirits Bay where they believe that the spirits of their ancestors collect together and rest before leaving on their journey to the afterlife (via the famous old tree at Cape Reinga). Although I could not discover any specific examples of other phenomena at the site, elsewhere I read that Spirits Bay is believed to be one of the most haunted places in New Zealand and a famous spot for supernatural happenings. According to legend, if visiting the bay at night you can observe multiple individual spirits travelling down the beach before disappearing at a single spot. I now realise that almost certainly we had camped at or very close to this spot the previous night. It is claimed that these spirits ignore any attempts to interact with them or delay them, since they are focused solely on getting to their destination. It should be borne in mind that I knew nothing about this prior to my uncomfortable night camping on the edge of Spirits Bay.

I was pleased – in more ways than one – when we finally got to the end of the walk, where we had lunch, whilst we waited for our lift. Today's walk took us exactly 3 hours equating to 7½ miles or 12 kilometres. A lad by the name of Liam came out as arranged from Waikiti Landing to collect us. Back at the hostel we sorted out our things, jumped in the car and then headed back South. On the way, we stopped at a Maori village. We also drove to various points along both the East coast and the West coast including at one point stopping to take in Ninety Miles Beach. We found lodgings at Kaitaia.

Saturday 21ˢᵗ August – Kauri Forest

Had a reasonably long lie in. Had breakfast in the communal kitchen and met two Israeli girls, one of whom was just about to do the same Cape Reinga walk that we'd just done, though she planned to do it on her own – thought it best not to tell her what happened. Will had a head of steam on and was getting impatient. We then drove down to a harbour area called Pawarenga. It was a very gloomy and rainy day and it provided a melancholy atmosphere to the beautiful countryside. We arrived just in time at Kohukohu where we took the ferry to cross Hokianga Harbour – we were one of only three cars to do so. Fun little journey. Had good lunch at Omapere. Good views. Then went to the Waipoua Kauri Forest. Saw some enormous trees, one of which was at least 2000 years old but reckoned to more likely be closer to 4000 years old. Gobsmacking to think it could go back as far as the early bronze age and almost as far as the Great Pyramid and Stonehenge. We saw the biggest tree in New Zealand which is currently 244 cubic metres; and were told that there had previously existed an even bigger one measuring over 400 cubic metres. Really fascinating stuff. We then headed to Auckland.

Had an ice cream for 80 cents on the way which was huge. Will suggested that we should have had one and shared it, which at 27 pence would have been a real cheapskate act – which caused much hilarity between us. Later in the evening I met Will's friend, Simon, and his wife, Mia. Will had planned that we would stay there the night. As we were sitting down for dinner, I trod on Simon's toes fairly quickly because I related to him the incident where I thought I had seen Will in front of me at Spirits Bay but then he appeared behind me. As a scientist, Simon immediately dismissed what I had seen as superstitious nonsense. Even though I had not intended to, he got my goat so much that I could not stop myself from rising to the bait and arguing my position. The talk became heated and really lively – to me, he seemed such an arrogant, bigoted person. Simon thought that I was pro-religion, spiritual and anti-science and was suggesting that people who believed in religion and/or ghosts were stupid. I reminded him that science is not fixed, that scientists were always discovering new things and that people should be open minded about what there is around us. Will and Mia, who was lovely, wisely kept out of it. It was an interesting evening.

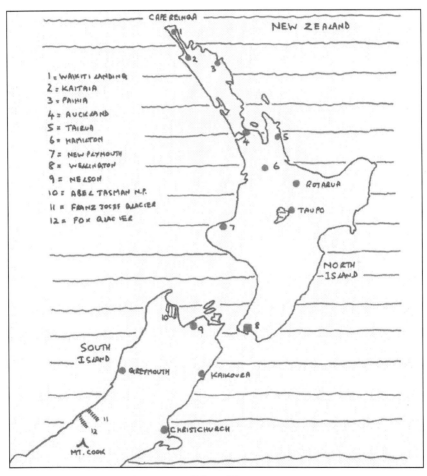

Map 49

Sunday 22nd August – Meeting Barry and Jane

Today all of us, that is me, Will, Simon and Mia, walked down to the beach after breakfast. We said our goodbyes and Will then helped me to try to find my schoolfriend Paul who had emigrated to New Zealand to live in Auckland several years ago. I had an address, so with that and his name I tried directory enquiries and rang a number that was given to me but the person at the other end didn't seem to know him. Will agreed to take me to the address. The number that I had for him in the street where I thought he lived was 166 but when we arrived there was no 166. However, there was a 16B, so it was entirely possible that I might just have misread my own handwriting when copying the address into my little red book. In any event, tried 16B but he was not there. The person that we spoke to at that address said that his name sounded familiar but he had no forwarding address or other details. Never mind.

We then headed back to Will's dad's place at Hamilton. Stopped on the way to visit Will's nephew Joe and his girlfriend, Maggie. Going from Simon and Mia's yuppie lifestyle to Joe and Maggie's drop-out hippy lifestyle was a real contrast. We then returned to Bob's farm where we dropped the stuff off before going for dinner to Will's sister, Jane, and her husband, Barry. Had a great meal and a great night. It was much more relaxing after my encounter with Simon last night. I related to them both my 'Spirits Bay' story and they were very interested, not dismissing any spiritual theory but thinking that I had probably had a classic episode of hallucination. They noted that I was tired, maybe felt a cold coming on, was possibly dehydrated (noting we had been unable to stock up our water at the Cape Reinga lighthouse), and I was on antibiotics. It seemed plausible, but to my way of thinking, it was almost as amazing to think that my brain could have planted that image in my mind, as if I had truly seen Will's doppelganger. They didn't completely rule out a supernatural cause, though, citing that Spirits Bay is a highly significant spiritual place for the Maoris and noting, after interrogating me closely, that I had never knowingly experienced an episode of hallucination before and observing that at the very least it was an amazing coincidence that I should have such an experience there. Received a letter – 8 pages of A4 – from Kitty. I am a very lucky guy.

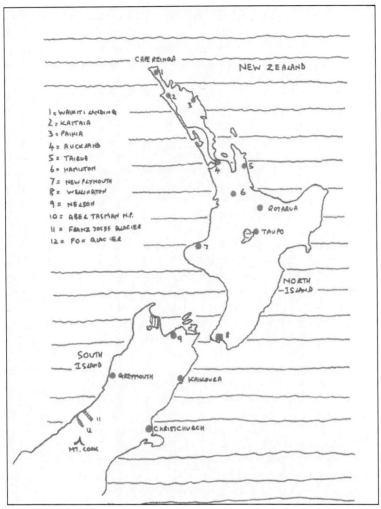

Map 50

<u>*Monday 23ʳᵈ August*</u>

I am getting now to the end of my trip and it seems unreal and a little frightening. Got up in good time, went off to breakfast and put some washing on. Will and I then spent time dodging in and out of rain showers to visit Bob's neighbour, another Bob, to return the tent that he had leant us. He had had a fire at his home yesterday and Will and I had a look around. Not too much damage done – considering. He and his daughter (and grandson) were great characters – true New Zealand farming types. We then went back to Bob's for lunch before I went off in Bob's car on my own into town, to do a couple of chores. The day was a mixture of bright sunshine, and squally showers, resulting in some very attractive rainbows. Back at the farm, I sorted out all my belongings ready to leave early tomorrow morning. I then did the cooking – a fry up. It's a slow and slightly deflating end to my mammoth trip. I am gradually planning all the things I've got to do when I get back home. Nightmare. Discovered that Kieren Fallon (an English jockey) *is alleged to have been having an affair with Henry Cecil's young wife, Natalie* (Henry Cecil being an English trainer – and Kieren Fallon's boss). *Bizarre. He's been sacked and is being replaced by Richard Quinn.*

Tuesday 24ᵗʰ August – Kelly Tarlton's World

Got up at 4.00 am and went with Will and his dad to Hamilton and then with Will to take Jane and Barry to Auckland Airport. I wasn't planning to remain at the airport or check anything in, but, as we were seeing Jane and Barry off, in part I used the chance to get my bearings and it also seemed like a good place for Will to drop me off. The location, South of Auckland, was good for connections into the city. We arrived at the airport at 6.30 am and Will and I had a coffee whilst I waited for the hostels to open up. Will and I then went our separate ways – even though we had spent over two weeks in each other's pockets it was an unemotional, dispassionate departure, knowing as we did that we would see each other back in the UK in a few weeks' time. I then took the shuttle to the Parnell area where I found accommodation – NZ$35. After a shower and a change, I went to Kelly Tarlton's Underwater World and Antarctic Encounter. Very good. There are two parts to it. The first part was the Underwater World – very cleverly done – I could see sharks and huge rays and other fish swimming above and beside me. Then I went to the Antarctic Encounter which included real penguins, snow and a poignant reconstruction of Captain Scott's hut – showing actual cinefilm footage taken by Scott's team and provided an interactive experience including music from the era, different smells and even a wind blowing through the set, which was all done to try to create the experience. It was very cleverly done and very eerie. I discovered something that I wasn't aware of and that is that Scott and most of his crew are still in the Antarctic and have never been found. Chilling.

To kill time, I then went back into town and seemed to make good eye contact with a real beauty, ironically at the same place where Kitty and I had an argument. Then walked to Westhaven Harbour, where I got talking to a female Maori security guard who was riding a bicycle. Great character. Then I walked to the Victoria Market. Finally, I went to the pictures where I hoped to be able to see a film called Waking Ned Devine, which had been recommended, but it was not on. Saw the latest Star Wars film instead – not my cup of tea.

Five people at a window, Pulau Muna

Kecak dancing, Bali

Haylee

Waitetuna country, North Island, New Zealand

Mt. Tarawera, New Zealand

Southern Alps, New Zealand

Trans Alpine Express NZ

Cape Reinga, New Zealand

Wednesday 25th August – Meeting Beatrice

Had a reasonable night's sleep. I'd omitted to bring one or two items from Will's that he said I could take for breakfast. Had shower, packed, had a cup of tea and then wandered out to kill time. I found a souvenir shop where I decided to buy polo style t-shirts for everyone, plus a mouse mat and mud soap for Robbyne. Then went back to wait for the shuttle. Made friends with a local cat. At the airport, I bought and sent two final postcards – one to Robbyne and one to Kitty. Then wandered through and onto the plane. It was half empty so I could stretch out. I saw the film, Entrapment. Quite good. Got to Kuala Lumpur in good time and it was all very strange to sit in the same seat in the departures lounge, to use the same loo and to be back where I started 6 months ago.

I arrived in New Zealand thinking about Kitty and it is true that, as I boarded the plane to fly out, I was still thinking about Kitty, as I would now be taking the opportunity afforded to me to properly re-read all her letters and cards. In between times, however, I had fallen in love with New Zealand, which had touched me in a very unexpected way. After my jaunt through exotic South-East Asia, I arrived assuming that it would be modern and Westernised and likely to be less interesting and less venturesome as a result, but there were adventures waiting for me aplenty and whilst there were many facets that were familiar, there were many more that were fantastical. I loved the wide, open spaces, the drama of the mountains, volcanoes, thermal activity and seascapes, and the healthy, vibrant, green and pleasant land; I loved the friendliness of the people, both Pakeha and Maori, and, whilst I was not so naïve as to think that issues over land rights and social attitudes between the races were fully resolved (a glance at any local newspaper tells you that), the experience for me personally was entirely positive, and I loved the apparent fusion of beliefs and utter respect for Maori history, culture and names; I loved the friendliness of the Kiwi bus driver – for whom it seems their job is a vocation, not a chore; I loved the fact that I had finally met Bob – my expectations had not been high, but I was pleasantly surprised by his openness, hospitality and overwhelming friendliness, and, of course, his dry sense of humour, not to mention his reliability when picking us up or meeting us from airports (it was easy to forget he was well into his eighties); I loved the complete respect that the peoples of New Zealand have for nature and their environment, and, whilst many of us in the West are a generation away from being fully trained to recycle and conserve resources and energy, the need for conservation is already deeply entrenched in the Kiwi psyche; I loved the tourist information centres, the informative and imaginative interactive displays and the way that the tourism industry encourages travellers and tourists to get close to nature, whilst causing least damage to the environment, by the provision, for example, of well-maintained trails and footpaths, and sleeping huts or bothies that are free and accessible to all; I was overwhelmed by the sense that New Zealand is a deeply spiritual place, which naturally was in part based on my own experiences, including the nervous encounter in Rotarua, the ghostly sound in my room at Greymouth and the supernatural event at Cape Reinga, but was also because so many towns, villages and spaces in New Zealand have an aura or resonance with, or are heavily influenced by Maori myths and beliefs – it seemed as if almost every place I visited had some important connection to Maori history; overall, I loved the fact that New Zealand has a culture that fuses traditional and modern, and allows their people the freedom to think differently. Of all the places that I had visited on this trip, New Zealand is the one place that I could seriously imagine me moving back to live.

Sitting on the plane, it was hard to fully take on board the fact that I was now going back home. Not wanting to completely let go of the journey just yet, I reflected on the last six months. One of the things that had particularly struck me from an early stage was the feeling that time had slowed down, which I first noticed and mentioned in my diary when I was in Laos almost four weeks into my trip. Prior to leaving, I would have thought that, with so many places to visit and so much to fit in, time would have flown by, whereas paradoxically the reverse was true. At home, the days would have skipped by with me rising with the alarm clock, racing around at work trying to keep to deadlines, programmed to eating pre-planned meals, in volumes that had been pre-ordained, and at designated set times, and going to bed early enough to ensure that I would be able to wake up in time for my next alarm call the following day. Instead, my pace had slackened so that I would wake up when I was ready to, I would eat when I was hungry and I would go to bed when I was tired. Time in the West goes by so quickly, and the older we get the faster time seems to fly. A few weeks into my trip, it was as though time had sharply applied the brakes. I was becoming accustomed to living life to the full each and every day, and experiencing the natural rhythms of daily life, and, more importantly, having the time to notice and take in everything around me, every song of a bird, or chirrup of an insect, or breeze on my face. It wasn't the case that I had no routine or pattern to my life. I did. But, instead of being dictated to by deadlines and diaries, I found that my life was more in sync with the ebb and flow of day and night, so that I would tend to get up with the sun, and retire to bed when I was tired. I became more observant of the world around me and had more time to absorb all that each day would bring. It was as though life expanded to fill the void left by time slowing down. I was not only able to tune into the natural world around me, but I was more aware of my own internal rhythms, by, for example, being more aware of what my body needed and when. I ate much more healthily, in so much as I would only consume sufficient to satisfy my hunger, and at times when my body told me I was hungry, not when my mind did. I also had sufficient time to be able to choose how long to stay at one place or when to move on, and, within the broad parameters of a rough itinerary, I could pick and choose when and where to go based on my own health, or mood or machinations. Consequently, if this trip taught me anything, it was that we should all of us try to find a way to switch off from the pressures of modern daily life and have the time to enjoy and experience every second of every day. This is easier said than done, of course, the problem being how to achieve this, short of each and every one of us having to go on a six-month backpacking trip.

As I was sitting there, another paradox occurred to me in that I realised that I had become accustomed to uncertainty and the unexpected, when every day would be different to the previous one. One day, I could be swimming or walking or sightseeing, and the next I could be relaxing reading a book or chatting with new friends or sitting out a storm. Now I would be heading back to routine, to alarm clocks, to monotony and to work – I would be starting my new job next Tuesday.

Of course, I had a lot to be thankful for and plenty to look forward to. I would be looking forward to seeing my family, including my niece, Robbyne, since it would be interesting to see how many postcards she had received. I had taken 69 rolls of film and I was looking forward to having them developed. I would be looking forward to seeing if my made-to-measure suit had arrived from Bangkok – my hopes were not high. I was looking forward to meeting up with my Great Aunt Olga, the widow of Great Uncle Durrant – she would be pleased that I had made good use of his camera. I was also looking forward to paying my respects to my late grandmother, Nan Thompson. I had stuck to my resolution to place her photograph in a prominent place in every hostel or room that I stayed in. To be honest, it was an easy resolution to keep, since the photograph I have of her captures her essence and her sweet, reassuring smile perfectly and having her photograph with me made me feel as though my nan had been on the journey with me, and perhaps had enjoyed it as much as I had, overseeing me like a Guardian Angel. I also fully acknowledged that, as difficult as it was to be thinking about going back to work, it was work, and saving up the money from having worked, that had financed this trip and it was also the very fact that I had a job lined up to go back to that had allowed me to relax and enjoy the time that I had.

And, of course, I had the lovely Kitty waiting for me. I was still basking in the after-glow of our meeting. I read and re-read all of Kitty's letters and cards. Although I had written to her, I had been nowhere near as prolific as she had been to me – I had been enjoying myself too much. I was struck yet again by how lucky I had been to have met her and to know that five weeks further on she was still waiting for me. I was also reminded that meeting Kitty had helped to make my time in New Zealand even more special. With New Zealand being the last leg of my journey, I could very well have slid into a deep depression knowing that the end of my trip and a return to work was fast approaching, but the very fact that she was waiting for me gave me something to look forward to, even though I was, of course, very impatient to see Kitty again some time soon.

On the flight from Auckland to Kuala Lumpur, I had plenty of time to contemplate the last amazing six months of my life and with the help of my diary, to reflect on the people I had met, the places I had seen and the experiences both good and bad that I had lived through. It was hard to fathom that I had had so many interesting and diverse experiences, from swimming with seven beautiful Indonesian girls in Penang, getting emotional at a classical concert in Kuala Lumpur, swimming with turtles and sharks off the coast of Malaysia, barricading myself in my hotel room in Xian, walking parts of the Great Wall of China, just breaking even when betting on horses in Hong Kong, staring into the smoking cauldron of Gunung Bromo in Java, sharing a meal with a widower at his wife's funeral in Sulawesi, dancing at a wedding in Sulawesi, nearly being ship-wrecked in Indonesia, playing football and scoring a goal in Australia, herding cattle into a truck in New Zealand and sharing a supernatural encounter with Will.

However, as I read through my diary I was struck most of all by the sheer number of chance brief encounters I had made with other persons of many different nationalities who were travelling themselves. As I read through my diary I noted that such people had included: eight Japanese men and a Singaporean girl and her cousin in Ipoh; a lad from Sweden and a girl from Denmark on a bus in Northern Malaysia; a couple from England on the island of Perhentian Kecil; a German woman teaching English to children in Borneo; a French girl in the Malaysian jungle; crossing into Laos with two Austrians; a Swede in a bar at Vientiane; an Aussie girl and an American lad in Vang Vieng; two Spaniards and a French war veteran on a bus from Luang Prabang; a teacher from Tibet in Kunming; a French lad from Budapest on the Yangtze River; a couple of English girls in Xian; twin sisters from Belgium on the flight to Ujung Pandang; a Kiwi in Singkang, Sulawesi; a Danish girl and a Swiss lad on a boat to Flores; a Scottish couple on a bemo in Flores; an English girl on a bus to Bali; a girl from Switzerland in Denpasar; an English lad, a Scottish bloke, an Irish girl, a Japanese girl and an American in Rotarua; an English girl on a bus to Mt. Cook; and two girls from Finland, and two girls from Israel in Northland, New Zealand. It was a fascinating thought that each one of those persons had been on their own epic journeys and poignant to think that at one tiny point within the infinitesimal stretches of time and space their movements in their personal pianolas coincided with my movements in my pianola.

It was a very strange feeling when later I was back at Kuala Lumpur airport, where my adventures had started six months before, and where everything looked so familiar, even to the extent, as I noted in my diary, that I used the same cubicle in the same toilet. It was as if I had closed the circle.

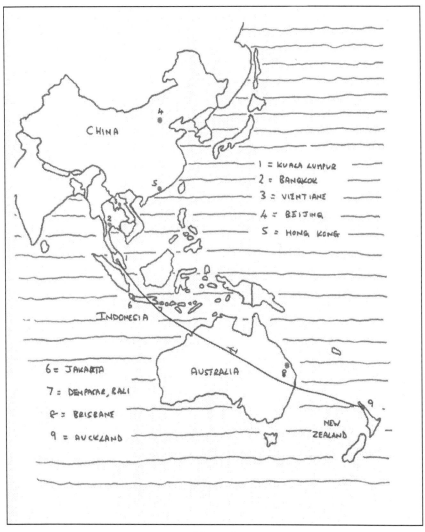

Map 51

It was with time to kill, and as I was ambling around the airport, that I came across a girl who looked familiar. I couldn't place her at first, and didn't want to approach her until I had worked out who she was, but it suddenly dawned on me that it was Beatrice, the girl from Switzerland who I had met over breakfast in Denpasar, Bali, whilst I was waiting for a bemo connection to take me North to Lovina Beach and back to Nur. What an amazing coincidence that I should meet somebody from my travels right here at Kuala Lumpur airport right at the very end of my trip. This was my pianola theory working its mesmerising magic once again. My recollection was that pretty Beatrice had seemed quite keen on me when we had first met, but either the bubble had burst or my original assessment had been arrogantly mistaken and the product of an overactive imagination, because when I approached Beatrice to speak to her, her reaction was distinctly cool, perhaps even of shock. She certainly wasn't as talkative as when we had first met. It was clear that she couldn't place me immediately, but when I explained where we'd met, she claimed to recall me and said that she was pleased to see me again. I was not wholly convinced, though she seemed to warm to me a little and even informed me that she was now on her way to London and that I might see her there. I could see quite clearly, however, that she was lost in thought and her mind was elsewhere and it suddenly dawned on me that her apparent coolness might simply have been dejection, perhaps even depression, in view of the fact that her own journey was now coming to an end. I seemed to recall that when we first met Beatrice had only just arrived in Bali and was trying to find her feet, but who knows what adventures she would have had, what people she would have met and what places she would have seen during the intervening two months since, and her low spirits – a reflection of my own – were symptomatic of the disappointment and sheer anti-climax that her own personal odyssey was now coming to an end. I could completely empathise with Beatrice and I shared her disappointment because it felt very unsettling. I, too, was going home.

EPILOGUE/POSTSCRIPT

To my amazement, the suit that I'd purchased in Bangkok was at mum's when I arrived back. I took some comfort from the fact that I'd not been (completely) duped.

I returned to Bali in 2011. Komang was still married, but her stock was lower than ever and she and her family were clearly struggling to make ends meet. By way of example, even in modern Indonesia, the shower of choice is often a rudimentary mandi, comprising a basin or bucket, filled with water, usually cold, from which water is scooped up using a plastic saucepan. Komang's house did not even have its own mandi. In the entire house – or shack – she had only one chair, a dirty, white plastic one, which was used only on important occasions when honoured guests, like me, visited. Her eldest son, Budi, is now a young man himself, and is working hard to help out his family. Komang continues to be always smiling, but now those bright eyes are jaded and tired and do little to hide her age.

I learnt that Parma had died in 2009, and his homestay, run by his widow, is becoming more and more run down.

I met up with Nur. Her English had much improved, having taken up English lessons after my departure. She had aged a bit, which didn't come as too much of a surprise once I'd learnt that her news was mixed. On the plus side, Nur had married a lad from Java in 2003. However, despite falling pregnant three times over the ensuing seven years, sadly all of the pregnancies failed, the longest pregnancy lasting seven months. Nur was very stoic about her fate, asserting that she and her husband would try again.

I wrote to most of the people that I had promised to write to. I never heard from Dao. I don't know if she ever received the money that I sent her, or if she ever made it to Norway. I also never heard from Cynthia.

I met up several times with both Valerie and Catherine, both in the UK and in Belgium. Their infectious laughter and child-like smiles continue to entrance.

After our initial meeting, the fires continued to burn brightly for Kitty

368

and I, and we regularly kept in touch by letter and telephone until she came over to visit me in the UK for an extended six-week stay in the spring of 2000. I can honestly say that we truly enjoyed being together again, but in that time, although we never fell out as such, I think on both our parts we came to realise that the spark was missing and we were not completely in sync with each other. Very soon after returning to Australia, fate dealt its hand and Kitty was offered – and accepted – the promotion of a lifetime within her bank, which would involve committing to regular trips between Brisbane and Hong Kong. Our relationship was not strong enough to survive the test of time and the distance between us. We continued to keep in touch for a while but the relationship fizzled out.

However, just over two years after returning from my trip, I was lucky enough to meet the love of my life, Sayara, a girl from Uzbekistan who I met in New York and later married, coincidentally the same year that Nur married. In a strange way, my adventures in 1999 potentially laid the groundwork for our meeting, partly because I came back from my trip buoyed with renewed enthusiasm and confidence, which is something Sayara saw in me, but partly also because, having conducted a truly trans-global relationship with somebody on the other side of the world, conducting a relationship which was merely transatlantic was peanuts in comparison.

BIBLIOGRAPHY

Ring of Fire, by Lawrence and Lorne Blair, published by Transworld Publishers Ltd, 1988.

Malaysia, Singapore & Brunei, published by Lonely Planet Publications, ed. 1996.

China, published by Lonely Planet Publications, ed. 1998.

South-East Asia on a Shoestring, published by Lonely Planet Publications, ed. 1997.

New Zealand, published by Lonely Planet Publications, ed. 1998.

Indonesia, published by Lonely Planet Publications, ed. 1997.

Nation's Favourite Poems, published by BBC Worldwide Ltd, 1996.

Behind the Wall: A Journey through China, by Colin Thubron, published by William Heinemann, 1987.

Foreign Devils on the Silk Road, by Peter Hopkirk, published by John Murray (Publishers Ltd.), 1984.

ABOUT THE AUTHOR

Born in King's Lynn in 1960, Mark is now a criminal defence solicitor with his own practice in Suffolk. Mark is married to Sayara.

Mark's interests include photography, walking, horse racing, canal boats, gardening, swimming, and reading. His two favourite genres of books are murder mysteries and travel books. His favourite authors include Agatha Christie, Ian Rankin, Colin Thubron, Peter Hopkirk and Simon Armitage. He also enjoys travelling. Once every two years he temporarily shuts down his business and takes himself off backpacking for a month with Sayara.

Mark is also an Okuden (i.e. level 2) Reiki practitioner and specialises in providing Reiki treatments to horses.

Although writing is an integral part of his day job, he has often wanted to write a book and *Travels With my Nan* is his first. He has up to three other book ideas.

Printed in Great Britain
by Amazon

51758572R00217